PHP 5 Objects, Patterns, and Practice

MATT ZANDSTRA

Apress®

PHP 5 Objects, Patterns, and Practice

Copyright © 2004 by Matt Zandstra

ISBN (pbk): 1-59059-380-4

Printed and bound in the United States of America 9 8 7 6 5 4 3 2 1

Trademarked names may appear in this book. Rather than use a trademark symbol with every occurrence of a trademarked name, we use the names only in an editorial fashion and to the benefit of the trademark owner, with no intention of infringement of the trademark.

Lead Editor: Jason Gilmore

Technical Reviewer: Tolan Blundell

Editorial Board: Steve Anglin, Dan Appleman, Ewan Buckingham, Gary Cornell, Tony Davis, Jason Gilmore, Chris Mills, Dominic Shakeshaft, Jim Sumser

Project Manager: Sofia Marchant

Copy Edit Manager: Nicole LeClerc

Copy Editor: Ami Knox

Production Manager: Kari Brooks-Copony

Production Editor: Janet Vail

Compositor: Susan Glinert Stevens

Proofreader: Sue Boshers

Indexer: Valerie Perry

Cover Designer: Kurt Krames

Manufacturing Manager: Tom Debolski

Distributed to the book trade in the United States by Springer-Verlag New York, Inc., 233 Spring Street, 6th Floor, New York, NY 10013, and outside the United States by Springer-Verlag GmbH & Co. KG, Tiergartenstr. 17, 69112 Heidelberg, Germany.

In the United States: phone 1-800-SPRINGER, fax 201-348-4505, e-mail orders@springer-ny.com, or visit http://www.springer-ny.com. Outside the United States: fax +49 6221 345229, e-mail orders@springer.de, or visit http://www.springer.de.

For information on translations, please contact Apress directly at 2560 Ninth Street, Suite 219, Berkeley, CA 94710. Phone 510-549-5930, fax 510-549-5939, e-mail info@apress.com, or visit http://www.apress.com.

The information in this book is distributed on an "as is" basis, without warranty. Although every precaution has been taken in the preparation of this work, neither the author(s) nor Apress shall have any liability to any person or entity with respect to any loss or damage caused or alleged to be caused directly or indirectly by the information contained in this work.

The source code for this book is available to readers at http://www.apress.com in the Downloads section.

For Louise, who is the whole point.

Contents at a Glance

PART ONE ▪▪▪ Introduction

PART TWO ▪▪▪ Objects

PART THREE ▪▪▪ Patterns

PART FOUR ■■■ Practice

PART FIVE ■■■ Conclusion

PART SIX ■■■ Appendixes

Contents

PART ONE ▪▪▪ Introduction

PART TWO ▪▪▪ Objects

PART THREE ■■■ Patterns

PART FOUR ■■■ Practice

PART FIVE ∎∎∎ Conclusion

PART SIX ∎∎∎ Appendixes

About the Author

MATT ZANDSTRA has worked as a Web programmer, consultant, and writer for a decade. He has been an object evangelist for most of that time. He is the author of *SAMS Teach Yourself PHP in 24 Hours* (three editions) and a contributor to *DHTML Unleashed*. He has written articles for *Linux Magazine* and Zend.com. He works primarily with PHP, Perl, and Java, building online applications. He is an engineer at Yahoo! in London.

Matt lives in Brighton with his wife, Louise, and two children, Holly and Jake. Because it has been so long since he has had any spare time, he only distantly recollects that he runs regularly to offset the effects of his liking for pubs and cafes, and for sitting around reading and writing fiction.

About the
Technical Reviewer

■**TOLAN BLUNDELL** is a partner in BGZ Consultants LLP. When not liaising with clients, designing applications, or writing specifications, he occasionally finds time to develop primarily Web-based applications in PHP and Java. He has designed and built systems for clients including the BBC and Red Bull.

The rare times that he escapes work find him writing code, animating and making music for pleasure, as well as more social activities such as making loud noises in fields.

Acknowledgments

When you first have an idea for a book (in my case while drinking good coffee in a Brighton cafe), it is the subject matter alone that grips you. In the enthusiasm of the moment, it is easy to forget the scale of the undertaking. I soon rediscovered the sheer hard work a book demands, and I learned once again that it's not something you can do alone. At every stage of this book's development, I have benefited from enormous support.

In fact, my thanks must predate the book's conception. The themes of this book first saw the light of day in a talk I gave for a Brighton initiative called Skillswap (`http://www.skillswap.org`) run by Andy Budd. It was Andy's invitation to speak that first planted the seeds of the idea in my mind. For that I still owe Andy a pint, and much thanks.

By chance, attending that meeting was Jessey White-Cinis, another Apress author, who put me in touch with Martin Streicher, who in turn commissioned the book for Apress straightaway. My thanks go out to both Jessey and Martin for seeing potential in the slightest of beginnings.

The Apress team has provided enormous support under considerable provocation as the commitments of a demanding job and a young family consistently ate away at deadline after deadline. I would particularly like to thank Chris Mills and Jason Gilmore for their enthusiastic lead, Sofia Marchant for her valiant struggle to prise chapters out of me, and Ami Knox for grappling with my words.

It's easy to lose sight of the plot when you're playing with code and writing about it. My friend and technical reviewer Tolan Blundell has done an excellent job of keeping me on track, and reminding me that details matter. Thanks Tolan.

Thanks to Steven John Metsker for his kind permission to reimplement in PHP a brutally simplified version of the parser API he presented in his book *Building Parsers in Java*.

I would also like to thank all at The Farm, the Brighton new media freelancers group, who still let me drink with them despite my permanent job. Aside from much needed light relief, Farm members have offered a welcome space to discuss themes and problems thrown up by the book.

Many people showed considerable patience in the face of my increasing preoccupation. Thanks to James Cowan and Paul Silver for cutting me slack on our project. Special thanks to Mark Lester, my boss at Yahoo!, who granted me leave at short notice so that I could concentrate on a tricky chapter.

Writing to a deadline is not conducive to family life, and so I must send my thanks and love to my wife, Louise, and to our children, Holly and Jake. I have missed you all.

The soundtrack to the writing of this book, in fact the soundtrack to much of my life in recent years, was provided by John Peel. John was a broadcaster who waged a 40-year war on the bland and mass-produced in music simply by championing everything original and eclectic he could lay his hands on. John died suddenly in October 2004, leaving listeners around the world bereft. He had an extraordinary impact on many lives, and I would like to add my thanks here.

Introduction

I have been using PHP in object-oriented projects since 2000. For most of that time, of course, PHP meant PHP 4, with its relatively limited support for objects. Even so, I found that I could do pretty much everything that I wanted with it, as long as I was careful and disciplined.

In early 2003, I began initial work on a book about PHP 4 and object-oriented programming. A good portion of the book was to focus on the strategies, disciplines, and workarounds required to get PHP to behave itself in an object-oriented context. Then I began to hear murmurs that PHP 5 was on its way, which dated my project before I had even started on it. I put the idea to one side and took up another book project.

It was for that project that I found myself investigating in detail the new features of PHP 5. It was a revelation! Almost every annoyance I had encountered in the past was addressed by the enhanced support of the Zend Engine 2 for object-oriented programming. I found myself once again making notes for a book, but this time a book that exploited the resources of the language, not a book that overcame its shortcomings.

This is that book. I have tried to write it for the programmer *I* was when I first started working with objects on larger projects. I have taken a basic understanding of PHP for granted. The typical reader of this book either knows PHP or can read up on a feature of syntax or particular function without help from me. The nuts and bolts of object orientation are not so transparent, though, and because many of them are new to the language, I cover them in full here.

What I lacked most, though, was a sense of how to use objects effectively, and the reasons for the choices I needed to make. At the same time I was adrift when it came to the best practices to deploy *around* my code—what tools and principles to use to test my code, to document it, and to install it.

These are the topics that this book attempts to address. I hope you find it as rewarding to read as it has been challenging to write!

Matt Zandstra
Brighton, UK
November 2004

PART ONE

■■■

Introduction

CHAPTER 1

■ ■ ■

PHP: Design and Management

Of the changes wrought by PHP 5, among the most important is its enhanced support for object-oriented programming. This has stimulated much interest in objects and design within the PHP community. In fact, this is an intensification of a process that began when PHP 4 first made object-oriented programming a serious reality.

In this chapter, we look at the needs that design can address. We very briefly summarize the evolution of patterns and related practices in the Java world. We look at the signs that a similar process is occurring among PHP coders.

We also outline the topics covered by this book.

We will look at

- *The evolution of disaster*: A project goes bad.

- *Design and PHP*: How object-oriented design techniques are infecting the PHP community.

- *This book*: Objects. Patterns. Practice.

The Problem

The problem is that PHP is just too easy. It tempts you to try out your ideas, and flatters you with good results. You write much of your code straight into your Web pages, because PHP is designed to support that. You add the heavier code to functions in library files, and before you know it you have a working Web application.

You are well on the road to ruin. You don't realize this, of course, because your site looks fantastic. It performs well, your clients are happy, and your users are spending money.

Trouble strikes when you go back to the code to begin a new phase. Now you have a larger team, some more users, a bigger budget. Yet without warning things begin to go wrong. It's as if your project has been poisoned.

Your new programmer is struggling to understand code that is second nature to you, though perhaps a little byzantine in its twists and turns. She is taking longer than you expected to reach full strength as a team member.

A simple change, estimated at a day, takes three days when you discover that you must update 20 or more Web pages as a result.

One of your coders saves his version of a file over major changes you made to the same code some time earlier . The loss is not discovered for three days, by which time you have amended your own local copy. It takes a day to sort out the mess, holding up a third developer who was also working on the file.

Because of the popularity of the application, you need to shift the code to a new server. The project needs to be installed by hand, and you discover that file paths, database names, and passwords are hard coded into many source files. You halt work during the move because you don't want to overwrite the configuration changes the migration entails. The estimated two hours becomes eight as it is revealed that someone did something clever involving the Apache module ModRewrite, and the application now requires this to operate properly.

You finally launch phase 2, and all is well. All is well for a day and a half. The first bug report comes in as you are about to leave the office. The client phones minutes later to complain. Her report is similar to the first, but a little more scrutiny reveals that it is a different bug causing similar behavior. You remember the simple change back at the start of the phase that necessitated extensive modifications throughout the rest of the project.

You realize that not all the required modifications are in place. This is either because they were omitted to start with, or because the files in question were overwritten in merge collisions. You hurriedly make the modifications needed to fix the bugs. You're in too much of a hurry to test the changes, but they are a simple matter of copy and paste, so what can go wrong?

The next morning you arrive at the office to find that a shopping basket module has been down all night. The last-minute changes you made omitted a leading quotation mark, rendering the code unusable. You fix the problem, mollify the client, and gather the team for another day's firefighting.

This everyday tale of coding folk may seem a little over the top, but I have seen all these things happen over and over again. Many PHP projects start their life small and evolve into monsters.

Because the presentation layer—the PHP pages containing HTML—also contains application logic, duplication creeps in early as database queries, authentication checks, form processing, and more are copied from page to page. Every time a change is required to one of these blocks of code, it must be made everywhere the code is found, or bugs will surely follow.

Lack of documentation makes the code hard to read, and lack of testing allows obscure bugs to go undiscovered until deployment. The changing nature of a client's business often means that code evolves away from its original purpose until it is performing tasks to which it is fundamentally unsuited. Because such code has often evolved as a seething intermingled lump, it is hard, if not impossible, to switch out and rewrite parts of it to suit the new purpose.

Now, none of this is bad news if you are a freelance PHP consultant. Assessing and fixing a system like this can fund expensive espresso drinks and DVD box sets for six months or more. More seriously, though, problems of this sort can mean the difference between a business's success or failure.

PHP and Other Languages

PHP's phenomenal popularity meant that its boundaries were tested hard and early. As we will see in the next chapter, PHP started life as a set of macros for managing personal home pages. With the advent of PHP 3 and, to a greater extent, PHP 4, the language was becoming the successful power behind large Enterprise Web sites. In many ways, though, the legacy of PHP's beginnings carried through into script design and project management. In some quarters PHP retained an unfair reputation as a hobbyist language, best suited for presentation tasks.

About this time (around the turn of the millennium), new ideas were gaining currency in other coding communities. An interest in object-oriented design galvanized the Java community. You may think that this is a truism, since Java is an object-oriented language. Java provides a grain that is easier to work with than against, of course, but using classes and objects does not in itself determine a particular design approach.

The concept of the design pattern as a way of describing a problem together with the essence of its solution was first discussed in the '70s. Perhaps aptly, the idea was developed in the field of architecture, and not computer science. By the early '90s object-oriented programmers were using the same technique to name and describe problems of software design. Perhaps the seminal book on design patterns, *Design Patterns: Elements of Reusable Object-Oriented Software*, by the affectionately nick-named *Gang of Four*, was published in 1995, and is still indispensable today. The patterns it contains are a required first step for anyone starting out in this field, which is why most of the patterns in this book are drawn from it.

The Java language itself deployed many core patterns in its API, but it wasn't until the late '90s that design patterns made the leap to the consciousness of the coding community at large. Patterns quickly infected the computer sections of high street bookstores, and the first hype or tripe flame wars began on mailing lists and forums.

Whether you think that patterns are a powerful way of communicating craft knowledge or largely hot air (and you can probably guess where I stand on that issue), it is hard to deny that the emphasis on software design they have encouraged is beneficial in itself.

Related topics also grew in prominence. Among them was eXtreme Programming (XP), championed by Kent Beck. XP is an approach to projects that encourages flexible, design-oriented, highly focused planning and execution.

Prominent among XP's principles is an insistence that testing is crucial to a project's success. Tests should be automated, run often, and preferably designed before their target code is written.

Projects should be broken down into small (very small) iterations. Both code and requirements should be scrutinized at all times. Architecture and design should be a shared and constant issue, leading to the frequent revision of code.

If XP is the militant wing of the design movement, then the moderate tendency was well represented by one of the best books about programming I have ever read: *The Pragmatic Programmer* by Andrew Hunt and David Thomas, which was published in 2000.

XP was deemed a tad cultish by some, but it grew out of two decades of object-oriented practice at the highest level and its principles were widely cannibalized. In particular, code revision, known as refactoring, was taken up as a powerful adjunct to patterns. Refactoring has evolved since the '80s, but it was codified in Martin Fowler's catalog of refactorings, *Refactoring: Improving the Design of Existing Code*, which was published in 1999 and defined the field.

Testing too became an increasingly hot issue with the rise in prominence of XP and patterns. The importance of automated tests was further underlined by the release of the powerful JUnit test platform, which became a key weapon in the Java programmer's armory. A landmark article on the subject, "Test Infected: Programmers Love Writing Tests" by Kent Beck and Erich Gamma (http://junit.sourceforge.net/doc/testinfected/testing.htm), provided an excellent introduction to the topic and remains hugely influential.

PHP 4 was released at about this time, bringing with it improvements in efficiency and, crucially, enhancements in its support for objects. These enhancements made fully object-oriented projects a possibility. Programmers embraced this feature, somewhat to the surprise of Zend founders Zeev Suraski and Andi Gutmans, who had joined Rasmus Lerdorf to manage PHP development. As we shall see in the next chapter, PHP's object support was by no means perfect, but with discipline and careful use of syntax one could really think in both objects and PHP at the same time.

Nevertheless, design disasters like the one that opened this chapter remained common. Design culture was some way off, and almost nonexistent in PHP publishing. Online, though, the interest was clear. Leon Atkinson wrote a piece about PHP and patterns for Zend in 2001 (`http://www.zend.com/zend/trick/tricks-app-patt-php.php`), and Harry Fuecks launched his excellent journal at `http://www.phppatterns.com` in 2002. Patterns-based framework projects such as BinaryCloud began to emerge, as well as tools for automated testing and documentation.

The release of the first PHP 5 beta in 2003 ensured the future of PHP as a language for object-oriented programming. The Zend 2 Engine provided greatly improved object support, as we shall see. Equally important, it sent a signal that objects and object-oriented design are now central to the PHP project.

About This Book

This book does not attempt to break new ground in the field of object-oriented design; in that respect it perches precariously upon the shoulders of giants. Instead, we examine, in the context of PHP, some well-established design principles, and some key patterns (particularly those inscribed in *Design Patterns*, the classic Gang of Four book). Finally, we move beyond the strict limits of code to look at tools and techniques that can help to ensure the success of a project. Aside from this introduction, and a brief conclusion, the book is divided into three main parts: objects, patterns, and practice.

Objects

We begin Part Two with a quick look at the history of PHP and objects, charting their shift from afterthought in PHP 3 to core feature in PHP 5.

You can be an experienced and successful PHP programmer with little or no knowledge of objects. We start from first principles to explain objects, classes, and inheritance. Even at this early stage, we look at some of the object enhancements that PHP 5 introduced.

The basics established, we delve deeper into our topic, examining PHP's more advanced object-oriented features. We also devote a chapter to the tools that PHP provides to help you work with objects and classes.

It is not enough, though, to know how to declare a class, and to use it to instantiate an object. You must first choose the right participants for your system, and decide the best ways for them to interact. These choices are harder to describe and to learn than the bald facts about object tools and syntax. We finish Part Two with an introduction to object-oriented design with PHP.

Patterns

Part Two far from exhausts the subject of design. A pattern describes a problem in software design, and provides the kernel of a solution. A solution here does not mean the kind of cut-and-paste code you might find in a cookbook (excellent as cookbooks are as resources for the programmer). Instead, a design pattern describes an approach that can be taken to solve a problem. A sample implementation may be given, but it is less important than the concept it serves to illustrate.

Part Three begins by defining design patterns and describing their structure. We also look at some of the reasons for their popularity.

Patterns tend to promote and follow certain core design principles. An understanding of these can help in analyzing a pattern's motivation, and can be applied usefully to all programming. We discuss some of these principles. We also examine the UML, a platform-independent way of describing classes and their interactions.

Although this book is not a pattern catalog, we examine some of the most famous and useful patterns over four chapters. I describe the problem that each pattern addresses, analyze the solution, and present an implementation example in PHP.

Practice

Even a beautifully balanced architecture will fail if it is not managed correctly. In Part Four we look at the tools available to help you create a framework that can ensure the success of your project. If the rest of the book is about the practice of design and programming, Part Four is about the practice of managing your code. The tools we examine can form a support structure for a project, helping to track bugs as they occur, promoting collaboration amongst programmers, providing ease of installation and clarity of code.

We have already discussed the power of the automated test. We kick off Part Four with an introductory chapter that also introduces PHPUnit2, a package based on the much ported JUnit testing tool. As usual, we examine the problem that automated testing is designed to address.

Many programmers are guilty of giving in to the impulse to do everything themselves. The PHP community maintains PEAR, a repository of quality-controlled packages that can be stitched into projects with ease. We look at the trade-offs between implementing a feature yourself and deploying a PEAR package.

While we are on the topic of PEAR, we look at the installation mechanism that makes the deployment of a package as simple as a single command. Best suited for stand-alone packages, this mechanism can be used to automate the installation of your own code. I show you how to do it.

Documentation is a pain, and along with testing, it is probably the easiest part of a project to jettison when deadlines loom. I argue that this is probably a mistake, and show you PHPDocumentor, a tool that helps you turn comments in your code into a set of hyperlinked HTML documents that describe every element of your API.

Every tool or technique discussed in this book directly concerns, or is deployed using, PHP. The one exception to this rule is Concurrent Versions System (CVS). CVS is a version control system that enables many programmers to work together on the same codebase without overwriting one another's work. CVS allows you to grab snapshots of your project at any stage in development, to see who has made which changes, and to split the project into mergeable branches. CVS will save your project one day.

PEAR provides a build tool that is ideal for installing self-enclosed packages. For a complete application, however, greater flexibility is required. Applications are messy. They may need files installed in nonstandard locations, or to set up databases, or to patch server configuration. In short, applications need *stuff* to be done during installation. Phing is a faithful port of a Java tool called Ant. Phing and Ant interpret a build file, and process your source files in any way you tell them to. At heart, this usually means copying them from a source directory to various target locations around your system, but as your needs get more complex, Phing scales effortlessly to meet them.

Summary

This is a book about object-oriented design and programming. It is also about tools for managing a codebase from collaboration through to deployment.

These two approaches address the same problem from different but complementary angles. The objective is to build systems that achieve their objectives and lend themselves well to ongoing collaborative development.

A secondary objective lies in the aesthetics of software systems. As programmers, we build machines that have shape and action. We invest many hours of our working day, and many days of our lives, writing these shapes into being. We want both those polls: the instruction, and the process it drives, the class and its objects, to form an elegant whole. The business of version control, testing, documentation, and build does more than support this objective, it is part of the shape we want to achieve. Just as we want clean and clever code, we want a codebase that is designed well for developers and users alike. The mechanics of sharing, reading, and deploying the project should be as important as the code itself.

PART TWO

Objects

CHAPTER 2

■ ■ ■

PHP and Objects

Objects were not always a key part of the PHP project. In fact, objects have been described as an afterthought by PHP's designers.

As afterthoughts go, this one has proved remarkably resilient. In this chapter, I introduce coverage of objects by summarizing the development of PHP's object-oriented features.

We will look at

- *PHP/FI 2.0*: PHP, but not as we know it.

- *PHP 3*: Objects make their first appearance.

- *PHP 4*: Object-oriented programming grows up.

- *PHP 5*: Objects at the heart of the language.

The Accidental Success of PHP Objects

With so many object-oriented PHP libraries and applications in circulation, to say nothing of PHP 5's extensive object enhancements, the rise of the object in PHP may seem like the culmination of a natural and inevitable process. In fact, nothing could be further from the truth.

In the Beginning: PHP/FI

The genesis of the PHP as we know it today lies with two tools developed by Rasmus Lerdorf using Perl. PHP stood for Personal Homepage Tools. FI stood for Form Interpreter. Together they comprised macros for sending SQL statements to databases, processing forms, and flow control.

These tools were rewritten in C and combined under the name PHP/FI 2.0. The language at this stage looked different from the syntax we recognize today, but not *that* different. There was support for variables, associative arrays, and functions. Objects, though, were not even on the horizon.

Syntactic Sugar: PHP 3

In fact, even as PHP 3 was in the planning stage, objects were off the agenda. As now, the principle architects of PHP 3 were Zeev Suraski and Andi Gutmans. PHP 3 was a complete rewrite of PHP/FI 2.0, but objects were not deemed a necessary part of the new syntax.

According to Zeev Suraski, support for classes was added almost as an afterthought (on 27 August 1997, to be precise). Classes and objects were actually just another way to define and access associative arrays.

Of course, the addition of methods and inheritance made classes much more than glorified associative arrays, but there were still severe limitations as to what you could do with your classes. In particular, you could not access a parent class's overridden methods (don't worry if you don't know what this means yet, I will cover it). Another disadvantage we will examine in the next section was the less than optimal way that objects were passed around in PHP scripts.

That objects were a marginal issue at this time is underlined by their lack of prominence in official documentation. The manual devoted one sentence and a code example to objects. The example did not illustrate inheritance or properties.

PHP 4 and the Quiet Revolution

If PHP 4 was yet another ground-breaking step for the language, most of the core changes took place beneath the surface. The Zend Engine (its name derived from **Zee**v and **And**i) was written from scratch to power the language.

From our *object*-ive perspective, the fact that it became possible to override parent methods and access them from child classes was a major benefit.

The main drawback remained, however. Assigning an object to a variable, passing it to a function, or returning it from a method, resulted in a copy being made. So an assignment like this:

```
$my_obj = new User('bob');
$other = $my_obj;
```

resulted in the existence of two User objects, rather than two references to the same User object. In most object-oriented languages you would expect assignment by reference, rather than by value as here. This means that you pass and assign handles that point to objects rather than copy the objects themselves. The default pass-by-value behavior resulted in many obscure bugs as programmers unwittingly modified objects in one part of a script, expecting the changes to be seen via references elsewhere. Throughout this book we will see many examples in which we maintain multiple references to the same object.

Luckily, there was a way of enforcing pass-by-reference, but it meant remembering to use a clumsy construction.

To assign by reference:

```
$other =& $my_obj;
// $other and $my_obj point to same object
```

To pass by reference:

```
function setSchool( & $school ) {
    // $school is now a reference to not a copy of passed object
}
```

To return by reference:

```
function & getSchool( ) {
    // returning a reference not a copy
    return $this->school;
}
```

Although this worked fine, it was easy to forget to add the ampersand, and it was all too easy for bugs to creep into object-oriented code. These were particularly hard to track down, because they rarely caused any reported errors, just nonsensical behavior.

Coverage of syntax in general, and objects in particular, was extended in the PHP manual, and object-oriented coding began to bubble up to the mainstream. Objects in PHP were not uncontroversial (then, as now, no doubt), and threads like "Do I need objects?" were common flame-bait in mailing lists. Indeed, the Zend site played host to articles that encouraged object-oriented programming side by side with others that sounded a warning note.

Pass-by-reference issues and controversy notwithstanding, many coders just got on and peppered their code with ampersand characters. Object-oriented PHP grew in popularity. As Zeev Suraski wrote recently in an article for DevX.com:

> *One of the biggest twists in PHP's history was that despite the very limited functionality, and despite a host of problems and limitations, object oriented programming in PHP thrived and became the most popular paradigm for the growing numbers of off-the-shelf PHP applications. This trend, which was mostly unexpected, caught PHP in a sub-optimal situation. It became apparent that objects were not behaving like objects in other OO languages, and were instead behaving like associating arrays.*

> [http://www.devx.com/webdev/Article/10007/0/page/1]

As noted in the previous chapter, interest in object-oriented design became obvious in sites and articles online. PHP's official software repository, PEAR, itself embraced object-oriented programming. Some of the best examples of deployed object-oriented design patterns are to be found in the packages that PEAR makes available to extend PHP's functionality.

Change Embraced: PHP 5

PHP 5 represents an explicit endorsement of objects and object-oriented programming. That is not to say that objects are now the only way to work with PHP (this book does not say that either, by the way). Objects, are, however, now recognized as a powerful and important means for developing enterprise systems, and PHP fully supports them in its core design.

Objects have moved from afterthought to language driver. Perhaps the most important change is the default pass-by-reference behavior in place of the evils of object copying. This is only the beginning though. Throughout the book, and particularly this part of it, we will encounter many more changes that extend and enhance PHP's object support, including argument hinting, private and protected methods and properties, the static keyword, and exceptions, among many others.

PHP remains a language that supports object-oriented development, rather than an object-oriented language. Its support for objects, however, is now well enough developed to justify books like this one that concentrate upon design from an exclusively object-oriented point of view.

Advocacy and Agnosticism, the Object Debate

Objects and object-oriented design seem to stir passions on both sides of the enthusiasm divide. Many excellent programmers have produced excellent code for years without using objects, and PHP continues to be a superb platform for procedural Web programming.

This book naturally displays an object-oriented bias throughout, a bias that reflects the author's object-infected outlook. Because this book *is* a celebration of objects, and an introduction to object-oriented design, it is inevitable that the emphasis is unashamedly object-oriented. Nothing in this book is intended, however, to suggest that objects are the one true path to coding success with PHP.

As you read, it is worth bearing in mind the famous Perl motto "There's more than one way to do it." This is especially true of smaller scripts, where getting a quick working example up and running is more important than building a structure that will scale well into a larger system (test projects of this sort are known as "spikes" in the XP world).

Code is a flexible medium. The trick is to know when your quick proof of concept is becoming the root of a larger development, and to call a halt before your design decisions are made for you by sheer weight of code. Now that you have decided to take a design-oriented approach to your growing project, there are plenty of books that will provide examples of procedural design for many different kinds of projects. This book offers some thoughts about designing with objects. I hope that it provides a valuable starting point.

Summary

This short chapter placed objects in their context in the PHP language. The future for PHP is very much bound up with object-oriented design. In the next few chapters, I take a snapshot of PHP's current support for object features, and introduce some design issues.

CHAPTER 3

■ ■ ■

Object Basics

Objects and classes lie at the heart of this book and, with the introduction of the Zend 2 Engine, they lie at the heart of PHP too. In this chapter, I lay down the groundwork and show you objects from first principles.

Things have changed quite radically since PHP 4, so even if you are an experienced PHP programmer, you will probably find something new here. If you are new to object-oriented programming, you should read this chapter carefully.

This chapter will cover

- *Classes and objects*: Declaring classes, instantiating objects

- *Constructor methods*: Automating the setup of your objects

- *Primitive and class types*: Why type matters

- *Inheritance*: Why we need inheritance, and how to use it

- *Visibility*: Streamlining your object interfaces and protecting your methods and properties from meddling

Classes and Objects

The first barrier to understanding object-oriented programming is the strange and wonderful relationship between the class and the object. For many people it is this relationship that represents the first moment of revelation, the first flash of object-oriented excitement. So let's not skimp on the basics.

A First Class

Classes are often defined in terms of objects. This is interesting because objects are often defined in terms of classes. This circularity can make the first steps in object-oriented programming hard going. Since classes define objects, we should begin by defining a class.

In short, a class is a code template used to generate objects. We declare a class with the class keyword and an arbitrary class name. Class names can be any combination of numbers and letters, although they must not begin with a number. The code associated with a class must be enclosed within braces. Let's combine these elements to build a class.

```
class ShopProduct {
    // class body
}
```

The ShopProduct class in the example is already a legal class, although it is not terribly useful yet. We have done something quite significant, however. We have defined a type. That is, we have created a category of data that we can use in our scripts. The power of this should become clearer as you work through the chapter.

A First Object (or Two)

If a class is a template for generating objects, it follows that an object is data that has been structured according to the template defined in a class. An object is said to be an instance of its class. It is of the type defined by the class.

We use our ShopProduct class as a mold for generating ShopProduct objects. To do this, we need the new operator. The new operator is used in conjunction with the name of a class, like this:

```
$product1 = new ShopProduct();
$product2 = new ShopProduct();
```

The new operator is invoked with a class name as its only operand and generates an instance of that class. That is, in our example, it generates a ShopProduct object.

We have used the ShopProduct class as a template to generate two ShopProduct objects. Although they are functionally identical (that is, empty), $product1 and $product2 are different objects of the same type generated from a single class.

If you are still confused, try this analogy. Think of a class as a cast in a plastic duck machine. Our objects are the ducks that this machine generates. The type of thing they are is determined by the mold from which they are pressed. They look identical in every way, but they are distinct entities. In other words, they are different instances of the same thing. The ducks may even have their own serial numbers to prove their identities. Every object that is created in a PHP script is also given its own unique identity (unique to that process, that is, not globally unique). We can prove this by printing out our $product1 and $product2 objects:

```
print "$product1\n";
print "$product2\n";
// output:
// Object id #1
// Object id #2
```

Objects are not meant to be printed directly, on the whole, but as you can see, printing an object reveals its identity number.

In order to make our objects more interesting, we can amend the ShopProduct class to support special data fields called properties.

Setting Properties in a Class

Classes can define special variables called properties. A property, also known as a member variable, holds data that can vary from object to object. So in the case of ShopProduct objects we may wish to manipulate title and price fields, for example.

A property in a class looks similar to a standard variable except that we must precede our declaration and assignment with a visiblity keyword. This can be public, protected, or private, and determines the scope from which the property can be accessed.

■**Note** Scope refers to the function or class context in which a variable has meaning. So a variable defined in a function exists in local scope, and a variable defined outside of the function exists in global scope. As a rule of thumb, it is not possible to access data defined in a scope that is more local than the current. So if you define a variable inside a function, you cannot then access it from outside that function. Objects are more permeable than this, in that some object variables can sometimes be accessed from other contexts. Which variables can be accessed and from what context is determined by the public, protected, and private keywords, as we shall see.

We will return to these keywords and the issue of visibility later in this chapter. For now, let's declare some properties using the public keyword:

```
class ShopProduct {
    public $title              = "default product";
    public $producerMainName   = "main name";
    public $producerFirstName  = "first name";
    public $price              = 0;
}
```

As you can see, we set up four properties, assigning a default value to each of them. Any objects that we instantiate from the ShopProduct class will now be prepopulated with default data. The public keyword in each property declaration ensures that we can access the property from outside of the object context.

■**Note** The visibility keywords public, private, and protected were introduced in PHP 5. If you are running PHP 4, these examples will not work for you. In PHP 4 all properties should be declared with the var keyword, which is identical in effect to using public:

```
class ShopProduct {
        var $title              = "default product";
        var $producerMainName   = "main name";
        var $producerFirstName  = "first name";
        var $price              = 0;
}
```

As the examples in this book become more complex, it will become more difficult to adapt them to work with PHP 4. If you have not yet done so, now might be the time to consider upgrading.

We can access property variables on an object-by-object basis using the characters '->' in conjunction with an object variable and property name, like this:

```
$product1 = new ShopProduct();
print $product1->title;
// outputs:
// default product
```

Because the properties are defined as public, we can assign values to them just as we can read them, replacing any default value set in the class:

```
$product1 = new ShopProduct();
$product2 = new ShopProduct();
$product1->title="My Antonia";
$product2->title="Catch 22";
```

By declaring and setting the $title property in the ShopProduct class, we ensure that all ShopProduct objects have this property. This means that client code can work with ShopProduct objects on that assumption. Because we can reset it, though, the value of $title may vary from object to object.

In fact, PHP does not force us to declare all our properties in the class. We could add properties dynamically to an object, like this:

```
$product1->arbitraryAddition = "treehouse";
```

This method of assigning properties to objects is not considered good practice in object-oriented programming, and is almost never used.

Note Is it bad practice to set properties dynamically? When you create a class you define a type. You inform the world that your class (and any object instantiated from it) consists of a particular set of fields and functions. If your ShopProduct class defines a $title property, then any code that works with ShopProduct objects can proceed on the assumption that a $title property will be available. There can be no guarantees about properties that have been dynamically set, though.

Our objects are still cumbersome at this stage. When we need to work with an object's properties, we must currently do so from outside the object. We reach in to set and get property information. Setting multiple properties on multiple objects will soon become a chore:

```
$product1 = new ShopProduct();
$product1->title = "My Antonia";
$product1->producerMainName  = "Cather";
$product1->producerFirstName = "Willa";
$product1->price = 5.99;
```

We work once again with the ShopProduct class, overriding all the default property values one by one until we have set all product details. Now that we have set some data we can also access it:

```
print "author: {$product1->producerFirstName} "
            ."{$product1->producerMainName}\n";
// output:
// author: Willa Cather
```

There are a number of problems with this approach to setting property values. Because PHP lets you set properties dynamically, you will not get warned if you misspell or forget a property name. For example, we might mistakenly write the line

```
$product1->producerMainName  = "Cather";
```

as

```
$product1->producerSecondName  = "Cather";
```

As far as the PHP engine is concerned, this code is perfectly legal, and we are not warned. When we come to print the author name, though, we will get unexpected results.

Another problem is that our objects are altogether too relaxed. We are not forced to set a title, or a price, or producer names. Client code can be sure that these properties exist, but is likely to be confronted with default values as often as not. Ideally, we would like to encourage anyone who instantiates a ShopProduct object to set meaningful property values.

Finally, we have to jump through hoops to do something that we will probably want to do quite often. Printing the full author name is a tiresome process:

```
print "author: {$product1->producerFirstName} "
            ."{$product1->producerMainName}\n";
```

It would be nice to have the object handle such drudgery on our behalf.

All of these problems can be addressed by giving our ShopProduct object its own set of functions that can be used to manipulate property data from within the object context.

Working with Methods

Just as properties allow your objects to store data, methods allow your objects to perform tasks. Methods are special functions declared within a class. As you might expect, a method declaration resembles a function declaration. The function keyword precedes a method name, followed by an optional list of argument variables in parentheses. The method body is enclosed by braces:

```
public function myMethod( $argument, $another ) {
    // ...
}
```

Unlike functions, methods must be declared in the body of a class. They can also accept a number of qualifiers, including a visibility keyword. Like properties, methods can be declared public, protected, or private. By declaring a method public, we ensure that it can be invoked from outside of the current object. If you omit the visibility keyword in your method declaration, the method will be declared public implicitly. We will return to method modifiers later in sthe chapter.

■ Note PHP 4 does not recognize visibility keywords for methods or properties. Adding `public`, `protected`, or `private` to a method declaration will cause a fatal error. All methods in PHP 4 are implicitly public.

In most circumstances you will invoke a method using an object variable in conjunction with ->, and the method name. You must use parentheses in your method call as you would if you were calling a function (even if you are not passing any arguments to the method).

```
$myObj = new MyClass();
$myObj->myMethod( "Harry", "Palmer" );
```

Let's declare a method in our ShopProduct class:

```
class ShopProduct {
        public $title           = "default product";
        public $producerMainName  = "main name";
        public $producerFirstName = "first name";
        public $price            = 0;

        function getProducer() {
            return "{$this->producerFirstName}".
                " {$this->producerMainName}";
        }
    }
```

```
$product1 = new ShopProduct();
$product1->title = "My Antonia";
$product1->producerMainName  = "Cather";
$product1->producerFirstName = "Willa";
$product1->price = 5.99;
```

```
print "author: ".$product1->getProducer()."\n";
// outputs:
// author: Willa Cather
```

We add the getProducer() method to the ShopProduct class. Notice that we do not include a visibility keyword. This means that getProducer() is a public method and can be called from outside the class.

We use a new feature in this method. The $this pseudo-variable is the mechanism by which a class can refer to an object instance. If you find this concept hard to swallow, try replacing $this with "the current instance." So the statement

```
$this->producerFirstName
```

translates to

```
the $producerFirstName property of the current instance.
```

So getProducer() combines and returns the $producerFirstName and $producerMainName properties, saving us from the chore of performing this task every time we need to quote the full producer name.

This has improved our class a little. We are still stuck with a great deal of unwanted flexibility, though. We rely upon the client coder to change a ShopProduct object's properties from their default values. This is problematic in two ways. Firstly, it takes five lines to properly initialize a ShopProduct object, and no coder will thank you for that. Secondly, we have no way of ensuring that any of the properties are set when a ShopProduct object is initialized. What we need is a method that is called automatically when an object is instantiated from a class.

Creating a Constructor Method

A constructor method is invoked when an object is created. You can use it to set things up, ensuring that essential properties are set, and any necessary preliminary work is completed. In PHP versions previous to 5, constructor methods took on the name of the class that enclosed them. So the ShopProduct class would use a ShopProduct() method as its constructor. As of PHP 5 you should name your constructor method __construct(). Note that the method name begins with two underscore characters. We will see this naming convention for many other special methods in PHP classes. Let's define a constructor for the ShopProduct class.

```
class ShopProduct {
        public $title;
        public $producerMainName;
        public $producerFirstName;
        public $price = 0;

        function __construct( $title,
                                $firstName, $mainName, $price ) {
            $this->title             = $title;
            $this->producerFirstName = $firstName;
            $this->producerMainName  = $mainName;
            $this->price             = $price;
        }

        function getProducer() {
            return "{$this->producerFirstName}".
                " {$this->producerMainName}";
        }
}
```

Once again we gather functionality into the class, saving effort and duplication in the code that uses it. The __construct() method is invoked when an object is created using the new operator.

```
$product1 = new ShopProduct( "My Antonia",
                                "Willa", "Cather", 5.99 );
print "author: ".$product1->getProducer()."\n";
// outputs:
// author: Willa Cather
```

Any arguments supplied are passed to the constructor. So in our example, we pass the title, the first name, the main name, and the product price to the constructor. The constructor method uses the pseudo-variable $this to assign values to each of the object's properties.

Note PHP 4 does not recognize the __construct() method as a constructor. If you are using PHP 4 you can create a constructor by declaring a method with the same name as the class that contains it. So for a class called ShopProduct, you would declare a constructor like this:

```
function ShopProduct( $title,
                     $firstName, $mainName, $price ) {
    //...
}
```

Php still honors this naming scheme, but unless you are writing for backwards compatibility, it is better to use __construct() when you name your constructor methods.

A ShopProduct object is now easier to instantiate and safer to use. Instantiation and setup are completed in a single statement. Any code that uses a ShopProduct object can be reasonably sure that all its properties are initialized.

This predictability is an important aspect of object-oriented programming. You should design your classes so that users of objects can be sure of their features. By the same token, when you use an object you should be sure of its type. In the next section, we examine a mechanism that we can use to enforce object types in method declarations.

Arguments and Types

Type determines the way that data can be managed in your scripts. You use the string type to display character data, for example, and manipulate such data with string functions. Integers are used in mathematical expressions, Booleans are used in test expressions, and so on. These categories are known as "primitive types." On a higher level, though, a class defines a type. A ShopProduct object, therefore, belongs to the primitive type "object," but it also belongs to the "ShopProduct" class type. In this section we will look at types of both kinds in relation to class methods.

Method and function definitions do not necessarily require that an argument should be of a particular type. This is both a curse and a blessing. The fact that an argument can be of any type offers you flexibility. You can build methods that respond intelligently to different data types, tailoring functionality to changing circumstances. This flexibility can also cause ambiguity to creep into code when a method body expects an argument to hold one type but gets another.

Primitive Types

PHP is a loosely typed language. This means that there is no necessity for a variable to be declared to hold a particular data type. The variable $number could hold the value 2 and the string "two" within the same scope. In strongly typed languages such as C or Java, you must declare the type of a variable before assigning a value to it, and, of course, the value must be of the specified type.

This does not mean that PHP has no concept of type. Every value that can be assigned to a variable has a type. You can determine the type of a variable's value using one of PHP's type-checking functions. Table 3-1 lists the primitive types recognized in PHP and their corresponding test functions. Each function accepts a variable or value and returns true if this argument is of the relevant type.

Table 3-1. *Primitive Types and Checking Functions in PHP*

Type Checking Function	Type	Description
is_bool()	Boolean	One of the two special values true or false
is_integer()	Integer	A whole number
is_double()	Double	A floating point number (a number with a decimal point)
is_string()	String	Character data
is_object()	Object	An object
is_array()	Array	An array
is_resource()	Resource	A handle for identifying and working with external resources such as databases or files
is_null()	NULL	An unassigned value

Checking the type of a variable can be particularly important when you work with method and function arguments.

Primitive Types Matter: An Example

You need to keep a close eye on type in your code. Let's look at an example of one of the many type-related problems that you could encounter.

Imagine that you are extracting configuration settings from an XML file. The <resolvedomains> XML element tells your application whether it should attempt to resolve IP addresses to domain names, a useful but relatively expensive process in terms of time. Here is some sample XML:

```
<settings>
    <resolvedomains>false</resolvedomains>
</settings>
```

The string "false" is extracted by your application and passed as a flag to a method called outputAddresses(), which displays IP address data. Here is outputAddresses():

```
    function outputAddresses( $resolve ) {
        foreach ( $this->addresses as $address ) {
            print $address;
            if ( $resolve ) {
                print " (".gethostbyaddr( $address ).")";
            }
            print "\n";
        }
    }
```

As you can see, the outputAddresses() method loops through an array of IP addresses, printing each one. If the $resolve argument variable itself resolves to true, the method outputs the domain name as well as the IP address.

Let's examine some code that might invoke this method:

```
$settings = simplexml_load_file("settings.xml");
$manager = new AddressManager();
$manager->outputAddresses( $settings->resolvedomains );
```

The code fragment uses the SimpleXML API (which was introduced with PHP 5) to acquire a value for the resolvedomains element. In our example, we know that this value is the string "false".

This code will not behave as you might expect. In passing the string "false" to the outputAddresses() method, we misunderstand the implicit assumption the method makes about the argument. The method is expecting a Boolean value (that is true or false). The string "false" will, in fact, resolve to true in a test. This is because PHP will helpfully cast a nonempty string value to the Boolean true for you in a test context. So

```
if ( "false" ) {
    // ...
}
```

is equivalent to

```
if ( true ) {
    // ...
}
```

There are a number of approaches you might take to fix this.

You could make the outputAddresses() method more forgiving so that it recognizes a string and applies some basic rules to convert it to a Boolean equivalent.

```
    function outputAddresses( $resolve ) {
        if ( is_string( $resolve ) ) {
            $resolve =
                ( preg_match("/false|no|off/i", $resolve ) )?
                    false:true;
        }
        // ...
    }
```

You could leave the outputAddresses() method as it is, but include a comment containing clear instructions that the $resolve argument should contain a Boolean value. This approach essentially tells the coder to read the small print or reap the consequences.

```
/**
 * Outputs the list of addresses.
 * If $resolve is true then each address will be resolved
 * @param      $resolve     Boolean     Resolve the address?
 */
function outputAddresses( $resolve ) {
    // ...
}
```

Finally, you could make outputAddresses() strict about the type of data it is prepared to find in the $resolve argument.

```
function outputAddresses( $resolve ) {
    if ( ! is_bool( $resolve ) ) {
        die( "outputAddress() requires a Boolean argument\n" );
    }
    //...
}
```

This approach forces client code to provide the correct data type in the $resolve argument. Converting a string argument on the client's behalf would be the more friendly approach, but would probably present other problems. In providing a conversion mechanism, we second-guess the context and intent of the client. By enforcing the Boolean data type, on the other hand, we leave the client to decide whether to map strings to Boolean values, and which word will map to which value. The outputAddresses() method, meanwhile, concentrates on the task it is designed to perform. This emphasis upon performing a specific task in deliberate ignorance of the wider context is an important principle in object-oriented programming, and we will return to it frequently throughout the book.

In fact, your strategies for dealing with argument types will depend upon the seriousness of any potential bugs. PHP casts most primitive values for you depending upon context. Numbers in strings are converted to their integer or floating point equivalents when used in a mathematical expression, for example. So your code might be naturally forgiving of type errors. If you expect one of your method arguments to be an array, however, you may need to be more careful. Passing a nonarray value to one of PHP's array functions will not produce a useful result, and could cause a cascade of errors in your method.

It is likely, therefore, that you will strike a balance between testing for type, converting from one type to another, and relying upon good, clear documentation (you should provide the documentation whatever else you decide to do).

However you address problems of this kind, you can be sure of one thing: type matters. The fact that PHP is loosely typed makes this all the more important. You cannot rely on a compiler to prevent type-related bugs. It is up to you to consider the potential impact of unexpected types when they find their way into your arguments. You cannot afford to trust client coders to read your thoughts, and you should always consider how your methods will deal with incoming garbage.

Taking the Hint: Object Types

Just as an argument variable can contain any primitive type, by default it can contain an object of any type. This flexibility has its uses, but can present problems in the context of a method definition.

Imagine a method designed to work with a ShopProduct object:

```
class ShopProductWriter {
    public function write( $shopProduct ) {
        $str  = "{$shopProduct->title}: ";
        $str .= $shopProduct->getProducer();
        $str .= " ({$shopProduct->price})\n";
        print $str;
    }
}
```

We can test this class like this:

```
$product1 = new ShopProduct( "My Antonia",
                             "Willa", "Cather", 5.99 );
$writer = new ShopProductWriter();
$writer->write( $product1 );
// output:
// My Antonia: Willa Cather (5.99)
```

The ShopProductWriter class contains a single method: write(). The write() method accepts a ShopProduct object and uses its properties and methods to construct and print a summary string. We use the name of the argument variable, $shopProduct, as a signal that the method expects a ShopProduct object, but we do not enforce this.

To address this problem, PHP 5 introduced class type hints. To add a type hint to a method argument, you simply place a class name in front of the method argument you need to constrain. So we can amend our write() method thus:

```
    public function write( ShopProduct $shopProduct ) {
        // ...
    }
```

Now the write() method will only accept the $shopProduct argument if it contains an object of type ShopProduct. Let's try to call write() with a dodgy object:

```
class Wrong { }
$writer = new ShopProductWriter();
$writer->write( new Wrong() );
```

Because the write() method contains a class type hint, passing it a Wrong object causes a fatal error.

```
Fatal error: Argument 1 must be an object of class ShopProduct ...
```

This saves us from having to test the type of the argument before we work with it. It also makes the method signature much clearer for the client coder. She can see the requirements of the write() method at a glance. She does not have to worry about some obscure bug arising from a type error, because the hint is rigidly enforced.

Even though this automating type checking is a great way of preventing bugs, it is important to understand that hints are checked at runtime. This means that a class hint will only report an error at the moment that an unwanted object is passed to the method. If a call to write() is buried in a conditional clause that only runs on Christmas morning, then you may find yourself working the holiday if you haven't checked your code carefully.

So far we have discussed types and classes as if they were synonymous. There is a key difference, however. When you define a class you also define a type, but a type can describe an entire family of classes. The mechanism by which different classes can be grouped together under a type is called inheritance. We discuss inheritance in the next section.

Inheritance

Inheritance is the mechanism by which one or more classes can be derived from a base class.

A class that inherits from another is said to subclass it. This relationship is often described in terms of parents and children. A child class is derived from and inherits characteristics from the parent. These characteristics consist of both properties and methods. The child class will typically add new functionality in addition to that provided by its parent (also known as a super class); for this reason a child class is said to "extend" its parent.

Before we dive into the syntax of inheritance, let's examine the problems it can help us to solve.

The Inheritance Problem

Look again at the ShopProduct class. At the moment it is nicely generic. It can handle all sorts of products.

```
$product1 = new ShopProduct(    "My Antonia", "Willa", "Cather", 5.99 );
$product2 = new ShopProduct(    "Exile on Coldharbour Lane",
                                "The", "Alabama 3", 10.99 );
print "author: ".$product1->getProducer()."\n";
print "artist: ".$product2->getProducer()."\n";
// output:
// author: Willa Cather
// artist: The Alabama 3
```

Separating the producer name into two parts works well with both books and CDs. We want to be able to sort on "Alabama 3" and "Cather", not on "The" and "Willa". Laziness is an excellent design strategy, so there is no need to worry about using ShopProduct for more than one kind of product at this stage.

If we add some new requirements to our example, however, things rapidly become more complicated. Imagine, for example, that you need to represent data specific to books and CDs. For CDs you must store the total playing time, for books the total number of pages. There could be any number of other differences, but these will serve to illustrate the issue.

How can we extend our example to accommodate these changes? Two options immediately present themselves. Firstly, we could throw all the data into the ShopProduct class. Secondly, we could split ShopProduct into two separate classes.

Let's examine the first approach. Here, we combine CD- and book-related data in a single class:

```php
class ShopProduct {
    public $numPages;
    public $playLength;
    public $title;
    public $producerMainName;
    public $producerFirstName;
    public $price;

    function __construct(   $title, $firstName,
                            $mainName, $price,
                            $numPages=0, $playLength=0 ) {
        $this->title             = $title;
        $this->producerFirstName = $firstName;
        $this->producerMainName  = $mainName;
        $this->price             = $price;
        $this->numPages          = $numPages;
        $this->playLength        = $playLength;
    }

    function getNumberOfPages() {
        return $this->numPages;
    }

    function getPlayLength() {
        return $this->playLength;
    }

    function getProducer() {
        return "{$this->producerFirstName}".
                " {$this->producerMainName}";
    }
}
```

An object instantiated from this class will include a redundant method, and possibly an unnecessary constructor argument. A CD will store information and functionality relating to book pages, and a book will support play-length data. This is probably something you could live with right now. But what would happen if we added more product types, each with its own methods, and then added more methods for each type? Our class would become increasingly complex and hard to manage.

So forcing fields that don't belong together into a single class leads to bloated objects with redundant properties and methods.

The problem doesn't end with data, either. We run into difficulties with functionality as well. Consider a method that summarizes a product. The sales department has requested a clear summary line for use in invoices. They want us to include the playing time for CDs and a page count for books, so we will be forced to provide different implementations for each type. We also need to use a flag to keep track of the object's format. Here's an example:

```
function getSummaryLine() {
    $base  = "{$this->title} ( {$this->producerMainName}, ";
    $base .= "{$this->producerFirstName} )";
    if ( $this->type == 'book' ) {
        $base .= ": page count - {$this->numPages}";
    } else if ( $this->type == 'cd' ) {
        $base .= ": playing time - {$this->playLength}";
    }
    return $base;
}
```

Once again our ShopProduct class has become more complex than necessary. As we add more differences to our formats, or add new formats, these functional differences will become harder to manage. Perhaps we should try the second approach to this problem.

Since ShopProduct is beginning to feel like two classes in one, we could accept this and create two types rather than one. Here's how we might do it:

```
class CdProduct {
    public $playLength;
    public $title;
    public $producerMainName;
    public $producerFirstName;
    public $price;

    function __construct(    $title, $firstName,
                             $mainName, $price,
                             $playLength ) {
        $this->title               = $title;
        $this->producerFirstName   = $firstName;
        $this->producerMainName    = $mainName;
        $this->price               = $price;
        $this->playLength          = $playLength;

    }

    function getPlayLength() {
        return $this->playLength;
    }

    function getSummaryLine() {
        $base  = "{$this->title} ( {$this->producerMainName}, ";
        $base .= "{$this->producerFirstName} )";
        $base .= ": playing time - {$this->playLength}";
        return $base;
    }
}
```

```
        function getProducer() {
            return "{$this->producerFirstName}".
                " {$this->producerMainName}";
        }
    }

class BookProduct {
    public $numPages;
    public $title;
    public $producerMainName;
    public $producerFirstName;
    public $price;

    function __construct(    $title, $firstName,
                             $mainName, $price,
                             $numPages ) {
        $this->title           = $title;
        $this->producerFirstName = $firstName;
        $this->producerMainName  = $mainName;
        $this->price             = $price;
        $this->numPages          = $numPages;
    }

    function getNumberOfPages() {
        return $this->numPages;
    }

    function getSummaryLine() {
        $base  = "{$this->title} ( {$this->producerMainName}, ";
        $base .= "{$this->producerFirstName} )";
        $base .= ": page count - {$this->numPages}";
        return $base;
    }

    function getProducer() {
        return "{$this->producerFirstName}".
            " {$this->producerMainName}";
    }
}
```

We have addressed the complexity issue, but at a cost. We can now create a getSummaryLine()
method for each format without having to test a flag. Neither class maintains fields or methods
that are not relevant to it.

The cost lies in duplication. The getProducerName() method is exactly the same in each
class. Each constructor sets a number of identical properties in the same way. This is another
unpleasant odor you should train yourself to sniff out.

If we need the getProducerName() method to behave identically for each class, any changes we make to one implementation will need to be made for the other. Our class will soon slip out of synchronization.

Even if we are confident that we can maintain the duplication, our worries are not over. We now have two types rather than one.

Remember the ShopProductWriter class? Its write() method is designed to work with a single type: ShopProduct. How can we amend this to work as before? We could remove the class type hint from the method declaration, but then we must trust to luck that write() is passed an object of the correct type. We could add our own type checking code to the body of the method:

```
class ShopProductWriter {
    public function write( $shopProduct ) {
        if ( ! ( $shopProduct instanceof CdWriter )  &&
             ! ( $shopProduct instanceof BookProduct ) ) {
            die( "wrong type supplied" );
        }
        $str  = "{$shopProduct->title}: ";
        $str .= $shopProduct->getProducer();
        $str .= " ({$shopProduct->price})\n";
        print $str;
    }
}
```

Notice the instanceof operator in the example. instanceof resolves to true if the object in the left-hand operand is of the type represented by the right-hand operand.

Once again we have been forced to include a new layer of complexity. Not only do we have to test the $shopProduct argument against two types in the write() method, but we have to trust that each type will continue to support the same fields and methods as the other. It was all much neater when we simply demanded a single type because we could use class type hinting, and because we could be confident that the ShopProduct class supported a particular interface.

The CD and book aspects of the ShopProduct class don't work well together, but can't live apart, it seems. We want to work with books and CDs as a single type while providing a separate implementation for each format. We want to provide common functionality in one place to avoid duplication but allow each format to handle some method calls differently. We need to use inheritance.

Working with Inheritance

The first step in building an inheritance tree is to find the elements of the base class that don't fit together, or that need to be handled differently.

We know that the getPlayLength() and getNumberOfPages() methods do not belong together. We also know that we would like to create different implementations for the getSummaryLine() method. Let's use these differences as the basis for two derived classes:

```php
class ShopProduct {
    public $numPages;
    public $playLength;
    public $title;
    public $producerMainName;
    public $producerFirstName;
    public $price;

    function __construct(   $title, $firstName,
                            $mainName, $price,
                            $numPages=0, $playLength=0 ) {
        $this->title            = $title;
        $this->producerFirstName = $firstName;
        $this->producerMainName  = $mainName;
        $this->price            = $price;
        $this->numPages         = $numPages;
        $this->playLength       = $playLength;
    }

    function getProducer() {
        return "{$this->producerFirstName}".
               " {$this->producerMainName}";
    }

    function getSummaryLine() {
        $base = "$this->title ( {$this->producerMainName}, ";
        $base .= "{$this->producerFirstName} )";
        return $base;
    }
}

class CdProduct extends ShopProduct {
    function getPlayLength() {
        return $this->playLength;
    }

    function getSummaryLine() {
        $base = "{$this->title} ( {$this->producerMainName}, ";
        $base .= "{$this->producerFirstName} )";
        $base .= ": playing time - {$this->playLength}";
        return $base;
    }
}
```

```
class BookProduct extends ShopProduct {
    function getNumberOfPages() {
        return $this->numPages;
    }

    function getSummaryLine() {
        $base  = "{$this->title} ( {$this->producerMainName}, ";
        $base .= "{$this->producerFirstName} )";
        $base .= ": page count - {$this->numPages}";
        return $base;
    }
}
```

To create a child class, you must use the extends keyword in the class declaration. In the example we created two new classes, BookProduct and CdProduct. Both extend the ShopProduct class.

Because the derived classes do not define constructors, the parent class's constructor is automatically invoked when they are instantiated. The child classes inherit access to all the parent's public and protected methods. This means that we can call the getProducer() method on an object instantiated from the CdProduct class, even though getProducer() is defined in the ShopProduct class.

```
$product2 =   new CdProduct(    "Exile on Coldharbour Lane",
                                "The", "Alabama 3",
                                10.99, null, 60.33 );
print "artist: ".$product2->getProducer()."\n";
```

So both our child classes inherit the behavior of the common parent. We can treat a BookProduct object as if it were a ShopProduct object. We can pass a BookProduct or CdProduct object to the ShopProductWriter class's write() method and all will work as expected.

Notice that both our CdProduct and BookProduct classes override the getSummaryLine() method, providing their own implementation. Derived classes can extend but also alter the functionality of their parents. At the same time, each class inherits its parent's properties. Both BookProduct and CdProduct access the $title property in their versions of getSummaryLine().

Inheritance can be a difficult concept to grasp at first. By defining a class that extends another, we ensure that an object instantiated from it is defined by the characteristics of first the child, and then the parent class. Another way of thinking about this is in terms of searching. When we invoke $product2->getProducer(), there is no such method to be found in the CdProduct class, and the invocation falls through to the default implementation in ShopProduct. When we invoke $product2->getSummaryLine(), on the other hand, the getSummaryLine() method is found in CdProduct and invoked.

The same is true of property accesses. When we access $title in the BookProduct class's getSummaryLine() method, the property is not found in the BookProduct class. It is acquired instead from the parent class, from ShopProduct. The $title property applies equally to both subclasses, and therefore it belongs in the super class.

A quick look at the ShopProduct constructor, however, shows that we are still managing data in the base class that should be handled by its children. The BookProduct class should handle the $numPages argument and property, and the CdProduct class should handle the

$playLength argument and property. To make this work, we will define constructor methods in each of the child classes.

Constructors and Inheritance

When you define a constructor in a child class, you become responsible for passing any arguments on to the parent. If you fail to do this, you can end up with a partially constructed object.

To invoke a method in a parent class, you must first find a way of referring to the class itself: a "handle." PHP provides us with the parent keyword for this purpose.

To refer to a method in the context of a class rather than an object we use :: rather than ->. So

```
parent::__construct()
```

means "Invoke the __construct() method of the parent class." Let's amend our example so that each class handles only the data that is appropriate to it.

```
class ShopProduct {
    public $title;
    public $producerMainName;
    public $producerFirstName;
    public $price;

    function __construct(   $title, $firstName,
                            $mainName, $price ) {
        $this->title             = $title;
        $this->producerFirstName = $firstName;
        $this->producerMainName  = $mainName;
        $this->price             = $price;
    }

    function getProducer() {
        return "{$this->producerFirstName}".
               " {$this->producerMainName}";
    }

      function getSummaryLine() {
        $base  = "{$this->title} ( {$this->producerMainName}, ";
        $base .= "{$this->producerFirstName} )";
        return $base;
    }
}

class CdProduct extends ShopProduct {
    public $playLength;
```

```php
    function __construct(    $title, $firstName,
                            $mainName, $price, $playLength ) {
        parent::__construct(    $title, $firstName,
                                $mainName, $price );
        $this->playLength = $playLength;
    }

    function getPlayLength() {
        return $this->playLength;
    }

    function getSummaryLine() {
        $base  = "{$this->title} ( {$this->producerMainName}, ";
        $base .= "{$this->producerFirstName} )";
        $base .= ": playing time - {$this->playLength}";
        return $base;
    }
}

class BookProduct extends ShopProduct {
    public $numPages;

    function __construct(    $title, $firstName,
                            $mainName, $price, $numPages ) {
        parent::__construct(    $title, $firstName,
                                $mainName, $price );
        $this->numPages = $numPages;
    }

    function getNumberOfPages() {
        return $this->numPages;
    }

    function getSummaryLine() {
        $base  = "$this->title ( $this->producerMainName, ";
        $base .= "$this->producerFirstName )";
        $base .= ": page count - $this->numPages";
        return $base;
    }
}
```

Each child class invokes the constructor of its parent before setting its own properties. The base class now knows only about its own data. Child classes are generally specializations of their parents. As a rule of thumb, you should avoid giving parent classes any special knowledge about their children.

Note Prior to PHP 5, constructors took on the name of the enclosing class. The new unified constructors use the name __construct(). Using the old syntax, a call to a parent constructor would tie you to that particular class:

```
parent::ShopProduct();
```

This could cause problems if the class hierarchy changed. Many bugs resulted from programmers changing the immediate parent of a class but forgetting to update the constructor. Using the unified constructor, a call to the parent constructor

```
parent::__construct()
```

invokes the immediate parent, no matter what changes are made in the hierarchy. Of course, you still need to ensure that the correct arguments are passed to an inserted parent!

Invoking an Overridden Method

The parent keyword can be used with any method that overrides its counterpart in a parent class. When we override a method, we may not wish to obliterate the functionality of the parent but rather extend it. We can achieve this by calling the parent class's method in the current object's context. If you look again at the getSummaryLine() method implementations, you will see that they duplicate a lot of code. It would be better to use rather than reproduce the functionality already developed in the ShopProduct class.

```
// ShopProduct class...
    function getSummaryLine() {
        $base  = "{$this->title} ( {$this->producerMainName}, ";
        $base .= "{$this->producerFirstName} )";
        return $base;
    }
```

```
// BookProduct class...
    function getSummaryLine() {
        $base = parent::getSummaryLine();
        $base .= ": page count - {$this->numPages}";
        return $base;
    }
```

We set up the core functionality for the getSummaryLine() method in the ShopProduct base class. Rather than reproduce this in the CdProduct and BookProduct subclasses, we simply call the parent method before proceeding to add more data to the summary string.

Now that we have seen the basics of inheritance, we can at last look at property and method visibility in light of the full picture.

public, private, protected: Managing Access to Your Classes

So far we have declared all properties public whether implicitly or otherwise. Public access is the default setting for methods, and for properties if you use the old var keyword in your property declaration.

Elements in your classes can be declared public, private, or protected.

Public properties and methods can be accessed from any context.

A private method or property can only be accessed from within the enclosing class. Even subclasses have no access.

A protected method or property can only be accessed from within either the enclosing class or from a subclass. No external code is granted access.

So how is this useful to us? Visibility keywords allow us to expose only those aspects of a class that are required by a client. This sets a clear interface for your object.

By preventing a client from accessing certain properties, access control can also help prevent bugs in your code. Imagine, for example, that we want to allow ShopProduct objects to support a discount. We could add a $discount property and a setDiscount() method.

```
// ShopProduct class
    public $discount = 0;
// ...
    function setDiscount( $num ) {
        $this->discount=$num;
    }
```

Armed with a mechanism for setting a discount, we can create a getPrice() method that takes account of the discount that has been applied.

```
// ShopProduct class
    function getPrice() {
        return ($this->price - $this->discount);
    }
```

At this point we have a problem. We only want to expose the adjusted price to the world, but a client can easily bypass the getPrice() method and access the $price property:

```
print "The price is {$product1->price}\n";
```

This will print the raw price, and not the discount-adjusted price we wish to present. We can put a stop to this straight away by making the $price property private. This will prevent direct access, forcing clients to use the getPrice() method. Any attempt from outside the ShopProduct class to access the $price property will fail. As far as the wider world is concerned, this property has ceased to exist.

Setting properties to private can be an overzealous strategy. A private property cannot be accessed by a child class. Imagine that our business rules state that books alone should be ineligible for discount. We could override the getPrice() method so that it returns the $price property, applying no discount.

```
// BookProduct class
    function getPrice() {
        return $this->price;
    }
```

Since the private $price property is declared in the ShopProduct class and not BookProduct, the attempt to access it here will fail. The solution to this problem is to declare $price protected, thereby granting access to child classes. Remember that a protected property or method cannot be accessed from outside the class hierarchy in which it was declared. It can only be accessed from within its originating class, or from within children of the originating class.

As a general rule, err on the side of privacy. Make properties private or protected at first and relax your restriction only as needed. Many (if not most) methods in your classes will be public, but once again, if in doubt, lock it down. A method that provides local functionality for other methods in your class has no relevance to your class's users. Make it private or protected.

Accessor Methods

Even when client programmers need to work with values held by your class, it is often a good idea to deny direct access to properties, providing methods instead that relay the needed values. Such methods are known as accessors or "getters and setters."

You have already seen one benefit afforded by accessor methods. You can use an accessor to filter a property value according to circumstances, as was illustrated with the getPrice() method.

You can also use a setter method to enforce a property type. We have seen that class type hints can be used to constrain method arguments, but we have no direct control over property types. Remember the ShopProductWriter class that uses a ShopProduct object to output list data? Let's develop this further so that it writes any number of ShopProduct objects at one time:

```
class ShopProductWriter {
    public $products = array();

    public function addProduct( ShopProduct $shopProduct ) {
        $this->products[] = $shopProduct;
    }

    public function write() {
        $str = "";
        foreach ( $this->products as $shopProduct ) {
            $str .= "{$shopProduct->title}: ";
            $str .= $shopProduct->getProducer();
            $str .= " ({$shopProduct->getPrice()})\n";
        }
        print $str;
    }
}
```

The ShopProductWriter class is now much more useful. It can hold many ShopProduct objects, and write data for them all in one go. We must trust our client coders to respect the intentions of our class, though. Despite the fact that we have provided an addProduct() method, we have not prevented programmers from manipulating the $products property directly. Not only could someone add the wrong kind of object to the $products array property, but they could even overwrite the entire array and replace it with a primitive value. We can prevent this by making the $products property private:

```
class ShopProductWriter {
    private $products = array();
//...
```

It's now impossible for external code to damage the $products property. All access must be via the addProduct() method, and the class type hint we use in the method declaration ensures that only ShopProduct objects can be added to the array property.

The ShopProduct Classes

Let's close this chapter by amending the ShopProduct class and its children to lock down access control:

```
class ShopProduct {
    private $title;
    private $producerMainName;
    private $producerFirstName;
    protected $price;
    private $discount = 0;

    public function __construct(  $title, $firstName,
                          $mainName, $price ) {
        $this->title            = $title;
        $this->producerFirstName = $firstName;
        $this->producerMainName  = $mainName;
        $this->price            = $price;
    }

    public function getProducerFirstName() {
        return $this->producerFirstName;
    }

    public function getProducerMainName() {
        return $this->producerMainName;
    }

    public function setDiscount( $num ) {
        $this->discount=$num;
    }

    public function getDiscount() {
        return $this->discount;
    }
```

```php
    public function getTitle() {
        return $this->title;
    }

    public function getPrice() {
        return ($this->price - $this->discount);
    }

    public function getProducer() {
        return "{$this->producerFirstName}".
               " {$this->producerMainName}";
    }

    function getSummaryLine() {
        $base  = "{$this->title} ( {$this->producerMainName}, ";
        $base .= "{$this->producerFirstName} )";
        return $base;
    }
}

class CdProduct extends ShopProduct {
    private $playLength = 0;

    public function __construct(  $title, $firstName,
                            $mainName, $price, $playLength ) {
        parent::__construct(   $title, $firstName,
                            $mainName, $price );
        $this->playLength = $playLength;
    }

    public function getPlayLength() {
        return $this->playLength;
    }

    function getSummaryLine() {
        $base = parent::getSummaryLine();
        $base .= ": playing time - {$this->playLength}";
        return $base;
    }

}

class BookProduct extends ShopProduct {
    private $numPages = 0;
```

```
    public function __construct(    $title, $firstName,
                            $mainName, $price, $numPages ) {
        parent::__construct(    $title, $firstName,
                            $mainName, $price );
        $this->numPages = $numPages;
    }

    public function getNumberOfPages() {
        return $this->numPages;
    }

    function getSummaryLine() {
        $base = parent::getSummaryLine();
        $base .= ": page count - {$this->numPages}";
        return $base;
    }

    public function getPrice() {
        return $this->price;
    }
}
```

There is nothing substantially new in this version of the ShopProduct family. All methods have been made explicitly public, and all properties are now either private or protected. We have added a number of accessor methods to round things off.

Summary

This chapter covered a lot of ground, taking a class from an empty implementation through to a fully featured inheritance hierarchy. You took in some design issues, particularly with regard to type and inheritance. You saw PHP's new support for visibility and explored some of its uses. In the next chapter, I will show you more features supported by the Zend 2 Engine that powers PHP 5.

CHAPTER 4

■ ■ ■

Advanced Features

PHP 5 opened new vistas of possibility for object-oriented programmers. We have already seen how class type hinting and access control afford greater control over a class's interface. In this chapter, we will delve deeper into PHP's enhanced object-oriented support.

This chapter will cover

- *Static methods and properties*: Accessing data and functionality through classes rather than objects

- *Abstract classes and interfaces*: Separating design from implementation

- *Error handling*: Introducing exceptions

- *Final classes and methods*: Limiting inheritance

- *Interceptor methods*: Automating delegation

- *Destructor methods*: Cleaning up after your objects

- *Cloning objects*: Making object copies

- *Resolving objects to strings*: Creating a summary method

Static Methods and Properties

All the examples in the previous chapter worked with objects. I characterized classes as templates from which objects are produced, and objects as active components, the things whose methods we invoke and whose properties we access. I implied that the action in object-oriented programming is to be found through instances of classes. Classes, after all, are merely templates for objects.

In fact, it is not that simple. We can access both methods and properties in the context of a class rather than that of an object. Such methods and properties are "static" and must be declared so using the `static` keyword.

```
class StaticExample {
    static public $aNum = 0;
    static public function sayHello() {
        print "hello";
    }
}
```

Note The `static` keyword was introduced with PHP 5. It cannot be used in PHP 4 scripts.

Because you access a static element via a class and not an instance, you do not need a variable that references an object. Instead, you use the class name in conjunction with `::`.

```
print StaticExample::$aNum;
print StaticExample::sayHello();
```

This syntax should be familiar to you from the previous chapter. We used `::` in conjunction with `parent` to access an overridden method. Now, as before, we are accessing class rather than object data. Class code can use the `parent` keyword to access a super class without using its class name. To access a static method or property from within the same class (rather than from a child), we would use the `self` keyword. `self` is to classes what the `$this` pseudo-variable is to objects. So from outside the `StaticExample` class we access the `$aNum` property using its class name:

```
StaticExample::$aNum;
```

From within the `StaticExample` class we can use the `self` keyword:

```
class StaticExample {
    static public $aNum = 0;
    static public function sayHello() {
        self::$aNum++;
        print "hello (".self::$aNum.")\n";
    }
}
```

Note Making a method call using `parent` is the only circumstance in which you can use a static reference to a nonstatic method using PHP 5. PHP 4 allowed you to treat any method as static simply by referencing it as such. This results in a fatal error in PHP 5.

Unless you are accessing an overridden method, you should only ever use `::` to access a method or property that has been explicitly declared static.

Note You will often see static syntax used in documentation to refer to a method or property. This does not mean that the item in question is necessarily static, just that it belongs to a certain class. The `write()` method of the `ShopProductWriter` class might be referred to as `ShopProductWriter::write()`, for example, even though the `write()` method is not static. You will see this syntax here when that level of specificity is appropriate.

By definition, static methods are not invoked in the context of an object. A consequence of this is you cannot use the $this pseudo-variable inside a static method without causing a fatal error.

So, why would we use a static method or property? Static elements have a number of characteristics that can be useful. Firstly, they are available from anywhere in your script (presuming that you have access to the class). This means you can access functionality without needing to pass an instance of the class around from object to object, or worse, storing an instance in a global variable. Secondly, a static property is available to every instance of a class, so you can set values that you wish to be available to all members of a type. Finally, the fact that you don't need an instance to access a static property or method can save you from instantiating an object purely to get at a simple function.

Let's build a static method for the ShopProduct class that automates the instantiation of ShopProduct objects. Using SQLite or MySQL, we might define a products table like this:

```
CREATE TABLE products (
                    id INT PRIMARY KEY,
                    type varchar(255),
                    firstname varchar(255),
                    mainname varchar(255),
                    title varchar(255),
                    price float,
                    numpages int,
                    playlength int,
                    discount int );
```

Let's build a getInstance() method that accepts a row ID and DB_common object, uses them to acquire a database row, then returns a ShopProduct object. We can add these methods to the ShopProduct class we created in the last chapter. The DB_common class is the parent for the connection objects in the PEAR::DB package.

```
// require_once("DB.php");
// ...
// ShopProduct class...
    private $id = 0;
    // ...
    public function setID( $id ) {
        $this->id = $id;
    }
    // ...
    public static function getInstance( $id, DB_common $db ) {
        $query = "select * from products where id='$id'";
        $query_result = $db->query( $query );

        if ( DB::isError( $query_result ) ) {
            die($query_result->getMessage());
        }
```

```
                $row = $query_result->fetchRow( DB_FETCHMODE_ASSOC );
                if ( empty( $row ) ) { return null; }

                if ( $row['type'] == "book" ) {
                    $product = new BookProduct(
                                        $row['title'],
                                        $row['firstname'],
                                        $row['mainname'],
                                        $row['price'],
                                        $row['numpages'] );
                } else if ( $row['type'] == "cd" ) {
                    $product = new CdProduct(
                                        $row['title'],
                                        $row['firstname'],
                                        $row['mainname'],
                                        $row['price'],
                                        $row['playlength'] );
                } else {
                    $product = new ShopProduct(
                                        $row['title'],
                                        $row['firstname'],
                                        $row['mainname'],
                                        $row['price'] );
                }
                $product->setId(          $row['id'] );
                $product->setDiscount(    $row['discount'] );
                return $product;
            }
        }
```

As you can see, the getInstance() method returns a ShopProduct object and, based on a type flag, is smart enough to work out the precise specialization it should instantiate. I have omitted any error handling in order to keep the example compact.

This method is more useful in a class context than an object context. It lets us convert raw materials into an object easily without requiring that we have a ShopProduct object to start with. The method does not use any instance properties or methods, so there is no reason why it should not be declared static. Given a valid DB_Common object, we can invoke the method from anywhere in an application:

```
require_once("DB.php");
$db = DB::connect("sqlite://./products.db");
$obj = ShopProduct::getInstance( 53, $db );
```

Methods like this act as "factories" in that they take raw materials and use them to produce objects. The term "factory" is applied to code designed to generate object instances. We will encounter factory examples again.

Constant Properties

Some properties should not be changed. Pi is pi, and you will want it to stay that way. Error and status flags will often be hard coded into your classes. Although they should be publicly and statically available, client code should not be able to change them.

PHP 5 allows us to define constant properties within a class. Like global constants, class constants cannot be changed once they are set. A constant property is declared with the const keyword. Constants are not prefixed with a dollar sign like regular properties. By convention, they are often named using only uppercase characters, like this:

```
class ShopProduct {
    const AVAILABLE      = 0;
    const OUT_OF_STOCK   = 1;
    // ...
```

Constant properties can contain only primitive values. You cannot assign an object to a constant. Like static properties, constant properties are accessed via the class and not an instance. You refer to a constant without a dollar sign, like this:

```
print ShopProduct::AVAILABLE;
```

An attempt to set a value on a constant once it has been declared will cause a parse error.

You should use constants when your property needs to be available across all instances of a class, and when the property value needs to be fixed and unchanging.

Abstract Classes

The introduction of abstract classes was one of the major changes ushered in with PHP 5 and the Zend 2 Engine. Its inclusion in the list of new features was another sign of PHP's extended commitment to object-oriented design.

An abstract class cannot be instantiated. Instead it defines (and optionally partially implements) the interface for any class that might extend it.

You define an abstract class with the abstract keyword. Let's redefine the ShopProductWriter class we created in the last chapter as an abstract class.

```
abstract class ShopProductWriter {
    protected $products = array();

    public function addProduct( ShopProduct $shopProduct ) {
        $this->products[]=$shopProduct;
    }
}
```

You can create methods and properties as normal, but any attempt to instantiate an abstract object will cause an error like this:

```
$writer = new ShopProductWriter();
// output:
// Fatal error: Cannot instantiate abstract class
// shopproductwriter ...
```

In most cases an abstract class will contain at least one abstract method. These are declared once again with the abstract keyword. An abstract method cannot have an implementation. You declare it as normal, but end the declaration with a semicolon rather than a method body. Here we add an abstract write() method to the ShopProductWriter class:

```
abstract class ShopProductWriter {
    protected $products = array();

    public function addProduct( ShopProduct $shopProduct ) {
        $this->products[]=$shopProduct;
    }

    abstract public function write();
}
```

In creating an abstract method, you ensure that an implementation will be available in all concrete child classes, but you leave the details of that implementation undefined.

If we were to create a class derived from ShopProductWriter that does not implement the write() method, we would face the following error:

```
class ErroredWriter extends ShopProductWriter{}
// output:
// Fatal error: Class ErroredWriter contains 1 abstract methods
// and must therefore be declared abstract
// (ShopProductWriter::write) in...
```

So any class that extends an abstract class must implement all abstract methods or must itself be declared abstract. An extending class is responsible for more than simply implementing an abstract method. In doing so it must reproduce the method signature. This means that the access control of the implementing method cannot be stricter than that of the abstract method. The implementing method should also require the same number of arguments as the abstract method, reproducing any class type hinting.

Let's define two implementations of ShopProductWriter():

```
class XmlProductWriter extends ShopProductWriter{
    public function write() {
        $str = "<products>\n";
         foreach ( $this->products as $shopProduct ) {
            $str .= "\t<product title=\"{$shopProduct->getTitle()}\">\n";
            $str .= "\t\t<summary>\n";
            $str .= "\t\t{$shopProduct->getSummaryLine()}\n";
            $str .= "\t\t</summary>\n";
            $str .= "\t</product>\n";
        }
        $str .= "</products>\n";
        print $str;
    }
}
```

```
class TextProductWriter extends ShopProductWriter{
    public function write() {
        $str = "PRODUCTS:\n";
        foreach ( $this->products as $shopProduct ) {
            $str .= $shopProduct->getSummaryLine()."\n";
        }
        print $str;
    }
}
```

We create two classes, each with its own implementation of the write() method. The first outputs XML, and the second outputs text. A method that requires a ShopProductWriter object will not know which of these two classes it is receiving but can be absolutely certain that a write() method will be implemented.

Abstract classes were often approximated in PHP 4 by creating methods containing warnings or even die() statements. This forces a derived class to implement the abstract methods or risk having them invoked.

```
class AbstractClass {
    function abstractFunction() {
        die( "AbstractClass::abstractFunction() is abstract\n" );
    }
}
```

The problem here is that the abstract nature of the base class is only tested when an abstract method is invoked. In PHP 5, abstract classes are tested when they are parsed, which is much safer.

Interfaces

While abstract classes let you provide some measure of implementation, interfaces are pure templates. An interface can only define functionality; it can never implement it. An interface is declared with the interface keyword. It can contain properties and method declarations, but not method bodies.

Let's define an interface:

```
interface Chargeable {
    public function getPrice();
}
```

As you can see, an interface looks very much like a class. Any class that incorporates this interface commits to implementing all the methods it defines, or it must be declared abstract.

A class can implement an interface using the implements keyword in its declaration. Once you have done this, the process of implementing an interface is the same as extending an abstract class that contains only abstract methods. Let's make the ShopProduct class implement Chargeable.

```
class ShopProduct implements Chargeable {
    // ...
    public function getPrice() {
        return ( $this->price - $this->discount );
    }
    // ...
```

ShopProduct already had a getPrice() method, so why might it be useful to implement the Chargeable interface? The answer lies in type once again. An implementing class takes on the type of the class it extends and the interface that it implements.

This means that the CdProduct class belongs to

CdProduct
ShopProduct
Chargeable

This can be exploited by client code. To know an object's type is to know its capabilities. So the method

```
public function cdInfo( CdProduct $prod ) {
    // ...
}
```

knows that the $prod object has got a getPlayLength() method in addition to all the methods defined in the ShopProduct class.

Passed the same object, the method

```
public function addProduct( ShopProduct $prod ) {
    // ..
}
```

knows that $prod supports all the methods in ShopProduct, but without further testing it will know nothing of the getPlayLength() method.

Once again, passed the same CdProduct object, the method

```
public function addChargeableItem( Chargeable $item ) {
    //...
}
```

knows nothing at all of the ShopProduct or CdProduct types. This method is only concerned that the $item argument contains a getPrice() method.

Because any class can implement an interface (in fact, a class can implement any number of interfaces), interfaces effectively join types that are otherwise unrelated. We might define an entirely new class that implements Chargeable:

```
class Shipping implements Chargeable {
    public function getPrice() {
        //...
    }
}
```

We can pass a Shipping object to the addChargeableItem() method just as we can pass it a ShopProduct object.

The important thing to a client working with a Chargeable object is that it can call a getPrice() method. Any other methods available are associated with other types, whether through the object's own class, a super class, or another interface. These are irrelevant to the client.

A class can both extend a super class and implement any number of interfaces. The extends clause should precede the implements clause:

```
class Consultancy extends TimedService implements Bookable, Chargeable {
    // ...
}
```

Notice that the Consultancy class implements more than one interface. Multiple interfaces follow the implements keyword in a comma-separated list.

PHP only supports inheritance from a single parent, so the extends keyword can precede a single class name only.

Handling Errors

Things go wrong. Files are misplaced, database servers are left uninitialized, URLs are changed, XML files are mangled, permissions are misset, disk quotas are exceeded. The list goes on and on. In the fight to anticipate every problem, a simple method can sometimes sink under the weight of its own error handling code.

Here is a simple Person class that stores some basic data:

```
class Person {
    private $name;
    private $age;
    private $id = 0;
    function __construct( $name, $age ) {
        $this->name = $name;
        $this->age  = $age;
    }

    function setID( $id ) {
        $this->id = $id;
    }

    function getName() {
        return $this->name;
    }
    function getAge() {
        return $this->age;
    }
}
```

The Person class does nothing but store $name, $age, and $id properties. $name and $age are set in the constructor, and are accessible with "getter" methods. The $id property can be set using the setID( ) method. To illustrate some of the issues surrounding error handling, let's create a class that writes Person object data to a database. The schema we will work with looks like this:

```
CREATE TABLE persons (
                    id INT PRIMARY KEY,
                    name varchar(255),
                    age int
                    );
```

The real error magnet in this example is a class called PersonPersist. PersonPersist takes a Person object and writes it to a database. At least, that's what we are hoping it will do.

```
require_once("DB.php");

class PersonPersist {
    private $dsn;
    private $db_obj;
    private $fields = array( "name", "age" );

    function __construct( $dsn ) {
        $this->dsn = $dsn;
    }

    public function connect( ) {
        $this->db_obj = DB::connect($this->dsn);
    }

    public function insert( Person $person ) {
        if ( empty( $this->db_obj) ) {
            $this->connect();
        }
        $row = array();
        foreach( $this->fields as $fieldname ) {
            $method = "get{$fieldname}";
            $row[$fieldname] = $person->$method();
        }
        $row['id'] = $this->db_obj->nextId('persons_sequence');
        $insert_result =
            $this->db_obj->autoExecute(
            'persons', $row, DB_AUTOQUERY_INSERT );
        $person->setId( $row['id'] );
        return $row['id'];
    }
}
```

The `PersonPersist` class uses the `PEAR::DB` package to write a `Person` object to a database table. With this package, we are able to write database-agnostic code. The `$fields` property contains an array of strings that match both database fields and the names of `Person` "getter" methods. We use this conjunction in the `insert()` method to construct an array of keys and values that can be passed to a `PEAR::DB` method called `autoexecute()`. This method uses an associative array to construct the SQL statement required to insert our `Person` data.

Of course, before we can make a query, we have to connect to the database. The `connect()` method uses a user-supplied Data Source Name (DSN) in conjunction with the static `DB::connect()` method to generate a `DB_Common` object. We store the `DB_Common` object in a property named `$db_obj`, and we can use it to work with our database. We use the `PersonPersist` class like this:

```
$person = new Person( 'bob', 44 );
$saver = new PersonPersist( "sqlite://./persons.db" );
$saver->insert( $person );
```

`PersonPersist` is highly simplified. In particular, it has no strategy for distinguishing between inserts and updates. It is also optimistic in outlook. It does not handle any of the errors that might arise when working with a database.

What will happen, for example, if the database connection fails, or if the expected table does not exist? A failed connection will cause a fatal error as we attempt to invoke methods on an invalid `$db_obj` method. Perhaps worse, a missing table will result in the database insert failing silently.

Testing for these error conditions is relatively trivial, but we must still decide how we should respond to them should they arise. We generally have two options:

Firstly, we could end execution. This is simple but drastic. Our humble method then presumes to take responsibility for bringing an entire script crashing down around it. Although methods like `connect()` and `insert()` are well placed to detect errors, they do not have the information to decide how to handle them.

Rather than handle the error in our method, then, we could return an error flag of some kind. This could be a Boolean or an integer value such as 0 or -1. Some classes will also set an error string or flag so that the client code can request more information after a failure.

Many PEAR packages combine these two approaches by returning an error object (an instance of `PEAR_Error`), which acts both as notification that an error has occurred and contains the error message within it.

The problem here is that we pollute our return value. PHP does not enforce a unified return value. There is no return class type hinting, so there is nothing to prevent us from returning an error flag instead of the promised object or primitive. When we do this, we have to rely on the client coder to test for the return type every time our error-prone method is called. This can be risky. Trust no one!

When we return an error value to the calling code, there is no guarantee that the client will be any more equipped than our method to decide how to handle the error. If this is the case, then the problem begins all over again. The client method will have to determine how to respond to the error condition, maybe even implementing a different error reporting strategy.

Exceptions

Zend Engine 2 introduces exceptions to PHP, a radically different way of handling error conditions. Different for PHP, that is. You will find them hauntingly familiar if you have Java or C++ experience. Exceptions address all of the issues that we have raised so far in this section.

An exception is a special object instantiated from the built-in Exception class (or from a derived class). Objects of type Exception are designed to hold and report error information.

The Exception class constructor accepts two optional arguments, a message string and an error code. The class provides some useful methods for analyzing error conditions. These are described in Table 4-1.

Table 4-1. *The Exception Class's Public Methods*

Method	Description
getMessage()	Get the message string that was passed to the constructor.
getCode()	Get the code integer that was passed to the constructor.
getFile()	Get the file in which the exception was generated.
getTrace()	Get a multidimensional array tracing the method calls that led to the exception, including method, class, file, and argument data.
getTraceAsString()	Get a string version of the data returned by getTrace().
__toString()	Called automatically when the Exception object is used in string context. Returns a string describing the exception details.

The Exception class is fantastically useful for providing error notification and debugging information (the getTrace() and getTraceAsString() methods are particularly helpful in this regard). In fact, it is almost identical to the PEAR_Error class that has already been discussed. There is much more to an exception than the information it holds, though.

Throwing an Exception

The throw keyword is used in conjunction with an Exception object. It halts execution of the current method and passes responsibility for handling the error back to the calling code. Let's amend the connect() method to use the throw statement:

```
public function connect( ) {
    $this->db_obj = DB::connect($this->dsn);
    if ( DB::isError( $this->db_obj )) {
        throw new Exception("A connection error occured");
    }
}
```

The insert() method can use a similar construct:

```
public function insert( Person $person ) {
    //...
    $insert_result =
        $this->db_obj->autoExecute(
        'persons', $row, DB_AUTOQUERY_INSERT );

    if ( DB::isError( $insert_result )) {
        throw new Exception( "Could not insert" );
    }
    //...
}
```

Our connect() and insert() methods can now check diligently for errors as they do their work, but let code more fitted for the purpose decide how to respond to any errors detected.

So how does client code know how to handle an exception when thrown? When you invoke a method that may throw an exception, you can wrap your call in a try clause. A try clause is made up of the try keyword followed by braces. The try clause must be followed by at least one catch clause in which you can handle any error, like this:

```
try {
    $saver = new PersonPersist( "sqlite://./persons.db" );
    $saver->insert( $person );
} catch ( Exception $e ) {
    die( $e->__toString() );
}
```

As you can see, the catch clause superficially resembles a method declaration. When an exception is thrown, the catch clause in the invoking scope is called. The Exception object is automatically passed to the argument variable.

Just as execution is halted within the throwing method when an exception is thrown, so it is within the try clause—control passes directly to the catch clause.

Subclassing Exception

You can create classes that extend the Exception class as you would with any user-defined class. There are two reasons why you might want to do this. Firstly, you can extend the class's functionality. Secondly, the fact that a derived class defines a new class type can aid error handling in itself.

You can, in fact, define as many catch clauses as you need for a try statement. The particular catch clause invoked will depend upon the type of the thrown exception and the class type hint in the argument list. Let's define some simple classes that extend Exception:

```
class DbException extends Exception {
    protected $pearError;
    function __construct( PEAR_Error $error ) {
        parent::__construct( $error->getMessage(), $error->getCode() );
        $this->pearError = $error;
    }

    function getPearError() {
        return $this->pearError;
    }
}

class DbConnectionException extends DbException{ }
class SqlException extends DbException{ }
```

The PEAR_Error class resembles the Exception class. It has getMessage() and getCode() methods. We take advantage of this similarity and use the PEAR_Error object in the DbException class. The SqlException and DbConnection classes do nothing more than subclass DbException. We can now use these classes in our code and amend both connect() and insert():

```
// PersonPersist class...
    public function connect( ) {
        $this->db_obj = DB::connect($this->dsn);
        if ( DB::isError( $db_obj )) {
            throw new DbConnectionException( $db_obj );
        }
    }

    public function insert( Person $person ) {
        if ( empty( $this->db_obj) ) {
            $this->connect();
        }
        $row = array();
        foreach( $this->fields as $fieldname ) {
            $method = "get{$fieldname}";
            $row[$fieldname] = $person->$method();
        }
        $row['id'] = $this->db_obj->nextId('persons_sequence');
        $insert_result =
            $this->db_obj->autoExecute(
            'persons', $row, DB_AUTOQUERY_INSERT );

        if ( DB::isError( $insert_result )) {
            throw new SqlException( $insert_result );
        }
        $person->setId( $row['id'] );
        return $row['id'];
    }
}
```

connect() throws a DbConnectionException and insert() throws an SqlException. Because the insert() method calls connect(), it might throw either exception. How does this work? PHP does not force a method to catch an exception. If an exception is uncaught within a method, then it is implicitly thrown to that method's own calling code, and so on until the exception is either caught or can be thrown no further. The insert() method *explicitly* throws an SqlException and *implicitly* throws a DbConnectionException. This kind of hidden exception can make it hard to trace what is happening in your code, so you may wish to manually rethrow any exceptions you do not want to handle to make your method clearer:

```
public function insert( Person $person ) {
    try {
        if ( empty( $this->db_obj ) ) {
            $this->connect();
        }
    } catch ( DbConnectionException $e ) {
        throw $e;
    }
    //...
```

This try/catch pair is ultimately redundant, but does have the virtue of clarity. Which approach you take is a matter of preference. Personally, I tend to let a calling method throw an exception implicitly, and include clear documentation to signal the fact.

So, we have established that connect() might throw one of two possible exceptions. How can we take advantage of this? Here's the code that invokes the insert() method:

```
try {
    $saver = new PersonPersist( "sqlite://./persons.db" );
    $saver->insert( $person );

} catch ( DbConnectionException $e ) {
    // perhaps try again with a new DSN?
    print $e->__toString();

} catch ( SqlException $e ) {
    // log and die?
    print $e->__toString();

} catch ( Exception $e ) {
    // should not currently get called
    print $e->__toString();
}
```

We provide a catch clause for each class type. The clause invoked depends upon the exception type thrown. The first to match will be executed, so remember to place the most generic type at the end and the most specialized at the start. For example, if you were to place the catch clause for Exception ahead of the clause for DbConnectionException and SqlException, neither of these would ever be invoked. This is because both of these classes belong to the Exception type, and would therefore match the first clause.

The first `catch` clause (`DbConnectionException`) is invoked if there is an error in connection (if the database file is unreadable, for example, or if the DSN is invalid). The second clause (`SqlException`) is invoked if an error occurs during the insert (if the "products" table does not exist or its schema does not match our fields, for example). The final clause (`Exception`) should not be reached because our methods only generate two exceptions, which are both explicitly handled. It is often a good idea to have a "backstop" clause like this, though, in case you add new exceptions to the code during development.

So what happens if an exception is not caught? You have seen that you can allow a method to rethrow an exception rather than handle it. You will have to deal with a thrown exception at some point in your code, though, or suffer a fatal error. Here's what would happen if we did not catch one of the exceptions in our example:

```
Fatal error: Uncaught exception "DbConnectionException"
with message 'DB Error: not found' in...
```

So when you throw an exception you force the client to take responsibility for handling it. This is not an abdication of responsibility. An exception should be thrown when a method has detected an error but does not have the contextual information to be able to handle it intelligently. The `connect()` method in our example knows when the attempt to connect has failed, and it knows why, but it does not know what to do about it. This is as it should be. If we were to make the `PersonPersist` class more knowing that it currently is, it would lose focus and become less reusable.

Final Classes and Methods

Inheritance allows for enormous flexibility within a class hierarchy. You can override a class or method so that a call in a client method will achieve radically different effects according to the particular class instance it has been passed. Sometimes, though, a class or method should remain fixed and unchanging. If you have achieved the definitive functionality for your class or method, and you feel that overriding it can only damage the ultimate perfection of your work, you may need the `final` keyword.

`final` puts a stop to inheritance. A final class cannot be subclassed. Less drastically, a final method cannot be overridden.

Let's declare a class final:

```
final class Checkout {
    // ...
}
```

Any attempt to subclass the `Checkout` class will now cause a fatal error like this:

```
class IllegalCheckout extends Checkout {
    // ...
}
// Fatal error: Class illegalcheckout may not inherit from
// final class (checkout) in...
```

We could relax matters somewhat by declaring a method in `Checkout` final, rather than the whole class. The `final` keyword should be placed in front of any other modifiers such as `protected` or `static`, like this:

```
class Checkout {
    final function totalize() {
        // calculate bill
    }
}
```

We can now subclass Checkout, but any attempt to override totalize() will cause a fatal error:

```
class IllegalCheckout extends Checkout {
    final function totalize() {
        // change bill calculation
    }
}
// Fatal error: Cannot override final method
// checkout::totalize() in ...
```

Good object-oriented code tends to emphasize the well-defined interface. Behind the interface, though, implementations will often vary. Different classes or combinations of classes conform to common interfaces but behave differently in different circumstances. By declaring a class or method final, you limit this flexibility. There will be times when this is desirable, and we will see some of them later in the book, but you should think carefully before declaring something final. Are there really no circumstances in which overriding would be useful? You could always change your mind later on, of course, but this might not be so easy if you are distributing a library for others to use. Use final with care.

Working with Interceptors

PHP provides built-in interceptor methods, which can intercept messages sent to undefined methods and properties. This is also known as "overloading," but since this term means something quite different in Java and C++, I think it is better to talk in terms of interception.

PHP 5 supports three built-in interceptor methods. Like __construct(), these are invoked for you when the right conditions are met. Table 4-2 describes the methods.

Table 4-2. *The Interceptor Methods*

Method	Description
__get($property)	Invoked when an undefined property is accessed
__set($property, $value)	Invoked when a value is assigned to an undefined property
__call($method, $arg_array)	Invoked when an undefined method is called

The __get() and __set() methods are designed for working with properties that have not been declared in a class (or its parents).

__get() is invoked when client code attempts to read an undeclared property. It is called automatically with a single string argument containing the name of the property that the client is attempting to access. Whatever you return from the __call() method will be sent back to the client as if the target property exists with that value. Here's a quick example:

```
class Person {
    function __get( $property ) {
        $method = "get{$property}";
        if ( method_exists( $this, $method ) ) {
            return $this->$method();
        }
    }

    function getName() {
        return "Bob";
    }

    function getAge() {
        return 44;
    }
}
```

When a client attempts to access an undefined property, the __get() method is invoked. We have implemented __get() to take the property name and construct a new string, prepending the word "get". We pass this string to a function called method_exists(), which accepts an object and a method name and tests for method existence. If the method does exist, we invoke it and pass its return value to the client. So if the client requests a $name property:

```
$p = new Person();
print $p->name;
// output:
// Bob
```

the getName() method is invoked behind the scenes. If the method does not exist, we do nothing. The property that the user is attempting to access will resolve to NULL.

The __set() method is invoked when client code attempts to assign to an undefined property. It is passed two arguments: the name of the property, and the value the client is attempting to set. You can then decide how to work with these arguments. Let's amend the Person class:

```
class Person {
    private $_name;
    private $_age;

    function __set( $property, $value ) {
        $method = "set{$property}";
        if ( method_exists( $this, $method ) ) {
            return $this->$method( $value );
        }
    }
}
```

```
    function setName( $name ) {
        $this->_name = strtoupper($name);
    }

    function setAge( $age ) {
        $this->_age = strtoupper($age);
    }
}
```

In this example we work with "setter" methods rather than "getters." If a user attempts to assign to an undefined property, the __set() method is invoked with the property name and the assigned value. We test for the existence of the appropriate method, and invoke it if it exists. In this way we can filter the assigned value.

■**Note** Remember that methods and properties in PHP documentation are frequently spoken of in static terms in order to identify them with their classes. So we might talk about the Person::$name property, even though the property is not declared static and would in fact be accessed via an object, like this:

$person->name;

So if we create a Person object and then attempt to set a property called Person::$name, the __set() method is invoked, because this class does not define a $name property. The method is passed the string "name" and the value we wish to set. It is up to us what we do with this information. In this example, we construct a method name out of the property argument combined with the string "set". The setName() method is found and duly invoked. This transforms the incoming value and stores it in a real property.

```
$p = new Person();
$p->name = "bob";
// the $_name property becomes 'BOB'
```

The __call() method is probably the most useful of all the interceptor methods. It is invoked when an undefined method is called by client code. __call() is invoked with the method name and an array holding all arguments passed by the client. Any value that you return from the __call() method is returned to the client as if it were returned by the method invoked.

The __call() method can be useful for delegation. Delegation is the mechanism by which one object passes method invocations on to a second. It is similar to inheritance in that a child class passes on a method call to its parent implementation. With inheritance the relationship between child and parent is fixed, so the fact that you can switch the receiving object at runtime means that delegation can be more flexible than inheritance. Let's clarify things a little with an example. Here is a simple class for formatting information from the Person class:

```
class PersonWriter {

    function writeName( Person $p ) {
        print $p->getName()."\n";
    }

    function writeAge( Person $p ) {
        print $p->getAge()."\n";
    }
}
```

We could, of course, subclass this to output `Person` data in various ways. Here is an implementation of the `Person` class that uses both a `PersonWriter` object and the `__call()` method:

```
class Person {
    private $writer;

    function __construct( PersonWriter $writer ) {
        $this->writer = $writer;
    }

    function __call( $methodname, $args ) {
        if ( method_exists( $this->writer, $methodname ) ) {
            return $this->writer->$methodname( $this );
        }
    }

    function getName()  { return "Bob"; }
    function getAge() { return 44; }
}
```

The `Person` class here demands a `PersonWriter` object as a constructor argument and stores it in a property variable. In the `__call()` method, we use the provided $methodname argument, testing for a method of the same name in the `PersonWriter` object we have stored. If we encounter such a method, we delegate the method call to the `PersonWriter` object, passing our current instance to it (in the $this pseudo-variable). So if the client makes this call to `Person`:

```
$person = new Person( new PersonWriter() );
$person->writeName();
```

the `__call()` method is invoked. We find a method called `writeName()` in our `PersonWriter` object, and invoke it. This saves us from manually invoking the delegated method like this:

```
function writeName() {
    $this->writer->writeName( $this );
}
```

The `Person` class has magically gained two new methods. Although automated delegation can save a lot of legwork if you have to delegate to too many methods, there is a cost in clarity. You present the world with a dynamic interface that will resist reflection (the runtime examination of class facets) and will not be clear to the client coder at first glance. The interceptor methods have their place, but they should be used with care, and classes that rely on them should document this fact very clearly.

We will return to the topics of delegation and reflection later in the book.

Defining Destructor Methods

We have seen that the __construct() method is automatically invoked when an object is instantiated. PHP 5 also introduced the __destruct() method. This is invoked just before an object is garbage-collected, that is, before it is expunged from memory. You can use this method to perform any final cleaning up that might be necessary.

Imagine, for example, a class that saves itself to a database when so ordered. We could use the __destruct() method to ensure that an instance saves its data when it is deleted.

```
class Person {
    private $name;
    private $age;
    private $id;

    function __construct( $name, $age ) {
        $this->name = $name;
        $this->age  = $age;
    }

    function setId( $id ) {
        $this->id = $id;
    }

    function __destruct() {
        if ( ! empty( $this->id ) ) {
            // save Person data
            print "saving person\n";
        }
    }
}
```

The __destruct() method is invoked whenever a Person object is removed from memory. This will happen either when you call the unset() function with the object in question or when no further references to the object exist in the process. So if we create and destroy a Person object, we can see the __destruct() method come into play.

```
$person = new Person( "bob", 44 );
$person->setId( 343 );
unset( $person );
// output:
// saving person
```

Copying Objects with __clone()

In PHP 4, copying an object was a simple matter of assigning from one variable to another.

```
class CopyMe {}
$first = new CopyMe();
$second = $first;
// PHP 4: $second and $first are 2 distinct objects
// PHP 5: $second and $first refer to one object
```

This "simple matter" was a source of many bugs, as object copies were accidentally spawned when variables were assigned, methods called, and objects returned. This was made worse by the fact that there was no way of testing two variables to see whether they referred to the same object. Equivalence tests would tell you whether all fields were the same (==) or whether both variables were objects (===), but not whether they pointed to the same object.

In PHP 5, objects are always assigned and passed around by reference. This means that when our previous example is run with PHP 5, $first and $second contain references to the same object instead of two copies. While this is generally what we want when working with objects, there will be occasions when we need to get a copy of an object rather than a reference to an object.

PHP 5 provides the clone keyword for just this purpose. clone operates upon an object instance, producing a by-value copy.

```
class CopyMe {}
$first  = new CopyMe();
$second = clone $first;
// PHP 5: $second and $first are 2 distinct objects
```

The issues surrounding object copying only start here. Consider the Person class that we implemented in the previous section. A default copy of a Person object would contain the identifier (the $id property) that in a full implementation we would use to locate the correct row in a database. If we allow this property to be copied, we will have two distinct objects referencing the same data source, which is probably not what we wanted when we made our copy. An update in one object will affect the other, and vice versa.

Luckily we can control what is copied when clone is invoked on an object. We do this by implementing a special method called __clone() (note the leading two underscores that are characteristic of built-in methods). __clone() is called automatically when the clone keyword is invoked on an object.

When you implement __clone(), it is important to understand the context in which the method runs. __clone() is run on the *copied* object and not the original. Let's add __clone() to yet another version of the Person class:

```
class Person {
    private $name;
    private $age;
    private $id;
```

```
function __construct( $name, $age ) {
    $this->name = $name;
    $this->age  = $age;
}

function setId( $id ) {
    $this->id = $id;
}



function __clone() {

    $this->id   = 0;
}
}
```

When clone is invoked on a Person object, a new shallow copy is made, and *its* __clone() method is invoked. This means that anything we do in __clone() overwrites the default copy already made. In this case, we ensure that the copied object's $id property is set to zero.

```
$person = new Person( "bob", 44 );
$person->setId( 343 );
$person2 = clone $person;
// $person2 :
//     name: bob
//     age: 44
//     id: 0.
```

A shallow copy ensures that primitive properties are copied from the old object to the new. Object properties though are copied by reference, which may not be what you want or expect when cloning an object. Say that we give our Person object an Account object property. This object holds a balance that we want copied to the cloned object. What we don't want, though, is for both Person objects to hold references to the *same* account.

```
class Account {
    public $balance;
    function __construct( $balance ) {
        $this->balance = $balance;
    }
}

class Person {
    private $name;
    private $age;
    private $id;
    public $account;
```

```
    function __construct( $name, $age, Account $account ) {
        $this->name = $name;
        $this->age  = $age;
        $this->account = $account;
    }

    function setId( $id ) {
        $this->id = $id;
    }

    function __clone() {
        $this->id   = 0;
    }
}

$person = new Person( "bob", 44, new Account( 200 ) );
$person->setId( 343 );
$person2 = clone $person;

// give $person some money
$person->account->balance += 10;
// $person2 sees the credit too
print $person2->account->balance;

// output:
// 210
```

$person holds a reference to an Account object that we have kept publicly accessible for the sake of brevity (as you know, we would usually restrict access to a property, providing an accessor method if necessary). When the clone is created, it holds a reference to the *same* Account object that $person references. We demonstrate this by adding to the $person object's Account, and confirming the increased balance via $person2.

If we do not want an object property to be shared after a clone operation, then it is up to us to clone it explicitly in the __clone() method:

```
    function __clone() {
        $this->id   = 0;
        $this->account = clone $this->account;
    }
```

Defining String Values for Your Objects

Another Java-inspired innovation in PHP 5 is the __toString() method. By default, when you print an object, it will resolve to a string like this:

```
class StringThing {}
$st = new StringThing();
print $st;
// output:
// Object id #1
```

By implementing a __toString() method, you can control the way that your objects represent themselves when printed. __toString() should be written to return a string value. The method is invoked automatically when your object is passed to print or echo, and its return value substituted. Let's add a __toString() version to a minimal Person class:

```
class Person {
    function getName()  { return "Bob"; }
    function getAge() { return 44; }
    function __toString() {
        $desc  = $this->getName();
        $desc .= " (age ".$this->getAge().")";
        return $desc;
    }
}
```

Now when we print a Person object, the object will resolve to this:

```
$person = new Person();
print $person;
// output:
// Bob (age 44)
```

The __toString() method is particularly useful for logging and error reporting, and for classes whose main task is to convey information. The Exception class, for example, summarizes exception data in its __toString() method.

Note At the time of writing, objects embedded within quotes are *not* converted into their string representation, although this is the ideal behavior. So

```
print "$person\n";
```

Does not resolve to the value returned by __toString(). This feature has been disabled by PHP's architects for developmental reasons. It may have been restored by the time you read this. Try it out!

Summary

In this chapter, we got to grips with PHP's advanced object-oriented features. Some of these will become familiar as you work through the book. In particular, we will return frequently to abstract classes, exceptions, and static methods.

In the next chapter, we take a step back from built-in object features and look at classes and functions designed to help you work with objects.

CHAPTER 5

Object Tools

As we have seen, PHP supports object-oriented programming through language constructs such as classes and methods. The language also provides wider support through object-related functions and classes.

In this chapter, we will look at some tools and techniques that you can use to organize, test, and manipulate objects and classes.

This chapter will cover

- *Packages*: PHP does not support packages explicitly, but that's no reason not to organize your code into package-like structures.

- *Include paths*: Setting central accessible locations for your library code.

- *Class and object functions*: Functions for testing objects, classes, properties, and methods.

- *The Reflection API*: A powerful suite of built-in classes that provide unprecedented access to class information at runtime.

PHP and Packages

A package is a set of related classes, usually grouped together in some way. Packages can be used to separate parts of a system from one another. Some programming languages formally recognize packages and provide them with distinct namespaces. Although the Zend 2 Engine has no concept of a package, we can still use the file system to organize our classes, and devise a strategy to guard against name collisions.

One of the themes of this book so far has been the shift away from trust to enforcement ushered in by some of the new features in PHP 5. Where once we trusted that an object's property would not be overwritten by client code, now we defend it with the `private` or `protected` keywords. Where we hoped that a child class would implement its parent's empty methods, now we use an abstract class to make certain of it.

This shift does not extend to support for packages. There were plans to introduce namespaces in PHP 5, but these were abandoned shortly before the first beta was released.

Nevertheless, we can organize classes using the file system, which affords us a kind of package structure. We might create `util` and `business` directories and include class files with the `require_once()` function, like this:

```
require_once('business/Customer.php');
require_once('util/WebTools.php');
```

Figure 5-1 shows the `util` and `business` packages from the point of view of the Nautilus file manager.

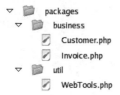

Figure 5-1. *PHP packages organized using the file system*

■**Note** `require_once()` accepts a path to a file and includes it evaluated in the current script. The function will only incorporate its target if it has not already been incorporated elsewhere. This "one-shot" approach is particularly useful when accessing library code because it prevents the accidental redefinition of classes and functions. This can happen when the same file is included by different parts of your script in a single process using a function like `require()` or `include()`.

It is customary to use `require()` and `require_once()` in preference to the similar `include()` and `include_once()` functions. This is because a fatal error encountered in a file accessed with the `require()` functions takes down the entire script. The same error encountered in a file accessed using the `include()` functions will cause the execution of the included file to cease, but will only generate a warning in the calling script. The former, more drastic, behavior is safer.

Remember PHP has no concept of a package. We are simply placing library scripts in different directories. Because of this, a class in one package can easily clash with a class in another that happens to have the same name. We might define a `User` class in our `business` package, for example, only to run into trouble later on when we include a third-party script that also defines a `User` class in a package called `forum`:

```
require_once('business/User.php'); // defines User class
require_once('forum/User.php'); // defines another User class
// Fatal error: Cannot redeclare class user in...
```

So how should we address the danger of name clashes? One answer is to use the naming convention common to PEAR packages.

■**Note** PEAR stands for the PHP Extension and Application Repository. It is an officially maintained archive of packages and tools that add to PHP's functionality. Core PEAR packages are included in the PHP distribution, and others can be added using a simple command line tool. You can browse the PEAR packages at `http://pear.php.net`. We will look at some other aspects of PEAR in Chapter 14.

PEAR uses the file system to define its packages as I have described. Every class is then named according to its package path, with each directory name separated by an underscore character.

For example, PEAR includes a package called XML, which has an RPC subpackage. The RPC package contains a file called Server.php. The class defined inside Server.php is not called Server as you might expect. Sooner or later that would clash with another Server class elsewhere in the PEAR project or in a user's code. Instead, the class is named XML_RPC_Server. This makes for unattractive class names. It does, however, make your code easy to read in that a class name always describes its own context.

In line with this convention, we might rename our User class business_User, in order to distinguish it from the User object in the forum package.

Include Paths

I have glossed over the issue of include paths so far in this section. When we include a file, we could refer to it using a relative path from the current working directory or an absolute path on the file system.

The examples we have seen so far seem to suggest a relative path:

```
require_once('business/User.php');
```

But this would require that our current working directory contain the business directory, which would soon become impractical. Using relative paths for our library inclusions, we would be more likely to see torturous require_once() statements:

```
require_once('../../projectlib/business/User.php');
```

We could use an absolute path, of course:

```
require_once('/home/john/projectlib/business/User.php');
```

Neither solution is ideal. By specifying paths in this much detail, we freeze the library file in place.

In using an absolute path, we tie the library to a particular file system. Whenever we install the project on a new server, all require statements will need changing to account for a new file path.

By using a relative path, we fix the relationship between the script's working directory and the library, making hard-to-move libraries and impractical-to-share libraries between projects without making copies. In either case, we lose the package idea in all the additional directories. Is it the business package, or is it the projectlib/business package?

In order to make included libraries work well in our code, we need to decouple the invoking code from the library so that

```
business/User.php
```

can be referenced from anywhere on a system. We can do this by putting the package in one of the directories to which the include_path directive refers. include_path is usually set in PHP's central configuration file, php.ini. It defines a list of directories separated by colons on Unix-like systems and semicolons on Windows systems.

```
include_path = ".:/usr/local/lib/php-libraries"
```

When you use a file system function such as fopen() or require() with a nonabsolute path that does not exist relative to the current working directory, the directories in the include path are searched automatically, beginning with the first in the list (in the case of fopen() you must include a flag in its argument list to enable this feature). When the target file is encountered, the search ends and the file function completes its task.

So by placing a package directory in an include directory, we need only refer to packages and files in our require() statements.

You may need to add a directory to the include_path so that you can maintain your own library directory. To do this, you can, of course, edit the php.ini file (remember that for the PHP server module you will need to restart your server for the changes to take effect).

If you do not have the privileges necessary to work with the php.ini file, you can set the include path from within your scripts using the set_include_path() function. set_include_path() accepts an include path (as it would appear in php.ini) and changes the include_path setting for the current process only. The php.ini file probably already defines a useful value for include_path, so rather than overwrite it, you can access it using the get_include_path() function, and append your own directory. Here's how you can add a directory to the current include path:

```
set_include_path( get_include_path().":/home/john/phplib/");
```

If you are working on a Windows platform, you should use semicolons rather than colons to separate each directory path.

Autoload

It is often a good idea to define each class in a project in a separate file. Each class file may bear a fixed relationship to the name of the class it contains. So we might define a ShopProduct class in a file named ShopProduct.php. Using the PEAR convention, on the other hand, we would name the file ShopProduct.php, but the class would be named according to its package address: business_ShopProduct, perhaps.

By splitting classes into individual files, and the files into separate packages, we promote reuse and flexibility. We can use an individual class in separate projects simultaneously without forcing the engine to parse irrelevant bundled classes.

The PEAR naming conventions make class name clashes unlikely. A project that consists of tens of distinct class files, however, will soon begin to fill up with require_once() statements as each file attempts to include its peers. This is not in itself a problem as long as the inclusions are necessary. As you improve your code, you may find that you are including some files unnecessarily.

PHP 5 introduces the __autoload() interceptor function to help automate the inclusion of class files. __autoload() should be implemented by the coder as a function requiring a single argument. When the PHP engine encounters an attempt to instantiate an unknown class, it invokes the __autoload() function (if defined), passing it the class name as a string. It is up to the implementor to define a strategy for locating and including the missing class file.

Let's define an __autoload() function:

```
function __autoload( $classname ) {
    include_once( "$classname.php" );
}
```

```
$product = new ShopProduct( 'The Darkening', 'Harry', 'Hunter', 12.99 );
```

Assuming that we have not already included a file that defines a class named ShopProduct, the instantiation of ShopProduct seems bound to fail. The PHP engine sees that we have defined an __autoload() function and passes it the string "ShopProduct". Our implementation simply attempts to include the file ShopProduct.php. This will only work, of course, if the file is in the current working directory or in one of our include directories. We have no easy way here of handling packages. This is another circumstance in which the PEAR naming scheme can pay off.

```
function __autoload( $classname ) {
    $path = str_replace('_', DIRECTORY_SEPARATOR, $classname );
    require_once( "$path.php" );
}

$y = new business_ShopProduct();
```

As you can see, the __autoload() function transforms underscores in the supplied $classname to the DIRECTORY_SEPARATOR character (/ on Unix systems). We attempt to include the class file (business/shopProduct.php). If the class file exists, and the class it contains has been named correctly, the object should be instantiated without error. Of course, this does require the programmer to observe a naming convention that forbids the underscore character in a class name except where it divides up packages.

According to the organization of your classes and files, the __autoload() function can be a useful way of managing your library inclusions.

The Class and Object Functions

PHP provides a powerful set of functions for testing classes and objects. Why is this useful? After all, you probably wrote most of the classes you are using in your script.

In fact, you don't always know at runtime about the classes that you are using. You may have designed a system to work transparently with third-party bolt-on classes, for example. In this case, you will typically instantiate an object given only a class name. PHP allows you to use strings to refer to classes dynamically like this:

```
// tasks/Task.php
class Task {
    function doSpeak() {
        print "hello";
    }
}

// TaskRunner.php
$classname = "Task";

require_once( "tasks/$classname.php" );
$myObj = new $classname();
$myObj->doSpeak();
```

You might acquire the string that we assign to $classname from a configuration file or by comparing a Web request with the contents of a directory. You can then use the string to load a class file and instantiate an object. Typically, you would do something like this when you want your system to be able to run user-created plug-ins. Before you do anything as risky as that in a real project, you would have to check that the class exists, that it has the methods you are expecting, and so on.

Some class functions have been superseded by the more powerful Reflection API, which we will examine later in the chapter. Their simplicity and ease of use make them a first port of call in some instances, however. For this reason, and because they can be used in PHP 4 compatible scripts, we will look at them here.

Looking for Classes

The class_exists() function accepts a string representing the class to check for and returns a boolean true value if the class exists and false otherwise.

Using this function, we can make our previous fragment a little safer.

```
$classname = "Task";
$path = "tasks/$classname.php";
if ( ! file_exists( $path ) ) {
    throw new Exception( "No such file as $path" );
}
require_once( $path );
if ( ! class_exists( $classname ) ) {
    throw new Exception( "No such class as $classname" );
}
```

Of course, we can't be sure that the class in question does not require constructor arguments. For that level of safety, you would have to turn to the Reflection API, covered later in the chapter. Nevertheless, we are able to ascertain that the class exists before we work with it.

You can also get an array of all classes defined in your script process using the get_declared_classes() function.

```
print_r( get_declared_classes() );
```

This will list user-defined and built-in classes. Remember that it only returns the classes declared at the time of the function call. You may run require() or require_once() later on and thereby add to the number of classes in your script.

Learning About an Object or Class

As you know, we can constrain the types of method arguments using class type hinting. Even with this tool we can't always be certain of an object's type. PHP 5 does not allow us to constrain class type returned from a method or function, for example.

There are a number of basic tools available to check the type of an object. First of all, we can check the class of an object with the get_class() function. This accepts any object as an argument and returns its class name as a string.

```
$product = getProduct();
if ( get_class( $product ) == 'CdProduct' ) {
    print "\$product is a CdProduct object\n";
}
```

In the fragment we acquire *something* from the getProduct() function. To be absolutely certain that it is a CdProduct object, we use the get_class() method.

Here's the getProduct() function:

```
function getProduct() {
    return new CdProduct(    "Exile on Coldharbour Lane",
                            "The", "Alabama 3", 10.99, 60.33 );
}
```

getProduct() simply instantiates and returns a CdProduct object. We will make good use of this function in this section.

The get_class() function is a very specific tool. We often want a more general confirmation of a class's type. We may want to know that an object belongs to the ShopProduct family, but we don't care whether its actual class is BookProduct or CdProduct. To this end, PHP 4 introduced the is_a() function. is_a() requires an object and the name of a class or interface. The function returns true if the object is an instance of the given type.

```
$product = getProduct();
if ( is_a( $product, 'ShopProduct' )  ) {
    print "\$product is a ShopProduct object\n";
}
```

PHP 5 has built this functionality into the heart of the language itself. The Zend 2 Engine supports the instanceof keyword. This operator works with two operands, the object to test on the left of the keyword and the class or interface name on the right.

```
$product = getProduct();
if ( $product instanceof ShopProduct  ) {
    print "\$product is a ShopProduct object\n";
}
```

Unless you need your code to be compatible with PHP 4, you should use instanceof in preference to is_a().

Learning About Methods

We can acquire a list of all the methods in a class using the get_class_methods() function. This requires a class name and returns an array containing the names of all the methods in the class.

```
print_r( get_class_methods( 'CdProduct' ) );
// Array
// (
//       [0] => __construct
//       [1] => getPlayLength
//       [2] => getSummaryLine
//       [3] => getProducerFirstName
//       [4] => getProducerMainName
//       [5] => setDiscount
//       [6] => getDiscount
//       [7] => getTitle
//       [8] => getPrice
//       [9] => getProducer

// )
```

In the example, we pass a class name to get_class_methods() and dump the returned array with the print_r() function. We could alternatively have passed an *object* to get_class_methods() with the same result.

There is no recognition of access control by the get_class_methods() function. All method names are returned whether declared as public, private, or protected.

As you have seen, you are given a method name in a string variable, and you can invoke it dynamically together with an object, like this:

```
$product = getProduct(); // acquire an object
$method = "getTitle";     // define a method name
print $product->$method(); // invoke the method
```

Of course, this can be dangerous. What happens if the method does not exist? As you might expect, your script will fail with an error. We have already encountered one way of testing that a method exists:

```
if ( in_array( $method, get_class_methods( $product ) ) ) {
    print $product->$method(); // invoke the method
}
```

We check that the method name exists in the array returned by get_class_methods() before invoking it. PHP provides us with more specialized tools for this purpose. We can check method names to some extent with the two functions is_callable() and method_exists(). is_callable() is the more sophisticated of the two functions. It accepts a string variable representing a function name as its first argument and returns true if the function exists and can be called. To apply the same test to a method, you should pass it an array in place of the function name. The array must contain an object or class name as its first element and the method name to check as its second element. The function will return true if the method exists in the class.

```
if ( is_callable( array( $product, $method) ) ) {
    print $product->$method(); // invoke the method
}
```

is_callable() optionally accepts a second argument: a Boolean. If you set this to true, the function will only check the syntax of the given method or function name and not its actual existence.

■Warning At the time of writing (PHP 5.0.1), the is_callable() function returns true when testing methods declared private and protected. While this remains the case (and it may have changed by the time you read this), the function should be used with caution in a PHP 5 context. If you are working with PHP 5, you should use the Reflection API to check the status of a method before attempting to invoke it. I cover the Reflection API later in the chapter.

The method_exists() function requires an object and a method name, and returns true if the given method exists in the object's class.

```
if ( method_exists( $product, $method ) ) {
    print $product->$method();  // invoke the method
}
```

Note that method_exists() does not accept a class name as its first argument—you must use an object. If you do not have an object at hand, you can work around this limitation by using get_class_methods() or is_callable(), both of which accept class names.

```
if ( in_array( $method, get_class_methods( 'CdProduct' ) ) ) {
    // do something with the class
}
```

■Warning Remember that in PHP 5 the fact that a method exists does not mean that it will be callable. method_exists() returns true for private and protected methods as well as for public ones.

Learning About Properties

Just as you can query the methods of a class, so can you query its fields. The get_class_vars() function requires a class name and returns an associative array. The returned array contains field names as its keys and field values as its values. Let's apply this test to the CdProduct object. For the purposes of illustration, we add a public property to the class: CdProduct::$coverUrl.

```
print_r( get_class_vars( 'CdProduct' ) );
Array
(
    [playLength] => 0
    [coverUrl] =>
    [price] =>
)
```

This function pays some attention to privacy. It reports only the properties that are visible to the class. It does not, however, tell you which properties are accessible to you, reporting `protected`, `private`, and `public` properties without distinction.

Note This is another function that has undergone marked evolution during the development of PHP 5. Because its output may have changed again, it is worth running a test before working with it.

Learning About Inheritance

The class functions also allow us to chart inheritance relationships. We can find the parent of a class, for example, with `get_parent_class()`. This function requires either an object or a class name, and it returns the name of the super class, if any. If no such class exists, that is, if the class we are testing does not have a parent, then the function returns `false`.

```
print get_parent_class( 'CdProduct' );
// ShopProduct
```

We can also test whether a class is a child of another using the `is_subclass_of()` function. This requires a child object and the name of the parent class. The function returns `true` if the second argument is a super class of the first argument.

```
$product = getProduct(); // acquire an object
if ( is_subclass_of( $product, 'ShopProduct' ) ) {
    print "CdProduct is a subclass of ShopProduct\n";
}
```

Method Invocation

We have already encountered an example in which we used a string to invoke a method dynamically:

```
$product = getProduct(); // acquire an object
$method = "getTitle";     // define a method name
print $product->$method();  // invoke the method
```

PHP also provides the `call_user_func()` method to achieve the same end. `call_user_func()` can invoke either methods or functions. To invoke a function, it requires a single string as its first argument:

```
$returnVal = call_user_func("myFunction");
```

To invoke a method, it requires an array. The first element of this should be an object and the second should be the name of the method to invoke.

```
$returnVal = call_user_func( array( $myObj, "methodName") );
```

You can pass any arguments that the target method or function requires in additional arguments to `call_user_func()`, like this:

```
$product = getProduct(); // acquire an object
call_user_func( array( $product, 'setDiscount' ), 20 );
```

Our dynamic call is, of course, equivalent to

```
$product->setDiscount( 20 );
```

Because we can equally use a string directly in place of the method name, like this:

```
$method = "setDiscount";
$product->$method(20);
```

the `call_user_func()` method doesn't change our lives greatly. Much more impressive, though, is the related `call_user_func_array()` function. This operates in the same way as `call_user_func()` as far as selecting the target method or function is concerned. Crucially, though, it accepts any arguments required by the target method as an array.

So why is this useful? Occasionally you are given arguments in array form. Unless you know in advance the number of arguments you are dealing with, it can be difficult to pass them on. In Chapter 4, we looked at the interceptor methods that can be used to create delegator classes. Here's a simple example of a `__call()` method:

```
function __call( $method, $args ) {
    if ( method_exists( $this->thirdpartyShop, $method ) ) {
        return $this->thirdpartyShop->$method( );
    }
}
```

As we have seen, the `__call()` method is invoked when an undefined method is called by client code. In this example, we maintain an object in a property called `$thirdpartyShop`. If we find a method in the stored object that matches the `$method` argument, we invoke it. We blithely assume that the target method does not require any arguments, which is where our problems begin. When we write the `__call()` method, we have no way of telling how large the `$args` array may be from invocation to invocation. If we pass `$args` directly to the delegate method, we will pass a single array argument, and not separate arguments it may be expecting. `call_user_func_array()` solves the problem perfectly:

```
function __call( $method, $args ) {
    if ( method_exists( $this->thirdpartyShop, $method ) ) {
        return call_user_func_array(
                    array( $this->thirdpartyShop,
                    $method ), $args );
    }
}
```

The Reflection API

The first beta version of PHP 5 was released in the summer of 2003 to much excitement. Developers descended upon PHP 5's long list of object-oriented features, analyzing and experimenting with the nascent capabilities. Oddly, PHP 5's Reflection application programming interface (API) was not part of that initial release, and was absent from the overview documentation.

In the following weeks, the Reflection API quietly found its way into the PHP 5 source tree without fuss or fanfare. Yet its stealthy arrival belies its importance: PHP 5's Reflection API is to PHP what the java.lang.reflect package is to Java.

The Reflection API consists of built-in classes for analyzing properties, methods, and classes. It's similar in some respects to existing object functions such as get_class_vars(), but is more flexible and provides much greater detail. It's also designed to work with PHP's newest object-oriented features, such as access control, interfaces, and abstract classes.

Getting Started

The Reflection API can be used to examine more than just classes. For example, the ReflectionFunction class provides information about a given function, and ReflectionExtension yields insight about an extension compiled into the language. Table 5-1 lists some of the classes in the API.

Table 5-1. *Some of the Classes in the Reflection API*

Class	Description
Reflection	Provides a static export() method for summarizing class information
ReflectionClass	Class information and tools
ReflectionMethod	Class method information and tools
ReflectionParameter	Method argument information
ReflectionProperty	Class property information
ReflectionFunction	Function information and tools
ReflectionExtension	PHP extension information
ReflectionException	An error class

Between them, the classes in the Reflection API provide unprecedented runtime access to information about the objects, functions, and extensions in your scripts.

Because of its power and reach, you should usually use the Reflection API in preference to the class and object functions. You will soon find it indispensable as a tool for testing classes. You might want to generate class diagrams or documentation, for example, or you might want to save object information to a database, examining an object's accessor ("getter" and "setter") methods to extract field names. Building a framework that invokes methods in module classes according to a naming scheme is another use of Reflection.

Time to Roll Up Your Sleeves

We have already encountered some functions for examining the attributes of classes. Many of them are not yet fully equipped to provide information about the newer features in PHP 5. Let's look at a tool that *is* up to the job. ReflectionClass provides methods that reveal information about every aspect of a given class, whether it's a user-defined or internal class. The constructor of ReflectionClass accepts a class name as its sole argument:

```
$prod_class = new ReflectionClass( 'CdProduct' );
Reflection::export( $prod_class );
```

Once you've created a ReflectionClass object, you can use the Reflection utility class to dump information about CdProduct. Reflection has a static export() method that outputs data on any of the Reflection classes (that is, any class that implements the Reflector interface, to be pedantic). Here's an extract from the output generated by a call to Reflection::export():

```
Class [ <user> class CdProduct extends ShopProduct ] {
  @@ /home/projects/sp/ShopProduct.php 59-80

  - Constants [0] {
  }

  - Static properties [0] {
  }

  - Static methods [0] {
  }

  - Properties [3] {
    Property [ <default> private $playLength ]
    Property [ <default> public $coverUrl ]
    Property [ <default> protected $price ]
  }

  - Methods [11] {
    Method [ <user> <ctor> public method __construct ] {
      @@ /home/projects/sp/ShopProduct.php 63 - 68

      - Parameters [5] {
        Parameter #0 [ $title ]
        Parameter #1 [ $firstName ]
        Parameter #2 [ $mainName ]
        Parameter #3 [ $price ]
        Parameter #4 [ $playLength ]
      }
    }

    Method [ <user> public method getPlayLength ] {
      @@ /home/projects/sp/ShopProduct.php 70 - 72
    }

    Method [ <user> public method getSummaryLine ] {
      @@ /home/projects/sp/ShopProduct.php 74 - 78
    }
}
```

As you can see, Reflection::export() provides remarkable access to information about a class. Reflection::export() provides summary information about almost every aspect of CdProduct, including the access control status of properties and methods, the arguments required by every method, and the location of every method within the script document. Compare that with a more established debugging function. The var_dump() function is a general-purpose tool for summarizing data. You must instantiate an object before you can extract a summary, and even then it provides nothing like the detail made available by Reflection::export().

```
var_dump( getProduct() );
```

```
// object(CdProduct)#1 (7) {
//    ["playLength:private"]=>
//    float(60.33)
//    ["coverUrl"]=>
//    string(0) ""
//    ["title:private"]=>
//    string(25) "Exile on Coldharbour Lane"
//    ["producerMainName:private"]=>
//    string(9) "Alabama 3"
//    ["producerFirstName:private"]=>
//    string(3) "The"
//    ["price:protected"]=>
//    float(10.99)
//    ["discount:private"]=>
//    int(0)
// }
```

var_dump() and its cousin print_r() are fantastically convenient tools for exposing the data in your scripts. For classes and functions, the Reflection API takes things to a whole new level, though.

Examining a Class

The Reflection ::export() method can provide a great deal of useful information for debugging, but we can use the API in more specialized ways. Let's work directly with the Reflection classes. You've already seen how to instantiate a ReflectionClass object:

```
$prod_class = new ReflectionClass( 'CdProduct' );
```

Next, let's use the ReflectionClass object to investigate CdProduct within a script. What kind of class is it? Can an instance be created? Here's a function to answer these questions:

```
$prod_class = new ReflectionClass( 'CdProduct' );
print classData( $prod_class );
```

```
function classData( ReflectionClass $class ) {
  $details = "";
  $name = $class->getName();
  if ( $class->isUserDefined() ) {
    $details .= "$name is user defined\n";
  }
  if ( $class->isInternal() ) {
    $details .= "$name is built-in\n";
  }
  if ( $class->isInterface() ) {
    $details .= "$name is interface\n";
  }
  if ( $class->isAbstract() ) {
    $details .= "$name is an abstract class\n";
  }
  if ( $class->isFinal() ) {
    $details .= "$name is a final class\n";
  }
  if ( $class->isInstantiable() ) {
    $details .= "$name can be instantiated\n";
  } else {
    $details .= "$name can not be instantiated\n";
  }
  return $details;
}
```

We create a ReflectionClass object, assigning it to a variable called $prod_class by passing the CdProduct class name to ReflectionClass's constructor. $prod_class is then passed to a function called classData() that demonstrates some of the methods that can be used to query a class.

The methods should be self-explanatory, but here's a brief description of each one:

- ReflectionClass::getName() returns the name of the class being examined.

- The ReflectionClass::isUserDefined() method returns true if the class has been declared in PHP code, and ReflectionClass::isInternal() yields true if the class is built-in.

- You can test whether a class is abstract with ReflectionClass::isAbstract(), and whether it's an interface with ReflectionClass::isInterface().

- If you want to get an instance of the class, you can test the feasibility of that with ReflectionClass::isInstantiable().

You can even examine a user-defined class's source code. The `ReflectionClass` object provides access to its class's file name, and to the start and finish lines of the class in the file.

Here's a quick-and-dirty method `ReflectionClass`:

```
class ReflectionUtil {
  static function getClassSource( ReflectionClass $class ) {
    $path = $class->getFileName();
    $lines = @file( $path );
    $from = $class->getStartLine();
    $to   = $class->getEndLine();
    $len = $to-$from+1;
    return implode( array_slice( $lines, $from-1, $len ));
  }
}


print ReflectionUtil::getClassSource(
  new ReflectionClass( 'CdProduct' ) );
```

`ReflectionUtil` is a simple class with a single static method, `ReflectionUtil::getClassSource()`. That method takes a `ReflectionClass` object as its only argument, and returns the referenced class's source code. `ReflectionClass::getFileName()` provides the path to the class's file as an absolute path, so the code should be able to go right ahead and open it. `file()` obtains an array of all the lines in the file. `ReflectionClass::getStartLine()` provides the class's start line; `ReflectionClass::getEndLine()` finds the final line. From there, it's simply a matter of using `array_slice()` to extract the lines of interest.

To keep things brief, this code omits error handling. In a real-world application, you'd want to check arguments and result codes.

Examining Methods

Just as `ReflectionClass` is used to examine a class, a `ReflectionMethod` object examines a method.

You can acquire a `ReflectionMethod` in two ways: you can get an array of `ReflectionMethod` objects from `ReflectionClass::getMethods()`, or if you need to work with a specific method, `ReflectionClass::getMethod()` accepts a method name and returns the relevant `ReflectionMethod` object.

Here we use `ReflectionClass::getMethods()` to put the `ReflectionMethod` class through its paces.

```
$prod_class = new ReflectionClass( 'CdProduct' );
$methods = $prod_class->getMethods();

foreach ( $methods as $method ) {
  print methodData( $method );
  print "\n----\n";
}
```

```
function methodData( ReflectionMethod $method ) {
  $details = "";
  $name = $method->getName();
  if ( $method->isUserDefined() ) {
    $details .= "$name is user defined\n";
  }
  if ( $method->isInternal() ) {
    $details .= "$name is built-in\n";
  }
  if ( $method->isAbstract() ) {
    $details .= "$name is abstract\n";
  }
  if ( $method->isPublic() ) {
    $details .= "$name is public\n";
  }
  if ( $method->isProtected() ) {
    $details .= "$name is protected\n";
  }
  if ( $method->isPrivate() ) {
    $details .= "$name is private\n";
  }
  if ( $method->isStatic() ) {
    $details .= "$name is static\n";
  }
  if ( $method->isFinal() ) {
    $details .= "$name is final\n";
  }
  if ( $method->isConstructor() ) {
    $details .= "$name is the constructor\n";
  }
  if ( $method->returnsReference() ) {
    $details .= "$name returns a reference (as opposed to a value)\n";
  }
  return $details;
}
```

The code uses ReflectionClass::getMethods() to get an array of ReflectionMethod objects, and then loops through the array, passing each object to methodData().

The names of the methods used in methodData() reflect their intent: the code checks whether the method is user-defined, built-in, abstract, public, protected, static, or final. You can also check whether the method is the constructor for its class, and whether or not it returns a reference.

One caveat: ReflectionMethod::returnsReference() doesn't return true if the tested method simply returns an object, even though objects are passed and assigned by reference in PHP 5. Instead, ReflectionMethod::returnsReference() only returns true if the method in question has been explicitly declared to return a reference (by placing an ampersand character in front of the method name).

As you might expect, you can access a method's source code using a technique similar to the one used previously with `ReflectionClass`:

```
class ReflectionUtil {
  static function getMethodSource( ReflectionMethod $method ) {
    $path = $method->getFileName();
    $lines = @file( $path );
    $from = $method->getStartLine();
    $to   = $method->getEndLine();
    $len  = $to-$from+1;
    return implode( array_slice( $lines, $from-1, $len ));
  }
}


$class = new ReflectionClass( 'CdProduct' );
$method = $class->getMethod( 'getSummaryLine' );
print ReflectionUtil::getMethodSource( $method );
```

Because `ReflectionMethod` provides us with `getFileName()`, `getStartLine()`, and `getEndLine()` methods, it's a simple matter to extract the method's source code.

Examining Method Arguments

Now that method signatures can constrain the types of object arguments, the ability to examine the arguments declared in a method signature becomes immensely useful. The Reflection API provides the `ReflectionParameter` class just for this purpose. To get a `ReflectionParameter` object, you need the help of a `ReflectionMethod` object. The `ReflectionMethod::getParameters()` method returns an array of `ReflectionParameter` objects.

`ReflectionParameter` can tell you the name of an argument, whether the variable is passed by reference (that is, with a preceding ampersand in the method declaration), and can also tell you the class required by argument hinting and whether the method will accept a null value for the argument.

Here are some of `ReflectionParameter`'s methods in action:

```
$prod_class = new ReflectionClass( CdProduct );
$method = $prod_class->getMethod( "__construct" );
$params = $method->getParameters();

foreach ( $params as $param ) {
  print argData( $param );
}
```

```
function argData( ReflectionParameter $arg ) {
  $details = "";
  $name  = $arg->getName();
  $class = $arg->getClass();

  if ( ! empty( $class )  ) {
    $classname = $class->getName();
    $details .= "\$$name must be a $classname object\n";
  }
  if ( $arg->allowsNull() ) {
    $details .= "\$$name can be null\n";
  }
  if ( $arg->isPassedByReference() ) {
    $details .= "\$$name is passed by reference\n";
  }
  return $details;
}
```

Using the `ReflectionClass::getMethod()` method, the code acquires a `ReflectionMethod` object. It then uses `ReflectionMethod::getParameters()` to get an array of `ReflectionParameter` objects. The `argData()` function uses the `ReflectionParameter` object it was passed to acquire information about the argument.

First, it gets the argument's variable name with `ReflectionParameter::getName()`. The `ReflectionParameter::getClass()` method returns a `ReflectionClass` object if a hint's been provided. Finally, the code checks whether the argument can be null with `allowsNull()`, and whether it's a reference with `isPassedByReference()`. This last method seems to confirm that all parameters can be null. I suspect that at some point there may have been plans for a `not_null` modifier for method parameters, but this does not seem to have come to pass.

An Example

With the basics of the Reflection API under your belt, you can now put the API to work.

Imagine that you're creating a class that calls `Module` objects dynamically. That is, it can accept plug-ins written by third parties and slotted into the application without the need for any hard coding. To achieve this, you might define an `execute()` method in the `Module` interface or abstract base class, forcing all child classes to define an implementation. You could allow the users of your system to list `Module` classes in an external XML configuration file. Your system can use this information to aggregate a number of `Module` objects before calling `execute()` on each one.

What happens, however, if each `Module` requires *different* information to do its job? In that case, the XML file can provide property keys and values for each `Module`, and the creator of each `Module` can provide setter methods for each property name. Given that foundation, it's up to your code to ensure that the correct setter method is called for the correct property name.

Here's some groundwork for the `Module` interface and a couple of implementing classes:

```php
class Person {
    public $name;
    function __construct( $name ) {
        $this->name = name;
    }
}

interface Module {
    function execute();
}

class FtpModule implements Module {
    function setHost( $host ) {
        print "FtpModule::setHost(): $host\n";
    }

    function setUser( $user ) {
        print "FtpModule::setUser(): $user\n";
    }

    function execute() {
        // do things
    }
}

class PersonModule implements Module {
    function setPerson( Person $person ) {
        print "PersonModule::setPerson(): {$person->name}\n";
    }

    function execute() {
        // do things
    }
}
```

Here, `PersonModule` and `FtpModule` both provide empty implementations of the `execute()` method. Each class also implements setter methods that do nothing but report that they were invoked. Our system lays down the convention that all setter methods must expect a single argument: either a string, or an object that can be instantiated with a single string argument. The `PersonModule::setPerson()` method expects a `Person` object so we include a `Person` class in our example.

To work with `PersonModule` and `FtpModule`, the next step is to create a `ModuleRunner` class. It will use a multidimensional array indexed by module name to represent configuration information provided in the XML file. Here's that code:

```
class ModuleRunner {
    private $configData
            = array(
                    "PersonModule" => array( 'person'=>'bob' ),
                    "FtpModule"    => array( 'host'
                                                  =>'example.com',
                                             'user'  =>'anon' )
              );
    private $modules = array();
  // ...
}
```

The `ModuleRunner::$configData` property contains references to the two `Module` classes. For each module element, the code maintains a subarray containing a set of properties. `ModuleRunner`'s `init()` method is responsible for creating the correct `Module` objects, as shown here:

```
class ModuleRunner {
  // ...

    function init() {
        $interface = new ReflectionClass('Module');
        foreach ( $this->configData as $modulename => $params ) {
            $module_class = new ReflectionClass( $modulename );
            if ( ! $module_class->isSubclassOf( $interface ) ) {
                throw new Exception( "unknown module type: $modulename" );
            }
            $module = $module_class->newInstance();
            foreach ( $module_class->getMethods() as $method ) {
                $this->handleMethod( $module, $method, $params );
                // we cover handleMethod() in a future listing!
            }
            array_push( $this->modules, $module );
        }
    }

  //...
}

$test = new ModuleRunner();
$test->init();
```

The `init()` method loops through the `ModuleRunner::$configData` array and for each module element it attempts to create a `ReflectionClass` object. An exception is generated when `ReflectionClass`'s constructor is invoked with the name of a nonexistent class, so in a real-world context we would want to include more error handling here. We use the `ReflectionClass::is_subclass_of()` method to ensure that the module class belongs to the `Module` type.

Before you can invoke the execute() method of each Module, an instance has to be created. That's the purpose of method::ReflectionClass::newInstance(). That method accepts any number of arguments, which it passes on to the relevant class's constructor method. If all's well, it returns an instance of the class. (For production code, be sure to code defensively: check that the constructor method for each Module object doesn't require arguments before creating an instance.)

ReflectionClass::getMethods() returns an array of all ReflectionMethod objects available for the class. For each element in the array, the code invokes the ModuleRunner::handleMethod() method, passing it a Module instance, the ReflectionMethod object, and an array of properties to associate with the Module. handleMethod() verifies and invokes the Module object's setter methods.

```
class ModuleRunner {
  // ...
  function handleMethod( Module $module, ReflectionMethod $method, $params ) {
    $name = $method->getName();
    $args = $method->getParameters();

    if ( count( $args ) != 1 ||
         substr( $name, 0, 3 ) != "set" ) {
      return false;
    }

    $property = strtolower( substr( $name, 3 ));
    if ( ! isset( $params[$property] ) ) {
      return false;
    }

    $arg_class = $args[0]->getClass();
    if ( empty( $arg_class ) ) {
      $method->invoke( $module, $params[$property] );
    } else {
      $method->invoke( $module,
          $arg_class->newInstance( $params[$property] ) );
    }
  }
}
```

handleMethod() first checks that the method is a valid setter. In the code, a valid setter method must be named setXXXX(), and must declare one and only one argument.

Assuming that the argument checks out, the code then extracts a property name from the method name by removing set from the beginning of the method name and converting the resulting substring to lowercase characters. That string is used to test the $params array argument. This array contains the user-supplied properties that are to be associated with the Module object. If the $params array doesn't contain the property, the code gives up and returns false.

If the property name extracted from the module method matches an element in the $params array, we can go ahead and invoke the correct setter method. To do that, the code must check the type of the first (and only) required argument of the setter method.

The ReflectionParameter::getClass() method provides this information. If the method returns an empty value, the setter expects a primitive of some kind; otherwise, it expects an object.

To call the setter method, we need a new Reflection API method. ReflectionMethod::invoke() requires an object and any number of method arguments to pass on to the method it represents. ReflectionMethod::invoke() throws an exception if the provided object does not match its method. We call this method in one of two ways. If the setter method doesn't require an object argument, we call ReflectionMethod::invoke() with the user-supplied property string. If the method requires an object, we use the property string to instantiate an object of the correct type, which is then passed to the setter.

The example assumes that the required object can be instantiated with a single string argument to its constructor. It's best, of course, to check this before calling ReflectionClass::newInstance().

By the time the ModuleRunner::init() method has run its course, the object has a store of Module objects, all primed with data. The class can now be given a method to loop through the Module objects, calling execute() on each one.

Summary

In this chapter, we covered some of the techniques and tools that you can use to manage your libraries and classes. Although PHP does not provide namespaces for packages, we saw that we can combine include paths, the PEAR class naming convention, and the file system to provide flexible organization for classes. We examined PHP's object and class functions, before taking things to the next level with the powerful Reflection API. Finally, we used the Reflection classes to build a simple example that illustrates one of the potential uses that Reflection has to offer.

■ ■ ■

CHAPTER 6

Objects and Design

Now that we have seen the mechanics of PHP's object support in some detail, we step back from the details in this chapter and consider how best to use the tools that we have encountered. In this chapter, I introduce you to some of the issues surrounding objects and design. We will also look at the UML, a powerful graphical language for describing object-oriented systems.

This chapter will cover

- *Design basics*: What do we mean by design? How does object-oriented design differ from procedural code?

- *Class scope*: How do you decide what to include in a class?

- *Polymorphism*: Hiding implementation behind interface.

- *Encapsulation*: Keeping your components independent of one another and the wider system.

- *The UML*: Using diagrams to describe object-oriented architectures.

Defining Code Design

This is a fair question given the title of this chapter. One sense of "code design" concerns the definition of a system: the determination of a system's requirements, scope, and objectives. What does the system need to do? Who does it need to do it for? What are the outputs of the system? Do they meet the stated need? On a lower level, design can be taken to mean the process by which you define the participants of a system and organize their relationships. This chapter is concerned with the second sense: the definition and disposition of classes and objects.

So what is a participant? An object-oriented system is made up of classes. It is important to decide the nature of these players in your system. Classes are made up of methods, so in defining your classes you must decide which methods belong together. As we will see, though, classes are often combined in inheritance relationships to conform to common interfaces. It is these interfaces, or types, that should be your first port of call in designing your system.

There are other relationships that you can define for your classes. You can create classes that are composed of other types or that manage lists of other type instances. You can design classes that simply use other objects. These relationships of composition or use are designed into your classes (through class type hints, for example), but the actual object relationships take place at runtime, which can add flexibility to your design. We will see how to model these relationships in this chapter and explore them further throughout the book.

As part of the design process, you must decide when an operation should belong to a type and when it should belong to another class used by the type. Everywhere you turn you are presented with choices, decisions that might lead to clarity and elegance, or might mire you in compromise.

In this chapter, we will examine some issues that might influence a few of these choices.

Object-Oriented and Procedural Programming

How does object-oriented design differ from the more traditional procedural code? It is tempting to say that the primary distinction is that object-oriented code has objects in it. This is neither true nor useful. In PHP, you will often find procedural code using objects. You may also come across classes that contain tracts of procedural code. The presence of classes does not guarantee object-oriented design, even in a language like Java, which forces you to do everything inside a class.

One core difference between object-oriented and procedural code can be found in the way that responsibility is distributed. Procedural code takes the form of a sequential series of commands and method calls. The controlling code tends to take responsibility for handling differing conditions. This top-down control can result in the development of duplications and dependencies across a project. Object-oriented code tries to minimize these dependencies by moving responsibility for handling tasks away from client code and toward the objects in the system.

Let's set ourselves a simple problem and analyze it in terms of both object-oriented and procedural code to illustrate these points. Our project is to build a quick tool for reading from and writing to configuration files. In order to maintain focus on the structures of the code, I will omit implementation code in these examples.

We begin with a procedural approach to this problem. To start with, we will read and write text in the format

```
key:value
```

We need only two functions for this purpose:

```
function readParams( $sourceFile) {
    $params = array();
    // read text parameters from $sourceFile
    return $params;
}

function writeParams( $params, $sourceFile) {
    // write text parameters to $sourceFile
}
```

The readParams() function requires the name of a source file. It attempts to open it, and reads each line, looking for key/value pairs. It builds up an array as it goes. Finally, it returns the array to the controlling code. writeParams() accepts an associative array and the path to a source file. It loops through the associative array, writing each key/value pair to the file. Here's some client code that works with the functions:

```
$file = "./param.txt";
$array['key1'] = "val1";
$array['key2'] = "val2";
$array['key3'] = "val3";
writeParams( $array, $file );  // array written to file
$output = readParams( $file ); // array read from file
print_r( $output );
```

This code is relatively compact and should be easy to maintain.

Now, though, we are informed that the tool should support a simple XML format that looks like this:

```
<params>
    <param>
        <key>my key</key>
        <val>my val</val>
    </param>
</params>
```

The parameter file should be read in XML mode if the parameter file ends in ".xml". Although this is not difficult to accommodate, it threatens to make our code much harder to maintain. We really have two options at this stage. We can check the file extension in the controlling code, or we can test inside our read and write functions. Let's go for the latter approach:

```
function readParams( $source ) {
    $params = array();
    if ( substr( $source, -4 ) == ".xml" ) {
        // read XML parameters from $source
    } else {
        // read text parameters from $source
    }
    return $params;
}

function writeParams( $params, $source ) {
    if ( substr( $source, -4 ) == ".xml" ) {
        // write XML parameters to $source
    } else {
        // write text parameters to $source
    }
}
```

As you can see, we have had to use the test for the XML extension in each of the functions. It is this repetition that might cause us problems down the line. If we are asked to include yet another parameter format, we will need to remember to keep the readParams() and writeParams() functions in line with one another.

Let's address the same problem with some simple classes. First we create an abstract base class that will define the interface for the type:

```php
abstract class ParamHandler {
    protected $source;
    protected $params = array();

    function __construct( $source ) {
        $this->source = $source;
    }

    function addParam( $key, $val ) {
        $this->params[$key] = $val;
    }

    function getAllParams() {
        return $this->params;
    }

    static function getInstance( $filename ) {
        if ( substr( $filename, -4 ) == ".xml" ) {
            return new XmlParam( $filename );
        }
        return new TextParam( $filename );
    }

    abstract function write();
    abstract function read();
}
```

We define the addParam() method to allow the user to add parameters to the protected $params property and getAllParams() to provide access to a copy of the array.

We also create a static getInstance() method that tests the file extension and returns a particular subclass according to the results. Crucially we define two abstract methods, read() and write(), ensuring that any subclasses will support this interface.

Now let's define the subclasses, once again omitting the details of implementation to keep the example clean:

```php
class XmlParam extends ParamHandler {

    function write() {
        // write XML
        // using $this->params
    }

    function read() {
        // read XML
        // and populate $this->params
    }

}
```

```
class TextParam extends ParamHandler {

    function write() {
        // write text
        // using $this->params
    }

    function read() {
        // read text
        // and populate $this->params
    }

}
```

These classes simply provide implementations of the write() and read() methods. Each class will write and read according to the appropriate format.

Client code will write to both text and XML formats entirely transparently according to the file extension:

```
$test = ParamHandler::getInstance( "./params.xml" );
$test->addParam("key1", "val1" );
$test->addParam("key2", "val2" );
$test->addParam("key3", "val3" );
$test->write(); // writing in XML format
```

We can also read from either file format:

```
$test = ParamHandler::getInstance( "./params.txt" );
$test->read(); // reading in text format
```

So, what can we learn from these two approaches?

Responsibility

The controlling code in the procedural example takes responsibility for deciding about format, not once but twice. The conditional code is tidied away into functions, certainly, but this merely disguises the fact of a single flow making decisions as it goes. The call to readParams() must always take place in a different context from a call to writeParams(), so we are forced to repeat the file extension test in each function (or to perform variations on this test).

In the object-oriented version, this choice about file format is made in the static getInstance() method, which tests the file extension only once, serving up the correct subclass. The client code takes no responsibility for implementation. It uses the provided object with no knowledge of, or interest in, the particular subclass it belongs to. It knows only that it is working with a ParamHandler object, and that it will support write() and read(). While the procedural code busies itself about details, the object-oriented code works only with an interface, unconcerned about the details of implementation. Because responsibility for implementation lies with the objects and not with the client code, it would be easy to switch in support for new formats transparently.

Cohesion

Cohesion is the extent to which proximate procedures are related to one another. Ideally, you should create components that share a clear responsibility. If your code spreads related routines widely, then you will find them harder to maintain as you have to hunt around to make changes.

Our `ParamHandler` classes collect related procedures into a common context. The methods for working with XML share a context in which they can share data, and where changes to one method can easily be reflected in another if necessary (if we needed to change an XML element name, for example). The `ParamHandler` classes can therefore be said to have "high cohesion."

The procedural example, on the other hand, separates related procedures. The code for working with XML is spread across functions.

Coupling

Tight coupling occurs when discrete parts of a system's code are tightly bound up with one another so that a change in one part necessitates changes in the others. Tight coupling is by no means unique to procedural code, though its sequential nature makes it prone to the problem.

We can see this kind of coupling in the procedural example. The `writeParams()` and `readParams()` functions run the same test on a file extension to determine how they should work with data. Any change in logic we make to one will have to be implemented in the other. If we were to add a new format, for example, we would have to bring the functions into line with one another so that they both implement a new file extension test in the same way. This problem can only get worse as we add new parameter-related functions.

The object-oriented example decouples the individual subclasses from one another and from the client code. If we were required to add a new parameter format, we could simply create a new subclass, amending a single test in the static `getInstance()` method.

Orthogonality

The killer combination in components of tightly defined responsibilities together with independence from the wider system is sometimes referred to as orthogonality (*The Pragmatic Programmer*).

Orthogonality, it is argued, promotes reuse in that components can be plugged into new systems without needing any special configuration. Such components will have clear inputs and outputs independent of any wider context. Orthogonal code makes change easier because the impact of altering an implementation will be localized to the component being altered. Finally, orthogonal code is safer. The effects of bugs should be limited in scope. An error in highly interdependent code can easily cause knock-on effects in the wider system.

There is nothing automatic about loose coupling and high cohesion in a class context. We could, after all, embed our entire procedural example into one misguided class. So how do we achieve this balance in our code? I usually start by considering the classes that should live in my system.

Choosing Your Classes

It can be surprisingly difficult to define the boundaries of your classes, especially as they will evolve with any system that you build.

It can seem straightforward when you are modeling the real world. Object-oriented systems often feature software representations of real things—Person, Invoice, and Shop classes abound. This would seem to suggest that defining a class is a matter of finding the *things* in your system and then giving them agency through methods. This is not a bad starting point, but it does have its dangers. If you see a class as a noun, a subject for any number of verbs, then you may find it bloating as ongoing development and requirement changes call for it to do more and more things.

Let's consider the ShopProduct example that we created in Chapter 3. Our system exists to offer products to a customer, so defining a ShopProduct class is an obvious choice, but is that the only decision we need to make? We provide methods such as getTitle() and getPrice() for accessing product data. When we are asked to provide a mechanism for outputting summary information for invoices and delivery notes, it seems to make sense to define a write() method. When the client asks us to provide the product summaries in different formats, we look again at our class. We duly create writeXML() and writeXHTML() methods in addition to the write() method. Or we add conditional code to write() to output different formats according to an option flag.

Either way, the problem here is that the ShopProduct class is now trying to do too much. It is struggling to manage strategies for display as well as for managing product data.

How *should* we think about defining classes? The best approach is to think of a class as having a primary responsibility, and to make that responsibility as singular and focused as possible. Put the responsibility into words. Peter Coad wrote that you should be able to describe a class's responsibility in 25 words or less, rarely using the words "and" or "or." If your sentence gets too long, or mired in clauses, it is probably time to consider defining new classes along the lines of some of the responsibilities you have described.

So ShopProduct classes are responsible for managing product data. If we add methods for writing to different formats, we begin to add a new area of responsibility: product display. As you saw in Chapter 3, we actually defined two types based on these separate responsibilities. The ShopProduct type remained responsible for product data, and the ShopProductWriter type took on responsibility for displaying product information. Individual subclasses refined these responsibilities.

■**Note** Very few design rules are entirely inflexible. You will sometimes see code for saving object data in an otherwise unrelated class, for example. While this would seem to violate the rule that a class should have a singular responsibility, it can be the most convenient place for the functionality to live because a method has to have full access to an instance's fields. Using local methods for persistence can also save us from creating a parallel hierarchy of persistence classes mirroring our savable classes, and thereby introducing unavoidable coupling. We deal with other stategies for object persistence in Chapter 12. Avoid religious adherence to design rules; they are not a substitute for analyzing the problem before you. Try to remain alive to the reasoning behind the rule, and emphasize that over the rule itself.

Polymorphism

Polymorphism, or class switching, is a common feature of object-oriented systems. We have encountered it several times already in this book.

Polymorphism is the maintenance of multiple implementations behind a common interface. This sounds complicated, but in fact it should be very familiar to you by now. The need for polymorphism is often signaled by the presence of extensive conditional statements in your code.

When we first created the ShopProduct class in Chapter 3, we experimented with a single class, which managed functionality for books and CDs in addition to generic products. In order to provide summary information, we relied upon a conditional statement:

```
function getSummaryLine() {
    $base  = "$this->title ( $this->producerMainName, ";
    $base .= "$this->producerFirstName )";
    if ( $this->type == 'book' ) {
        $base .= ": page count - $this->numPages";
    } else if ( $this->type == 'cd' ) {
        $base .= ": playing time - $this->playLength";
    }
    return $base;
}
```

These statements suggested the shape for the two subclasses: CdProduct and BookProduct.

By the same token, the conditional statements in our procedural parameter example contained the seeds of the object-oriented structure we finally arrived at. We repeated the same condition in two parts of the script.

```
function readParams( $source ) {
    $params = array();
    if ( substr( $source, -4 ) == ".xml" ) {
        // read XML parameters from $source
    } else {
        // read text parameters from $source
    }
    return $params;
}

function writeParams( $params, $source ) {
    if ( substr( $source, -4 ) == ".xml" ) {
        // write XML parameters to $source
    } else {
        // write text parameters to $source
    }
}
```

Each clause suggested one of the subclasses we finally produced: XmlParam and TextParam, extending the abstract base class ParamHandler's write() and read() methods.

```
// could return XmlParam or TextParam
$test = ParamHandler::getInstance( $file );
```

```
$test->read();  // could be XmlParam::read() or TextParam::read()
$test->addParam("key1", "val1" );
$test->write(); // could be XmlParam::write() or TextParam::write()
```

It is important to note that polymorphism doesn't banish conditionals. Methods like `ParamHandler::getInstance()` will often determine which objects to return based upon `switch` or `if` statements. These tend to centralize the conditional code into one place, though.

As we have seen, PHP 5 enforces the interfaces defined by abstract classes. This is useful because we can be sure that a child class will implement a method signature in exactly the same way as defined by an abstract parent. This includes all class type hints and access control. Client code can therefore treat all members of a type interchangeably. There is an important exception to this rule: there is no way of constraining the return type of a method. This means that it is possible for methods in different subclasses to return different class types or primitives, which can undermine the interchangeability of types. You should try to be consistent with your return values. Some methods may be defined to take advantage of PHP's loose typing and return different types according to circumstances. Other methods enter into a contract with client code, effectively promising that they will return a particular type. If this contract is laid down in an abstract super class, it should be honored by its concrete children so that clients can be sure of consistent behavior. If you commit to return an object of a particular type, you can, of course, return an instance of a subtype. Although the interpreter does not enforce return types, you can make it a convention in your projects that certain methods will behave consistently. Use comments in the source code to specify a method's return type.

Encapsulation

Encapsulation simply means the hiding of data and functionality from a client. And once again it is a key object-oriented concept.

On the simplest level we encapsulate data by declaring properties `private` or `protected`. By hiding a property from client code, we enforce an interface and prevent the accidental corruption of an object's data.

Polymorphism illustrates another kind of encapsulation. By placing different implementations behind a common interface, we hide these underlying strategies from the client. This means that any changes that are made behind this interface are transparent to the wider system. We can add new classes or change the code in a class without causing errors. The interface is what matters, and not the mechanisms working beneath it. The more independent these mechanisms are kept, the less chance that changes or repairs will have a knock-on effect in your projects.

Encapsulation is in some ways the key to object-oriented programming. Our objective should be to make each part as independent as possible from its peers. Classes and methods should receive as much information as is necessary to perform their allotted tasks, which should be limited in scope and clearly identified.

The introduction of the `private`, `protected`, and `public` keywords have made encapsulation easier. Encapsulation is also a state of mind, though. Working with PHP 4 privacy was signaled using documentation and naming conventions alone. An underscore, for example, is a common way of signaling a private property:

```
var $_touchezpas;
```

Code had to be checked closely, of course, because privacy was not strictly enforced. Interestingly, though, errors were rare, because the structure and style of the code made it pretty clear which properties wanted to be left alone.

By the same token even in PHP 5, we could break the rules and discover the exact subtype of an object that we are using in a class-switching context, simply by passing it to the get_class() method.

```
function workWithProducts( ShopProduct $prod ) {
    if ( get_class( $prod ) == "cdproduct" ) {
        // do cd thing
    } else if ( get_class( $prod ) == "bookproduct" ) {
        // do book thing
    }
}
```

You may have a very good reason to do this, but in general it carries with it a slightly uncertain odor. By querying the specific subtype in the example, we are setting up a dependency. While the specifics of the subtype were hidden by polymorphism, it would have been possible to have changed our ShopProduct inheritance hierarchy entirely with no ill effects. Our code ends that. Now if we need to rationalize the CdProduct and BookProduct classes, we may cause unexpected side effects in the workWithProducts() method.

There are two lessons to take away from this example. Firstly, encapsulation helps you to create orthogonal code. Secondly, the extent to which encapsulation is enforceable is beside the point. Encapsulation is a technique that should be observed equally by classes and their clients.

Forget How to Do It

If you are like me, the mention of a problem will set your mind racing, looking for mechanisms that might provide a solution. You might select functions that will address an issue, revisit clever regular expressions, track down PEAR packages. You probably have some paste-able code in an old project that does something somewhat similar. At the design stage, you can profit by setting all that aside for a while. Empty your head of procedures and mechanisms.

Think only about the key participants of your system: the types it will need, and their interfaces. Of course, your knowledge of process will inform your thinking. A class that opens a file will need a path, database code will need to manage table names and passwords, and so on. Let the structures and relationships in your code lead you, though. You will find that the implementation falls into place easily behind a well-defined interface. You then have the flexibility to switch out, improve, or extend an implementation should you need to without affecting the wider system.

In order to emphasize interface, think in terms of abstract base classes rather than concrete children. In our parameter-fetching code, for example, the interface is the most important aspect of the design. We want a type that reads and writes name/value pairs. It is this responsibility that is important about the type, not the actual persistence medium or the means of storing and retrieving data. We design the system around the abstract `ParamHandler` class, and only add in the concrete strategies for actually reading and writing parameters later on. In this way we build both polymorphism and encapsulation into our system from the start. The structure lends itself to class switching.

Having said that, of course, we knew from the start that there would be text and XML implementations of `ParamHandler`, and there is no question that this influenced our interface. There is always a certain amount of mental juggling to do when designing interfaces.

The Gang of Four (*Design Patterns*) summed up this principle with the phrase "Program to an interface, not an implementation." It is a good one to add to your little book of wisdom.

Four Signposts

Very few people get it absolutely right at the design stage. Most of us amend our code as requirements change, or as we gain a deeper understanding of the nature of the problem we are addressing.

As we amend our code, it can easily drift beyond our control. An added method here, and a new class there, and gradually our system begins to decay. As we have seen already, your code can point the way to its own improvement. These pointers in code are sometimes referred to as "code smells"—that is, features in code that *may* suggest particular fixes, or at least call you to look again at your design. In this section, I distill some of the points already made into four signs that you should watch out for as you code.

Code Duplication

Duplication is one of the great evils in code. If you get a strange sense of déjà vu as you write a routine, the chances are you have a problem.

Take a look at the instances of repetition in your system. Perhaps they belong together. Duplication generally means tight coupling. If you change something fundamental about one routine, will the similar routines need amendment? If this is the case, they probably belong in the same class.

The Class Who Knew Too Much

It can be a pain passing parameters around from method to method. Why not simply reduce the pain by using a global variable? With a global, everyone can get at the data.

Global variables have their place, but they do need to be viewed with some level of suspicion. That's quite a high level of suspicion, by the way. By using a global variable, or by giving a class any kind of knowledge about its wider domain, you anchor it into its context, making it less reusable and dependent upon code beyond its control. Remember, you want to decouple your classes and routines, and not create interdependence. Try to limit a class's knowledge of its context. We will look at some strategies for doing this later in the book.

The Jack of All Trades

Is your class trying to do too many things at once? If so, see if you can list the responsibilities of the class. You may find that one of them will form the basis of a good class itself.

Leaving an overzealous class unchanged can cause particular problems if you subclass. Which responsibility are you extending by subclassing? What would you do if you needed to subclass for more than one responsibility? You are likely to end up with too many subclasses, or an overreliance on conditional code.

Conditional Statements

You will use `if` and `switch` statements with perfectly good reason throughout your projects. Sometimes, though, such structures can be a cry for polymorphism.

If you find that you are testing for certain conditions frequently within a class, and especially if you find these tests mirrored across more than one method, this could be a sign that your one class should be two or more. See whether the structure of the conditional code suggests responsibilities that could be expressed in classes. The new classes should implement a shared abstract base class. The chances are that you will then have to work out how to pass the right class to client code. I will cover some patterns for creating objects in Chapter 9.

The UML

So far in this book, we have let the code speak for itself. We have used short examples to illustrate concepts such as inheritance and polymorphism.

This is useful because PHP is a common currency here. It's a language we have in common if you have read this far. As our examples grow, though, it becomes something of an absurdity to use code alone to illustrate the broad sweep of design. It is hard to see an overview in a few lines of code.

UML stands for Unified Modeling Language. The initials are correctly used with the definite article. This isn't just *a* unified modeling language, it is *the* Unified Modeling Language.

Perhaps this magisterial tone derives from the circumstances of the language's forging. According to Martin Fowler (*UML Distilled*, 1999), the UML emerged as a standard only after long years of intellectual and bureaucratic sparring amongst the great and good of the object-oriented design community.

The result of this struggle is a powerful graphical syntax for describing object-oriented systems. We will only scratch the surface in this section, but you will soon find that a little UML (sorry, a little of *the* UML) goes a long way.

Class diagrams in particular can describe structures and patterns so that their meaning shines through. This luminous clarity is often harder to find in code fragments and bullet points.

Class Diagrams

Although class diagrams are only one aspect of the UML, they are perhaps the most ubiquitous. Because they are particularly useful for describing object-oriented relationships, I will focus on them in this book.

Representing Classes

As you might expect, classes are the main constituents of class diagrams. A class is represented by a named box, as in Figure 6-1.

Figure 6-1. *A class*

The class is divided into three sections, with the name displayed in the first. These dividing lines are optional when we present no more information than the class name. In designing a class diagram, we may find that the level of detail in Figure 6-1 is enough for some classes. We are not obligated to represent every field and method, or even every class in a class diagram.

Abstract classes are represented either by italicizing the class name as in Figure 6-2 or by adding {abstract} to the class name as in Figure 6-3. The first method is the more common of the two, but the second is more useful when you are making notes.

■**Note** The {abstract} syntax is an example of a constraint. Constraints are used in class diagrams to describe the way in which specific elements should be used. There is no special structure for the text between the braces; it should simply provide a short clarification of any conditions that may apply to the element.

Figure 6-2. *An abstract class*

Figure 6-3. *An abstract class defined using a constraint*

Interfaces are defined in the same way as classes, except that they must include a "stereotype" (that is an extension to the UML), as in Figure 6-4.

Figure 6-4. *An interface*

Attributes

Broadly speaking, attributes describe a class's properties.

Attributes are listed in the section directly beneath the class name as in Figure 6-5.

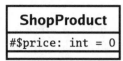

Figure 6-5. *An attribute*

Let's take a close look at the attribute in the example. The initial symbol represents the level of visibility, or access control, for the attribute. Table 6-1 shows the three symbols available.

Table 6-1. *Visibility Symbols*

Symbol	Visibility	Explanation
+	Public	Available to all code
-	Private	Available to the current class only
#	Protected	Available to the current class and its subclasses only

The visibility symbol is followed by the name of the attribute. In this case, we are describing the ShopProduct::$price property. A colon is used to separate the attribute name from its type (and optionally its default value).

Once again, you need only include as much detail as is needed for clarity. It is quite common to see an unqualified attribute name in a class diagram.

Operations

Operations describe methods. Or more properly, they describe the calls that can be made on an instance of a class. Figure 6-6 shows two operations in the ShopProduct class.

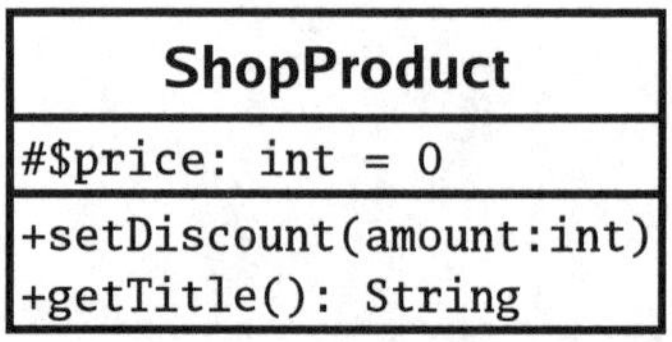

```
ShopProduct
#$price: int = 0
+setDiscount(amount:int)
+getTitle(): String
```

Figure 6-6. *Operations*

As you can see, operations use a similar syntax to that used by attributes. The visibility symbol precedes the method name. A list of parameters is enclosed in parentheses. The method's return type, if any, is delineated by a colon. Parameters are separated by commas, and follow the attribute syntax, with the attribute name separated from its type by a colon.

As you might expect, this syntax is relatively flexible. You can omit the visibility flag and the return type. Parameters are often represented by their type alone, as the argument name is not usually significant.

Describing Inheritance and Implementation

The UML describes the inheritance relationship as "generalization." This relationship is signified by a line leading from the subclass to its parent. The line is tipped with an empty closed arrow.

Figure 6-7 shows the relationship between the ShopProduct class and its child classes.

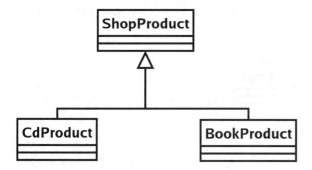

Figure 6-7. *Describing inheritance*

The UML describes the relationship between interfaces and the classes that implement them as "realization." So if the ShopProduct class were to implement the Chargeable interface, we could add it to our class diagram as in Figure 6-8.

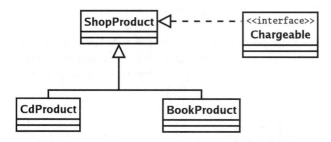

Figure 6-8. *Describing interface implementation*

Associations

Inheritance is only one of a number of relationships in an object-oriented system. An association occurs when a class property is declared to hold a reference to an instance (or instances) of another class.

In Figure 6-9, we model two classes and create an association between them.

Figure 6-9. *An association*

At this stage, we are vague about the nature of this relationship. We have only specified that a Teacher object will have a reference to one or more Pupil objects or vice versa. This relationship may or may not be reciprocal.

We can use arrows to describe the direction of the association. If the Teacher class has an instance of the Pupil class but not the other way round, then we should make our association an arrow leading from the Teacher to the Pupil class. This association, which is called "unidirectional," is shown in Figure 6-10.

Figure 6-10. *A unidirectional association*

If each class has a reference to the other, we can use a double-headed arrow to describe a "bidirectional" relationship as in Figure 6-11.

Figure 6-11. *A bidirectional association*

We can also specify the number of instances of a class that are referenced by another in an association. We do this by placing a number or range beside each class. We can also use * to stand for any number. So in Figure 6-12 there can be one Teacher object and any number of Pupil objects.

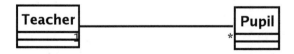

Figure 6-12. *Defining multiplicity for an association*

In Figure 6-13, there can be one Teacher object and between 5 and 10 Pupil objects in the association.

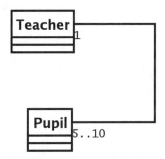

Figure 6-13. *Defining multiplicity for an association*

Aggregation and Composition

Aggregation and composition are similar to association. All describe a situation in which a class holds a permanent reference to one or more instances of another. With aggregation and composition, though, the referenced instances form an intrinsic part of the referring object.

In the case of aggregation, the contained objects are a core part of the container, but they can also be contained by other objects at the same time. The aggregation relationship is illustrated by a line that begins with an unfilled diamond.

In Figure 6-14 we define two classes, SchoolClass and Pupil. The SchoolClass class aggregates Pupil.

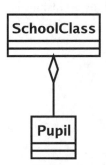

Figure 6-14. *Aggregation*

Pupils make up a class, but the same Pupil object can be referred to by different SchoolClass instances at the same time. If we were to dissolve a school class, we would not necessarily delete the pupil, who may attend other classes.

Composition represents an even stronger relationship than this. In composition, the contained object can be referenced by its container only. It should be deleted when the container is deleted. Composition relationships are depicted in the same way as aggregation relationships, except that the diamond should be filled. We illustrate a composition relationship in Figure 6-15.

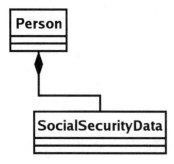

Figure 6-15. *Composition*

A Person class maintains a reference to a SocialSecurityData object. The contained instance can belong only to the containing Person object.

Describing Use

The use relationship is described as a dependency in the UML. It is the most transient of the relationships discussed in this section because it does not describe a permanent link between classes.

A used class may be passed as an argument or acquired as a result of a method call.

The Report class in Figure 6-16 uses a ShopProductWriter object. It does not, however, maintain this reference as a property in the same way that a ShopProductWriter object maintains an array of ShopProduct objects.

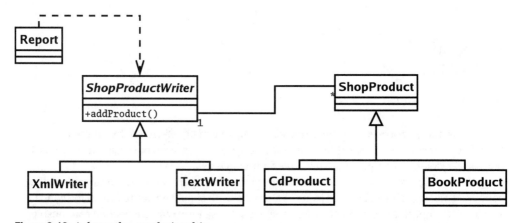

Figure 6-16. *A dependency relationship*

Using Notes

Class diagrams can capture the structure of a system, but they provide no sense of process.

Figure 6-16 tells us about the classes in our system. We know that a `Report` object uses a `ShopProductWriter`, but we don't know the mechanics of this. In Figure 6-17 we use a note to clarify things somewhat.

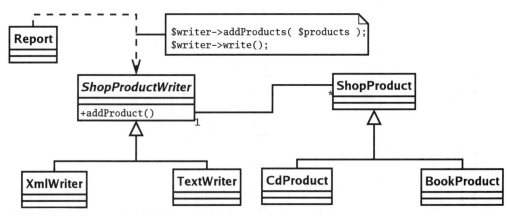

Figure 6-17. *Using a note to clarify a dependency*

As you can see, a note consists of a box with a folded corner. It will often contain scraps of pseudo-code.

This clarifies our diagram; we can now see that the `Report` object uses a `ShopProductWriter` to output product data. This is hardly a revelation, but then use relationships are not always so obvious. In some cases, even a note might not provide enough information. Luckily, we can model the interactions of objects in our system as well as the structure of our classes.

Sequence Diagrams

A sequence diagram is object based rather than class based. It is used to model a process in a system step by step.

Let's build up a simple diagram, modeling the means by which a `Report` object writes product data. A sequence diagram presents the participants of a system from left to right as in Figure 6-18.

Figure 6-18. *Objects in a sequence diagram*

We have labeled our objects with class names alone. If we had more than one instance of the same class working independently in our diagram, we would include an object name using the format `label:class` (`product1:ShopProduct`, for example).

We show the lifetime of the process we are modeling from top to bottom as in Figure 6-19.

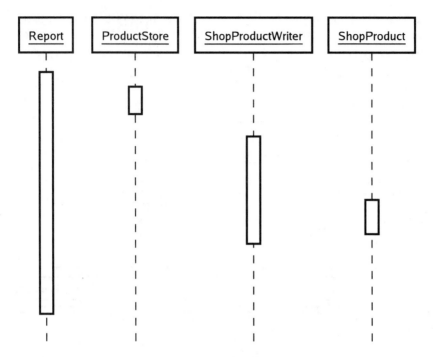

Figure 6-19. *Object lifelines in a sequence diagram*

The vertical broken lines represent the lifetime of the objects in the system. The larger boxes that follow the lifelines represent the focus of a process. If you read Figure 6-19 from top to bottom, you can see how the process moves between objects in the system. This is hard to read without showing the messages that are passed between the objects. We add these in Figure 6-20.

The arrows represent the messages sent from one object to another. Return values are often left implicit (though they can be represented by a broken line, passing from the invoked object to the message originator). Each message is labeled using the relevant method call. You can be quite flexible with your labeling, though there is some syntax. Square brackets represent a condition. So

```
[okToPrint]
write()
```

means that the write() invocation should only be made if the correct condition is met. An asterisk is used to indicate a repetition, optionally with further clarification in square brackets:

```
*[for each ShopProduct]
write()
```

So we can interpret Figure 6-20 from top to bottom. First a Report object acquires a list of ShopProduct objects from a ProductStore object. It passes these to a ShopProductWriter object, which stores references to them (though we can only infer this from the diagram). The ShopProductWriter object calls ShopProduct::getSummaryLine() for every ShopProduct object it references, adding the result to its output.

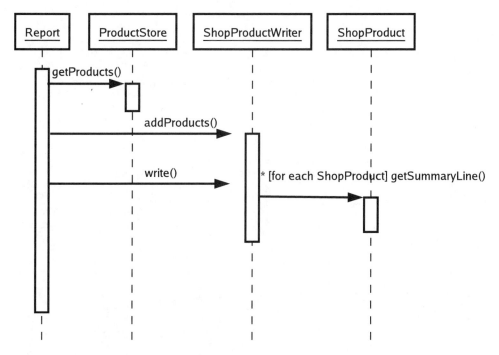

Figure 6-20. *The complete sequence diagram*

As you can see, sequence diagrams can model processes, freezing slices of dynamic inter-action and presenting them with surprising clarity.

■**Note** Look at Figures 6-16 and 6-20. Notice how the class diagram illustrates polymorphism, showing the classes derived from ShopProductWriter and ShopProduct. Now notice how this detail becomes trans-parent when we model the communication between objects. Where possible, we want objects to work with the most general types available so that we can hide the details of implementation.

Summary

In this chapter, we went beyond the nuts and bolts of object-oriented programming to look at some key design issues. We examined features such as encapsulation, loose coupling, and cohesion that are essential aspects of a flexible and reusable object-oriented system. We went on to look at the UML, laying groundwork that will be essential in working with patterns later in the book.

PART THREE

Patterns

■ ■ ■

CHAPTER 7

What Are Design Patterns? Why Use Them?

Most problems we encounter as programmers have been handled time and again by others in our community. Design patterns can provide us with the means to mine that wisdom. Once a pattern becomes a common currency, it enriches our language, making it easy to share design ideas and their consequences. Design patterns simply distill common problems, define tested solutions, and describe likely outcomes. They take up where the nuts-and-bolts how-to books end.

In this chapter, I introduce you to design patterns and look at some of the reasons for their popularity.

This chapter will cover

- *Pattern basics*: What are design patterns?

- *Pattern structure*: The key elements of a design pattern.

- *Pattern benefits*: Why patterns are worth your time.

What Are Design Patterns?

In the world of software, a pattern is a tangible manifestation of an organization's tribal memory.

—Grady Booch, *Core J2EE Patterns* (introduction)

[A pattern is] a solution to a problem in a context.

—*Design Patterns*, p. 3

A design pattern is a problem analyzed, and good practice for its solution explained.

Problems tend to recur, and as Web programmers we must solve them time and time again. How are we going to handle an incoming request? How can we translate this data into instructions for our system? How should we acquire data? Present results? Over time, we answer these questions with a greater or lesser degree of elegance, and evolve an informal set of techniques that we use and reuse in our projects. These techniques are patterns of design.

Design patterns inscribe and formalize these problems and solutions, making hard-won experience available to the wider programming community. Patterns are (or should be) essentially bottom-up and not top-down. They are rooted in practice and not theory. That is not to say that there isn't a strong theoretical element to design patterns (as we will see in the next chapter), but patterns are based upon real-world techniques used by real programmers. Renowned pattern-hatcher Martin Fowler says that he discovers patterns, he does not invent them. For this reason, many patterns will engender a sense of déjà vu as you recognize techniques you have used yourself.

A catalog of patterns is not a cookbook. Recipes can be followed slavishly, code can be copied and slotted into a project with minor changes. You do not always need even to understand all the code used in a recipe. Design patterns inscribe *approaches* to particular problems. The details of implementation may vary enormously according to the wider context. This context might include the programming language you are using, the nature of your application, the size of your project, and the specifics of the problem.

The very act of naming a pattern is valuable; it provides the kind of common vocabulary that has arisen naturally over the years in the older crafts and professions. Such shorthand greatly aids collaborative design as alternative approaches, and their consequences are weighed and tested.

Finally, it is illegal, according to international law, to write about patterns without quoting Christopher Alexander, an architecture academic whose work heavily influenced the original object-oriented pattern advocates:

> *Each pattern describes a problem which occurs over and over again in our environment, and then describes the core of the solution to that problem, in such a way that you can use this solution a million times over, without ever doing it the same way twice.*

> —*A Pattern Language*

It is significant that this definition (which applies to architectural problems and solutions) begins with the problem and its wider setting and proceeds to a solution. There has been some criticism in recent years that design patterns have been overused, especially by inexperienced programmers. This is often a sign that solutions have been applied where the problem and context are not present. Patterns are more than a particular organization of classes and objects, cooperating in a particular way. Patterns are structured to define the conditions in which solutions should be applied, and to discuss the effects of the solution.

In this book, we will focus upon a particularly influential strand in the patterns field: the form described in *Design Patterns: Elements of Reusable Object-Oriented Software* by Erich Gamma, Richard Helm, Ralph Johnson, and John Vlissides. The authors of this book are often referred to as the Gang of Four and the book itself as the Gang of Four book. It concentrates upon patterns in object-oriented software development and inscribes some of the classic patterns that are present in most modern object-oriented projects.

The Gang of Four book is important because it inscribes key patterns, but also because it describes the design principles that inform and motivate these patterns. We will look at some of these principles in the next chapter.

A Design Pattern Overview

At heart, a design pattern consists of four parts:

Name

Names matter. They enrich the language of programmers, a few short words standing in for quite complex problems and solutions. They must balance brevity and description. The Gang of Four claim:

> *Finding good names has been one of the hardest parts of developing our catalog.*

> *—Design Patterns*, p. 3

Martin Fowler agrees:

> *Pattern names are crucial, because part of the purpose of patterns is to create a vocabulary that allows developers to communicate more effectively.*

> *—Patterns of Enterprise Application Architecture*, p. 11

In *Patterns of Enterprise Application Architecture*, Martin Fowler refines a database access pattern I first encountered in *Core J2EE Patterns*. He defines two patterns that describe specializations of the older pattern. The logic of his approach is clearly correct (one of the new patterns models domain objects, while the other models database tables, a distinction that was vague in the earlier work). It was hard to train myself to think in terms of the new patterns. I had been using the name of the original in design sessions and documents for so long that it had become part of my language.

The Problem

No matter how elegant the solution (and some are very elegant indeed), the problem and its context are the grounds of a pattern. Recognizing a problem is harder than applying any one of the solutions in a pattern catalog. This is one reason that some pattern solutions can be misapplied or overused.

Patterns describe a problem space with great care. The problem is described in brief, and then contextualized, often with a typical example and one or more diagrams. It is broken down into its specifics, its various manifestations. Any warning signs that might help in identifying the problem are described.

The Solution

The solution is summarized initially in conjunction with the problem. It is also described in detail often using UML class and interaction diagrams. The pattern usually includes a code example.

Although code may be presented, the solution is never cut and paste. The pattern describes an approach to a problem. There may be hundreds of nuances in implementation. Think about instructions for sowing a food crop. If you simply follow a set of steps blindly, you are likely to go hungry come harvest time. More useful would be a pattern-based approach that covers the various conditions that may apply. The basic solution to the problem (making your crop grow) will always be the same (plant seeds, irrigate, harvest crop), but the actual steps you take will depend on all sorts of factors such as your soil type, your location, the orientation of your land, local pests, and so on.

Martin Fowler refers to solutions in patterns as "half-baked." That is, the coder must take away the concept and finish it for himself (*Patterns of Enterprise Application Architecture*, p. 11).

Consequences

Every design decision you make will have wider consequences. This should include the satisfactory resolution of the problem in question, of course. A solution, once deployed, may be ideally suited to work with other patterns. There may also be dangers to watch for.

The "Gang of Four" Format

As I write, I have five pattern catalogs on the desk in front of me. A quick look at the patterns in each confirms that not one uses the same structure as the others. Some are more formal than others, some are fine-grained, with many subsections, others are discursive.

There are a number of well-defined pattern structures, including the original form developed by Christopher Alexander (the "Alexandrian Form"), the narrative approach favored by the Portland Pattern Repository (the "Portland Form"). Because the Gang of Four book is so influential, and because we will cover many of the patterns they describe, let's examine a few of the sections they include in their patterns.

- *Intent*: A brief statement of the pattern's purpose. You should be able to see the point of the pattern at a glance.

- *Motivation*: The problem described, often in terms of a typical situation. The anecdotal approach can help make the pattern easy to grasp.

- *Applicability*: An examination of the different situations in which you might apply the pattern. While the motivation describes a typical problem, this section defines specific situations, and weighs the merits of the solution in the context of each.

- *Structure/Interaction*: These sections may contain UML class and interaction diagrams describing the relationships between classes and objects in the solution.

- *Implementation*: This section looks at the details of the solution. It examines any issues that may come up when applying the technique and provides tips for deployment.

- *Sample Code*: I always skip ahead to this section. I find that a simple code example often provides a way into a pattern. The example is often chopped down to the basics in order to lay the solution bare. It could be in any object-oriented language. Of course, in this book it will always be PHP.

- *Known Uses*: Real systems in which the pattern (problem, context, and solution) occur. Some people say that for a pattern to be genuine it must be found in at least three publicly available contexts. This is sometimes called the "rule of three."

- *Related Patterns*: Some patterns imply others. In applying one solution, you can create the context in which another becomes useful. This section examines these synergies. It may also discuss patterns that have similarities in problem or solution and any antecedents: patterns defined elsewhere upon which the current pattern builds.

Why Use Design Patterns?

So what benefits can patterns bring? Given that a pattern is a problem defined and solution described, the answer should be obvious. Patterns can help you to solve common problems.

There is more to patterns, of course:

A Design Pattern Defines a Problem

How many times have your reached a stage in a project and found that there is no going forward? The chances are you must backtrack some way before starting out again.

By defining common problems, patterns can help you to improve your design. Sometimes the first step to a solution is recognizing that you have a problem.

A Design Pattern Defines a Solution

Having defined and recognized the problem (and made certain that it is the right problem), a pattern gives you access to a solution, together with an analysis of the consequences of its use. Although a pattern does not absolve you of the responsibility to consider the implications of a design decision, you can at least be certain that you are using a tried-and-tested technique.

Design Patterns Are Language Independent

When I first started using patterns, I read code examples in C++ and Smalltalk and deployed my solutions in a Java context. Patterns define objects and solutions in object-oriented terms. This means that many patterns apply equally in more than one language. Others transfer with modifications to the pattern's applicability or consequences but remain valid. Either way, patterns can help you as you move between languages. Equally, an application that is built upon good object-oriented design principles can be relatively easy to port between languages (although there are always issues that must be addressed).

Patterns Define a Vocabulary

By providing developers with names for techniques, patterns make communication richer. Imagine a design meeting. I'm describing my plans to Bob.

ME: I'm thinking of using a Composite.

BOB: I don't think you've thought that through.

OK, Bob didn't agree with me. He never does. But he knew what I was talking about, and therefore why my idea sucked. Let's play that scene through again without a design vocabulary.

ME: I intend to use a tree of objects that share the same type. The type's interface will provide methods for adding child objects of its own type. In this way, we can build up complex combinations of implementing objects at runtime.

BOB: Huh?

Patterns, or the techniques they describe, tend to interoperate. The Composite pattern lends itself to collaboration with Visitor:

ME: And then we can use Visitors to summarize the data.

BOB: You're missing the point.

Ignore Bob. I won't describe the tortuous nonpattern version of this. We will cover Composite in Chapter 10 and Visitor in Chapter 11.

The point is that without a pattern language we would still use these techniques. They *precede* their naming and organization. If patterns did not exist, they would evolve on their own anyway. Any tool that is used sufficiently will eventually acquire a name.

Patterns Are Tried and Tested

So if patterns document good practice, is naming the only truly original thing about pattern catalogs? In some senses, that would seem to be true. Patterns represent best practice in an object-oriented context. To some highly experienced programmers, this may seem an exercise in repackaging the obvious. To the rest of us, patterns provide access to problems and solutions we would otherwise have to discover the hard way.

Patterns make design accessible. As pattern catalogs emerge for more and more specializations, even the highly experienced can find benefits as they move into new aspects of their field. A GUI programmer can gain fast access to common problems and solutions in enterprise programming, for example. A Web programmer can quickly chart strategies for avoiding the pitfalls that lurk in PDA and cell phone projects.

Patterns Are Designed for Collaboration

By their nature, patterns should be "generative" and "composable." This means that you should be able to apply one pattern and thereby create conditions suitable for the application of another. In other words, in using a pattern you may find other doors opened for you.

Pattern catalogs are usually designed with this kind of collaboration in mind, and the potential for pattern composition is always documented in the pattern itself.

Design Patterns Promote Good Design

Design patterns demonstrate and apply principles of object-oriented design. So a study of design patterns can yield more than a specific solution in a context. You can come away with a new perspective on the ways that objects and classes can be combined to achieve an objective.

PHP and Design Patterns

There is little in this chapter that is specific to PHP, which is characteristic of our topic to some extent. Many patterns apply to many object-capable languages with few or no implementation issues.

This is not always the case, of course. Some enterprise patterns work well in languages in which an application process continues to run between server requests. PHP does not work that way. A new script execution is kicked off for every request. This means that some patterns need to be treated with more care. Front Controller, for example, often requires some serious initialization time. This is fine when the initialization takes place once at application startup, but more of an issue when it must take place for every request. That is not to say that we can't use the pattern; I have deployed it with very good results in the past. We must simply ensure that we take account of PHP-related issues when we discuss the pattern. PHP forms the context for all the patterns that this book examines.

I referred to object-capable languages earlier in this section. You can code in PHP without defining any classes at all (although with PEAR's continuing development you will probably manipulate objects to some extent). Although this book focuses almost entirely upon object-oriented solutions to programming problems, it is not a broadside in an advocacy war. Patterns and PHP can be a powerful mix, and they form the core of this book; they can, however, coexist quite happily with more traditional approaches. PEAR is an excellent testament to this. PEAR packages use design patterns elegantly. They tend to be object-oriented in nature. This makes them more, not less, useful in procedural projects. Because PEAR packages are self-enclosed, and hide their complexity behind clean interfaces, they are easy to stitch into any kind of project.

Summary

In this chapter, I introduced design patterns, showed you their structure (using the Gang of Four form), and suggested some reasons why you might want to use design patterns in your scripts.

It is important to remember that design patterns are not snap-on solutions that can be combined like components to build a project. They are suggested approaches to common problems. These solutions embody some key design principles. It is these that we will examine in the next chapter.

CHAPTER 8

■ ■ ■

Some Pattern Principles

Although design patterns simply describe solutions to problems, they tend to emphasize solutions that promote reusability and flexibility. To achieve this, they manifest some key object-oriented design principles. We will encounter some of them in this chapter and in more detail throughout the rest of the book.

This chapter will cover

- *Composition*: How to use object aggregation to achieve greater flexibility than you could with inheritance alone

- *Decoupling*: How to reduce dependency between elements in a system

- *The power of the interface*: Patterns and polymorphism

- *Pattern categories*: The types of pattern that this book will cover

The Pattern Revelation

I first started working in an object-oriented context using the Java language. As you might expect, it took a while before some concepts clicked. When it did happen, though, it happened very fast, almost with the force of revelation. The elegance of inheritance and encapsulation bowled me over. I could sense that this was a different way of defining and building systems. I "got" polymorphism, working with a type and switching implementations at runtime.

All the books on my desk at the time focused on language features and the very many APIs available to the Java programmer. Beyond a brief definition of polymorphism, there was little attempt to examine design strategies.

Language features alone do not engender object-oriented design. Although my projects fulfilled their functional requirements, the kind of design that inheritance, encapsulation, and polymorphism had seemed to offer continued to elude me.

My inheritance hierarchies grew wider and deeper as I attempted to build new classes for every eventuality. The structure of my systems made it hard to convey messages from one tier to another without giving intermediate classes too much awareness of their surroundings, binding them into the application and making them unusable in new contexts.

It wasn't until I discovered *Design Patterns*, otherwise known as the Gang of Four book, that I realized I had missed an entire design dimension. By that time I had already discovered some of the core patterns for myself, but others contributed to a new way of thinking.

I discovered that I had overprivileged inheritance in my designs, trying to build too much functionality into my classes. But where else can functionality go in an object-oriented system?

I found the answer in composition. Software components can be defined at runtime by combining objects in flexible relationships. The Gang of Four boiled this down into a principle: "favor composition over inheritance." The patterns described ways in which objects could be combined at runtime to achieve a level of flexibility impossible in an inheritance tree alone.

Composition and Inheritance

Inheritance is a powerful way of designing for changing circumstances or contexts. It can limit flexibility, however, especially when classes take on multiple responsibilities.

The Problem

As you know, child classes inherit the methods and properties of their parents (as long as they are protected or public elements). We use this fact to design child classes that provide specialized functionality.

Figure 8-1 presents a simple example using the UML.

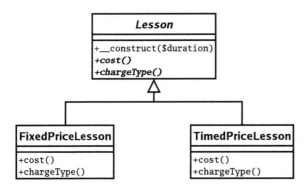

Figure 8-1. *A parent class and two child classes*

The abstract Lesson class in Figure 8-1 models a lesson in a college. It defines abstract cost() and chargeType() methods. The diagram shows two implementing classes, FixedPriceLesson and TimedPriceLesson, which provide distinct charging mechanisms for lessons.

Using this inheritance scheme, we can switch between lesson implementations. Client code will know only that it is dealing with a Lesson object, so the details of costing will be transparent.

What happens, though, if we introduce a new set of specializations? We need to handle lectures and seminars. Because these organize enrollment and lesson notes in different ways, they require separate classes. So now we have two forces that operate upon our design. We need to handle pricing strategies and separate lectures and seminars.

Figure 8-2 shows a brute-force solution.

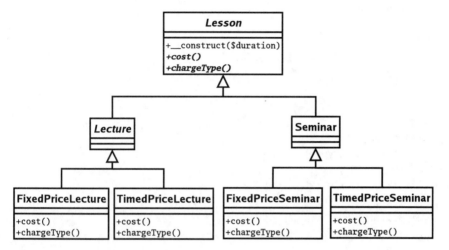

Figure 8-2. *A poor inheritance structure*

Figure 8-2 shows a hierarchy that is clearly faulty. We can no longer use the inheritance tree to manage our pricing mechanisms without duplicating great swathes of functionality. The pricing strategies are mirrored across the Lecture and Seminar class families.

At this stage, we might consider using conditional statements in the Lesson super class, removing those unfortunate duplications. Essentially, we remove the pricing logic from the inheritance tree altogether, moving it up into the super class. This is the reverse of the usual refactoring where we replace a conditional with polymorphism. Here is an amended Lesson class:

```
abstract class Lesson {
    protected $duration;
    const    FIXED = 1;
    const    TIMED = 2;
    private  $costtype;

    function __construct( $duration, $costtype=1 ) {
        $this->duration = $duration;
        $this->costtype = $costtype;
    }
}
```

```php
    function cost() {
        switch ( $this->costtype ) {
            CASE self::TIMED :
                return (5 * $this->duration);
                break;
            CASE self::FIXED :
                return 30;
                break;
            default:
                $this->costtype = self::FIXED;
                return 30;
        }
    }

    function chargeType() {
        switch ( $this->costtype ) {
            CASE self::TIMED :
                return "hourly rate";
                break;
            CASE self::FIXED :
                return "fixed rate";
                break;
            default:
                $this->costtype = self::FIXED;
                return "fixed rate";
        }
    }

    // more lesson methods...
}

class Lecture extends Lesson {
    // Lecture-specific implementations ...
}

class Seminar extends Lesson {
    // Seminar-specific implementations ...
}
```

You can see the new class diagram in Figure 8-3.

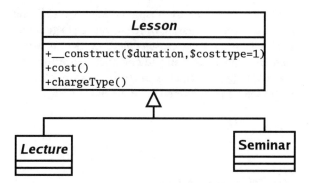

Figure 8-3. *Inheritance hierarchy improved by removing cost calculations from subclasses*

We have made the class structure much more manageable, but at a cost. Using conditionals in this code is a retrograde step. Usually, we would try to replace a conditional statement with polymorphism. Here we have done the opposite. As you can see, this has forced us to duplicate the conditional statement across the chargeType() and cost() methods.

We seem doomed to duplicate code.

Using Composition

We can use the Strategy pattern to compose our way out of trouble. Strategy is used to move a set of algorithms into a separate type. In moving cost calculations, we can simplify the Lesson type. You can see this in Figure 8-4.

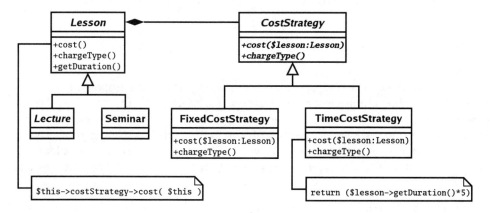

Figure 8-4. *Moving algorithms into a separate type*

We create an abstract class, CostStrategy, which defines the abstract methods cost() and chargeType(). The cost() method requires an instance of Lesson, which it will use to generate cost data. We provide two implementations for CostStrategy. Lesson objects work only with the CostStrategy type, not a specific implementation, so we can add new cost algorithms at any time by subclassing CostStrategy. This would require no changes at all to any Lesson classes.

Here's a simplified version of the new Lesson class illustrated in Figure 8-4:

```php
abstract class Lesson {
    private    $duration;
    private    $costStrategy;

    function __construct( $duration, CostStrategy $strategy ) {
        $this->duration = $duration;
        $this->costStrategy = $strategy;
    }

    function cost() {
        return $this->costStrategy->cost( $this );
    }

    function chargeType() {
        return $this->costStrategy->chargeType( );
    }

    function getDuration() {
        return $this->duration;
    }

    // more lesson methods...
}
```

The Lesson class requires a CostStrategy object, which it stores as a property. The Lesson::cost() method simply invokes CostStrategy::cost(). Equally, Lesson::chargeType() invokes CostStrategy::chargeType(). This explicit invocation of another object's method in order to fulfill a request is known as delegation. In our example, the CostStrategy object is the delegate of Lesson. The Lesson class washes its hands of responsibility for cost calculations and passes on the task to a CostStrategy implementation. Here it is caught in the act of delegation:

```php
function cost() {
    return $this->costStrategy->cost( $this );
}
```

Here is the CostStrategy class, together with its implementing children:

```php
abstract class CostStrategy {
    abstract function cost( Lesson $lesson );
    abstract function chargeType();
}
```

```
class TimedCostStrategy extends CostStrategy {
    function cost( Lesson $lesson ) {
        return ( $lesson->getDuration() * 5 );
    }
    function chargeType() {
        return "hourly rate";
    }
}

class FixedCostStrategy extends CostStrategy {
    function cost( Lesson $lesson ) {
        return 30;
    }

    function chargeType() {
        return "fixed rate";
    }
}
```

We can change the way that any Lesson object calculates cost by passing it a different CostStrategy object at runtime. This approach then makes for highly flexible code. Rather than building functionality into our code structures statically, we can combine and recombine objects dynamically.

```
$lessons[] = new Seminar( 4, new TimedCostStrategy() );
$lessons[] = new Lecture( 4, new FixedCostStrategy() );

foreach ( $lessons as $lesson ) {
    print "lesson charge {$lesson->cost()}. ";
    print "Charge type: {$lesson->chargeType()}\n";
}

// output:
// lesson charge 20. Charge type: hourly rate
// lesson charge 30. Charge type: fixed rate
```

As you can see, one effect of this structure is that we have focused the responsibilities of our classes. CostStrategy objects are responsible solely for calculating cost, and Lesson objects manage lesson data.

So, composition can make your code more flexible because objects can be combined to handle tasks dynamically in many more ways than you can anticipate in an inheritance hierarchy alone. There can be a penalty with regard to readability, though. Because composition tends to result in more types, with relationships that aren't fixed with the same predictability as they are in inheritance relationships, it can be slightly harder to digest the relationships in a system.

Decoupling

We saw in Chapter 6 that it makes sense to build independent components. A system with highly interdependent classes can be hard to maintain. A change in one location can require a cascade of related changes across the system.

The Problem

Reusability is one of the key objectives of object-oriented design, and tight-coupling is its enemy. We diagnose tight coupling when we see that a change to one component of a system necessitates many changes elsewhere. We aspire to create independent components so that we can make changes in safety.

We saw an example of tight coupling in Figure 8-2. Because the costing logic was mirrored across the Lecture and Seminar types, a change to TimedPriceLecture would necessitate a parallel change to the same logic in TimedPriceSeminar. By updating one class and not the other, we would break our system, but without any warning from the PHP engine. Our first solution, using a conditional statement, produced a similar dependency between the cost() and chargeType() methods.

By applying the Strategy pattern, we distilled our costing algorithms into the CostStrategy type, locating them behind a common interface, and implementing each only once.

Coupling of another sort can occur when many classes in a system are embedded explicitly into a platform or environment. Let's say that you are building a system that works with a MySQL database, for example. You might use functions such as mysql_connect() and mysql_query() to speak to the database server.

Should you be required to deploy the system on a server that does not support MySQL, you *could* convert your entire project to use SQLite. You would be forced to make changes throughout your code, though, and face the prospect of maintaining two parallel versions of your application.

The problem here is not the dependency of the system upon an external platform. Such a dependency is inevitable. We need to work with code that speaks to a database. The problem comes when such code is scattered throughout a project. Talking to databases is not the primary responsibility of most classes in a system, so the best strategy is to extract such code, and group it together behind a common interface. In this way you promote the independence of your classes. At the same time, by concentrating your "gateway" code in one place, you make it much easier to switch to a new platform without disturbing your wider system.

Loosening Your Coupling

To handle database code flexibly, we should decouple the application logic from the specifics of the database platform it uses. Fortunately, this is as easy as using a PEAR package: PEAR::DB.

Here is some code that uses PEAR::DB to work first with MySQL, and then with SQLite:

```
require_once("DB.php");
$dsn_array[] = "mysql://bob:bobs_pass@localhost/bobs_db";
$dsn_array[] = "sqlite://./bobs_db.db";
```

```
foreach ( $dsn_array as $dsn ) {
    print "$dsn\n\n";
    $db = DB::connect($dsn);
    $query_result = $db->query( "SELECT * FROM bobs_table" );
    while ( $row = $query_result->fetchRow( DB_FETCHMODE_ARRAY ) ) {
        printf( "| %-4s| %-4s| %-25s|", $row[0], $row[2], $row[1] );
        print "\n";
    }
    print "\n";
    $query_result->free();
    $db->disconnect();
}
```

Note that we have stripped this example of error handling for the sake of brevity. I covered PEAR errors and the DB package in Chapter 4.

The DB class provides a static method called connect() that accepts a Data Source Name (DSN) string. According to the makeup of this string, it returns a particular implementation of a class called DB_Common. So for the string "mysql://", the connect() method returns a DB_mysql object, and for a string that starts with "sqlite://", it returns a DB_sqlite object. You can see the class structure in Figure 8-5.

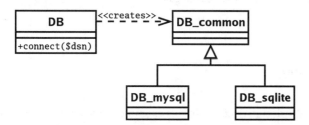

Figure 8-5. *PEAR::DB decouples client code from database objects*

The PEAR::DB package, then, enables you to decouple your application code from the specifics of your database platform. As long as you use uncontroversial SQL, you should be able to run a single system with MySQL, SQLite, MSSQL, and many others without changing a line of code (apart from the DSN, of course, which is the single point at which the database context must be configured).

This design bears some resemblance to the Abstract Factory pattern described in the Gang of Four book, and later in this book. Although it is simpler in nature, it has the same motivation, to generate an object that implements an abstract interface without requiring the client to instantiate the object directly.

Of course, by decoupling your system from the specifics of a database platform, the DB package still leaves you with your own work to do. If your (now database-agnostic) SQL code is sprinkled throughout your project, you may find that a single change in one aspect of your project causes a cascade of changes elsewhere. An alteration in the database schema would be the most common example here, where an additional field in a table might necessitate changes to many duplicated database queries. You should consider extracting this code and placing it in a single package, thereby decoupling your application logic from the details of a relational database.

Code to an Interface Not an Implementation

This principle is one of the all-pervading themes of this book. We saw in Chapter 6 (and in the last section) that we can hide different implementations behind the common interface defined in a super class. Client code can then require an object of the super class's type rather than that of an implementing class, unconcerned by the specific implementation it is actually getting.

Parallel conditional statements, like the ones we built into Lesson::cost() and lesson::chargeType(), are a common signal that polymorphism is needed. They make code hard to maintain because a change in one conditional expression necessitates a change in its twins. Conditional statements are occasionally said to implement a "simulated inheritance."

By placing the cost algorithms in separate classes that implement CostStrategy, we remove duplication. We also make it much easier should we need to add new cost strategies in the future.

From the perspective of client code, it is often a good idea to require abstract or general types in your methods' parameter lists. By requiring more specific types, you could limit the flexibility of your code at runtime.

Having said that, of course, the level of generality you choose in your argument hints is a matter of judgment. Make your choice too general, and your method may become less safe. If you require the specific functionality of a subtype, then accepting a differently equipped sibling into a method could be risky.

Still, make your choice of argument hint too restricted, and you lose the benefits of polymorphism. Take a look at this altered extract from the Lesson class:

```
function __construct( $duration,
    FixedPriceStrategy $strategy ) {
    $this->duration = $duration;
    $this->costStrategy = $strategy;
}
```

There are two issues arising from the design decision in this example. Firstly, the Lesson object is now tied to a specific cost strategy, which closes down our ability to compose dynamic components. Secondly, the explicit reference to the FixedPriceStrategy class forces us to maintain that particular implementation.

By requiring a common interface, you can combine a Lesson object with any CostStrategy implementation.

```
function __construct( $duration, CostStrategy $strategy ) {
    $this->duration = $duration;
    $this->costStrategy = $strategy;
}
```

You have, in other words, decoupled your Lesson class from the specifics of cost calculation. All that matters is the interface and the guarantee that the provided object will honor it.

Of course, coding to an interface can often simply defer the question of how to instantiate your objects. When we say that a Lesson object can be combined with any CostStrategy interface at runtime, we beg the question, "But where does the CostStrategy object come from?"

When you create an abstract super class, there is always the issue as to how its children should be instantiated. Which one do you choose in which condition? This subject forms a category of its own in the GoF pattern catalog, and we will examine some of these in the next chapter.

The Concept That Varies

It's easy to interpret a design decision once it has been made, but how do you decide where to start?

The Gang of Four recommend that you "encapsulate the concept that varies." In terms of our lesson example, the "varying concept" is the cost algorithm. Not only is the cost calculation one of two possible strategies in the example, but it is obviously a candidate for expansion: special offers, overseas student rates, introductory discounts, all sorts of possibilities present themselves.

We quickly established that subclassing for this variation was inappropriate and we resorted to a conditional statement. By bringing our variation into the same class, we underlined its suitability for encapsulation.

The Gang of Four recommend that you actively seek varying elements in your classes and assess their suitability for encapsulation in a new type. Each alternative in a suspect conditional may be extracted to form a class extending a common abstract parent. This new type can then be used by the class or classes from which it was extracted. This has the effect of

- Focusing responsibility

- Promoting flexibility through composition

- Making inheritance hierarchies more compact and focused

- Reducing duplication

So how do we spot variation? One sign is the misuse of inheritance. This might include inheritance deployed according to multiple forces at one time (lecture/seminar, fixed/timed cost). It might also include subclassing on an algorithm where the algorithm is incidental to the core responsibility of the type. The other sign of variation suitable for encapsulation is, of course, a conditional expression.

Patternitis

One problem for which there is no pattern is the unnecessary or inappropriate use of patterns. This has earned patterns a bad name in some quarters. Because pattern solutions are neat, it is tempting to apply them wherever you see a fit, whether they truly fulfill a need or not.

The eXtreme Programming methodology offers a couple of principles that might apply here. The first is "You aren't going to need it" (often abbreviated to YAGNI). This is generally applied to application features, but it also makes sense for patterns.

When I build large environments in PHP, I tend to split my application into layers, separating application logic from presentation and persistence layers. I use all sorts of core and enterprise patterns in conjunction with one another.

When I am asked to build a feedback form for a small business Web site, however, I may simply use procedural code in a single page script. I do not need enormous amounts of flexibility, I won't be building upon the initial release. I don't need to use patterns that address problems in larger systems. Instead I apply the second XP principle: "Do the simplest thing that works."

When you work with a pattern catalog, the structure and process of the solution are what stick in the mind, consolidated by the code example. Before applying a pattern, though, pay close attention to the "problem" or "when to use it" section, and read up on the pattern's consequences. In some contexts, the cure may be worse than the disease.

The Patterns

This book is not a pattern catalog. Nevertheless, in the coming chapters, I will introduce a few of the key patterns in use at the moment, providing PHP implementations and discussing them in the broad context of PHP programming.

The patterns described will be drawn from key catalogs including *Design Patterns*, *Patterns of Enterprise Application Architecture*, and *Core J2EE Patterns*. I follow the Gang of Four's categorization, dividing patterns as follows:

Patterns for Generating Objects

These patterns are concerned with the instantiation of objects. This is an important category given the principle "Code to an interface." If we are working with abstract parent classes in our design, then we must develop strategies for instantiating objects from concrete subclasses. It is these objects that will be passed around our system.

Patterns for Organizing Objects and Classes

These patterns help us to organize the compositional relationships of our objects. More simply, these patterns show how we combine objects and classes.

Task-oriented Patterns

These patterns describe the mechanisms by which classes and objects cooperate to achieve objectives.

Enterprise Patterns

We look at some patterns that describe typical Internet programming problems and solutions. Drawn largely from *Patterns of Enterprise Application Architecture* and *Core J2EE Patterns*, the patterns deal with database persistence, presentation, and application logic.

Summary

In this chapter, we looked at some of the principles that underpin many design patterns. We looked at the use of composition to enable object combination and recombination at runtime, resulting in more flexible structures than would be available using inheritance alone. We introduced decoupling, the practice of extracting software components from their context to make them more generally applicable. We reviewed the importance of interface as a means of decoupling clients from the details of implementation.

In the coming chapters, we will examine some design patterns in detail.

■ ■ ■

CHAPTER 9

Generating Objects

Creating objects is a messy business. So many object-oriented designs deal with nice, clean abstract classes, taking advantage of the impressive flexibility afforded by polymorphism (the switching of concrete implementations at runtime). To achieve this flexibility though, we must devise strategies for object generation. This is the topic we will look at here.

This chapter will cover

- *The Singleton pattern*: A special class that generates one and only one object instance

- *The Factory Method pattern*: Building an inheritance hierarchy of creator classes

- *The Abstract Factory pattern*: Grouping the creation of functionally related products

- *The Prototype pattern*: Using clone to generate objects

Problems and Solutions in Generating Objects

Object creation can be a weak point in object-oriented design. In the previous chapter, we saw the principle "Code to an interface, not to an implementation." To this end, we are encouraged to work with abstract supertypes in our classes. This makes code more flexible, allowing you to use objects instantiated from different concrete subclasses at runtime. This has the side effect that object instantiation is deferred.

Here's a class that accepts a name string and instantiates a particular object:

```
abstract class Employee {
    protected $name;
    function __construct( $name ) {
        $this->name = $name;
    }
    abstract function fire();
}

class Minion extends Employee {
    function fire() {
        print "{$this->name}: I'll clear my desk\n";
    }
}
```

```
class CluedUp extends Employee {
    function fire() {
        print "{$this->name}. I'll call my lawyer\n";
    }
}

class NastyBoss {
    private $employees = array();

    function addEmployee( $employeeName ) {
        $this->employees[] = new Minion( $employeeName );
    }

    function projectFails() {
        if ( count( $this->employees ) ) {
            $emp = array_pop( $this->employees );
            $emp->fire();
        }
    }
}

$boss = new NastyBoss();
$boss->addEmployee( "harry" );
$boss->addEmployee( "bob" );
$boss->addEmployee( "mary" );
$boss->projectFails();

// output:
// mary: I'll clear my desk
```

As you can see, we define an abstract base class: Employee, with a downtrodden implementation: Minion. Given a name string, the NastyBoss::addEmployee() method instantiates a new Minion object. Whenever a NastyBoss object runs into trouble (via the NastyBoss::projectFails() method), it looks for a Minion to fire.

By instantiating a Minion object directly in the NastyBoss class, we limit flexibility. If a NastyBoss object could work with *any* instance of the Employee type, we could make our code amenable to variation at runtime as we add more Employee specializations. You should find the polymorphism in Figure 9-1 familiar.

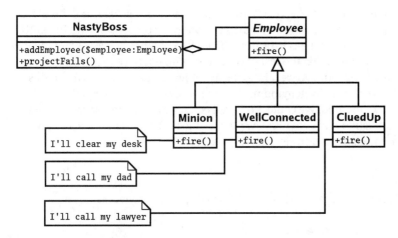

Figure 9-1. *Working with an abstract type enables polymorphism*

If the NastyBoss class does not instantiate a Minion object, where does it come from? Authors often duck out of this problem by constraining an argument type in a method declaration and then conveniently omitting to show the instantiation in anything other than a test context.

```
class NastyBoss {
    private $employees = array();

    function addEmployee( Employee $employee ) {
        $this->employees[] = $employee;
    }

    function projectFails() {
        if ( count( $this->employees ) ) {
            $emp = array_pop( $this->employees );
            $emp->fire();
        }
    }
}
$boss = new NastyBoss();
$boss->addEmployee( new Minion( "harry" ) );
$boss->addEmployee( new CluedUp( "bob" ) );
$boss->addEmployee( new Minion( "mary" ) );
$boss->projectFails();
$boss->projectFails();
// output:
// mary: I'll clear my desk
// bob: I'll call my lawyer
// harry: I'll clear my desk
```

Although this version of the NastyBoss class works with the Employee type, and therefore benefits from polymorphism, we still haven't defined a strategy for object creation. Instantiating objects is a dirty business, but it has to be done. This chapter is about classes and objects that work with concrete classes so that the rest of your classes do not have to.

If there is a principle to be found, here it is "Delegate object instantiation." We did this implicitly in the previous example by demanding that an Employee object is passed to the NastyBoss::addEmployee() method. We could, however, equally delegate to a separate class or method that takes responsibility for generating Employee objects. Let's add a static method to the Employee class that implements a strategy for object creation:

```
abstract class Employee {
    protected $name;
    private static $types = array( 'minion', 'cluedup', 'wellconnected' );

    static function recruit( $name ) {
        $num = rand( 1, count( self::$types ) )-1;
        $class = self::$types[$num];
        return new $class( $name );
    }

    function __construct( $name ) {
        $this->name = $name;
    }
    abstract function fire();
}
```

As you can see, this takes a name string and uses it to instantiate a particular Employee subtype at random. We can now delegate the details of instantiation to the Employee class's recruit() method.

```
$boss = new NastyBoss();
$boss->addEmployee( Employee::recruit( "harry" ) );
$boss->addEmployee( Employee::recruit( "bob" ) );
$boss->addEmployee( Employee::recruit( "mary" ) );
```

We saw a simple example of such a class in Chapter 4. We placed a static method in the ShopProduct class called getInstance(). getInstance() is responsible for generating the correct ShopProduct subclass based upon a database query. The ShopProduct class, therefore, has a dual role. It defines the ShopProduct type, but it also acts as a factory for concrete ShopProduct objects.

```
// class ShopProduct
public static function getInstance( $id, DB_common $db ) {
        $query = "select * from products where id='$id'";
        $query_result = $db->query( $query );

        if ( DB::isError( $query_result ) ) {
            die($query_result->getMessage());
        }
```

```
$row = $query_result->fetchRow( DB_FETCHMODE_ASSOC );
if ( empty( $row ) ) { return null; }

if ( $row['type'] == "book" ) {
    // instantiate a BookProduct object
} else if ( $row['type'] == "cd" ) {
    // instantiate a CdProduct object
} else {
    // instantiate a ShopProduct object
}
$product->setId(          $row['id'] );
$product->setDiscount(    $row['discount'] );
return $product;
}
```

Note We use the term "factory" frequently in this chapter. A factory is a class or method with responsibility for generating objects.

The getInstance() method uses a large switch statement to determine which subclass to instantiate. Conditionals like this are quite common in factory code. Although we often attempt to excise large conditional statements from our projects, this often has the effect of pushing the conditional back to the moment at which an object is generated. This is not generally a serious problem, because we remove parallel conditionals from our code in pushing the decision making back to this point.

In this chapter, then, we will examine some of the key Gang of Four patterns for generating objects.

Note "Gang of Four" is the affectionate nickname of Erich Gamma, Richard Helm, Ralph Johnson, and John Vlissides, who are the authors of *Design Patterns: Elements of Reusable Object-Oriented Software*. This book is one of the most important design pattern catalogs, which is often known as the "Gang of Four book."

The Singleton Pattern

The global variable is one of the great bugbears of the object-oriented programmer. The reasons should be familiar to you by now. Global variables tie classes into context, undermining encapsulation. A class that relies on global variables becomes impossible to pull out of an application and use in another, without first ensuring that the new application itself defines the same global variables.

Although this is undesirable, the unprotected nature of global variables can be a greater problem. Once you start relying upon global variables, it is perhaps just a matter of time before one of your libraries declares a global that clashes with another declared elsewhere. We have seen already that PHP is vulnerable to class name clashes, but this is much worse. PHP will not warn you when globals collide. The first you will know about it is when your script begins to behave oddly.

Globals remain a temptation, however. This is because there are times when the sin inherent in global access seems a price worth paying in order to give all your classes access to an object.

The Problem

Well-designed systems generally pass object instances around via method calls. Each class retains its independence from the wider context, collaborating with other parts of the system via clear lines of communication. Sometimes, though, you find that this forces you to use some classes as conduits for objects that do not concern them, introducing dependencies in the name of good design.

Imagine a Preferences class that holds application-level information. We might use a Preferences object to store data such as DSN strings (Data Source Names hold table and user information about a database), URL roots, file paths, and so on. This is the sort of information that will vary from installation to installation. The object may also be used as a "notice board," a central location for messages that could be set or retrieved by otherwise unrelated objects in a system.

Passing a Preferences object around from object to object may not always be a good idea. Many classes that do not otherwise use the object could be forced to accept it simply so that they could pass it on to the objects that they work with. This is just another kind of coupling.

We also need to be sure that all objects in our system are working with the *same* Preferences object. We do not want objects setting values on one object, while others read from an entirely different one.

Let's distill the forces in this problem:

- A Preferences object should be available to any object in our system.

- A Preferences object should not be stored in a global variable, which can be overwritten.

- There should be no more than one Preferences object in play in the system. This means that *object Y* can set a property in the Preferences object, and *object Z* can retrieve the same property, without either one talking to the other directly.

Implementation

To address this problem, we can start by asserting control over object instantiation. Here we create a class that cannot be instantiated from outside of itself. That may sound difficult, but it's simply a matter of defining a private constructor:

```php
class Preferences {
    private $props = array();

    private function __construct() { }

    public function setProperty( $key, $val ) {
        $this->props[$key] = $val;
    }

    public function getProperty( $key ) {
        return $this->props[$key];
    }
}
```

Of course, at this point the Preferences class is entirely unusable. We have taken access restriction to an absurd level. Because the constructor is declared private, no client code can instantiate an object from it. The setProperty() and getProperty() methods are therefore redundant.

We can use a static method and a static property to mediate object instantiation.

```php
class Preferences {
    private $props = array();
    private static $instance;

    private function __construct() { }

    public static function getInstance() {
        if ( empty( self::$instance ) ) {
            self::$instance = new Preferences();
        }
        return self::$instance;
    }

    public function setProperty( $key, $val ) {
        $this->props[$key] = $val;
    }

    public function getProperty( $key ) {
        return $this->props[$key];
    }
}
```

The $instance property is private and static, so it cannot be accessed from outside the class. The getInstance() method has access though. Because getInstance() is public and static, it can be called via the class from anywhere in a script.

```
$pref = Preferences::getInstance();
$pref->setProperty( "name", "matt" );
unset( $pref );

$pref2 = Preferences::getInstance();
print $pref2->getProperty( "name" );
```

A static method cannot access object properties because it is, by definition, invoked in a class and not an object context. It can, however, access a static property. When getInstance() is called, we check the Preferences::$instance property. If it is empty, then we create an instance of the Preferences class and store it in the property. Then we return the instance to the calling code. Because the static getInstance() method is part of the Preferences class, we have no problem instantiating a Preferences object even though the constructor is private.

Figure 9-2 shows this structure in the UML.

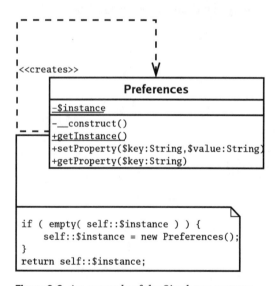

Figure 9-2. *An example of the Singleton pattern*

Consequences

So, how does the Singleton approach compare to using a global variable? First the bad news. Both Singletons and global variables can be misused. Because Singletons can be accessed from anywhere in a system, they can serve to create dependencies that can be hard to debug. Change a Singleton, and classes that use it may be affected. Dependencies are not a problem in themselves. After all, we create a dependency every time we declare that a method requires an argument of a particular type. The problem is that the global nature of the Singleton lets a programmer bypass the lines of communication defined by class interfaces. When a Singleton is used, the dependency is hidden away inside a method and not declared in its signature. This can make it harder to trace the relationships within a system. Singleton classes should therefore be deployed sparingly and with care.

Nevertheless, I think that moderate use of the Singleton pattern can improve the design of a system, saving you from horrible contortions as you pass objects unnecessarily around your system.

Singletons represent an improvement over global variables in an object-oriented context. You cannot overwrite a Singleton with the wrong kind of data. This kind of protection is especially important in PHP, which does not support namespaces. Any name clash will be caught at compile time, ending script execution.

Factory Method Pattern

Object-oriented design emphasizes the abstract class over the implementation. That is, we work with generalizations rather than specializations. The Factory Method pattern addresses the problem of how to create object instances when your code focuses on abstract types. The answer? Let specialist classes handle instantiation.

The Problem

Imagine a personal organizer project. Among others, we manage Appointment objects. Our business group has forged a relationship with another company, and we must communicate appointment data to them using a format called BloggsCal. The business group warns us that we may face yet more formats as time wears on, though.

Staying at the level of interface alone, we can identify two participants right away. We need a data encoder that converts our Appointment objects into a proprietary format. Let's call that class ApptEncoder. We need a manager class that will retrieve an encoder, and maybe work with it to communicate with a third party. We can call that CommsManager. Using the terminology of the pattern, the CommsManager is the creator, and the ApptEncoder is the product. You can see this structure in Figure 9-3.

Figure 9-3. *Abstract creator and product classes*

How do we get our hands on a real concrete ApptEncoder, though?

We could demand that an ApptEncoder is passed to the CommsManager, but that simply defers our problem, and we want the buck to stop about here. Let's instantiate a BloggsApptEncoder object directly within the CommsManager class:

```
abstract class ApptEncoder {
    abstract function encode();
}

class BloggsApptEncoder extends ApptEncoder {
    function encode() {
        return "Appointment data encoded in BloggsCal format\n";
    }
}

class MegaApptEncoder extends ApptEncoder {
    function encode() {
        return "Appointment data encoded in MegaCal format\n";
    }
}
class CommsManager {
    function getApptEncoder() {
        return new BloggsApptEncoder();
    }
}
```

The CommsManager class is responsible for generating BloggsApptEncoder objects. When
the sands of corporate allegiance inevitably shift and we are asked to convert our system
to work with a new format called MegaCal, we can simply add a conditional into the
CommsManager::getApptEncoder() method. This is the strategy we have used in the past,
after all. Let's build a new implementation of CommsManager that handles both BloggsCal
and MegaCal formats:

```
class CommsManager {
    const BLOGGS = 1;
    const MEGA = 2;
    private $mode = 1;

    function __construct( $mode ) {
        $this->mode = $mode;
    }

    function getApptEncoder() {
        switch ( $this->mode ) {
            case ( self::MEGA ):
                return new MegaApptEncoder();
            default:
                return new BloggsApptEncoder();
        }
    }
}
```

```
$comms = new CommsManager( CommsManager::MEGA );
$apptEncoder = $comms->getApptEncoder();
print $apptEncoder->encode();
```

We use constant flags to define two modes in which the script might be run: MEGA and
BLOGGS. We use a switch statement in the getApptEncoder() method to test the $mode property
and instantiate the appropriate implementation of ApptEncoder.

There is little wrong with this approach. Conditionals are sometimes considered examples
of bad "code smells," but object creation often requires a conditional at some point. We should
be less sanguine if we see duplicate conditionals creeping into our code. The CommsManager
class provides functionality for communicating calendar data. Imagine that the protocols we
work with require us to provide header and footer data. Let's extend our previous example to
support a getHeaderText() method:

```
class CommsManager {
    const BLOGGS = 1;
    const MEGA = 2;
    private $mode = 1;

    function __construct( $mode ) {
        $this->mode = $mode;
    }

    function getHeaderText() {
        switch ( $this->mode ) {
            case ( self::MEGA ):
                return "MegaCal header\n";
            default:
                return "BloggsCal header\n";
        }
    }
    function getApptEncoder() {
        switch ( $this->mode ) {
            case ( self::MEGA ):
                return new MegaApptEncoder();
            default:
                return new BloggsEncoder();
        }
    }
}
```

As you can see, the need to support header output has forced us to duplicate the protocol
conditional test. This will become unwieldy as we add new protocols, especially if we also add
a getFooterText() method.

So, to summarize our problem:

- We do not know until runtime the kind of object we need to produce (`BloggsApptEncoder` or `MegaApptEncoder`).

- We need to be able to add new product types with relative ease. (SyncML support is just a new business deal away!)

- Each product type is associated with a context that requires other customized operations (`getHeaderText()`, `getFooterText()`).

Additionally, we might note that we are using conditional statements, and we have seen already that these are naturally replaceable by polymorphism. The Factory Method pattern enables us to use inheritance and polymorphism to encapsulate the creation of concrete products. In other words, we create a `CommsManager` subclass for each protocol, each one implementing the `getApptEncoder()` method.

Implementation

The Factory Method pattern splits creator classes from the products they are designed to generate. The creator is a factory class that defines a method for generating a product object. If no default implementation is provided, it is left to creator child classes to perform the instantiation. Typically, each creator subclass instantiates a parallel product child class.

Let's redesignate `CommsManager` as an abstract class. That way we keep a flexible super class and put all our protocol-specific code in the concrete subclasses. You can see this alteration in Figure 9-4.

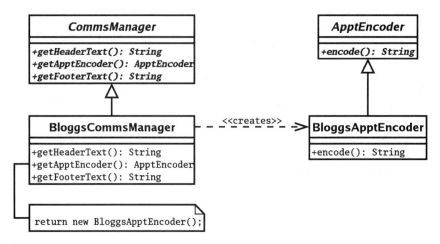

Figure 9-4. *Concrete creator and product classes*

Here's some simplified code:

```
abstract class ApptEncoder {
    abstract function encode();
}

class BloggsApptEncoder extends ApptEncoder {
    function encode() {
        return "Appointment data encode in BloggsCal format\n";
    }
}

abstract class CommsManager {
    abstract function getHeaderText();
    abstract function getApptEncoder();
    abstract function getFooterText();
}

class BloggsCommsManager extends CommsManager {
    function getHeaderText() {
        return "BloggsCal header\n";
    }

    function getApptEncoder() {
        return new BloggsApptEncoder();
    }

    function getFooterText() {
        return "BloggsCal footer\n";
    }
}
```

The `BloggsCommsManager::getTtdEncoder()` method returns a `BloggsApptEncoder` object. Client code calling `getApptEncoder()` can expect an object of type `ApptEncoder`, and will not necessarily know about the concrete product it has been given. In some languages, method return types are enforced, so client code calling a method like `getApptEncoder()` can be absolutely certain that it will receive an `ApptEncoder` object. In PHP 5, this is a matter of convention. It is important to document return types or otherwise signal them through naming conventions.

So when we are required to implement MegaCal, supporting it is simply a matter of writing a new implementation for our abstract classes. Figure 9-5 shows the MegaCal classes.

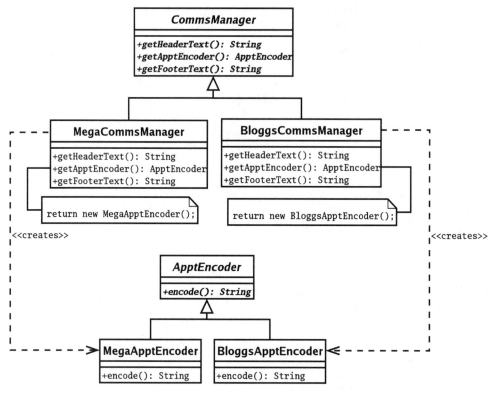

Figure 9-5. *Extending the design to support a new protocol*

Consequences

Notice that our creator classes mirror the product hierarchy. This is a common consequence of the Factory Method pattern and disliked by some as a special kind of code duplication. Another issue is the possibility that the pattern could encourage unnecessary subclassing. If your only reason for subclassing a creator is to deploy the Factory Method pattern, you may need to think again (that's why we introduced the header and footer constraints to our example here).

We have focused only on appointments in our example. If we extend it somewhat to include "to do" items and contacts, we face a new problem. We need a structure that will handle sets of related implementations at one time. The Factory Method pattern is often used with the Abstract Factory pattern, as we will see in the next section.

Abstract Factory

In large applications, you may need factories that produce related sets of classes. The Abstract Factory pattern addresses this problem.

The Problem

Let's look again at our organizer example. We manage encoding in two formats, BloggsCal and MegaCal. We can grow this structure "horizontally" by adding more encoding formats, but how can we grow "vertically," adding encoders for different types of PIM object? In fact, we have been working toward this pattern already.

In Figure 9-6, you can see the parallel families with which we will want to work.

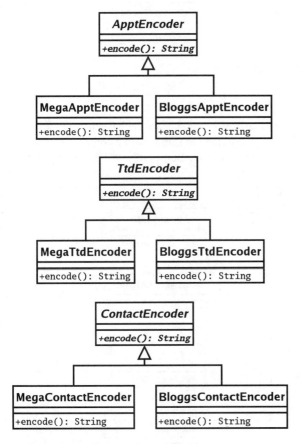

Figure 9-6. *Three product families*

The BloggsCal classes are unrelated to one another by inheritance (although they could implement a common interface), but they are functionally parallel. If our system is currently working with BloggsTtdEncoder, it should also be working with BloggsContactEncoder.

To see how we enforce this, we can begin with the interface as we did with the Factory Method pattern (see Figure 9-7).

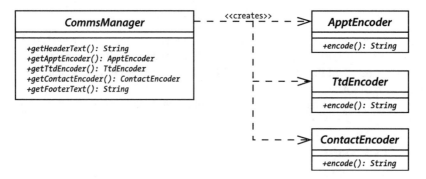

Figure 9-7. *An abstract creator and its abstract products*

Implementation

The abstract CommsManager class defines the interface for generating each of the three products (ApptEncoder, TtdEncoder, and ContactEncoder). We need to implement a concrete creator in order to actually generate the concrete products for a particular family. We do that for the BloggsCal format in Figure 9-8.

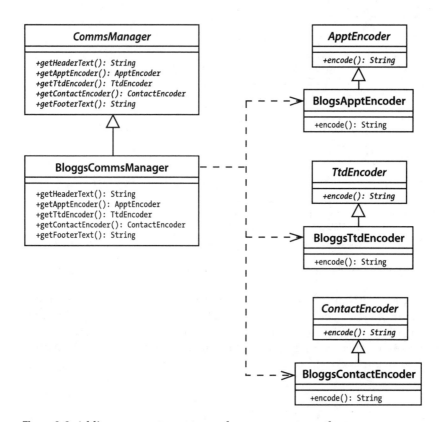

Figure 9-8. *Adding a concrete creator and some concrete products*

Here is a code version of CommsManager and BloggsCommsManager:

```
abstract class CommsManager {
    abstract function getHeaderText();
    abstract function getApptEncoder();
    abstract function getTtdEncoder();
    abstract function getContactEncoder();
    abstract function getFooterText();
}

class BloggsCommsManager extends CommsManager {
    function getHeaderText() {
        return "BloggsCal header\n";
    }

    function getApptEncoder() {
        return new BloggsApptEncoder();
    }

    function getTtdEncoder() {
        return new BloggsTtdEncoder();
    }

    function getContactEncoder() {
        return new BloggsContactEncoder();
    }

    function getFooterText() {
        return "BloggsCal footer\n";
    }
}
```

Notice that we use the Factory Method pattern in this example. getContact() is abstract in CommsManager and implemented in BloggsCommsManager. Design patterns tend to work together in this way, one pattern creating the context that lends itself to another. In Figure 9-9, we add support for the MegaCal format.

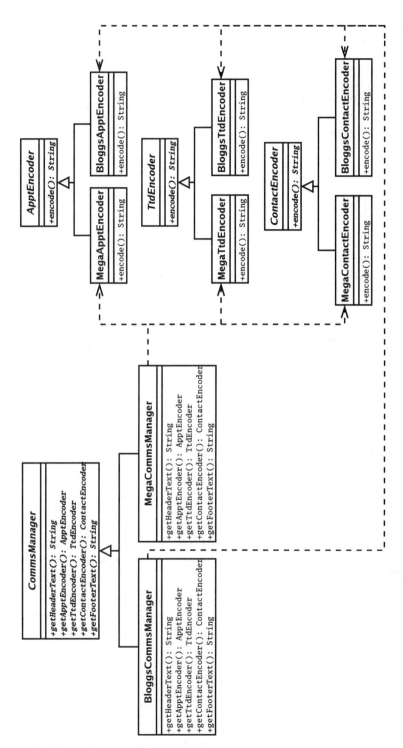

Figure 9-9. *Adding concrete creators and some concrete products*

Consequences

So what does this pattern buy us?

- Firstly, we decouple our system from the details of implementation. We can add or remove any number of encoding formats to our example without causing a knock on effect.

- We enforce the grouping of functionally related elements of our system. So by using BloggsCommsManager, we are guaranteed that we will work only with BloggsCal-related classes.

- Adding new products can be a pain. Not only do we have to create concrete implementations of the new product, but also we have to amend the abstract creator and every one of its concrete implementers in order to support it.

Many implementations of the Abstract Factory pattern use the Factory Method pattern. This may be because most examples are written in Java or C++. PHP, however, does not enforce a return type for a method, which affords us some flexibility that we might leverage.

Rather than create separate methods for each Factory Method, we can create a single make() method that uses a flag argument to determine which object to return.

```
abstract class CommsManager {
    const APPT    = 1;
    const TTD     = 2;
    const CONTACT = 3;
    abstract function getHeaderText();
    abstract function make( $flag_int );
    abstract function getFooterText();
}

class BloggsCommsManager extends CommsManager {
    function getHeaderText() {
        return "BloggsCal header\n";
    }
    function make( $flag_int ) {
        switch ( $flag_int ) {
            case self::APPT:
                return new BloggsApptEncoder();
            case self::CONTACT:
                return new BloggsContactEncoder();
            case self::TTD:
                return new BloggsTtdEncoder();
        }
    }

    function getFooterText() {
        return "BloggsCal footer\n";
    }
}
```

As you can see, we have made the class interface more compact. We've done this at a considerable cost, though. In using Factory Methods, we define a clear interface and force all concrete factory objects to honor it. In using a single make() method, we must remember to support all product objects in all the concrete creators. We also introduce parallel conditionals, as each concrete creator must implement the same flag tests. A client class cannot be certain that concrete creators generate all the products because the internals of make() are a matter of choice in each case.

On the other hand, we can build more flexible creators. The base creator class can provide a make() method that guarantees a default implementation of each product family. Concrete children could then modify this behavior selectively. It would be up to implementing creator classes to call the default make() method after providing their own implementation.

We will see another variation on the Abstract Factory pattern in the next section.

Prototype

The emergence of parallel inheritance hierarchies can be a problem with the Factory Method pattern. This is a kind of coupling that makes some programmers uncomfortable. Every time you add a product family, you are forced to create an associated concrete creator (the BloggsCal encoders are matched by BloggsCommsManager, for example). In a system that grows fast to encompass many products, maintaining this kind of relationship can quickly become tiresome.

One way of avoiding this dependency is to use PHP's clone keyword to duplicate existing concrete products. The concrete product classes themselves then become the basis of their own generation. This is the Prototype pattern. It enables us to replace inheritance with composition. This in turn promotes runtime flexibility and reduces the number of classes we must create.

The Problem

Imagine a Civilization-style Web game in which units operate on a grid of tiles. Each tile can represent sea, plains, or forests. The terrain type constrains the movement and combat abilities of units occupying the tile. We might have a TerrainFactory object that serves up Sea, Forest, and Plains objects. We decide that we will allow the user to choose between radically different environments, so the Sea object is an abstract super class implemented by MarsSea and EarthSea. Forest and Plains objects are similarly implemented. The forces here lend themselves to the Abstract Factory pattern. We have distinct product hierarchies (Sea, Plains, Forests), with strong family relationships cutting across inheritance (Earth, Mars). Figure 9-10 presents a class diagram that shows how we might deploy the Abstract Factory and Factory Method patterns to work with these products.

As you can see, we rely on inheritance to group the terrain family for the products that a factory will generate. This is a workable solution, but it requires a large inheritance hierarchy, and it is relatively inflexible. When you do not want parallel inheritance hierarchies, and when you need to maximize runtime flexibility, the Prototype pattern can be used in a powerful variation on the Abstract Factory pattern.

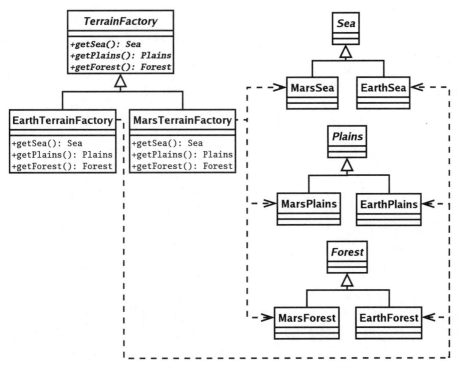

Figure 9-10. *Handling terrains with the Abstract Factory method*

Implementation

When we work with the Abstract Factory/Factory Method patterns, we must decide at some point which concrete creator we wish to work with, probably by checking some kind of preference flag. Since we must do this anyway, why not simply create a factory class that stores concrete products, and populate this during initialization? We can cut down on a couple of classes this way, and, as we shall see, take advantage of other benefits. Here's some simple code that uses the Prototype pattern in a factory:

```
class Sea {}
class EarthSea extends Sea {}
class MarsSea extends Sea {}

class Plains {}
class EarthPlains extends Plains {}
class MarsPlains extends Plains {}

class Forest {}
class EarthForest extends Forest {}
class MarsForest extends Forest {}
```

```
class TerrainFactory {
    private $sea;
    private $forest;
    private $plains;

    function __construct( Sea $sea, Plains $plains, Forest $forest ) {
        $this->sea = $sea;
        $this->plains = $plains;
        $this->forest = $forest;
    }

    function getSea( ) {
        return clone $this->sea;
    }

    function getPlains( ) {
        return clone $this->plains;
    }

    function getForest( ) {
        return clone $this->forest;
    }
}

$factory = new TerrainFactory( new EarthSea(),
    new EarthPlains(),
    new EarthForest() );
print_r( $factory->getSea() );
print_r( $factory->getPlains() );
print_r( $factory->getForest() );
```

As you can see, we load up a concrete `TerrainFactory` with instances of our product objects. When a client calls `getSea()`, we return a clone of the Sea object that we cached during initialization. Not only have we saved a couple of classes, but also we have bought additional flexibility. Want to play a game on a new planet with Earth-like seas and forests, but Mars-like plains? No need to write a new creator class—we can simply change the mix of classes we add to `TerrainFactory`.

```
$factory = new TerrainFactory( new EarthSea(),
    new MarsPlains(),
    new EarthForest() );
```

So the Prototype pattern allows us to take advantage of the flexibility afforded by composition. We get more than that, though. Because we are storing and cloning objects at runtime, we reproduce object state when we generate new products. Imagine that Sea objects have a $navigability property. The property influences the amount of movement energy a sea tile saps from a vessel, and can be set to adjust the difficulty level of a game.

```
class Sea {
    private $navigability = 0;
    function __construct( $navigability ) {
        $this->navigability = $navigability;
    }
}
```

Now when we initialize the TerrainFactory object, we can add a Sea object with a navigability modifier. This will then hold true for all Sea objects served by TerrainFactory.

```
$factory = new TerrainFactory( new EarthSea( -1 ),
    new EarthPlains(),
    new EarthForest() );
```

This flexibility is also apparent when the object you wish to generate is composed of other objects. Perhaps all Sea objects can contain Resource objects (FishResource, OilResource, etc.). According to a preference flag, we might give all Sea objects a FishResource by default. Remember that if your products reference other objects, you should implement a __clone() method in order to ensure that you make a deep copy.

■**Note** We covered object cloning in Chapter 4. The clone keyword generates a shallow copy of any object to which it is applied. This means that the product object will have the same properties as the source. If any of the source's properties are objects, then these will not be copied into the product. Instead, the product will reference the *same* object properties. It is up to us to change this default, and to customize object copying in any other way, by implementing a __clone() method. This is called automatically when the clone keyword is used.

```
class Contained { }

class Container {
    public $contained;
    function __construct() {
        $this->contained = new Contained();
    }

    function __clone() {
        // Ensure that cloned object holds a
        // clone of self::$contained and not
        // a reference to it
        $this->contained = clone $this->contained;
    }
}
```

But That's Cheating!

I promised that this chapter would deal with the logic of object creation, doing away with the sneaky buck-passing of many object-oriented examples. Yet some patterns here have slyly dodged the decision-making part of object creation, if not the creation itself.

The Singleton pattern is not guilty. The logic for object creation is built in and unambiguous. The Abstract Factory pattern groups the creation of product families into distinct concrete creators. How do we decide which concrete creator to use though? The Prototype pattern presents us with a similar problem. Both these patterns handle the creation of objects, but they defer the decision as to which object, or group of objects, should be created.

The particular concrete creator that a system chooses is often decided according to the value of a configuration switch of some kind. This could be located in a database, a configuration file, a server file (such as Apache's local server configuration file, usually called .htaccess) or it could even be hard coded as a PHP variable or property. Because PHP applications must be reconfigured for every request, we need script initialization to be as painless as possible. For this reason, I often opt to hard code configuration flags in PHP code. This can be done by hand, or by writing a script that auto-generates a class file. Here's a crude class that includes a flag for calendar protocol types:

```php
class Settings {
    static $COMMSTYPE = 'Mega';
}
```

Now that we have a flag (however inelegant), we can create a class that uses it to decide which CommsManager to serve on request. It is quite common to see a Singleton used in conjunction with the Abstract Factory pattern, so let's do that:

```php
require_once( 'Settings.php' );

class AppConfig {
    private static $instance;
    private $commsManager;

    private function __construct() {
        // will run once only
        $this->init();
    }

    private function init() {
        switch ( Settings::$COMMSTYPE ) {
            case 'Mega':
                $this->commsManager = new MegaCommsManager();
                break;
            default:
                $this->commsManager = new BloggsCommsManager();
        }
    }
}
```

```
    public static function getInstance() {
        if ( empty( self::$instance ) ) {
            self::$instance = new self();
        }
        return self::$instance;
    }

    public function getCommsManager() {
        return $this->commsManager;
    }
}
```

The AppConfig class is a standard Singleton. For that reason, we can get an AppConfig instance anywhere in our system, and we will always get the same one. The init() method is invoked by the class's constructor, and is therefore only run once in a process. It tests the Settings::$COMMSTYPE property, instantiating a concrete CommsManager object according to its value. Now our script can get a CommsManager object and work with it without ever knowing about its concrete implementations or the concrete classes they generate.

```
$commsMgr = AppConfig::getInstance()->getCommsManager();
$commsMgr->getApptEncoder()->encode();
```

Summary

This chapter covered some of the tricks you can use to generate objects. We examined the Singleton pattern, which provides global access to a single instance. We looked at the Factory Method pattern, which applies the principle of polymorphism to object generation. We combined Factory Method with the Abstract Factory pattern to generate creator classes that instantiate sets of related objects. Finally, we looked at the Prototype pattern and saw how object cloning can allow composition to be used in object generation.

CHAPTER 10

Designing for Object Relations

With strategies for generating objects covered, we're free now to look at some strategies for structuring classes and objects. We will focus in particular on the principle that composition provides greater flexibility than inheritance. The patterns we examine in this chapter are once again drawn from the Gang of Four catalog.

This chapter will cover

- *The Composite pattern*: Composing structures in which groups of objects can be used as if they were individual objects

- *The Decorator pattern*: A flexible mechanism for combining objects at runtime to extend functionality

- *The Facade pattern*: Creating a simple interface to complex or variable systems

Structuring Classes to Allow Flexible Objects

Way back in Chapter 4, I said that beginners often confuse objects and classes. This was only half true. In fact, most of the rest of us occasionally scratch our heads over UML class diagrams, attempting to reconcile the static inheritance structures they show with the dynamic object relationships their objects will enter into off the page.

Remember the pattern principle "Favor composition over inheritance"? This principle distills this tension between the organization of classes and of objects. In order to build flexibility into our projects, we structure our classes so that their objects can be built into useful structures at runtime.

This is a common theme running through the first two patterns of this chapter. Inheritance is an important feature in both, but it is important in part for providing the mechanism by which composition can be used to represent structures and extend functionality.

The Composite Pattern

The Composite pattern is perhaps the most extreme example of inheritance deployed in the service of composition. It is a simple and yet breathtakingly elegant design. It is also fantastically useful. Be warned, though, it is so neat, you might be tempted to overuse this strategy.

The Composite pattern is a simple way of aggregating and then managing groups of similar objects such that an individual object is indistinguishable to a client from a collection of objects. The pattern is, in fact, very simple, but it is also often confusing. One reason for this is the similarity in structure of the classes in the pattern to the organization of its objects. Inheritance hierarchies are trees, beginning with the super class at the root, and branching out into specialized subclasses. The inheritance tree of *classes* laid down by the Composite pattern is designed to allow the easy generation and traversal of a tree of *objects*.

If you are not already familiar with this pattern, you have every right to feel confused at this point. Let's try an analogy to illustrate the way that single entities can be treated in the same way as collections of things. Given broadly irreducible ingredients such as cereals and meat (or soya if you prefer), we can make a food product—a sausage, for example. We then act on the result as a single entity. Just as we eat, cook, buy, or sell meat, we can eat, cook, buy, or sell the sausage that the meat in part composes. We might take the sausage and combine it with the other composite ingredients to make a pie, thereby rolling a composite into a larger composite. We behave in the same way to the collection as we do to the parts. The Composite pattern helps us to model this relationship between collections and components in our code.

The Problem

Managing groups of objects can be quite a complex task, especially if the objects in question might also contain objects of their own. This kind of problem is very common in coding. Think of invoices, with line items that summarize additional products or services, or things-to-do lists with items that themselves contain multiple subtasks. In content management, we can't move for trees of sections, pages, articles, media components. Managing these structures from the outside can quickly become daunting.

Let's return to a previous scenario. We are designing a system based on a game called Civilization. A player can move units around hundreds of tiles that make up a map. Individual counters can be grouped together to move, fight, and defend themselves as a unit. Let's define a couple of unit types:

```
abstract class Unit {
    abstract function bombardStrength();
}

class Archer extends Unit {
    function bombardStrength() {
        return 4;
    }
}

class LaserCanonUnit extends Unit {
    function bombardStrength() {
        return 44;
    }
}
```

The Unit class defines an abstract bombardStrength() method, which sets the attack strength of a unit bombarding an adjacent tile. We implement this in both the Archer and

LaserCanonUnit classes. These classes would also contain information about movement and defensive capabilities, but let's keep things simple. We could define a separate class to group units together like this:

```
class Army {
    private $units = array();

    function addUnit( Unit $unit ) {
        array_push( $this->units, $unit );
    }

    function bombardStrength() {
        $ret = 0;
        foreach( $this->units as $unit ) {
            $ret += $unit->bombardStrength();
        }
        return $ret;
    }
}
```

The Army class has an addUnit() method that accepts an addUnit() object. Unit objects are stored in an array property called $units. We calculate the combined strength of our army in the bombardStrength() method. This simply iterates through the aggregated Unit objects, calling the bombardStrength() method of each one.

This model is perfectly acceptable as long as the problem remains as simple as this. What happens, though, when we add some new requirements? Let's say that an army should be able to combine other armies. Each army should retain its own identity, so we can't just decant the units from each army into a new force.

We could amend the Army class to accept Army objects as well as Unit objects:

```
function addArmy( Army $army ) {
    array_push( $this->armies, $army );
}
```

We need to amend the bombardStrength() method to iterate through all armies as well as units:

```
function bombardStrength() {
    $ret = 0;
    foreach( $this->units as $unit ) {
        $ret += $unit->bombardStrength();
    }

    foreach( $this->armies as $army ) {
        $ret += $army->bombardStrength();
    }

    return $ret;
}
```

This additional complexity is not too problematic at the moment. Remember, though, we need to do something similar in methods like defensiveStrength(), movementRange(), and so on. Our game is going to be richly featured. Already the client is calling for troop carriers that can hold up to 10 units to improve their movement range on certain terrains. Clearly a troop carrier is similar to an army in that it groups units. It also has its own characteristics. We could further amend the Army class to handle TroopCarrier objects, but we know that there will be a need for still more unit groupings. It is clear that we need a more flexible model.

Let's look again at the model we have been building. All the classes we created shared the need for a bombardStrength() method. In effect, a client does not need to distinguish between an army, a unit, or a troop carrier. They are functionally identical. They need to move, attack, and defend. Those objects that contain others need to provide methods for adding and removing. These similarities lead us to an inevitable conclusion. Because container objects share an interface with the objects that they contain, they are naturally suited to share a type family.

Implementation

The Composite pattern defines a single inheritance hierarchy that lays down two distinct sets of responsibilities. We have already seen both of these in our example. Classes in the pattern must support a common set of operations as their primary responsibility. For us, that means the bombardStrength() method. Classes must also support methods for adding and removing child objects.

Figure 10-1 shows a class diagram that illustrates the Composite pattern as applied to our problem.

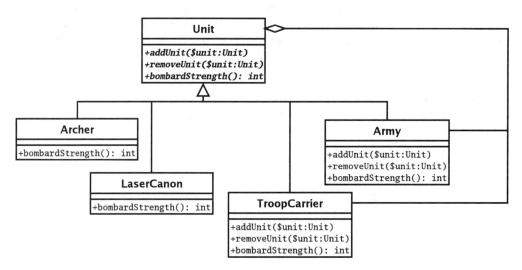

Figure 10-1. *The Composite pattern*

As you can see, all the units in our model extend the Unit class. A client can be sure, then, that any Unit object will support the bombardStrength() method. So an Army can be treated in exactly the same way as an Archer.

The Army and TroopCarrier classes are *composites*: designed to hold Unit objects. The Archer and LaserCanon classes are *leaves*, designed to support unit operations but not to hold

other Unit objects. There is actually an issue as to whether leaves should honor the same interface as composites, but we will return to this shortly. Here is the abstract Unit class:

```
class UnitException extends Exception {}

abstract class Unit {
    abstract function addUnit( Unit $unit );
    abstract function removeUnit( Unit $unit );
    abstract function bombardStrength();
}
```

As you can see, we lay down the basic functionality for all Unit objects here. Now let's see
how a composite object might implement these abstract methods:

```
class Army extends Unit {
    private $units = array();

    function addUnit( Unit $unit ) {
        foreach ( $this->units as $thisunit ) {
            if ( $unit === $thisunit ) {
                return;
            }
        }
        $this->units[] = $unit;
    }

    function removeUnit( Unit $unit ) {
        $units = array();
        foreach ( $this->units as $thisunit ) {
            if ( $unit !== $thisunit ) {
                $units[] = $thisunit;
            }
        }
        $this->units = $units;
    }

    function bombardStrength() {
        $ret = 0;
        foreach( $this->units as $unit ) {
            $ret += $unit->bombardStrength();
        }
        return $ret;
    }
}
```

The addUnit() method checks that we have not yet added the same Unit object before
storing it in the private $units array property. removeUnit() uses a similar loop to remove a
given Unit object from the property.

■**Note** At the time of writing, functions such as in_array() do not check properly for object instances. in_array() returns true for two different objects instantiated from the same class if their property values are equivalent. This forces us to loop through the $units property and test for the $unit object manually using the === operator. The correct operation of === is a great step forward in PHP 5, however. In order to test object identity in PHP 4, it was necessary to assign a unique value to every object used in the Composite pattern.

Army objects, then, can store Units of any kind, including other Army objects, or leaves such as Archer or LaserCanonUnit. Because all units are guaranteed to support bombardStrength(), our Army::bombardStrength() method simply iterates through all the child Unit objects stored in the $units property, calling the same method on each.

One problematic aspect of the Composite pattern is the implementation of add and remove functionality. The classic pattern places add() and remove() methods in the abstract super class. This ensures that all classes in the pattern share a common interface. As you can see here, though, it also means that leaf classes must provide an implementation:

```php
class Archer extends Unit {
    function addUnit( Unit $unit ) {
        throw new UnitException( get_class($this)." is a leaf" );
    }

    function removeUnit( Unit $unit ) {
        throw new UnitException( get_class($this)." is a leaf" );
    }

    function bombardStrength() {
        return 4;
    }
}
```

We do not want to make it possible to add a Unit object to an Archer object, so we throw exceptions if addUnit() or removeUnit() are called. We will need to do this for all leaf objects, so we could perhaps improve our design by replacing the abstract addUnit()/removeUnit() methods in Unit with default implementations like the one in the preceding example.

```php
class UnitException extends Exception {}

abstract class Unit {
    abstract function bombardStrength();

    function addUnit( Unit $unit ) {
        throw new UnitException( get_class($this)." is a leaf" );
    }
```

```
    function removeUnit( Unit $unit ) {
        throw new UnitException( get_class($this)." is a leaf" );
    }
}

class Archer extends Unit {
    function bombardStrength() {
        return 4;
    }
}
```

This removes duplication in leaf classes but has the drawback that a Composite is not forced at compile time to provide an implementation of addUnit() and removeUnit(), which could cause problems down the line.

We will look in more detail at some of the problems presented by the Composite pattern in the next section. Let's end this section by reminding ourselves of some of the benefits.

- *Flexibility*: Because everything in the Composite pattern shares a common super type, it is very easy to add new composite or leaf objects to the design without changing a program's wider context.

- *Simplicity*: A client using a Composite structure has a straightforward interface. There is no need for a client to distinguish between an object that is composed of others, and a leaf object. A call to Army::bombardStrength() may cause a cascade of delegated calls behind the scenes, but to the client the process and result are exactly equivalent to those associated with calling Archer::bombardStrength().

- *Implicit reach*: Objects in the Composite pattern are organized in a tree. Each composite holds references to its children. An operation on a particular part of the tree therefore can have a wide effect. We might remove a single Army object from its Army parent, and add it to another. This simple act is wrought on one object, but it has the effect of changing the status of the Army object's referenced Unit objects and of their own children.

- *Explicit reach*: Tree structures are easy to traverse. They can be iterated in order to gain information or to perform transformations. We will look at a particularly powerful technique for this in the next chapter when we deal with the Visitor pattern.

Often you really see the benefit of a pattern from a client's perspective, so let's create a couple of armies:

```
// create an army
$main_army = new Army();

// add some units
$main_army->addUnit( new Archer() );
$main_army->addUnit( new LaserCanonUnit() );

// create a new army
$sub_army = new Army();
```

```
// add some units
$sub_army->addUnit( new Archer() );
$sub_army->addUnit( new Archer() );
$sub_army->addUnit( new Archer() );

// add the second army to the first
$main_army->addUnit( $sub_army );

// all the calculations handled behind the scenes
print "attacking with strength: {$main_army->bombardStrength()}\n";
```

We create a new Army object and add some primitive Unit objects. We repeat the process for a second Army object that we then add to the first. When we call Unit::bombardStrength() on the first Army object, all the complexity of the structure that we have built up is entirely hidden.

Consequences

If you're anything like me, you would have heard alarm bells ringing when you saw the code extract for the Archer class. Why do we put up with these redundant addUnit() and removeUnit() methods in leaf classes that do not need to support them? An answer of sorts lies in the transparency of the Unit type.

If a client is passed a Unit object, it knows that the addUnit() method will be present. The Composite pattern principle that primitive (leaf) classes have the same interface as composites is upheld. This does not actually help us much because we still do not know how safe we might be calling addUnit() on any Unit object we might come across.

If we move these add/remove methods down so that they are available only to composite classes, then passing a Unit object to a method leaves us with the problem that we do not know by default whether or not it supports addUnit(). Nevertheless, leaving booby-trapped methods lying around in leaf classes makes me uncomfortable.

We can split composite classes off into their own subtype quite easily. First of all, we excise add/remove behavior from Unit.

```
abstract class Unit {
    function getComposite() {
        return null;
    }

    abstract function bombardStrength();
}
```

Notice the new getComposite() method. We will return to this in a little while. Now we need a new abstract class to hold addUnit() and removeUnit(). We can even provide default implementations.

```
abstract class CompositeUnit extends Unit {
    private $units = array();

    function getComposite() {
        return $this;
    }

    protected function units() {
        return $this->units;
    }

    function removeUnit( Unit $unit ) {
        $units = array();
        foreach ( $this->units as $thisunit ) {
            if ( $unit !== $thisunit ) {
                $units[] = $thisunit;
            }
        }
        $this->units = $units;
    }

    function addUnit( Unit $unit ) {
        foreach ( $this->units as $thisunit ) {
            if ( $unit === $thisunit ) {
                return;
            }
        }
        $this->units[] = $unit;
    }
}
```

The CompositeUnit class is declared abstract, even though it does not itself declare an abstract method. It does, however, extend Unit, and does not implement the abstract bombardStrength() method. Army (and any other composite classes) can now extend CompositeUnit. The classes in our example are now organized as in Figure 10-2.

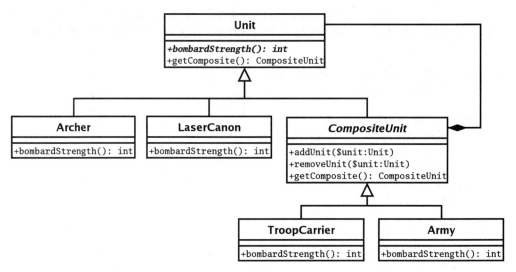

Figure 10-2. *Moving add/remove methods out of the base class*

We have lost the annoying, useless implementations of add/remove methods in the leaf classes, but the client must still check to see whether it has a CompositeUnit before it can use addUnit().

This is where the getComposite() method comes into its own. By default this method returns a null value. Only in a CompositeUnit class does it return CompositeUnit. So if a call to this method returns an object, we should be able to call addUnit() on it. Here's a client that uses this technique:

```
class UnitScript {
    static function joinExisting( Unit $newUnit,
                                  Unit $occupyingUnit ) {

        $comp;
        if ( $comp = $occupyingUnit->getComposite() ) {
            $comp->addUnit( $newUnit );
        } else {
            $comp = new Army();
            $comp->addUnit( $occupyingUnit );
            $comp->addUnit( $newUnit );
        }
        return $comp;
    }
}
```

The joinExisting() method accepts two Unit objects. The first is a newcomer to a tile, and the second is a prior occupier. If the second Unit is a CompositeUnit, then the first will attempt to join it. If not, then a new Army will be created to cover both units. We have no way of knowing at first whether the $occupyingUnit argument contains a CompositeUnit. A call to getComposite() settles the matter, though. If getComposite() returns an object, we can add the new Unit object to it directly. If not, then we create the new Army object, and add both.

These contortions are symptomatic of a drawback to the Composite pattern. Simplicity is achieved by ensuring that all classes are derived from a common base. The benefit of simplicity is sometimes bought at a cost to type safety. The more complex your model becomes, the more manual type checking you are likely to have to do. Let's say that we have a Cavalry object. If the rules of our game state that you cannot put a horse on a troop carrier, we have no automatic way of enforcing this with the Composite pattern.

```
class TroopCarrier {

    function addUnit( Unit $unit ) {
        if ( $unit instanceof Cavalry ) {
            throw new UnitException("Can't get a horse on the vehicle");
        }
        super::addUnit( $unit );
    }

    function bombardStrength() {
        return 0;
    }
}
```

We are forced to use the instanceof operator to test the type of the object passed to addUnit(). Too many special cases of this kind, and the drawbacks of the pattern begin to outweigh its benefits. Composite works best when most of the components are interchangeable.

Another issue to bear in mind is the cost of some Composite operations. The Army::bombardStrength() method is typical in that it sets off a cascade of calls to the same method down the tree. For a large tree with lots of sub-armies, a single call can cause an avalanche behind the scenes. bombardStrength() is not itself very expensive, but what would happen if some leaves performed a complex calculation in order to arrive at their return value? One way around this problem is to cache the result of a method call of this sort in the parent object, so that subsequent invocations are less expensive. You need to be careful, though, to ensure that the cached value does not grow stale. You should devise strategies to wipe any caches whenever any operations take place on the tree. This may require that you give child objects references to their parents.

Finally, a note about persistence. The Composite pattern is elegant, but it doesn't lend itself neatly to storage in a relational database. This is because, by default, you access the entire structure only through a cascade of references. So to construct a Composite structure from a database in the natural way you would have to make multiple expensive queries. We can get round this problem by assigning an ID to the whole tree, so that all components can be drawn from the database in one go. Having acquired all the objects, however, we would still have the task of recreating the parent/child references which themselves would have to be stored in the database. This is not difficult, but it is somewhat messy.

While Composites sit uneasily with relational databases, they lend themselves very well indeed to XML. This is because XML elements are often themselves composed of trees of subelements.

Composite in Summary

So the Composite pattern is useful when you need to treat a collection of things in the same way as you would an individual, either because the collection is intrinsically like a component (armies and archers), or because the context gives the collection the same characteristics as the component (line items in an invoice). Composites are arranged in trees, so an operation on the whole can affect the parts, and data from the parts is transparently available via the whole. The Composite pattern makes such operations and queries transparent to the client. Trees are easy to traverse (as we shall see in the next chapter). It is easy to add new component types to Composite structures. On the downside, Composites rely on the similarity of their parts. As soon as we introduce complex rules as to which composite object can hold which set of components, our code can become hard to manage. Composites do not lend themselves well to storage in relational databases, but are well suited to XML persistence.

The Decorator Pattern

While the Composite pattern helps us to create a flexible representation of aggregated components, the Decorator pattern uses a similar structure to help us to modify the functionality of concrete components. Once again, the key to this pattern lies in the importance of composition at runtime. Inheritance is a neat way of building on characteristics laid down by a parent class. This neatness can lead you to hard code variation into your inheritance hierarchies, often causing inflexibility.

The Problem

Building all your functionality into an inheritance structure can result in an explosion of classes in a system. Even worse, as you try to apply similar modifications to different branches of your inheritance tree, you are likely to see duplication emerge.

Let's return to our game. Here we define a `Tile` class, and a derived type:

```
abstract class Tile {
    abstract function getWealthFactor();
}

class Plains extends Tile {
    private $wealthfactor = 2;
    function getWealthFactor() {
        return $this->wealthfactor;
    }
}
```

We define a `Tile` class. This represents a square upon which our units might be found. Each tile has certain characteristics. In this example, we have defined a `getWealthFactor()` method that affects the revenue a particular square might generate if owned by a player. As you can see, `Plains` objects have a wealth factor of 2. Obviously, tiles manage other data. They might also hold a reference to image information so that the board could be drawn. Once again, we keep things simple here.

We need to modify the behavior of the Plains object to handle the effects of natural resources and human abuse. We wish to model the occurrence of diamonds on the landscape, and the damage caused by pollution. One approach might be to inherit from the Plains object:

```
class DiamondPlains extends Plains {
    function getWealthFactor() {
        return parent::getWealthFactor() + 2;
    }
}

class PollutedPlains extends Plains {
    function getWealthFactor() {
        return parent::getWealthFactor() - 4;
    }
}
```

We can now acquire a polluted tile very easily:

```
$tile = new PollutedPlains();
print $tile->getWealthFactor();
```

You can see the class diagram for this example in Figure 10-3.

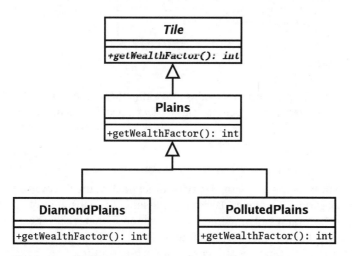

Figure 10-3. *Building varation into an inheritance tree*

This structure is obviously inflexible. We can get plains with diamonds. We can get polluted plains. But can we get them both? Clearly not, unless we are willing to perpetrate the horror that is PollutedDiamondPlains. This situation can only get worse when we introduce the Forest class, which can also have diamonds and pollution.

This is an extreme example, of course, but the point is made. Relying entirely upon inheritance to define your functionality can lead to a multiplicity of classes, and a tendency toward duplication.

Let's take a more realistic example at this point. Serious web applications often have to perform a range of actions upon a request before a task is initiated to form a response. We might need to authenticate the user, for example, and to log the request. Perhaps we should process the request to build a data structure from raw input. Finally, we must perform our core processing. We are presented with the same problem.

We can extend the functionality of a base `ProcessRequest` class with additional processing in a derived `LogRequest` class, in a `StructureRequest` class, and in an `AuthenticateRequest` class. You can see this class hierarchy in Figure 10-4.

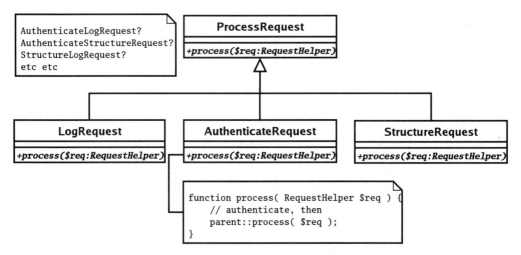

Figure 10-4. *More hard-coded variations*

What happens, though, when we need to perform logging *and* authentication but *not* data preparation? Do we create a `LogAndAuthenticateProcessor` class? Clearly it is time to find a more flexible solution.

Implementation

Rather than use only inheritance to solve the problem of varying functionality, the Decorator pattern uses composition and delegation. In essence, Decorator classes hold an instance of another class of their own type. A Decorator will implement an operation so that it calls the same operation on the object to which it has a reference before (or after) performing its own actions. In this way it is possible to build a pipeline of decorator objects at runtime.

Let's rewrite our game example to illustrate this.

```
abstract class Tile {
    abstract function getWealthFactor();
}

class Plains extends Tile {
    private $wealthfactor = 2;
    function getWealthFactor() {
        return $this->wealthfactor;
    }
}

abstract class TileDecorator extends Tile {
    protected $tile;
    function __construct( Tile $tile ) {
        $this->tile = $tile;
    }
}
```

Here we have declared Tile and Plains classes as before, but introduced a new class: TileDecorator. This does not implement getWealthFactor(), so it must be declared abstract. We define a constructor that requires a Tile object, which it stores in a property called $tile. We make this property protected so that child classes can gain access to it. Let's redefine our Pollution and Diamond classes:

```
class DiamondDecorator extends TileDecorator {
    function getWealthFactor() {
        return $this->{tile}->getWealthFactor()+2;
    }
}

class PollutionDecorator extends TileDecorator {
    function getWealthFactor() {
        return $this->{tile}->getWealthFactor()-4;
    }
}
```

Each of these classes extends TileDecorator. This means that they have a reference to a Tile object. When getWealthFactor() is invoked, each of these classes invokes the same method on its Tile reference before making its own adjustment.

By using composition and delegation like this, we make it easy to combine objects at runtime. Because all the objects in the pattern extend Tile, the client does not need to know which combination it is working with. It can be sure that a getWealthFactor() method is available for any Tile object, whether it is decorating another behind the scenes or not.

```
$tile = new Plains();
print $tile->getWealthFactor(); // 2
// Plains is a component. It simply returns 2

$tile = new DiamondDecorator( new Plains );
print $tile->getWealthFactor(); // 4
// DiamondDecorator has a reference to a Plains object. It invokes
// getWealthFactor() before adding its own weighting of 2

$tile = new PollutionDecorator(
          new DiamondDecorator( new Plains() ));
print $tile->getWealthFactor(); // 0
// PollutionDecorator has a reference to a DiamondDecorator
// object which as its own Tile reference.
```

You can see the class diagram for this example in Figure 10-5.

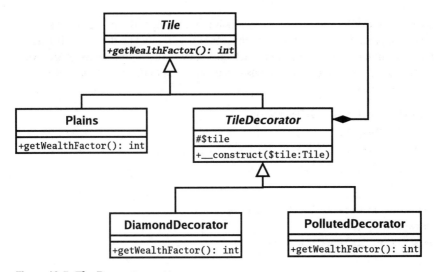

Figure 10-5. *The Decorator pattern*

This model is very extensible. We can add new decorators and components very easily. With lots of decorators we can build very flexible structures at runtime. The component class, Plains in this case, can be significantly modified in very many ways without the need to build the totality of the modifications into the class hierarchy. In plain English, this means we can have a polluted Plains object that has diamonds without having to create a PollutedDiamondPlains object.

The Decorator pattern builds up pipelines that are very useful for creating filters. The Java IO package makes great use of decorator classes. The client coder can combine decorator objects with core components to add filtering, buffering, compression, and so on to core methods like read(). Our Web request example can also be developed into a configurable pipeline. Here's a simple implementation that uses the Decorator pattern:

```
class RequestHelper{}

abstract class ProcessRequest {
    abstract function process( RequestHelper $req );
}

class MainProcess extends ProcessRequest {
    function process( RequestHelper $req ) {
        print __CLASS__.": doing something useful with request\n";
    }
}

abstract class DecorateProcess extends ProcessRequest {
    protected $processrequest;
    function __construct( ProcessRequest $pr ) {
        $this->processrequest = $pr;
    }
}
```

As before, we define an abstract super class (ProcessRequest), a concrete component (MainProcess), and an abstract decorator (DecorateProcess). MainProcess::process() does nothing but report that it has been called. DecorateProcess stores a ProcessRequest object on behalf of its children. Here are some simple concrete decorator classes:

```
class LogRequest extends DecorateProcess {
    function process( RequestHelper $req ) {
        print __CLASS__.": logging request\n";
        $this->processrequest->process( $req );
    }
}

class AuthenticateRequest extends DecorateProcess {
    function process( RequestHelper $req ) {
        print __CLASS__.": authenticating request\n";
        $this->processrequest->process( $req );
    }
}

class StructureRequest extends DecorateProcess {
    function process( RequestHelper $req ) {
        print __CLASS__.": structuring request data\n";
        $this->processrequest->process( $req );
    }
}
```

Each process() method outputs a message before calling the referenced ProcessRequest object's own process() method. We can now combine objects instantiated from these classes at runtime to build filters that perform different actions on a request and in different orders. Here's some code to combine objects from all these concrete classes into a single filter:

```
$process = new AuthenticateRequest( new StructureRequest(
                                    new LogRequest (
                                    new MainProcess()
                                    )));
$process->process( new RequestHelper() );
```

This code will give the following output:

```
AuthenticateRequest: authenticating request
StructureRequest: structuring request data
LogRequest: logging request
MainProcess: doing something useful with request
```

▓**Note** This example is, in fact, also an instance of an enterprise pattern called Intercepting Filter. Intercepting Filter is described in *Core J2EE Patterns*.

Consequences

Like the Composite pattern, Decorator can be confusing. It is important to remember that both composition and inheritance are coming into play at the same time. So LogRequest inherits its interface from ProcessRequest, but it is acting as a wrapper around another ProcessRequest object.

Because a decorator object forms a wrapper around a child object, it is important to keep the interface as sparse as possible. If we build a heavily featured base class, then decorators are forced to delegate to all public methods in their contained object. This can be done in the abstract decorator class, but still introduces the kind of coupling that can lead to bugs.

Some programmers create decorators that do not share a common type with the objects they modify. As long as they fulfill the same interface as these objects, this strategy can work well. You get the benefit of being able to use the built-in interceptor methods to automate delegation (implementing __call() to catch calls to nonexistent methods and invoking the same method on the child object automatically). However, by doing this you also lose the safety afforded by class type checking. In our examples so far, client code can demand a Tile or a ProcessRequest object in its argument list and be certain of its interface, whether or not the object in question is heavily decorated.

The Facade Pattern

You may have had occasion to stitch third-party systems into your own projects in the past. Whether or not the code is object-oriented, it will often be daunting, large, and complex. Your own code, too, may become a challenge to the client programmer who needs only to access a few features. The Facade pattern is a way of providing a simple, clear interface to complex systems.

The Problem

Systems tend to evolve large amounts of code that is really only useful within the system itself. Just as classes define clear public interfaces and hide their guts away from the rest of the world, so should discreet systems. However, it is not always clear which parts of a system are for public consumption and which are best hidden.

As you work with subsystems (like Web forums or gallery applications) you may find yourself making calls deep into the logic of the code. If the subsystem code is subject to change over time, and your code interacts with it at many different points, you may find yourself with a serious maintenance problem as the subsystem evolves.

Similarly, when you build your own systems, it is a good idea to organize distinct parts into separate tiers. Typically, you may have a tier responsible for application logic, another for database interaction, another for presentation, and so on. You should aspire to keep these tiers as independent of one another as you can, so that a change in one area of your project will have minimal repercussions elsewhere. If code from one tier is tightly integrated into code from another, then this objective is hard to meet.

Here is some deliberately confusing procedural code that makes a song-and-dance routine of the simple process of getting log information from a file and turning it into object data:

```php
function getProductFileLines( $file ) {
    return file( $file );
}

function getProductObjectFromId( $id, $productname ) {
    // some kind of database lookup
    return new Product( $id, $productname );
}

function getNameFromLine( $line ) {
    if ( preg_match( "/.*-(.*)\s\d+/", $line, $array ) ) {
        return str_replace( '_',' ', $array[1] );
    }
    return '';
}

function getIDFromLine( $line ) {
    if ( preg_match( "/^(\d{1,3})-/", $line, $array ) ) {
        return $array[1];
    }
    return -1;
}
```

```
class Product {
    public $id;
    public $name;
    function __construct( $id, $name ) {
        $this->id = $id;
        $this->name = $name;
    }
}
```

Let's imagine that the internals of this code are more complicated than they actually are, and that we are therefore stuck with using it rather than rewriting it from scratch. In order to turn a file that contains lines like

```
234-ladies_jumper 55
532-gents_hat 44
```

into an array of objects, we must call all of these functions (note that for the sake of brevity we don't extract the final number, which represents a price):

```
$lines = getProductFileLines( 'test.txt' );
$objects = array();
foreach ( $lines as $line ) {
    $id = getIDFromLine( $line );
    $name = getNameFromLine( $line );
    $objects[$id] = getProductObjectFromID( $id, $name  );
}
```

If we call these functions directly like this throughout our project, our code will become tightly wound into the subsystem it is using. This could cause problems if the subsystem changes, or if we decide to switch it out entirely. We really need to introduce a gateway between the system and the rest of our code.

Implementation

Here is a simple class that provides an interface to the procedural code we encountered in the previous section:

```
class ProductFacade {
    private $products = array();

    function __construct( $file ) {
        $this->file = $file;
        $this->compile();
    }
```

```
    private function compile() {
        $lines = getProductFileLines( $this->file );
        foreach ( $lines as $line ) {
            $id = getIDFromLine( $line );
            $name = getNameFromLine( $line );
            $this->products[$id] = getProductObjectFromID( $id, $name );
        }
    }

    function getProducts() {
        return $this->products;
    }

    function getProduct( $id ) {
        return $this->products[$id];
    }
}
```

From the point of view of client code, now access to Product objects from a log file is much simplified:

```
$facade = new ProductFacade( 'test.txt' );
$facade->getProduct( 234 );
```

Consequences

A Facade is really a very simple concept. It is just a matter of creating a single point of entry for a tier or subsystem. This has a number of benefits. It helps to decouple distinct areas in a project from one another. It is useful and convenient for client coders to have access to simple methods that achieve clear ends. It reduces errors by focusing use of a subsystem in one place so changes to the subsystem should cause failure in a predictable location. Errors are also minimized by Facade classes in complex subsystems where client code might otherwise use internal functions incorrectly.

Despite the simplicity of the Facade pattern, it is all too easy to forget to use it, especially if you are familiar with the subsystem you are working with. There is a balance to be struck, of course. On the one hand the benefit of creating simple interfaces to complex systems should be clear. On the other hand, one could abstract systems with reckless abandon, and then abstract the abstractions. If you are making significant simplifications for the clear benefit of client code, and/or shielding it from systems that might change, then you are probably right to implement the Facade pattern.

Summary

In this chapter, we looked at a few of the ways that classes and objects can be organized in a system. In particular, we focused on the principle that composition can be used to engender flexibility where inheritance fails. In both the Composite and Decorator patterns, inheritance is used to promote composition, and to define a common interface that provides guarantees for client code. We also saw delegation used effectively in these patterns. Finally, we looked at the simple but powerful Facade pattern. Facade is one of those patterns that many people have been using for years without having a name to give it. Facade lets us provide a clean point of entry to a tier or subsystem. In PHP, the Facade pattern is also used to create object wrappers that encapsulate blocks of procedural code.

CHAPTER 11

Performing and Representing Tasks

In this chapter, we get active. We look at patterns that help us to get things done, whether interpreting a mini-language or encapsulating an algorithm.

This chapter will cover

- *The Interpreter pattern*: Building a mini-language interpreter that can be used to create scriptable applications

- *The Strategy pattern*: Identifying algorithms in a system and encapsulating them into their own types

- *The Observer pattern*: Creating hooks for alerting disparate objects about system events

- *The Visitor pattern*: Applying an operation to all the nodes in a tree of objects

- *The Command pattern*: Command objects that can be saved and passed around

The Interpreter Pattern

Languages are written in other languages (at least at first). PHP itself, for example, is written in C. By the same token, odd as it may sound, we can define and run our own languages using PHP. Of course, any language we might create will be slow and somewhat limited. Nonetheless, mini-languages can be very useful, as we will see in this chapter.

When we create Web (or command line) interfaces in PHP, we give the user access to functionality. The trade-off in interface design is between power and ease of use. As a rule, the more power you give your user, the more cluttered and confusing your interface becomes. Good interface design can help a lot here, of course, but if 90 percent of users are using the same 30 percent of your features, the costs of piling on the functionality may outweigh the benefits. You may wish to consider simplifying your system for most users. But what of the power users, that 10 percent who use your system's advanced features? Perhaps you can accommodate them in a different way. By offering such users a domain language, you might actually extend the power of your application.

Of course, we have a programming language to hand right away. It's called PHP. Here's how we could allow our users to script our system:

```
$form_input = "print file_get_contents('/etc/passwd');";
eval( $form_input );
```

This approach to making an application scriptable is clearly insane. Just in case the reasons are not blatantly obvious, they boil down to two issues: security and complexity. The security issue is well addressed in our example. By allowing users to execute PHP via our script, we are effectively giving them access to the server the script runs on. The complexity issue is just as big a drawback. No matter how clear your code is, the average user is unlikely to extend it easily, and certainly not from the browser window.

A mini-language, though, can address both these problems. You can design flexibility into the language, reduce the possibility that the user can do damage, and keep things focused.

Imagine an application for authoring quizzes. Producers design questions and establish rules for marking the answers submitted by contestants. It is a requirement that quizzes must be marked without human intervention, even though some answers can be typed into a text field by users.

Here's a question:

```
How many members in the Design Patterns gang?
```

We can accept "four" or "4" as correct answers. We might create a Web interface that allows a producer to use regular expression for marking responses:

```
^4|four$
```

Most producers are not hired for their knowledge of regular expressions, however. To make everyone's life easier, we might implement a more user-friendly mechanism for marking responses:

```
$input equals "4" or $input equals "four"
```

We propose a language that supports variables, an operator called equals and Boolean logic (or and and). Programmers love naming things, so let's call it MarkLogic. It should be easy to extend, as we envisage lots of requests for richer features. Let's leave aside the issue of parsing input for now and concentrate on a mechanism for plugging these elements together at runtime to produce an answer. This, as you might expect, is where the Interpreter pattern comes in.

Implementation

Our language is made up of expressions (that is, things that resolve to a value). As you can see in Table 11-1, even a tiny language like MarkLogic needs to keep track of a lot of elements.

Table 11-1. *Elements of the MarkLogic Grammar*

Description	EBNF Name	Class Name	Example
Variable	variable	VariableExpression	*$input*
String literal	<stringLiteral>	LiteralExpression	*"four"*
Boolean and	andExpr	BooleanAndExpression	$input equals '4' *and* $other equals '6'
Boolean or	orExpr	BooleanOrExpression	$input equals '4' *or* $other equals '6'
Equality test	equalsExpr	EqualsExpression	$input *equals* '4'

Table 11-1 lists EBNF names. So what is EBNF all about? It's a notation that we can use to describe a language grammar. EBNF stands for Extended Backus-Naur Form. It consists of a series of lines (called productions), each one consisting of a name, and a description that takes the form of references to other productions and to terminals (that is, elements that are not themselves made up of references to other productions). Here is one way of describing our grammar using EBNF:

```
expr     ::= operand (orExpr | andExpr )*
operand  ::= ( '(' expr ')' | <stringLiteral> | variable ) ( eqExpr )*
orExpr   ::= 'or' operand
andExpr  ::= 'and' operand
eqExpr   ::= 'equals' operand
variable ::= '$' <word>
```

Some symbols have special meanings (that should be familiar from regular expression notation): * means zero or more, for example, and | means "or." We can group elements using brackets. So in the example, an expression (expr) consists of an operand followed by zero or more of either orExpr, andExpr, or eqExpr. An operand can be a bracketed expression, a quoted string (I have omitted the production for this), or a variable. Once you get the hang of referring from one production to another, EBNF becomes quite easy to read.

In Figure 11-1, we represent the elements of our grammar as classes.

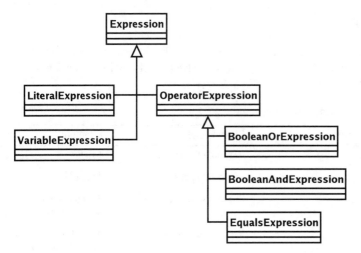

Figure 11-1. *The Interpreter classes that make up the MarkLogic language*

As you can see, BooleanAndExpression and its siblings inherit from OperatorExpression. This is because these classes all perform their operations upon other Expression objects. VariableExpression and LiteralExpression work directly with values.

All Expression objects implement an interpret() method that is defined in the abstract base class, Expression. The interpret() method expects a Context object that is used as a shared data store. Each Expression object can store data in the Context object. The Context will then be passed along to other Expression objects. So that data can be retrieved easily from the Context, the Expression base class implements a getKey() method that returns a unique handle. Let's see how this works in practice with an implementation of Expression:

```
abstract class Expression {
    abstract function interpret( Context $context );

    function getKey() {
        return (string)$this;
    }
}

class LiteralExpression extends Expression {
    private $value;

    function __construct( $value ) {
        $this->value = $value;
    }

    function interpret( Context $context ) {
        $context->replace( $this, $this->value );
    }
}
```

```
class Context {
    private $expressionstore = array();
    function replace( Expression $exp, $value ) {
        $this->expressionstore[$exp->getKey()] = $value;
    }

    function lookup( Expression $exp ) {
        return $this->expressionstore[$exp->getKey()];
    }
}

$context = new Context();
$literal = new LiteralExpression( 'four');
$literal->interpret( $context );
print $context->lookup( $literal );
```

Let's start with the Context class. As you can see, it is really only a front end for an associative array, $expressionstore, which we use to hold data. The replace() method accepts an Expression object as key and a value of any type, and adds the pair to $expressionstore. It also provides a lookup() method for retrieving data.

The Expression class defines the abstract interpret() method and a concrete getKey() method that uses the current object (as stored in $this) to generate a label. We do this by casting $this to a string. The default behavior for an object in string context is for it to be replaced with a string containing the object's identifier.

```
class PrintMe{}
$test = new PrintMe();
print "$test";

// output: Object id #1
```

The getKey() method makes good use of this behavior to generate a key. This method is used by Context::lookup() and Context::replace() to convert their Expression arguments to their string equivalents.

Note Casting objects to strings for use as associative array keys is useful, but may not always be safe. At the time of writing, PHP 5 will always generate an object ID string when an object is cast to a string. It seems likely that at some time in the future the engine will respect the __toString() method in this context. This would mean that you would no longer be guaranteed a unique string from an object to string cast if you also implement __toString(). The return value from __toString() would be substituted instead. One way around this problem might be to implement a __toString() method that enforces the default behavior and declare it final to prevent child classes from providing their own implementation:

```
final function __toString() {
    return (string)$this;
}
```

The LiteralExpression class defines a constructor that accepts a value argument. The interpret() method requires a Context object. We simply call replace(), using getKey() to define the key for retrieval and the $value property. This will become a familiar pattern as we examine the other expression classes. The interpret() method always inscribes its results upon the Context object.

We include some client code as well, instantiating both a Context object and a LiteralExpression object (with a value of "four"). We pass the Context object to LiteralExpression::interpret(). The interpret() method stores the key/value pair in Context, from where we retrieve the value by calling lookup().

Let's define the remaining terminal class. VariableExpression is a little more complicated.

```
class VariableExpression extends Expression {
    private $name;
    private $val;

    function __construct( $name, $val=null ) {
        $this->name = $name;
        $this->val = $val;
    }

    function interpret( Context $context ) {
        if ( ! is_null( $this->val ) ) {
            $context->replace( $this, $this->val );
            $this->val = null;
        }
    }

    function setValue( $value ) {
        $this->val = $value;
    }

    function getKey() {
        return $this->name;
    }
}
$context = new Context();
$myvar = new VariableExpression( 'input', 'four' );
$myvar->interpret( $context );
print $context->lookup( $myvar );
// output: four

$newvar = new VariableExpression( 'input' );
$newvar->interpret( $context );
print $context->lookup( $newvar );
// output: four
```

```
$myvar->setValue("five");
$myvar->interpret( $context );
print $context->lookup( $myvar );
// output: five
print $context->lookup( $newvar );
// output: five
```

The VariableExpression class accepts both name and value arguments for storage in property variables. We provide the setValue() method so that client code can change the value at any time.

The interpret() method checks whether or not the $val property has a nonnull value. If the $val property has a value, it sets it on the Context. We then set the $val property to null in case interpret() is called again later after another instance of VariableExpression with the same name has changed the value in the context. This is quite a limited variable, accepting only string values as it does. If we were going to extend our language, we should consider having it work with other Expression objects, so that it could contain the results of tests and operations. For now, though, VariableExpression will do the work we need of it. Notice that we have overridden the getKey() method so that variable values are linked to the variable name and not to the object ID.

Operator expressions in our language all work with two other Expression objects in order to get their job done. It makes sense therefore to have them extend a common super class. Here is the OperatorExpression class:

```
abstract class OperatorExpression extends Expression {
    protected $l_op;
    protected $r_op;

    function __construct( Expression $l_op, Expression $r_op ) {
        $this->l_op = $l_op;
        $this->r_op = $r_op;
    }

    function interpret( Context $context ) {
        $this->l_op->interpret( $context );
        $this->r_op->interpret( $context );
        $result_l = $context->lookup( $this->l_op );
        $result_r = $context->lookup( $this->r_op );
        $this->doOperation( $context, $result_l, $result_r );
    }

    protected abstract function doOperation( Context $context,
                                             $result_l,
                                             $result_r );

}
```

OperatorExpression is an abstract class. It implements interpret(), but it also defines the abstract doInterpret() method.

The constructor demands two Expression objects, $l_op and $r_op, which it stores in properties.

The interpret() method begins by invoking interpret() on both its operand properties. (If you have read the previous chapter, you might notice that we are creating an instance of the Composite pattern here.) Once the operands have been run, interpret() still needs to acquire the values that this yields. It does this by calling Context::lookup() for each property. It then calls doInterpret(), leaving it up to child classes to decide what to do with the results of these operations.

Here's the EqualsExpression class, which tests two Expression objects for equality:

```
class EqualsExpression extends OperatorExpression {
    protected function doOperation( Context $context,
                                    $result_l, $result_r ) {
        $context->replace( $this, $result_l == $result_r );
    }
}
```

EqualsExpression only implements the doInterpret() method, which tests the equality of the operand results it has been passed by the interpret() method, placing the result in the Context object.

To wrap up the Expression classes, here are BooleanOrExpression and BooleanAndExpression:

```
class BooleanOrExpression extends OperatorExpression {
    protected function doOperation( Context $context,
                                    $result_l, $result_r ) {
        $context->replace( $this, $result_l || $result_r );
    }
}

class BooleanAndExpression extends OperatorExpression {
    protected function doOperation( Context $context,
                                    $result_l, $result_r ) {
        $context->replace( $this, $result_l && $result_r );
    }
}
```

Instead of testing for equality, the BooleanOrExpression class applies a logical or operation and stores the result of that via the Context::replace() method. BooleanAndExpression, of course, applies a logical and operation.

We now have enough code to execute the mini-language fragment we quoted earlier. Here it is again:

```
$input equals "4" or $input equals "four"
```

Here's how we can build this statement up with our Expression classes:

```
$context = new Context();
$input = new VariableExpression( 'input' );
$statement = new BooleanOrExpression(
    new EqualsExpression( $input, new LiteralExpression( 'four' ) ),
    new EqualsExpression( $input, new LiteralExpression( '4' ) )
);
```

We instantiate a variable called 'input', but hold off from providing a value for it. We then create a BooleanOrExpression object that will compare the results from two EqualsExpression objects. The first of these objects compares the VariableExpression object stored in $input with a LiteralExpression containing the string "four", the second compares $input with a LiteralExpression object containing the string "4".

Now with our statement prepared, we are ready to provide a value for the input variable, and run the code:

```
foreach ( array( "four", "4", "52" ) as $val ) {
    $input->setValue( $val );
    print "$val:\n";
    $statement->interpret( $context );
    if ( $context->lookup( $statement ) ) {
        print "top marks\n\n";
    } else {
        print "dunce hat on\n\n";
    }
}
```

In fact, we run the code three times, with three different values. First time through we set the temporary variable $val to "four", assigning it to the input VariableExpression object using its setValue() method. We then call interpret() on our topmost Expression object (the BooleanOrExpression object that contains references to all other expressions in the statement). Let's step through the internals of this invocation:

- $statement calls interpret() on its $l_op property (the first EqualsExpression object).

- The first EqualsExpression object calls interpret() on *its* $l_op property (a reference to the input VariableExpression object which is currently set to "four").

- The input VariableExpression object writes its current value to the provided Context object by calling Context::replace().

- The first EqualsExpression object calls interpret() on its $r_op property (a LiteralExpression object charged with the value "four").

- The LiteralExpression object registers its key and its value with Context.

- The first EqualsExpression object retrieves the values for $l_op ("four") and $r_op ("four") from the Context object.

- The first EqualsExpression object compares these two values for equality and registers the result (true) together with its key with the Context object.

- Back at the top of the tree the $statement object (BooleanOrExpression) calls interpret() on its $r_op property. This resolves to a value (false, in this case) in the same way as the $l_op property did.

- The $statement object retrieves values for each of its operands from the Context object and compares them using ||. It is comparing true and false, so the result is true. This final result is stored in the Context object.

And all that is only for the first iteration through our loop. Here is our final output:

```
four:
top marks

4:
top marks

52:
dunce hat on
```

You may need to read through this section a few times before the process clicks. The old issue of object versus class trees might confuse you here. Expression classes are arranged in an inheritance hierarchy just as Expression objects are composed into a tree at runtime. As you read back through the code, keep this distinction in mind.

Figure 11-2 shows the complete class diagram for our example.

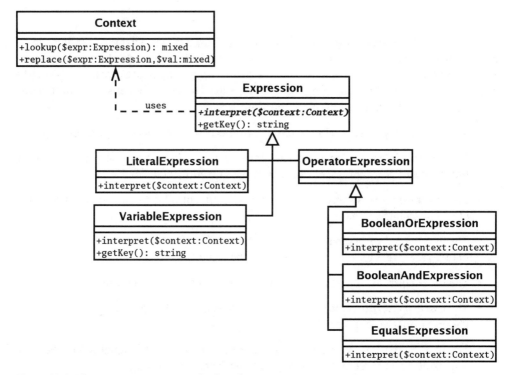

Figure 11-2. *The Interpreter pattern deployed*

Interpreter Issues

Once you have set up the core classes for an Interpreter pattern implementation, it becomes easy to extend. The price you pay is in the sheer number of classes you could end up creating. For this reason, Interpreter is best applied to relatively small languages. If you have a need for a full programming language, you would do better to look for a third-party tool to use.

Because Interpreter classes often perform very similar tasks, it is worth keeping an eye on the classes you create with a view to factoring out duplication.

Many people approaching the Interpreter pattern for the first time are disappointed after some initial excitement to discover that it does not address parsing. This means that we are not yet in a position to offer our users a nice friendly language. Appendix B contains some rough code to illustrate one strategy for parsing a mini-language.

The Strategy Pattern

Classes often try to do too much. It's understandable: you create a class that performs a few related actions. As you code, some of these actions need to be varied according to circumstances. At the same time, your class needs to be split into subclasses. Before you know it, your design is being pulled apart by competing forces.

The Problem

Since we have recently built a marking language, let's stick with the quiz example. Quizzes need questions, so we build a Question class, giving it a mark() method. All is well until we need to support different marking mechanisms.

Let's say that we are asked to support the simple MarkLogic language, marking by straight match and marking by regular expression. Your first thought might be to subclass for these differences, as in Figure 11-3.

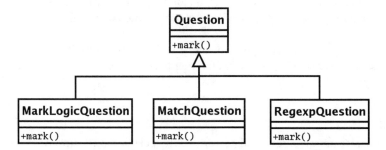

Figure 11-3. *Defining subclasses according to marking strategies*

This would serve us well as long as marking remains the only aspect of the class that varies. Imagine, though, that we are called upon to support different kinds of question: those that are text based and those that support rich media. This presents us with a problem when it comes to incorporating these forces in one inheritance tree as you can see in Figure 11-4.

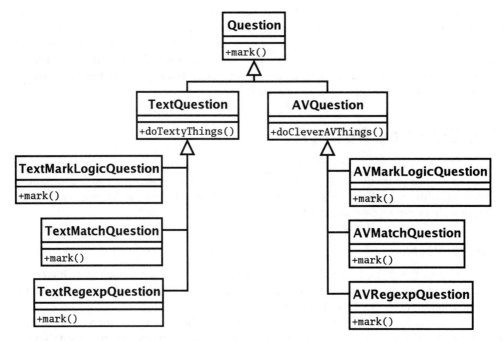

Figure 11-4. *Defining subclasses according to two forces*

Not only have the number of classes in the hierarchy ballooned, but we also necessarily introduce repetition. Our marking logic is reproduced across each branch of the inheritance hierarchy.

Whenever you find yourself repeating an algorithm across siblings in an inheritance tree (whether through subclassing or repeated conditional statements), consider abstracting these behaviors into their own type.

Implementation

As with all the best patterns, Strategy is simple and powerful. When classes must support multiple implementations of an interface (multiple marking mechanisms, for example), the best approach is often to extract these implementations and place them in their own type, rather than to extend the original class to handle them.

So, in our example, our approach to marking might be placed in a Marker type. Figure 11-5 shows the new structure.

Remember the Gang of Four principle "Favor composition over inheritance"? This is an excellent example. By defining and encapsulating the marking algorithms, we reduce subclassing and increase flexibility. We can add new marking strategies at any time without the need to change the Question classes at all. All Question classes know is that they have an instance of a Marker at their disposal, and that it is guaranteed by its interface to support a mark() method. The details of implementation are entirely somebody else's problem.

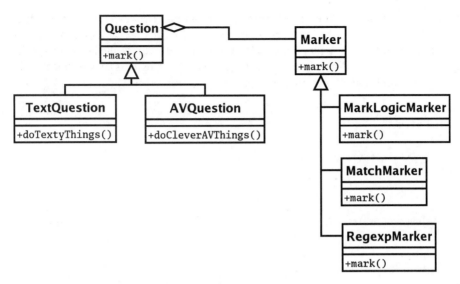

Figure 11-5. *Extracting algorithms into their own type*

Here are the Question classes rendered as code:

```
abstract class Question {
    protected $prompt;
    protected $marker;

    function __construct( $prompt, Marker $marker ) {
        $this->marker=$marker;
        $this->prompt = $prompt;
    }

    function mark( $response ) {
        return $this->marker->mark( $response );
    }
}

class TextQuestion extends Question {
    // do text question specific things
}

class AVQuestion extends Question {
    // do audiovisual question specific things
}
```

As you can see, we have left the exact nature of the difference between TextQuestion and AVQuestion to the imagination. The Question base class provides all the real functionality, storing a prompt property and a Marker object. When Question::mark() is called with a response from the end user, the method simply delegates the problem solving to its Marker object.

Let's define some simple Marker objects:

```
abstract class Marker {
    protected $test;

    function __construct( $test ) {
        $this->test = $test;
    }

    abstract function mark( $response );
}

class MarkLogicMarker extends Marker {
    private $engine;
    function __construct( $test ) {
        parent::__construct( $test );
        //$this->engine = new MarkParse( $test );
    }

    function mark( $response ) {
        //return $this->engine->evaluate( $response );
        // dummy return value
        return true;
    }
}
class MatchMarker extends Marker {
    function mark( $response ) {
        return ( $this->test == $response );
    }
}

class RegexpMarker extends Marker {
    function mark( $response ) {
        return ( preg_match( $this->test, $response ) );
    }
}
```

There should be little if anything that is particularly surprising about the Marker classes themselves. Note that the MarkParse object is designed to work with the simple parser developed in Appendix B. This isn't necessary for the sake of this example though, so we simply return a dummy value of true from MarkLogicMarker::mark().The key here is in the structure that we have defined, rather than in the detail of the strategies themselves. We can swap RegexpMarker for MatchMarker, with no impact on the Question class.

Of course, you must still decide what method to use to choose between concrete Marker objects. I have seen two real-world approaches to this problem. In the first, producers used radio buttons to select the marking strategy they preferred. In the second, the structure of the marking condition was itself used: a match statement was left plain:

```
five
```

A MarkLogic statement was preceded by a colon:

```
:$input equals 'five'
```

And a regular expression used forward slashes:

```
/f.ve/
```

Here is some code to run our classes through their paces:

```
$markers = array(   new RegexpMarker( "/f.ve/" ),
                    new MatchMarker( "five" ),
                    new MarkLogicMarker( '$input equals "five"' )
        );

foreach ( $markers as $marker ) {
    print get_class( $marker )."\n";
    $question = new TextQuestion( "how many beans make five", $marker );
    foreach ( array( "five", "four" ) as $response ) {
        print "\tresponse: $response: ";
        if ( $question->mark( $response ) ) {
            print "well done\n";
        } else {
            print "never mind\n";
        }
    }
}
```

We construct three strategy objects, using each in turn to help construct a TextQuestion object. The TextQuestion object is then tried against two sample responses.

The MarkLogicMarker class shown here is a placeholder at present, and its mark() method always returns true. The commented out code does work, however, with the parser example shown in Appendix B, or could be made to work with a third-party parser.

Here is the output:

```
RegexpMarker
        response: five: well done
        response: four: never mind
MatchMarker
        response: five: well done
        response: four: never mind
MarkLogicMarker
        response: five: well done
        response: four: well done
```

Remember that the MarkLogicMarker class is a dummy at present. It always returns true, so always marks the user correct.

In our example, we passed specific data (the $response variable) from the client to the strategy object via the mark() method. Sometimes you may encounter circumstances in which you don't always know in advance how much information the strategy object will require when its operation is invoked. You can delegate the decision as to what data to acquire by passing the strategy an instance of the client itself. The strategy can then query the client in order to build the data it needs.

The Observer Pattern

Orthogonality is a virtue we have discussed before. One of our objectives as programmers should be to build components that can be altered or moved with minimal impact upon other components. If every change you make to one component necessitates a ripple of changes elsewhere in the codebase, the task of development can quickly become a spiral of bug creation and elimination.

Of course, orthogonality is often just a dream. Elements in a system must have embedded references to other elements. You can, however, deploy various strategies to minimize this. We have seen various examples of polymorphism in which the client understands a component's interface but where the actual component may vary at runtime.

In some circumstances, you may wish to drive an even greater wedge between components than this. Consider a class responsible for handling a user's access to a system.

```
class Login {
    const LOGIN_USER_UNKNOWN = 1;
    const LOGIN_WRONG_PASS = 2;
    const LOGIN_ACCESS = 3;
    private $status = array();

    function handleLogin( $user, $pass, $ip ) {
        switch ( rand(1,3) ) {
            case 1:
                $this->setStatus( self::LOGIN_ACCESS, $user, $ip );
                $ret = true; break;
            case 2:
                $this->setStatus( self::LOGIN_WRONG_PASS, $user, $ip );
                $ret = false; break;
            case 3:
                $this->setStatus( self::LOGIN_USER_UNKNOWN, $user, $ip );
                $ret = false; break;
        }
        return $ret;
    }
```

```
    private function setStatus( $status, $user, $ip ) {
        $this->status = array( $status, $user, $ip );
    }
    function getStatus() {
        return $this->status;
    }


}
```

This class fakes the login process using the rand() function. There are three potential outcomes of a call to handleLogin(). The status flag may be set to LOGIN_ACCESS, LOGIN_WRONG_PASS, or LOGIN_USER_UNKNOWN.

Because the Login class is a gateway guarding the treasures of your business team, it may excite much interest during development and in the months beyond. Marketing might call you up and ask that you keep a log of domain names. You can add a call to your system's Logger class:

```
    function handleLogin( $user, $pass, $ip ) {
        switch ( rand(1,3) ) {
            case 1:
                $this->setStatus( self::LOGIN_ACCESS, $user, $ip );
                $ret = true; break;
            case 2:
                $this->setStatus( self::LOGIN_WRONG_PASS, $user, $ip );
                $ret = false; break;
            case 3:
                $this->setStatus( self::LOGIN_USER_UNKNOWN, $user, $ip );
                $ret = false; break;
        }
        Logger::logIP( $user, $ip, $this->getStatus() );
        return $ret;
    }
```

Worried about security, the system administrators might ask for notification of failed logins. Once again, you can return to the login method and add a new call.

```
    if ( ! $ret ) {
        Notifier::mailWarning( $user, $ip,
                                $this->getStatus()  );
    }
```

The business development team might announce a tie-in with a particular ISP and ask that a cookie be set when particular users log in. And so on. And on.

These are all easy enough requests to fulfill, but at a cost to our design. The Login class soon becomes very tightly embedded into this particular system. We cannot pull it out and drop it into another product without going through the code line by line and removing everything that is specific to the old system. This isn't too hard, of course, but then we are off down the road of cut'n'paste coding. Now that we have two similar but distinct Login classes in our systems, we find that an improvement to one will necessitate the same changes in the other, until inevitably and gracelessly they fall out of alignment with one another.

So what can we do to save the Login class? The Observer pattern is a powerful fit here.

Implementation

At the core of the Observer pattern is the unhooking of client elements (the observers) from a central class (the subject). Observers need to be informed when events occur that the subject knows about. At the same time, we do not want the subject to have a hard-coded relationship with its observer classes.

To achieve this, we can allow observers to register themselves with the subject. We give the Login class three new methods, attach(), detach(), and notify(), enforcing this using an interface called Observable.

```
interface Observable {
    function attach( Observer $observer );
    function detach( Observer $observer );
    function notify();
}

// ... Login class
    private $observers;
    //...
    function attach( Observer $observer ) {
        $this->observers[] = $observer;
    }

    function detach( Observer $observer ) {
        $this->observers =
            array_diff( $this->observers, array($observer) );
    }

    function notify() {
        foreach ( $this->observers as $obs ) {
            $obs->update( $this );
        }
    }
}
//...
```

So the Login class manages a list of observer objects. These can be added by a third party using the attach() method, and removed via detach(). The notify() method is called to tell the observers that something of interest has happened. The method simply loops through the list of observers, calling update() on each one.

The Login class itself calls notify() from its handleLogin() method.

```
function handleLogin( $user, $pass, $ip ) {
    switch ( rand(1,3) ) {
        case 1:
            $this->setStatus( self::LOGIN_ACCESS, $user, $ip );
            $ret = true; break;
        case 2:
            $this->setStatus( self::LOGIN_WRONG_PASS, $user, $ip );
            $ret = false; break;
```

```
        case 3:
            $this->setStatus( self::LOGIN_USER_UNKNOWN, $user, $ip );
            $ret = false; break;
    }
    $this->notify();
    return $ret;
}
```

Let's define the interface for the Observer class:

```
interface Observer {
    function update( Observable $observable );
}
```

Any object that uses this interface can be added to the Login class via the attach() method. Let's create a few concrete instances:

```
class SecurityMonitor extends Observer {
    function update( Observable $observable ) {
        $status = $observable->getStatus();
        if ( $status[0] == Login::LOGIN_WRONG_PASS ) {
            // send mail to sysadmin
            print __CLASS__.":\tsending mail to sysadmin\n";
        }
    }
}

class GeneralLogger extends Observer {
    function update( Observable $observable ) {
        $status = $observable->getStatus();
        // add login data to log
        print __CLASS__.":\tadd login data to log\n";
    }
}

class PartnershipTool extends Observer {
    function update( Observable $observable ) {
        $status = $observable->getStatus();
        // check $ip address
        // set cookie if it matches a list
        print __CLASS__.":\tset cookie if it matches a list\n";
    }
}
```

Notice how the observer objects use the instance of Observable to get more information about the event. It is up to the subject class to provide methods that observers can query to learn about state. In this case, we have defined a method called getStatus() that observers can call to get a snapshot of the current state of play.

Instances of any classes that implement Observable can be registered with Login.

```
$login = new Login();
$login->attach( new SecurityMonitor() );
$login->attach( new GeneralLogger() );
$login->attach( new PartnershipTool() );
```

So now we have created a flexible association between the subject classes and the observers. You can see the class diagram for our example in Figure 11-6.

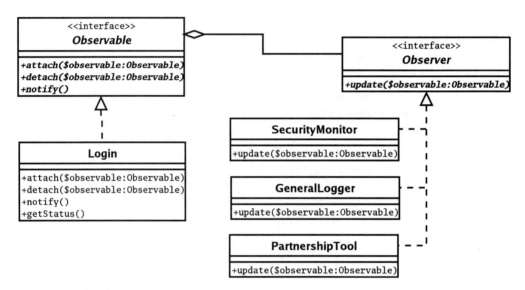

Figure 11-6. *The Observer pattern*

We have seen most of the parts of our Observer pattern example. For the sake of clarity, here is the whole lot in one listing:

```
interface Observable {
    function attach( Observer $observer );
    function detach( Observer $observer );
    function notify();
}

class Login implements Observable {
    private $observers = array();
    const LOGIN_USER_UNKNOWN = 1;
    const LOGIN_WRONG_PASS   = 2;
    const LOGIN_ACCESS       = 3;
    private $status = array();
```

```php
    function attach( Observer $observer ) {
        $this->observers[] = $observer;
    }

    function detach( Observer $observer ) {
        $this->observers = array_diff( $this->observers, array($observer) );
    }

    function notify() {
        foreach ( $this->observers as $obs ) {
            $obs->update( $this );
        }
    }

    function handleLogin( $user, $pass, $ip ) {
        switch ( rand(1,3) ) {
            case 1:
                $this->setStatus( self::LOGIN_ACCESS, $user, $ip );
                $ret = true; break;
            case 2:
                $this->setStatus( self::LOGIN_WRONG_PASS, $user, $ip );
                $ret = false; break;
            case 3:
                $this->setStatus( self::LOGIN_USER_UNKNOWN, $user, $ip );
                $ret = false; break;
        }
        $this->notify();
        return $ret;
    }

    private function setStatus( $status, $user, $ip ) {
        $this->status = array( $status, $user, $ip );
    }

    function getStatus() {
        return $this->status;
    }

}

interface Observer {
    function update( Observable $observer );
}
```

```
class SecurityMonitor extends Observer {
    function update( Observable $observable ) {
        $status = $observable->getStatus();
        if ( $status[0] == Login::LOGIN_WRONG_PASS ) {
            // send mail to sysadmin
            print __CLASS__.":\tsending mail to sysadmin\n";
        }
    }
}

class GeneralLogger extends Observer {
    function update( Observable $observable ) {
        $status = $observable->getStatus();
        // add login data to log
        print __CLASS__.":\tadd login data to log\n";
    }
}

class PartnershipTool extends Observer {
    function update( Observable $observable ) {
        $status = $observable->getStatus();
        // check $ip address
        // set cookie if it matches a list
        print __CLASS__.":\tset cookie if it matches a list\n";
    }
}
```

There are, of course, some variations and issues relating to this pattern. Firstly, the state method (getStatus()) is not inscribed in the Observable interface. This means that Observable is extremely flexible, but it also loses us a measure of type safety. What would happen if one of the observer objects that uses getStatus() found itself attached to an Observable class that did implement such a method? Well, we know what would happen.

As always, there is a trade-off. Omitting the specifics of state data retrieval from the Observable interface makes it flexible, but allows some risk that the wrong Observer may attach to the wrong Observable. Adding getStatus() to the Observable interface, on the other hand, is safe but might be limiting. Some Observable classes may need to provide several status methods, for example.

Another approach to this problem could be to pass specific state information via the update() method, rather than an instance of the subject class. For a quick-and-dirty solution, this is often the approach I would take initially. So in our example, update() would expect a status flag, the username, and IP address (probably in an array for portability), rather than an instance of Login. This saves us from having to write a state method in the Login class. On the other hand, where the subject class stores a lot of state, passing an instance of it to update() allows observers much more flexibility.

You could also lock down type completely, by making the Login class refuse to work with anything other than a specific type of observer class (LoginObserver perhaps). If you want to do that, then you may consider some kind of runtime check on objects passed to the attach() method; otherwise, you may need to reconsider the Observable interface altogether.

Once again we have used composition at runtime to build a flexible and extensible model. The Login class can be extracted from the context and dropped into an entirely different project without qualification. There, it might work with a different set of observers.

The Visitor Pattern

As we have seen, many patterns aim to build structures at runtime, following the principle that composition is more flexible than inheritance. The ubiquitous Composite pattern is an excellent example of this. When you work with collections of objects, you may need to apply various operations to the structure that involve working with each individual component. Such operations can be built into the components themselves. After all, components are often best placed to invoke one another.

This approach is not without issues. You do not always know about all the operations you may need to perform on a structure. If you add support for new operations to your classes on a case-by-case basis, you can bloat your interface with responsibilities that don't really fit. As you might guess, the Visitor pattern addresses these issues.

The Problem

Think back to the Composite example from the previous chapter. For a game, we created an army of components such that the whole and its parts can be treated interchangeably. We saw that operations can be built into components. Typically, leaf objects perform an operation and composite objects call upon their children to perform the operation.

```
class Army extends CompositeUnit {

    function bombardStrength() {
        $ret = 0;
        foreach( $this->units() as $unit ) {
            $ret += $unit->bombardStrength();
        }
        return $ret;
    }
}
class LaserCanonUnit extends Unit {
    function bombardStrength() {
        return 44;
    }
}
```

Where the operation is integral to the responsibility of the composite class, there is no problem. There are more peripheral tasks, however, that may not sit so happily on the interface.

Here's an operation that dumps textual information about leaf nodes. It could be added to the abstract Unit class.

```
// Unit
function textDump( $num=0 ) {
    $ret = "";
    $pad = 4*$num;
    $ret .= sprintf( "%{$pad}s", "" );
    $ret .= get_class($this).": ";
    $ret .= "bombard: ".$this->bombardStrength()."\n";
    return $ret;
}
```

This method can then be overridden in the CompositeUnit class:

```
// CompositeUnit
    function textDump( $num=0 ) {
    $ret = "";
    $pad = 4*$num;
    $ret .= sprintf( "%{$pad}s", "" );
    $ret .= get_class($this).": ";
    $ret .= "bombard: ".$this->bombardStrength()."\n";
    foreach ( $this->units as $unit ) {
        $ret .= $unit->textDump( $num + 1 );
    }
    return $ret;
}
```

We could go on to create methods for counting the number of units in the tree, for saving components to a database, and for calculating the food units consumed by an army.

Why would we want to include these methods in the composite's interface? There is only one really compelling answer. We include these disparate operations here because this is where an operation can gain easy access to related nodes in the composite structure.

Although it is true that ease of traversal is part of the Composite pattern, it does not follow that every operation that needs to traverse the tree should therefore claim a place in the Composite's interface.

So these are the forces at work. We want to take full advantage of the easy traversal afforded by our object structure, but we want to do this without bloating the interface.

Implementation

Let's start with our interfaces. In the abstract Unit class we define an accept() method.

```
function accept( ArmyVisitor $visitor ) {
    $method = "visit".get_class( $this );
    $visitor->$method( $this );
}
```

As you can see, the accept() method expects an ArmyVisitor object to be passed to it. PHP allows us dynamically to define the method on the ArmyVisitor we wish to call. This saves us from implementing accept() on every leaf node in our class hierarchy. The only other accept() method we need to define is in the abstract composite class.

```
function accept( ArmyVisitor $visitor ) {
    $method = "visit".get_class( $this );
    $visitor->$method( $this );
    foreach ( $this->units as $thisunit ) {
        $thisunit->accept( $visitor );
    }
}
```

This method does the same as Unit::accept(), with one addition. It constructs a method name based on the name of the current class, and invokes that method on the provided ArmyVisitor object. So if the current class is Army, then it invokes ArmyVisitor::visitArmy(), and if the current class is TroopCarrier, it invokes ArmyVisitor::visitTroopCarrier(), and so on. Having done this, it then loops through any child objects calling accept(). In fact, because accept() overrides its parent operation, we could factor out the repetition here:

```
function accept( ArmyVisitor $visitor ) {
    parent::accept( $visitor );
    foreach ( $this->units as $thisunit ) {
        $thisunit->accept( $visitor );
    }
}
```

Eliminating repetition in this way can be very satisfying, though in this case we have saved only one line, arguably at some cost to clarity. In either case, the accept() method allows us to do two things:

- Invoke the correct visitor method for the current component.

- Pass the visitor object to all the current element children via the accept() method (assuming the current component is composite).

We have yet to define the interface for ArmyVisitor. The accept() methods should give you some clue. The visitor class should define accept() methods for each of the concrete classes in the class hierarchy. This allows us to provide different functionality for different objects. In my version of this class, I also define a default visit() method that is automatically called if implementing classes choose not to provide specific handling for particular Unit classes.

```
abstract class ArmyVisitor  {
    abstract function visit( Unit $node );

    function visitArcher( Archer $node ) {
        $this->visit( $node );
    }
    function visitCavalry( Cavalry $node ) {
        $this->visit( $node );
    }

    function visitLaserCanonUnit( LaserCanonUnit $node ) {
        $this->visit( $node );
    }
```

```
    function visitTroopCarrierUnit( TroopCarrierUnit $node ) {
        $this->visit( $node );
    }

    function visitArmy( Army $node ) {
        $this->visit( $node );
    }
}
```

So now it's just a matter of providing implementations of ArmyVisitor, and we are ready to go. Here is our simple text dump code reimplemented as an ArmyVisitor object:

```
class TextDumpArmyVisitor extends ArmyVisitor {
    private $text="";

    function visit( Unit $node ) {
        $ret = "";
        $pad = 4*$node->getDepth();
        $ret .= sprintf( "%{$pad}s", "" );
        $ret .= get_class($node).": ";
        $ret .= "bombard: ".$node->bombardStrength()."\n";
        $this->text .= $ret;
    }
    function getText() {
        return $this->text;
    }
}
```

Let's look at some client code, and then walk through the whole process:

```
$main_army = new Army();
$main_army->addUnit( new Archer() );
$main_army->addUnit( new LaserCanonUnit() );
$main_army->addUnit( new Cavalry() );

$textdump = new TextDumpArmyVisitor();
$main_army->accept( $textdump  );
print $textdump->getText();
```

This code yields the following output:

```
Army: bombard: 50
    Archer: bombard: 4
    LaserCanonUnit: bombard: 44
    Cavalry: bombard: 2
```

We create an Army object. Because Army is composite, it has an addUnit() method that we use to add some more Unit objects. We then create the TextDumpArmyVisitor object. We pass this to the Army::accept(). The accept() method constructs a method call and invokes TextDumpArmyVisitor::visitArmy(). In this case, we have provided no special handling for

Army objects, so the call is passed on to the generic visit() method. visit() has been passed a reference to our Army object. It invokes its methods (including a new one, getDepth(), which tells anyone who needs to know how far down the object hierarchy it is) in order to generate summary data. The call to visitArmy() complete, the Army::accept() operation now calls accept() on its children in turn, passing the visitor along. In this way, the ArmyVisitor class visits every object in the tree.

With the addition of just a couple of methods, we have created a mechanism by which new functionality can be plugged into our composite classes without compromising their interface, and without lots of duplicated traversal code.

On certain squares in our game, our armies are subject to tax. The tax collector visits the army and levies a fee for each unit it finds. Different units are taxable at different rates. Here's where we can take advantage of the specialized methods in the visitor class:

```php
class TaxCollectionVisitor extends ArmyVisitor {
    private $due=0;
    private $report="";

    function visit( Unit $node ) {
        $this->levy( $node, 1 );
    }

    function visitArcher( Archer $node ) {
        $this->levy( $node, 2 );
    }

    function visitCavalry( Cavalry $node ) {
        $this->levy( $node, 3 );
    }

    function visitTroopCarrierUnit( TroopCarrierUnit $node ) {
        $this->levy( $node, 5 );
    }

    private function levy( Unit $unit, $amount ) {
        $this->report .= "Tax levied for ".get_class( $unit );
        $this->report .= ": $amount\n";
        $this->due += $amount;
    }

    function getReport() {
        return $this->report;
    }

    function getTax() {
        return $this->due;
    }
}
```

In this simple example, we make no direct use of the Unit objects passed to the various visit methods. We do, however, use the specialized nature of these methods, levying different fees according to the specific type of the invoking Unit object.

Here's some client code:

```
$main_army = new Army();
$main_army->addUnit( new Archer() );
$main_army->addUnit( new LaserCanonUnit() );
$main_army->addUnit( new Cavalry() );

$taxcollector = new TaxCollectionVisitor();
$main_army->accept( $taxcollector );
print "TOTAL: ";
print $taxcollector->getTax()."\n";
```

The TaxCollectionVisitor object is passed to the Army object's accept() method as before. Once again Army passes a reference to itself to the visitArmy() method, before calling accept() on its children. The components are blissfully unaware of the operations performed by their visitor. They simply collaborate with its public interface, each one passing itself dutifully to the correct method for its type.

In addition to the methods defined in the ArmyVisitor class, TaxCollectionVisitor provides two summary methods, getReport() and getTax(). Invoking these provides the data you might expect:

```
Tax levied for Army: 1
Tax levied for Archer: 2
Tax levied for LaserCanonUnit: 1
Tax levied for Cavalry: 3
TOTAL: 7
```

Figure 11-7 shows the participants in this example.

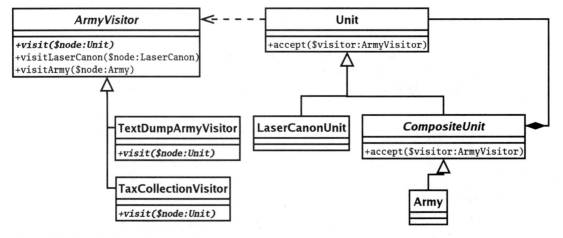

Figure 11-7. *The Visitor pattern*

Visitor Issues

The Visitor pattern, then, is another that combines simplicity and power. There are a few things to bear in mind when deploying this pattern, however.

Firstly, although it is perfectly suited to the Composite pattern, Visitor can, in fact, be used with any collection of objects. So you might use it with a list of objects where each object stores a reference to its siblings, for example.

By externalizing operations, you may risk compromising encapsulation. That is, you may need to expose the guts of your visited objects in order to let visitors do anything useful with them. We saw, for example, that for our first Visitor example, we were forced to provide an additional method in the Unit interface in order to provide information for TextDumpArmyVisitor objects.

Because iteration is separated from the operations that visitor objects perform, you must relinquish a degree of control. For example, you cannot easily create a visit() method that does something both before and after child nodes are iterated. One way around this would be to move responsibility for iteration into the visitor objects. The trouble with this is that you may end up duplicating the traversal code from visitor to visitor.

By default, I prefer to keep traversal internal to the visited classes, but externalizing it provides you with one distinct advantage. You can vary the way that you work through the visited classes on a visitor-by-visitor basis.

The Command Pattern

In recent years, I have rarely completed a Web project without deploying this pattern. Originally conceived in the context of graphical user interface design, command objects make for good enterprise application design, encouraging a separation between the controller (request and dispatch handling) and domain model (application logic) tiers. Put more simply, the Command pattern makes for systems that are well organized and easy to extend.

The Problem

All systems must make decisions about what to do in response to a user's request. In PHP, that decision-making process is often handled by a spread of point-of-contact pages. In selecting a page (feedback.php), the user clearly signals the functionality and interface she requires. Increasingly, PHP developers are opting for a single point-of-contact approach (as I will discuss in the next chapter). In either case, however, the receiver of a request must delegate to a tier more concerned with application logic. This delegation is particularly important where the user can make requests to different pages. Without it, duplication inevitably creeps into the project.

So, imagine we have a project with a range of tasks that need performing. In particular, our system must allow some users to log in and others to submit feedback. We could create login.php and feedback.php pages that handle these tasks, instantiating specialist classes to get the job done. Unfortunately, views in a system rarely map neatly to the tasks that the system is designed to complete. We may require login and feedback capabilities on every page, for example. If pages must handle many different tasks, then perhaps we should think of tasks as things that can be encapsulated. In doing this, we make it easy to add new tasks to our system, and we build a boundary between our system's tiers. This, of course, brings us to the Command pattern.

Implementation

The interface for a command object could not get much simpler. It requires a single method: execute().

In Figure 11-8, I have represented Command as an abstract class. At this level of simplicity, it could be defined instead as an interface. I tend to use abstracts for this purpose because I often find that the base class can also provide useful common functionality for its derived objects.

Figure 11-8. *The Command class*

There are up to three other participants in the Command pattern: the client, which instantiates the command object, the invoker, which deploys the object, and the receiver upon which the command operates.

The receiver can be given to the command in its constructor by the client, or it can be acquired from a factory object of some kind. I like the latter approach, keeping the constructor method clear of arguments. All Command objects can then be instantiated in exactly the same way.

Let's build a concrete Command class:

```
abstract class Command {
    abstract function execute();
}

class LoginCommand extends Command {

    function execute( CommandContext $context ) {
        $manager = ReceiverFactory::getAccessManager();
        $user = $context->get( 'username' );
        $pass = $context->get( 'pass' );
        $user = $manager->login( $user, $pass );
        if ( ! $user ) {
            $this->context->setError( $manager->getError() );
            return false;
        }
        $context->addParam( "user", $user );
        return true;
    }
}
```

The LoginCommand is designed to work with an AccessManager object. AccessManager is an imaginary class whose task is to handle the nuts and bolts of logging users into the system. Notice that our Command::execute() method demands a CommandContext object (known as RequestHelper in *Core J2EE Patterns*). This is a mechanism by which request data can be passed to Command objects, and by which responses can be channeled back to the view layer. Using an object in this way is useful, because we can pass different parameters to commands without breaking the interface. The CommandContext is essentially an object wrapper around an associative array variable, though it is frequently extended to perform additional helpful tasks. Here is a simple CommandContext implementation:

```
class CommandContext {
    private $params = array();
    private $error = "";

    function __construct() {
        $this->params = $_REQUEST;
    }

    function addParam( $key, $val ) {
        $this->params[$key]=$val;
    }

    function get( $key ) {
        return $this->params[$key];
    }

    function setError( $error ) {
        $this->error = $error;
    }
    function getError() {
        return $this->error;
    }
}
```

So, armed with a Context object, the LoginCommand can access request data: the submitted username and password. We use ReceiverFactory, a simple class with static methods for generating common objects, to return the AccessManager object with which LoginCommand needs to work. If AccessManager reports an error, the command lodges the error message with the Context object for use by the presentation layer, and returns false. If all is well, LoginCommand simply returns true. Note that Command objects do not themselves perform much logic. They check input, handle error conditions, and cache data as well as calling on other objects to perform the operations they must report on.

Now we are only missing the client: the class that generates command objects, and the invoker. The easiest way of selecting which command to instantiate in a Web project is by using a parameter in the request itself. Here is a simplified client:

```
class CommandNotFoundException extends Exception {}

class CommandFactory {
    private static $dir = 'commands';
```

```
function getCommand( $action='Default' ) {
    $class = ucfirst(strtolower($action))."Command";
    $file = self::$dir."/$class.php";
    if ( ! file_exists( $file ) ) {
        throw new CommandNotFoundException( "could not find '$file'" );
    }
    require_once( $file );
    if ( ! class_exists( $class ) ) {
        throw new CommandNotFoundException( "no '$class' class located" );
    }
    $cmd = new $class();
    return $cmd;
}
}
```

The `CommandFactory` class simply looks in a directory called `commands` for a particular class file. The file name is constructed using the `CommandContext` object's `$action` parameter, which in turn should have been passed to our system from the request. If the file is there, and the class exists, then it is returned to the caller. We could add even more error checking here, ensuring that the found class belongs to the `Command` family, that the user supplied `$class` string does not contain a directory path, and that constructor is expecting no arguments, but this version will do fine for our purposes. The strength of this approach is that you can drop a new `Command` object into the `commands` directory at any time, and the system will immediately support it.

The invoker is now simplicity itself:

```
class Controller {
    private $context;
    function __construct() {
        $this->context = new CommandContext();
    }

    function getContext() {
        return $this->context;
    }

    function process() {
        $cmd = CommandFactory::getCommand( $this->context->get('action') );
        if ( ! $cmd->execute( $this->context ) ) {
            // handle failure
        } else {
            print "all is well";
            // success
        }
    }
}
```

```
$controller = new Controller();
// fake user request
$context = $controller->getContext();
$context->addParam('action', 'login' );
$context->addParam('username', 'bob' );
$context->addParam('pass', 'tiddles' );
$controller->process();
```

Before we call `Controller::process()`, we fake up a Web request by setting parameters on the `CommandContext` object instantiated in the controller's constructor. The `process()` method delegates object instantiation to the `CommandFactory` object. It then invokes `execute()` on the returned command. Notice how the controller has no idea about the command's internals. It is this independence from the details of command execution that makes it possible for us to add new `Command` classes with a relatively small impact on this framework.

Let's create one more `Command` class:

```
class FeedbackCommand extends Command {

    function execute( CommandContext $context ) {
        $msgSystem = ReceiverFactory::getMessageSystem();
        $email = $context->get( 'email' );
        $msg = $context->get( 'pass' );
        $topic = $context->get( 'topic' );
        $result = $msgSystem->despatch( $email, $msg, $topic );
        if ( ! $user ) {
            $this->context->setError( $msgSystem->getError() );
            return false;
        }
        $context->addParam( "user", $user );
        return true;
    }
}
```

■Note We will return to the Command pattern in Chapter 12 with a fuller implementation of a Command factory class. The framework for running commands presented here is a simplified version of another pattern that we will encounter: the Front Controller.

As long as this class is contained within a file called `FeedbackCommand.php`, and is saved in the correct `commands` folder, it will be run in response to a "feedback" action string, without the need for any changes in the controller or `CommandFactory` classes.

Figure 11-9 shows the participants of the Command pattern.

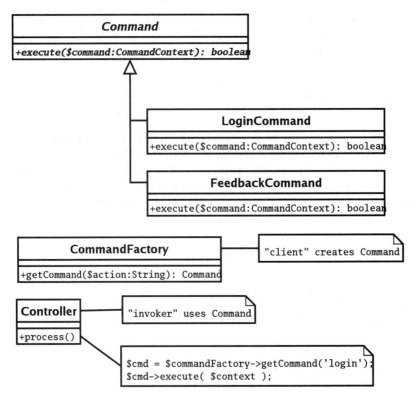

Figure 11-9. *Command pattern participants*

Summary

In this chapter, we wrapped up our examination the Gang of Four patterns. We designed a mini-language and built its engine with the Interpreter pattern. We encountered in the Strategy pattern another way of using composition to increase flexibility and reduce the need for repetitive subclassing. The Observer pattern solved the problem of notifying disparate and varying components about system events. We revisited our Composite example, and with the Visitor pattern learned how to pay a call on, and apply many operations to, every component in a tree. Finally, we saw how the Command pattern can help us to build an extensible tiered system.

In the next chapter, we will step beyond the Gang of Four to examine some patterns specifically oriented toward Enterprise programming.

■ ■ ■

CHAPTER 12

Enterprise Patterns

PHP is first and foremost a language designed for the Web. And with its newly extended support for objects, it can also derive greater benefit from patterns hatched in other Enterprise languages, particularly Java.

This chapter will cover

- *Presentation patterns*: Tools for managing and responding to requests, and for presenting data to the user

- *Business logic patterns*: Getting to the real purpose of your system: addressing business problems

- *Data patterns*: Taming the relational database

- *Summary*: A bullet point list covering all the patterns in this chapter

Introduction

Many (most, in fact) of the patterns in this chapter are designed to promote the independent operation of several distinct tiers in an application. Just as classes represent specializations of responsibilities, so do the tiers of an Enterprise system, albeit on a coarser scale. Figure 12-1 shows a typical breakdown of the layers in a system.

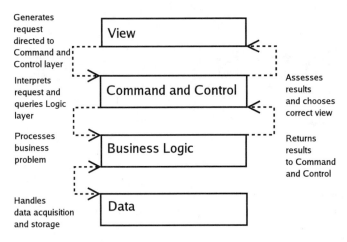

Figure 12-1. *The layers or tiers in a typical Enterprise system*

The structure shown in Figure 12-1 is not written in stone: some of these tiers may be combined and different strategies used for communication between them depending upon the complexity of your system. Nonetheless, Figure 12-1 illustrates a model that emphasizes flexibility and reuse, and many Enterprise applications follow it to a large extent.

- The *View layer* contains the interface that a system's users actually see and interact with. It is responsible for presenting the results of a user's request, and providing the mechanism by which the next request can be made to the system.

- The *Command and Control layer* processes the request from the user. Based on this analysis, it delegates to the Business Logic layer to perform any processing required in order to fulfill the request. It then chooses which view is best suited to present the results to the user. In practice, this and the View layer are often combined into a single *Presentation layer*. Even so, the role of display tends to be strictly separated from those of request handling and business logic invocation.

- The *Business Logic layer* is responsible for seeing to the business of a request. It performs any required calculations and marshals the resulting data.

- The *Data layer* insulates the rest of the system from the mechanics of saving and acquiring persistent information. In some systems, the Command and Control layer uses the Data layer to acquire the business objects with which it needs to work. In other systems, the Data layer is hidden as far as possible. Later in the chapter, I will demonstrate a near-transparent Data layer.

So what is the point of dividing a system in this way? As with so much else in the book, the answer lies with decoupling. By keeping business logic independent of the View layer, you make it possible to add new interfaces to your system with little or no rewriting.

Imagine a system for managing event listings (this will be a very familiar example by the end of the chapter). The end user will naturally require a slick HTML interface. Technicians maintaining the system may then require a command line interface for building into automated systems. At the same time, you may be developing versions of the system to work with cell phones and other handheld devices. You may even begin to consider Web Services like XML-RPC and SOAP.

If you originally combined the underlying logic of your system with the HTML View layer (which is still a common strategy whatever project managers might tell you), these requirements would trigger an instant rewrite. If, on the other hand, you had created a tiered system, you would be able to bolt on new presentation strategies without the need to reconsider your Business Logic and Data layers.

By the same token, persistence strategies are subject to change. Once again, you should be able to switch between storage models with minimal impact upon the other tiers in a system.

Testing is another good reason for creating systems with separated tiers. Web applications are notoriously hard to test. Any kind of automated test tends to get caught up in the need to parse the HTML interface at one end, and work with live databases at the other. This means that tests must work with fully deployed systems, and risk undermining the very system that they were written to protect. The classes in a tier that face other layers should be written so that they extend an abstract super class or implement an interface. This supertype can then support polymorphism. In a test context, an entire tier can be replaced by a set of dummy objects (often called "stubs" or "mock objects"). In this way, you can test business logic using a fake Data layer, for example.

Layers are useful even if you think that testing is for wimps, and your system will only ever have a single interface. By creating tiers with distinct responsibilities, you build a system whose constituent parts are easier to extend and debug. You limit duplication by keeping code with the same kinds of responsibility in one place (rather than lacing a system with database calls, for example, or with display strategies). Adding to a system is relatively easy because your changes tend to be nicely vertical as opposed to messily horizontal.

A new feature, in a tiered system, might require a new interface component, additional request handling, some more business logic, and an amendment to your storage mechanism. That's vertical change. In a nontiered system you might add your feature, and then remember that five separate pages reference your amended database table, or was it six? There may be dozens of places where your new interface may potentially be invoked, so you need to work through your system adding code for that. This is horizontal amendment.

In reality, of course, you never entirely escape from horizontal dependencies of this sort, especially when it comes to navigation elements in the interface. A tiered system can help to minimize the need for horizontal amendment, however.

■Note While many of these patterns have been around for a while (that's what patterns mean, after all), the names and boundaries are drawn either from Martin Fowler's key work on Enterprise patterns, *Patterns of Enterprise Application Architecture*, or from the influential *Core J2EE Patterns* by Alur et al. For the sake of consistency, I have tended to use Martin Fowler's naming conventions where the two sources diverge. This is because the latter's work is less focused upon a single technology, and therefore has the wider application. Alur et al. tend to concentrate upon Enterprise Java Beans in their work, which means that many patterns are optimized for distributed architectures. This is clearly a niche concern in the PHP world.

If you find this chapter useful, I would recommend both books as a next step. Even if you don't know Java, as an object-oriented PHP programmer you should find the examples reasonably easy to decipher.

All the examples in this chapter revolve around a fictional listings system with the whimsical-sounding name "Woo," which stands for something like "What's On Outside."

Participants of the system include venues (theaters, clubs, and cinemas), spaces ("screen 1," "the stage upstairs") and events (*The Long Good Friday, The Importance of Being Earnest*).

The operations I will cover include creating a venue, adding a space to a venue, and listing all venues in the system.

Remember that the aim of this chapter is to illustrate key Enterprise design patterns, and not to build a working system. Reflecting the interdependent nature of design patterns, most of these examples overlap to a large extent with code examples, making good use of ground covered elsewhere in the chapter. Addressing the needs of demonstration code, though, does not fulfill the criteria demanded by a production system. You should approach the examples as a means of illustrating the patterns they implement, rather than as building blocks in a framework or application.

Cheating Before We Start

Most of the patterns in this book find a natural place in the layers of an Enterprise architecture. Some patterns are so basic that they stand outside of this structure. The Registry pattern is a good example of this. In fact, Registry is a powerful way of breaking out of the constraints laid down by layering. It is the exception that allows for the smooth running of the rule.

Registry

It is an article of faith that globals are bad. Like other sins, though, global data is fatally attractive. This is so much the case that object-oriented architects have felt it necessary to reinvent globals under a new name. We encountered the Singleton pattern in Chapter 9. This is unfair, of course, because Singleton objects do not suffer from all the ills that beset global variables. In particular, you cannot overwrite a Singleton by accident. Singletons, then, are low-fat globals. We remain suspicious of Singleton objects, though, because they invite us to anchor our classes into a system, thereby introducing coupling.

Even so, Singletons are so useful at times, that many programmers (including me) can't bring themselves to give them up.

The Problem

As you may know, many Enterprise systems are divided into layers, with each layer communicating with its neighbors only through tightly defined conduits. This separation of tiers makes an application flexible. You can replace or otherwise develop each tier with the minimum impact on the rest of the system. What happens, though, when you acquire information in a tier that you later need in another noncontiguous layer?

■Note Some of the examples in this chapter use the PEAR class naming convention. That is, they include the package path in class names. This guards against name clashes, but can also be hard on the eye in discussion. For that reason, where I discuss a class, I will use only its core name. So woo_controller_ApplicationHelper in an example may be referred to as ApplicationHelper in the text.

Let's say that we acquire configuration data in an ApplicationHelper class:

```
// woo_controller_ApplicationHelper
function getOptions() {
    if ( ! file_exists( "data/woo_options.xml" ) ) {
        throw new woo_base_AppException(
            "Could not find options file" );
    }
    $options = SimpleXml_load_file( "data/woo_options.xml" );
    $dsn = (string)$options->dsn;
    // what do we do with this now?
    // ...
}
```

Acquiring the information is easy enough, but how do we get it to the Data layer where it is later used? And what about all the other configuration information we must disseminate throughout our system?

One answer would be to pass this information around the system from object to object: from a controller object responsible for handling requests, through to objects in the Business Logic layer, and on to an object responsible for talking to the database.

This is entirely feasible. In fact, you could pass the ApplicationHelper object itself around, or alternatively a more specialized Context object. Either way, contextual information is transmitted through the layers of your system to the object or objects that need it.

The trade-off is that in order to do this, you must alter the interface of all the objects that relay the context object whether they need to use it or not. Clearly this undermines loose coupling to some extent.

The Registry pattern provides an alternative that is not without its own consequences.

A Registry is simply a class that provides access to data (usually, but not exclusively, objects) via static methods (or via instance methods on a Singleton). Every object in a system therefore has access to these objects.

The term "Registry" is drawn from Martin Fowler's *Patterns of Enterprise Application Architecture*, but like all patterns, implementations pop up everywhere. David Hunt and David Thomas (*The Pragmatic Programmer*) liken a Registry class to a police incident notice board. Detectives on one shift leave evidence and sketches on the board, which are then picked up by new detectives on another shift. I have also seen Registry classes called Whiteboard and Blackboard.

Implementation

Figure 12-2 shows a Registry object whose job it is to store and serve Request objects:

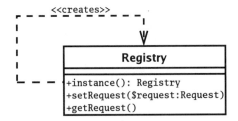

Figure 12-2. *A simple registry*

Here is this class in code form:

```php
class Registry {
    private static $instance;
    private $request;

    static function instance() {
        if ( ! self::$instance ) { self::$instance = new self(); }
        return self::$instance;
    }

    function getRequest() {
        return $this->request;
    }

    function setRequest( Request $request ) {
        $this->request = $request;
    }
}
// empty class for testing
class Request {}
```

You can then add a Request object in one part of a system.

```php
$reg = Registry::instance();
$reg->setRequest( new Request() );
```

And access it from another part of the system.

```
$reg = Registry::instance();
print_r( $reg->getRequest() );
```

As you can see, the Registry is simply a Singleton (see Chapter 9 if you need a reminder about Singleton classes). The code creates and returns a sole instance of the Registry class via the instance() method. This can then be used to set and retrieve a Request object. Despite the fact that PHP does not enforce return types, the value returned by getRequest() is *guaranteed* to be a Request object because of the type hint in setRequest().

I have been known to throw caution to the winds and use a key-based system, like this:

```
class Registry {
    private static $instance;
    private $values = array();

    static function instance() {
        if ( ! self::$instance ) { self::$instance = new self(); }
        return self::$instance;
    }

    function get( $key ) {
        return $this->values[$key];
    }

    function set( $key, $value ) {
        $this->values[$key] = $value;
    }
}
```

The benefit here is that you don't need to create methods for every object you wish to store and serve. The downside, though, is that you reintroduce global variables by the back door. The use of arbitrary strings as keys for the objects you store means that there is nothing stopping one part of your system overwriting a key/value pair when adding an object. I have found it useful to use this map-like structure during development, and shift over to explicitly named methods when I'm clear about the data I am going to need to store and retrieve.

Registry, Scope, and PHP

The term "scope" is often used to describe the visibility of an object or value in the context of code structures. The lifetime of a variable can also be measured over time. There are three levels of scope you might consider in this sense. The standard is the period covered by an HTTP request. In terms of real in-memory scope, this is as far as it goes in the PHP world. We do not have access to pools of memory in which we might store data for longer than a single request.

PHP also provides built-in support for session variables. These are serialized and saved to the file system or the database at the end of a request, and then restored at the start of the next. A session ID stored in a cookie or passed around in query strings is used to keep track of the session owner. Because of this, you can think of some variables having session scope. You can take advantage of this by storing some objects between requests, saving a trip to the database.

Clearly, you need to be careful that you don't end up with multiple versions of the same object, so you may need to consider a locking strategy when you check an object that also exists in a database into a session.

In other languages, notably Java and Perl (running on the ModPerl Apache module), there is the concept of application scope. Variables that occupy this space are available across all instances of the application. This is fairly alien to PHP, but in larger applications it is very useful to have access to an application-wide space for accessing configuration variables. You can build a Registry class that emulates application scope, though you must be aware of some pretty considerable caveats.

Figure 12-3 shows a possible structure for Registry classes that work on the three levels I have described:

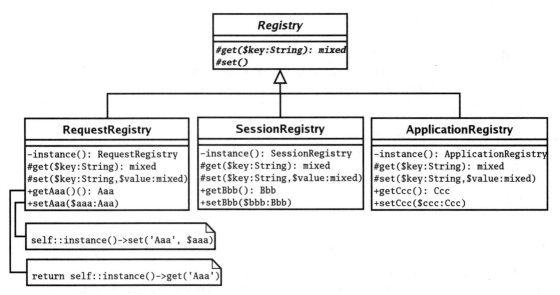

Figure 12-3. *Implementing Registry classes for different scopes*

The base class defines two protected methods, get() and set(). They are not available to client code because we want to enforce type for get and set operations. The base class may define other public methods such as isEmpty(), isPopulated(), and clear(), but I'll leave those as an exercise for you to do.

■Note In a real-world system, you might want to extend this structure to include another layer of inheritance. You might keep the concrete get() and set() methods in their respective implementations, but specialize the public getAaa() and setAaa() methods into domain-specific classes. The new specializations would become the Singletons. That way you could reuse the core save and retrieve operations across multiple applications.

Here is the abstract class as code:

```
abstract class woo_base_Registry {
    private function __construct() {}
    abstract protected function get( $key );
    abstract protected function set( $key, $val );
}
```

The request level class is pretty straightforward. In another variation from our previous example, we keep the Registry sole instance hidden, and provide static methods to set and get objects. Apart from that, it's simply a matter of maintaining an associative array.

```
class woo_base_RequestRegistry extends woo_base_Registry {
    private $values = array();
    private static $instance;

    static function instance() {
        if ( ! self::$instance ) { self::$instance = new self(); }
        return self::$instance;
    }

    protected function get( $key ) {
        return $this->values[$key];
    }

    protected function set( $key, $val ) {
        $this->values[$key] = $val;
    }

    static function getRequest() {
        return self::instance()->get('request');
    }

    static function setRequest( woo_controller_Request $request ) {
        return self::instance()->set('request', $request );
    }
}
```

The session-level implementation simply uses PHP's built-in session support:

```
class woo_base_SessionRegistry extends woo_base_Registry {
    private static $instance;
    private function __construct() {
        session_start();
    }
```

```
    static function instance() {
        if ( ! self::$instance ) { self::$instance = new self(); }
        return self::$instance;
    }

    protected function get( $key ) {
        return $_SESSION[__CLASS__][$key];
    }

    protected function set( $key, $val ) {
        $_SESSION[__CLASS__][$key] = $val;
    }

    function setComplex( Complex $complex ) {
        self::instance()->set('complex', $complex);
    }

    function getComplex( ) {
        return self::instance()->get('complex');
    }
}
```

As you can see, this class uses the $_SESSION superglobal to set and retrieve values. We kick off the session in the constructor with the session_start() method. As always with sessions, you must ensure that you have not yet sent any text to the user before using this class.

As you might expect, the application-level implementation is more of an issue. As with all code examples in this chapter, this is an illustration rather than production-quality code:

```
class woo_base_ApplicationRegistry extends woo_base_Registry {
    private static $instance;
    private $freezefile = "data/applicationRegistry.txt";
    private $values = array();
    private $dirty = false;

    private function __construct() {
        $this->doReload( $this );
    }

    static function instance() {
        if ( ! self::$instance ) { self::$instance = new self(); }
        return self::$instance;
    }

    function __destruct() {
        if ( $this->dirty ) {
            $this->save();
        }
    }
```

```php
    static function reload() {
        self::instance()->doReload();
    }

    private function doReload() {
        if ( ! file_exists( $this->freezefile ) ) { return false; }
        $serialized = file_get_contents( $this->freezefile, true );
        $array = unserialize( $serialized );
        if ( is_array( $array ) ) {
            $array = array_merge( $array, $this->values );
            $this->values = $array;
            return true;
        }
        return false;
    }

    private function save() {
        $frozen = serialize( $this->values );
        file_put_contents(  $this->freezefile, $frozen,
                            FILE_USE_INCLUDE_PATH  );
        $this->dirty = false;
    }

    protected function get( $key ) {
        return $this->values[$key];
    }

    protected function set( $key, $val ) {
        $this->dirty = true;
        $this->values[$key] = $val;
    }

    static function isEmpty() {
        return empty( self::instance()->values );
    }

    static function getDSN() {
        return self::instance()->get('dsn');
    }

    static function setDSN( $dsn ) {
        return self::instance()->set('dsn', $dsn);
    }
}
```

This class uses serialization to save and restore the $values property. The doReload()
method handles data acquisition, first checking for the file's existence and then reading its
contents. Contents acquired, the method uses unserialize() to generate an array. reload()

is called when the ApplicationRegistry is first instantiated to ensure that the object starts out with a populated $values array. It can also be invoked at any time via the static reload() method.

Whenever a client sets a value, a private flag, $dirty, is set to true (in the set() method). The class implements a __destruct() method, which is automatically invoked when the ApplicationRegistry object is destroyed. If the $dirty property is set to true, then the save() method is called. This works like reload() in reverse. The $values array is serialized and saved to the storage file.

If you intend to use a variation on this code example, make sure you check out the next section: there are some serious issues that you should consider.

Consequences

Because both SessionRegistry and ApplicationRegistry serialize data to the file system, it is important to restate the obvious point that objects retrieved in different requests are identical copies and not references to the same object. This should not matter with SessionRegistry, because the same user is accessing the object in each instance. With ApplicationRegistry, this could be a serious problem. If you are saving data promiscuously, you could arrive at a situation where two processes conflict. Take a look at these steps:

```
Process 1 retrieves an object
Process 2 retrieves an object
Process 1 alters object
Process 2 alters object
Process 1 saves object
Process 2 saves object
```

The changes made by Process 1 are overwritten by the save of Process 2. If you really want to create a shared space for data, you will need to work on ApplicationRegistry to implement a locking scheme to prevent collisions like this. Alternatively, you can treat ApplicationRegistry as a largely read-only resource. This is the way that I use the class in examples later in this chapter. Data is set on it only once, and thereafter all interactions with it are read-only. The code only calculates new values and writes them if the storage file cannot be found. You can therefore force a reload of configuration data only by deleting the storage file. You may wish to enhance the class so read-only behavior is enforced.

Another point to remember is that not every object is suitable for serialization. In particular, if you are storing a resource of any type (a database connection handle, for example), it will not serialize. You will have to devise strategies for disposing of the handle on serialization and reacquiring it on unserialization.

Note One way of managing serialization is to implement the magic methods __sleep() and __wakeup(). __sleep() is called automatically when an object is serialized. You can use it to perform any cleaning up before the object is saved. In order to work, the method should return an array. The __wakeup() method is invoked when an object is unserialized. You can use this to resume any file or database handles the object may have been using at the time of storage.

Although serialization is a pretty efficient business in PHP, you should be careful of what you save. A simple-seeming object may contain a reference to an enormous collection of objects pulled from a database.

`Registry` objects make their data globally available. This means that any class that acts as a client for a Registry will exhibit a dependency that is not declared in its interface. This can become a serious problem if you begin to rely on `Registry` objects for lots of data in your system. `Registry` objects are best used sparingly, for a well-defined set of data items.

The Presentation Layer

When a request hits your system, you must interpret the requirement it carries, then you must invoke any business logic needed, and finally return a response. For simple scripts, this whole process often takes place entirely inside the view itself, with only the heavyweight logic and persistence code split off into libraries.

■**Note** A *view* is an individual element in the View layer. It is usually a PHP page whose primary responsibility is to display data and provide the mechanism by which new requests can be generated by the user. It could also be a template in a templating system such as Smarty.

As systems grow in size, this default strategy becomes less tenable with request processing, business logic invocation, and view dispatch logic necessarily duplicated from view to view.

In this section, we look at strategies for managing these three key responsibilities of the Presentation layer. Because the boundaries between the View layer and the Command and Control layer are often fairly blurred, it makes sense to treat them together under the common term "Presentation layer."

Front Controller

This pattern is diametrically opposed to the traditional PHP application with its multiple points of entry. The Front Controller pattern presents a central point of access for all incoming requests, ultimately delegating to a view to present results back to the user. This is a key pattern in the Java Enterprise community. It is covered in great detail in *Core J2EE Patterns*, which remains one of the most influential Enterprise patterns resources. The pattern is not universally loved in the PHP community partly because of the overhead that initialization sometimes incurs.

Most systems I write tend to gravitate toward the Front Controller. That is, I may not deploy the entire pattern to start with, but I will be aware of the steps necessary to evolve my project into a Front Controller implementation should I need the amazing power and flexibility it affords.

The Problem

Where requests are handled at multiple points throughout a system, it is hard to keep duplication from the code. You may need to authenticate a user, translate terms into different languages, or simply access common data. When a request requires common actions from view to view, you may find yourself copying and pasting operations. This makes changes very difficult, as a simple change to an operation must be repeated throughout your system. It is very easy for some parts of your code to fall out of alignment with others. Of course, a first step might be to centralize common operations into library code, but you are still left with the calls to the library functions or methods distributed throughout your system.

Difficulty in managing the progression from view to view is another problem that can arise in a system where control is distributed among its views. In a complex system, a submission in one view may lead to any number of result pages, according to the input and the success of any operations performed at the logic layer. Forwarding from view to view can get messy, especially if the same view might be used in different flows.

Implementation

At heart, the Front Controller pattern defines a central point of entry for every request. It processes the request and uses it to select an operation to perform. Operations are often defined in specialized command objects organized according to the Command pattern.

Figure 12-4 shows an overview of a Front Controller implementation.

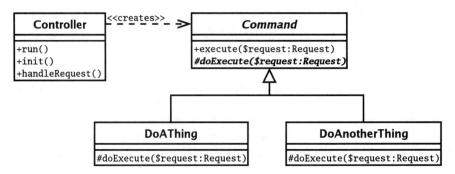

Figure 12-4. *A Controller class and a command hierarchy*

In fact, you are likely to deploy a few helper classes to smooth the process, but let's begin with the core participants. Here is a simple Controller class:

```
class woo_controller_Controller {
    private $applicationHelper;

    private function __construct() {}

    static function run() {
        $instance = new woo_controller_Controller();
        $instance->init();
        $instance->handleRequest();
    }
```

```
function init() {
    $applicationHelper
        = woo_controller_ApplicationHelper::instance();
    $applicationHelper->init();
}

function handleRequest() {
    $request = new woo_controller_Request();
    $cmd_r = new woo_command_CommandResolver();
    $cmd = $cmd_r->getCommand( $request );
    $cmd->execute( $request );
}
}
```

Simplified as this is, and bereft of error handling, there isn't much more to the Controller class. A controller sits at the tip of a system delegating to other classes. It is these other classes that do most of the work.

run() is merely a convenience method that calls init() and handleRequest(). It is static and the constructor is private, so the only option for client code is to kick off execution of our system. I usually do this in a file called index.php that contains only a couple of lines of code:

```
require( "woo/controller/Controller.php" );
woo_controller_Controller::run();
```

The distinction between the init() and handleRequest() methods is really one of category in PHP. In some languages, init() would be run only at application startup, and handleRequest() or equivalent would be run for each user request. This class observes the same distinction between setup and request handling, even though init() is called for each request.

The init() method obtains an instance of a class called ApplicationHelper. This class manages configuration data for the application as a whole. init() calls a method in ApplicationHelper, also called init(), which, as you will see, initializes data used by the application.

The handleRequest() method uses a CommandResolver to acquire a Command object, which it runs by calling Command::execute().

ApplicationHelper

The ApplicationHelper class is not essential to Front Controller. Most implementations must acquire basic configuration data, though, so it's as well to discuss a strategy for this. Here is a simple ApplicationHelper:

```
class woo_controller_ApplicationHelper {
    private static $instance;
    private $config = "data/woo_options.xml";

    private function __construct() {}
```

```
    static function instance() {
        if ( ! self::$instance ) {
            self::$instance = new self();
        }
        return self::$instance;
    }

    function init() {
        if ( ! woo_base_ApplicationRegistry::isEmpty() ) {
            return;
        }
        $this->getOptions();
    }
     private function getOptions() {
        $this->ensure( file_exists( $this->config ),
                            "Could not find options file" );
        $options = @SimpleXml_load_file( $this->config );
        $this->ensure( $options instanceof SimpleXMLElement,
                            "Could not resolve options file" );
        $dsn = (string)$options->dsn;
        $this->ensure( $dsn, "No DSN found" );
        woo_base_ApplicationRegistry::setDSN( $dsn );
        // set other values
    }

    private function ensure( $expr, $message ) {
        if ( ! $expr ) {
            throw new woo_base_AppException( $message );
        }
    }

    function DB() {
        $dsn = woo_base_ApplicationRegistry::getDSN();
        $this->ensure( $dsn, "No DSN" );
        if ( ! $this->db ) {
            $this->db = DB::connect( $dsn );
        }
        $this->ensure(  (! DB::isError( $this->db )),
                        "Unable to connect to DB" );
        return $this->db;
    }
}
```

This class simply reads a configuration file and makes values available to clients. As you
can see, it is another Singleton, which is a useful way of making it available to any class in our
system. You could equally make it a standard class, and ensure that it is passed around to any
interested objects. I have already discussed the trade-offs involved there.

The fact that we are using an ApplicationRegistry here suggests a refactoring. It may be worth making ApplicationHelper itself the Registry rather than have two Singletons in a system with overlapping responsibilities. This would involve the refactoring suggested in the previous section (splitting core ApplicationRegistry functionality from storage and retrieval of domain-specific objects). I will leave that for you to do!

So the init() method is responsible for loading configuration data. In fact, it checks the ApplicationRegistry to see if the data is already cached. If the Registry object is already populated, init() does nothing at all. This is useful for systems that do lots of very expensive initialization. Complicated setup may be acceptable in a language that separates application initialization from individual requests. In PHP, you need to minimize initialization in favor of the request.

Caching is very useful for ensuring that complex and time-consuming initialization processes take place in an initial request only (probably one run by you), with all subsequent requests benefiting from the results.

If this *is* the first run (or if the cache file has been deleted—a crude but effective way of forcing the configuration file to be re-created), then the setOptions() method is invoked.

In real life, this would probably do a lot more work than the example shows. This version satisfies itself with acquiring a DSN. setOptions() first checks that the configuration file exists (the path is stored in a property called $config). It then attempts to load XML data from the file, and sets the DSN.

Notice that the class uses a trick to throw exceptions. Rather than pepper the code with conditionals and throw statements like this:

```
if ( ! file_exists( "data/woo_options.txt" ) ) {
    throw new woo_base_AppException(
        "Could not find options file" );
}
```

the class centralizes the test expression and the throw statement in a method called ensure(). You can confirm that a condition is true (and throw an exception otherwise) in a single (albeit split) line:

```
$this->ensure( file_exists( $this->config ),
                    "Could not find options file" );
```

Finally, ApplicationHelper includes a DB() method, which serves up a DB_common object (or throws an exception if things go wrong).

The cache approach taken here allows for the best of both worlds. The system can maintain an easy-to-use XML configuration file, but caching means that its values can be accessed at near native speed. Of course, if your end users are programmers too, or if you don't intend to change configuration very often, you could include PHP data structures directly in the helper class. While inflexible, this approach is certainly the fastest.

CommandResolver

A controller needs a way of deciding how to interpret an HTTP request so that it can invoke the right code in order to fulfill that request. You could easily include this logic within the Controller class itself, but I prefer to use a specialist class for the purpose. That makes it easy to refactor for polymorphism if necessary.

A Front Controller often invokes application logic by running a Command object (we covered the Command pattern in Chapter 11). The Command that is chosen is usually selected according to a parameter in the request or according to the structure of the URL itself (you might, for example, use Apache configuration in order to make concrete-seeming URLs yield a key for use in selecting a Command). In these examples, I will use a simple parameter: cmd.

There is more than one way of using the given parameter to select a Command. You can test the parameter against a configuration file or data structure (a *logical* strategy). Or you can test it directly against class files on the file system (a *physical* strategy).

A logical strategy is more flexible, but also more labor intensive, both in terms of setup and maintenance. You can see an example of this approach in the "Application Controller" section.

You saw an example of a command factory that used a physical strategy in the last chapter. Here is a slight variation that uses reflection for added safety:

```php
class woo_command_CommandResolver {
    private static $base_cmd;
    private static $default_cmd;

    function __construct() {
        if ( ! self::$base_cmd ) {
            self::$base_cmd = new ReflectionClass( "woo_command_Command" );
            self::$default_cmd = new woo_command_DefaultCommand();
        }
    }

    function getCommand( woo_controller_Request $request ) {
        $cmd = $request->getProperty( 'cmd' );
        if ( ! $cmd ) {
            return self::$default_cmd;
        }
        $cmd=str_replace( array('.','/'), "", $cmd );
        $filepath = "woo/command/$cmd.php";
        $classname = "woo_command_$cmd";
        if ( file_exists( $filepath ) ) {
            @require_once( "$filepath" );
            if ( class_exists( $classname) ) {
                $cmd_class = new ReflectionClass($classname);
                if ( $cmd_class->isSubClassOf( self::$base_cmd ) ) {
                    return $cmd_class->newInstance();
                } else {
                    $request->addFeedback( "command '$cmd' is not a Command" );
                }
            }
        }
        $request->addFeedback( "command '$cmd' not found" );
        return clone self::$default_cmd;
    }
}
```

This simple class looks for a request parameter called cmd. Assuming that this is found, and that it maps to a real class file in the command directory, *and* that the class file contains the right kind of class, the method creates and returns an instance of the relevant class.

If any of these conditions are not met, the getCommand() method degrades gracefully by serving up a default Command object.

You may wonder why this code takes it on trust that the Command class it locates does not require parameters:

```
if ( $cmd_class->isSubClassOf( self::$base_cmd ) ) {
    return $cmd_class->newInstance();
}
```

The answer to this lies in the signature of the Command class itself.

```
abstract class woo_command_Command {
    final function __construct() { }

    function execute( woo_controller_Request $request ) {
        $this->doExecute( $request );
    }

    abstract function doExecute( woo_controller_Request $request );
}
```

By declaring the constructor method final, we make it impossible for a child class to override it. No Command class therefore will ever require arguments to its constructor.

Remember that you should never use input from the user without checking it first. I have included a test to ensure that there is no path element to the provided "cmd" string, so that only files in the correct directory can be invoked (and not something like ../../../tmp/ DodgyCommand.php). You can make code even safer by only accepting command strings that match values in a configuration file.

Request

Requests are magically handled for us by PHP and neatly packaged up in superglobal arrays. You might have noticed that we still use a class to represent a request. A Request object is passed to CommandResolver, and later on to Command.

Why do we not let these classes simply query the $_REQUEST, $_POST, or $_GET arrays for themselves? We could do that, of course, but by centralizing request operations in one place we open up new options. You could, for example, apply filters to the incoming request. Or, as the next example shows, you could gather request parameters from somewhere other than an HTTP request, allowing the application to be run from the command line or from a test script. Of course, if your application uses sessions, you may have to provide an alternative storage mechanism for use in a command line context. The Registry pattern would work well for you there, allowing you to generate different Registry classes according to the context of the application.

The Request object is also a useful repository for data that needs to be communicated to the View layer. In that respect, Request can also provide response capabilities.

Here is a simple Request class:

```
class woo_controller_Request {
    private $appreg;
    private $properties;
    private $feedback = array();

    function __construct() {
        $this->init();
        woo_base_RequestRegistry::setRequest($this );
    }

    function init() {
        if ( $_SERVER['REQUEST_METHOD'] ) {
            $this->properties = $_REQUEST;
            return;
        }
        foreach( $_SERVER['argv'] as $arg ) {
            if ( strpos( $arg, '=' ) ) {
                list( $key, $val )=explode( "=", $arg );
                $this->setProperty( $key, $val );
            }
        }
    }

    function getProperty( $key ) {
        return $this->properties[$key];
    }

    function setProperty( $key, $val ) {
        $this->properties[$key] = $val;
    }


    function addFeedback( $msg ) {
        array_push( $this->feedback, $msg );
    }

    function getFeedback( ) {
        return $this->feedback;
    }
    function getFeedbackString( $separator="\n" ) {
        return implode( $separator, $this->feedback );
    }
}
```

As you can see, most of this class is taken up with mechanisms for setting and acquiring properties. The init() method is responsible for populating the private $properties array. Notice that it works with command line arguments as well as the HTTP requests. This is extremely useful when it comes to testing and debugging.

Once you have a Request object, you should be able to access an HTTP parameter via the getProperty() method, which accepts a key string and returns the corresponding value (as stored in the $properties array). You can also add data via setProperty().

The class also manages a $feedback array. This is a simple conduit through which controller classes can pass messages to the user.

A Command

You have already seen the Command base class, and Chapter 11 covered the Command pattern in detail, so there's no need to go too deep into Commands. It would be a shame to round up this pattern without showing at least a simple concrete Command object:

```
class woo_command_DefaultCommand extends woo_command_Command {
    function doExecute( woo_controller_Request $request ) {
        $request->addFeedback( "Welcome to WOO" );
        include( "woo/view/main.php");
    }
}
```

This is the Command object that is served up by CommandResolver if no explicit request for a particular Command is received.

As you may have noticed, the abstract base class implements execute() itself, calling down to the doExecute() implementation of its child class. This allows us to add setup and cleanup code to all commands simply by altering the base class.

The execute() method is passed a Request object that gives access to user input, as well as to the setFeedback() method. DefaultCommand makes use of this to set a welcome message.

Finally, the command dispatches control to a view, simply by calling include(). Embedding the map from command to view in the Command classes is the simplest dispatch mechanism, but for small systems it can be perfectly adequate. A more flexible strategy can be seen in the "Application Controller" section.

Overview

It is possible that the detail of the classes covered in this section might disguise the simplicity of the Front Controller pattern. Figure 12-5 shows a sequence diagram that illustrates the life-cycle of a request.

As you can see, the Front Controller delegates initialization to the ApplicationHelper object (which uses caching to short-circuit any expensive setup). The Controller then acquires a Command object from the CommandResolver object. Finally, it invokes Command::execute() in order to kick off the application logic.

In this implementation of the pattern, the Command itself is responsible for delegating to the View layer. You can see a refinement of this in the next section.

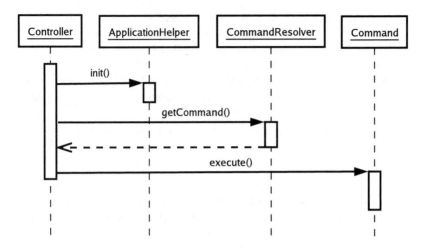

Figure 12-5. *The Front Controller in operation*

Consequences

So Front Controller is not for the fainthearted. It does require a lot of up-front development before you begin to see benefits. This is a serious drawback if your project requires fast turnaround, or if it is small enough that the Front Controller framework would weigh in heavier than the rest of the system.

Having said that, once you have successfully deployed a Front Controller in one project, you will find that you can reuse it for others with lightning speed. You can abstract much of its functionality into library code, effectively building yourself a reusable framework.

The requirement that all configuration information is loaded up for every request is another drawback. All approaches will suffer from this to some extent, but Front Controller often requires additional information, such as logical maps of commands and views.

This overhead can be eased considerably by caching such data. The most efficient way of doing this is to add the data to your system as native PHP. This is fine if you are the sole maintainer of a system, but if you have nontechnical users, you may need to provide a configuration file. You can still automate the native PHP approach, though, by creating a system that builds PHP data structures from and writes them to an include file. Less efficient but much easier is the approach I took in the ApplicationRegistry class—simply serialize the data.

On the plus side, Front Controller centralizes the presentation logic of your system. This means that you can exert control over the way that requests are processed and views selected in one place (well, in one set of classes, anyway). This reduces duplication and decreases the likelihood of bugs.

Front Controller is also very extensible. Once you have a core up and running, you can add new Command classes and views very easily.

In this example, Commands handled their own view dispatch. If you use the Front Controller pattern with an object that helps with view (and possibly Command) selection, then the pattern allows for excellent control over navigation, which is harder to maintain elegantly when presentation control is distributed throughout a system. I cover such an object in the next section.

Application Controller

Allowing commands to invoke their own views is acceptable for smaller systems, but it is not ideal. It is preferable to decouple your Commands from your View layer as much as possible.

An Application Controller takes responsibility for mapping requests to commands, and commands to views. This decoupling means that it becomes easier to switch in alternative sets of views without changing the codebase. It also allows the system owner to change the flow of the application, again without the need for touching any internals. By allowing for a logical system for Command resolution, the pattern also makes it easier for the same Command to be used in different contexts within a system.

The Problem

Remember the nature of our example problem. An administrator needs to be able to add a venue to the system, and to associate a space with it. The system might therefore support the AddVenue and AddSpace commands. According to the examples so far, these commands would be selected using a direct map from a request parameter (cmd=AddVenue) to a class (AddVenue).

Broadly speaking, a successful call to the AddVenue command should lead to an initial call to the AddSpace command. This relationship might be hard coded into the classes themselves, with AddVenue invoking AddSpace on success. AddSpace might then include a view that contains the form for adding the space to the venue.

Both commands may be associated with at least two different views, a core view for presenting the input form and an error or "thank you" screen. According to the logic already discussed, the Command classes themselves would include those views (using conditional tests to decide which view to present in which circumstances).

This level of hard coding is fine, as long as the commands will always be used in the same way. It begins to break down, though, if we want a special view for AddVenue in some circumstances, and if we want to alter the logic by which one command leads to another (perhaps one flow might include an additional screen between a successful venue addition and the start of a space addition). If each of your commands is only used once, in one relationship to other commands, and with one view, then you should hard code your commands' relationship with each other and their views. Otherwise you should read on.

An Application Controller class can take over this logic, freeing up Command classes to concentrate on their job, which is to process input, invoke application logic, and handle any results.

Implementation

As always, the key to this pattern is the interface. An Application Controller is a class (or a set of classes) that the Front Controller can use to acquire commands based on a user request, and to find the right view to present after the command has been run. You can see the bare bones of this relationship in Figure 12-6.

As with all patterns in this chapter, the aim is to make things as simple as possible for the client code—hence our spartan Front Controller class. Behind the interface, though, we must deploy an implementation. The approach laid out here is just one way of doing it. As you work through this section, remember that the essence of the pattern lies in the way that the participants, the Application Controller, the commands, and the views, interact, and not with the specifics of this implementation.

Let's begin with the code that uses the Application Controller.

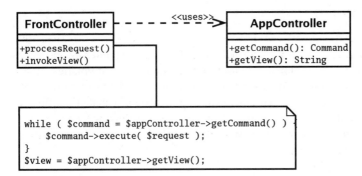

Figure 12-6. *The Application Controller pattern*

The Front Controller

Here is how the FrontController might work with the AppController class (simplified and stripped of error handling):

```
function handleRequest() {
    $request = new woo_controller_Request();
    $app_c = $this->applicationHelper->appController();
    while( $cmd = $app_c->getCommand( $request ) ) {
        $cmd->execute( $request );
    }
    $this->invokeView( $app_c->getView( $request ) );
}

function invokeView( $target ) {
    include( "woo/view/$target.php" );
    exit;
}
```

As you can see, the principle difference from the previous Front Controller example is that here Command objects are retrieved and executed in a loop. The code also uses AppController to get the name of the view that it should include.

So how do we move from a cmd parameter to a chain of commands and ultimately a view?

Implementation Overview

A Command class might demand a different view according to different stages of operation. The default view for the AddVenue command might be a data input form. If the user adds the wrong kind of data, the form may be re-presented, or an error page may be shown. If all goes well, and the venue is created in the system, then we may wish to forward to another in a chain of Command objects: AddSpace, perhaps.

The Command objects tell the system of their current state by setting a status flag. Here are the flags that this minimal implementation recognizes (as set as a property in the Command super class):

```
private static $STATUS_STRINGS = array (
    'CMD_DEFAULT'=>0,
    'CMD_OK' => 1,
    'CMD_ERROR' => 2,
    'CMD_INSUFFICIENT_DATA' => 3
);
```

The Application Controller finds and instantiates the correct Command class using the Request object. Once it has been run, the Command will be associated with a status. This combination of Command and status can be compared against a data structure to determine which command should be run next, or if no more commands should be run, which view to serve up.

The Configuration File

The system's owner can determine the way that commands and views work together in a set of configuration directives. Here is an extract:

```
<control>
    <view>main</view>
    <view status="CMD_OK">menu</view>
    <view status="CMD_ERROR">error</view>

    <command name="ListVenues">
        <view>listvenues</view>
    </command>

    <command name="QuickAddVenue">
        <classroot name="AddVenue" />
        <view>quickadd</view>
    </command>

    <command name="AddVenue">
        <view>addvenue</view>
        <status value="CMD_OK">
          <forward>AddSpace</forward>
        </status>
    </command>

    <command name="AddSpace">
        <view>addspace</view>
        <status value="CMD_OK">
            <forward>ListVenues</forward>
        </status>
    </command>
    ...
</control>
```

This simplified XML fragment shows one strategy for abstracting the flow of commands and their relationship to views from the Command classes themselves. The directives are all contained within a control element. The logic here is search-based. The outermost elements defined are the most generic. They can be overridden by their equivalents within command elements.

So the first element, view, defines the default view for all commands if no other directive contradicts this order. The other view elements on the same level declare status attributes (which correspond to flags set in the Command class). Each status represents a flag that might be set by a Command object to signal its progress with a task. Because these elements are more specific than the first view element, they have priority. If a command sets the CMD_OK flag, then the corresponding view "menu" is the one that will be included, unless an even more specific element overrides this.

Having set these defaults, the document presents the command elements. By default these elements map directly to Command classes (and their class files on the file system) as in the previous CommandResolver example. So if the cmd parameter is set to AddVenue, then the corresponding element in the configuration document is selected. The string "AddVenue" is used to construct a path to the AddVenue.php class file.

Aliases are supported, however. So if cmd is set to QuickAddVenue, then the following element is used:

```
<command name="QuickAddVenue">
    <classroot name="AddVenue" />
    <view>quickadd</view>
</command>
```

Here the command element named QuickAddVenue does not map to a class file. That mapping is defined by the classroot element. This makes it possible to reference the AddVenue class in the context of many different flows, and many different views.

Command elements work from outer elements to inner elements, with the inner, more specific, elements having priority. By setting a view element within a command, we ensure that the command is tied to that view.

```
<command name="AddVenue">
    <view>addvenue</view>
    <status value="CMD_OK">
      <forward>AddSpace</forward>
    </status>
</command>
```

So here the addvenue view is associated with the AddVenue command (as set in the Request object's cmd parameter). This means that the addvenue.php view will always be included when the AddVenue command is invoked. Always, that is, unless the status condition is matched. If the AddVenue class sets a flag of CMD_OK, the default view for the Command is overridden.

The status element could simply contain another view that would be included in place of the default. Here, though, the forward element comes into play. By forwarding to another command, the configuration file delegates all responsibility for handling views to the new element.

Parsing the Configuration File

This is a reasonably flexible model for controlling display and command flow logic. The document, though, is not something that you would want to parse for every single request. We have already seen a solution to this problem. The ApplicationHelper class provides a mechanism for caching configuration data.

Here is an extract:

```
private function getOptions() {
    $this->ensure( file_exists( $this->config ),
                       "Could not find options file" );
    $options = @SimpleXml_load_file( $this->config );

    // ...set DSN...

    $map = new woo_controller_ControllerMap();

    foreach ( $options->control->view as $default_view ) {
        $stat_str = trim($default_view['status']);
        $status = woo_command_Command::statuses( $stat_str );
        $map->addView( 'default', $status, (string)$default_view );
    }
    // ... more parse code omitted ...
    woo_base_ApplicationRegistry::setControllerMap( $map );
}

function appController() {
    $map = woo_base_ApplicationRegistry::getControllerMap();
    $this->ensure( is_object($map), "No ControllerMap" );
    return new woo_controller_AppController( $map );
}
```

Parsing XML, even with the excellent SimpleXML package, is a wordy business, and not particularly challenging, so I leave most of the details out here. The key thing to note is that the getOptions() method is only invoked if configuration has not been cached into the ApplicationRegistry object.

Storing the Configuration Data

The cached object in question is a ControllerMap. ControllerMap is essentially a wrapper around three arrays. We could use raw arrays, of course, but ControllerMap gives us the security of knowing that each array will follow a particular format. Here is the ControllerMap class:

```
class woo_controller_ControllerMap {
    private $viewMap = array();
    private $forwardMap = array();
    private $classrootMap = array();

    function addClassroot( $command, $classroot ) {
        $this->classrootMap[$command]=$classroot;
    }

    function getClassroot( $command ) {
        return ($name = $this->classrootMap[$command])?
            $name : $command;
    }

    function addView( $command='default', $status=0, $view ) {
        $this->viewMap[$command][$status]=$view;
    }

    function getView( $command, $status ) {
        return $this->viewMap[$command][$status];
    }

    function addForward( $command, $status=0, $newCommand ) {
        $this->forwardMap[$command][$status]=$newCommand;
    }

    function getForward( $command, $status ) {
        return $this->forwardMap[$command][$status];
    }
}
```

The $classroot property is simply an associative array that maps command handles (that is, the names of the command elements in configuration) to the roots of Command class names (that is, AddVenue, as opposed to woo_command_AddVenue). This is used to determine whether the cmd parameter is an alias to a particular class file. During the parsing of the configuration file, the addClassroot() method is called to populate this array.

The $forwardMap and $viewMap arrays are both two-dimensional, supporting combinations of commands and statuses.

Returning to this fragment:

```
<command name="AddVenue">
    <view>addvenue</view>
    <status value="CMD_OK">
      <forward>AddSpace</forward>
    </status>
</command>
```

Here is the call the parse code will make to add the correct element to the $viewMap property:

```
$map->addView( 'AddVenue', 0, 'addvenue' );
```

And here is the call for populating the $forwardMap property:

```
$map->addForward( 'AddVenue', 1, 'AddSpace' );
```

The Application Controller class uses these combinations in a particular search order. Let's say the AddVenue command has returned CMD_OK (which maps to 1, while 0 is CMD_DEFAULT). The Application Controller will search the $forwardMap array from the most specific combination of Command and status flag to the most general. The first match found will be the command string that is returned:

```
$viewMap['AddVenue'][1];   //  AddVenue CMD_OK [MATCHED]
$viewMap['AddVenue'][0];   //  AddVenue CMD_DEFAULT
$viewMap['default'][1];    //  DefaultCommand CMD_OK
$viewMap['default'][0];    //  DefaultCommand CMD_DEFAULT
```

The same hierarchy of array elements is searched in order to retrieve a view.
Here is an Application Controller:

```
class woo_controller_AppController {
    private static $base_cmd;
    private static $default_cmd;
    private $controllerMap;
    private $invoked = array();

    function __construct( ControllerMap $map ) {
        $this->controllerMap = $map;
        if ( ! self::$base_cmd ) {
            self::$base_cmd = new ReflectionClass( "woo_command_Command" );
            self::$default_cmd = new woo_command_DefaultCommand();
        }
    }

    function getView( woo_controller_Request $req ) {
        $view = $this->getResource( $req, "View" );
        return $view;
    }

    function getForward( woo_controller_Request $req ) {
        $forward = $this->getResource( $req, "Forward" );
        if ( $forward ) {
            $req->setProperty( 'cmd', $forward );
        }
        return $forward;
    }
```

```
    private function getResource( woo_controller_Request $req,
                                  $res ) {
    $cmd_str = $req->getProperty( 'cmd' );
    $previous = $req->getLastCommand();
    $status = $previous->getStatus();
    if (! $status ) { $status = 0; }
    $acquire = "get$res";
    $resource = $this->controllerMap->$acquire(
                        $cmd_str, $status );
    if ( ! $resource ) {
        $resource = $this->controllerMap->$acquire( $cmd_str,
                    0 );
    }
    if ( ! $resource ) {
        $resource = $this->controllerMap->$acquire( 'default',
                    $status );
    }
    if ( ! $resource ) {
        $resource = $this->controllerMap->$acquire( 'default',
                    0 );
    }
    return $resource;
}

function getCommand( woo_controller_Request $req ) {
    $previous = $req->getLastCommand();
    if ( ! $previous ) {
        // this is the first command this request
        $cmd = $req->getProperty('cmd');
        if ( ! $cmd ) {
            // no cmd property - using default
            $req->setProperty('cmd', 'default' );
            return  self::$default_cmd;
        }
    } else {
        // a command has been run already this request
        $cmd = $this->getForward( $req );
        if ( ! $cmd ) { return null; }
    }
    // we now have a command name in $cmd

    // turn it into a Command object
    $cmd_obj = $this->resolveCommand( $cmd );
    if ( ! $cmd_obj ) {
        throw new woo_base_AppException( "couldn't
            resolve '$cmd'" );
    }
```

```
        $cmd_class = get_class( $cmd_obj );
        $this->invoked[$cmd_class]++;
        if ( $this->invoked[$cmd_class] > 1 ) {
            throw new woo_base_AppException( "circular forwarding" );
        }
        // return the Command object
        return $cmd_obj;
    }

    function resolveCommand( $cmd ) {
        $cmd=str_replace( array('.','/'), "", $cmd );
        $classroot = $this->controllerMap->getClassroot( $cmd );
        $filepath = "woo/command/$classroot.php";
        $classname = "woo_command_$classroot";
        if ( file_exists( $filepath ) ) {
            require_once( "$filepath" );
            if ( class_exists( $classname ) ) {
                $cmd_class = new ReflectionClass($classname);
                if ( $cmd_class->isSubClassOf( self::$base_cmd ) ) {
                    return $cmd_class->newInstance();
                }
            }
        }
        return null;
    }
}
```

The getResource() method implements the search for both forwarding and view selection. It is called by getView() and getForward(), respectively. Notice how it searches from the most specific combination of command string and status flag to the most generic.

getCommand() is responsible for returning as many commands as have been configured into a forwarding chain. It works like this: when the initial request is received, there should be a cmd property available, and no record of a previous Command having been run in this request. The Request object stores this information. If the cmd request property has not been set, then the method uses "default", and returns the default Command class. The $cmd string variable is passed to resolveCommand(), which uses it to acquire a Command object.

When getCommand() is called for the second time in the request, the Request object will be holding a reference to the Command previously run. getCommand() then checks to see if any forwarding is set for the combination of that Command and its status flag (by calling getForward()). If getForward() finds a match, it returns a string that can be resolved to a Command and returned to the Controller.

Another thing to note in getCommand() is the essential check we impose to prevent circular forwarding. We maintain an array indexed by Command class names. If the tally for any element exceeds 1, we know that this command has been retrieved previously. This puts us at risk of falling into an infinite loop, which is something we *really* don't want, so we throw an exception if this happens.

The Command Class

You may have noticed that the AppController class relies upon previous commands having been stored in the Request object. This is done by the Command base class:

```
abstract class woo_command_Command {

    private static $STATUS_STRINGS = array (
        'CMD_DEFAULT'=>0,
        'CMD_OK' => 1,
        'CMD_ERROR' => 2,
        'CMD_INSUFFICIENT_DATA' => 3
    );

    private $status = 0;

    final function __construct() { }

    function execute( woo_controller_Request $request ) {
        $this->status = $this->doExecute( $request );
        $request->setCommand( $this );
    }

    function getStatus() {
        return $this->status;
    }

    static function statuses( $str='CMD_DEFAULT' ) {
        if ( empty( $str ) ) { $str = 'CMD_DEFAULT'; }
        // convert string into a status number
        return self::$STATUS_STRINGS[$str];
    }
    abstract function doExecute( woo_controller_Request $request );
}
```

The Command class defines an array of status strings (severely cut for the sake of this example). It provides the statuses() method for converting a string ("CMD_OK") to its equivalent number, and getStatus() for revealing the current Command object's status flag. If you want to be strict, statuses() could throw an Exception on failure. As it is, the method returns null by default if the right element is not defined. The execute() method uses the return value of the abstract doExecute() to set the status flag, and to cache itself in the Request object.

A Concrete Command

Here is how a simple AddVenue command might look:

```
class woo_command_AddVenue extends woo_command_Command {
    function doExecute( woo_controller_Request $request ) {
        $name = $request->getProperty("venue_name");
        if ( ! $name ) {
            $request->addFeedback( "no name provided" );
            return self::statuses('CMD_INSUFFICIENT_DATA');
        } else {
            $venue_obj = new woo_domain_Venue( null, $name );
            $request->setObject( 'venue', $venue_obj );
            $request->addFeedback( "'$name' added ({$venue_obj->getId()})" );
            return self::statuses('CMD_OK');
        }

    }
}
```

Some of this code will make more sense later in the chapter. The key thing to note is that the doExecute() method returns a status flag that the abstract base class stores in a property. The decision as to how to respond to the fact that this object has been invoked and has set this status is entirely driven by the configuration file. So according to the example XML, if CMD_OK is returned, the forwarding mechanism will cause the AddSpace class to be instantiated. This chain of events is triggered in this way only if the request contains cmd=AddVenue. If the request contains cmd=QuickAddVenue, then no forwarding will take place, and the quickaddvenue view will be displayed.

Incidentally, although this example looks to be stripped of any code for saving a Venue object to the database, such is the magic of the patterns still to come that persistence is actually handled for us behind the scenes!

Consequences

This pattern is a pain to set up because of the sheer amount of work that must go into acquiring and applying metadata that describes the relationship between command and request, command and command, and command and view.

For this reason, I tend to implement something like this when my application tells me it is needed. This is generally when I find myself adding switches to my commands that invoke different views or invoke other commands according to circumstances. It is at about this time that I feel that command flow and display logic are beginning to spiral out of my control.

Once you have implemented an Application Controller, though, things should become much easier, as long as you have built adequate functionality into your system. In our implementation, for example, we omitted one feature I would probably consider—the ability to include subcommands within a Composite command and define this at runtime. This is not difficult to implement on top of the current implementation.

Page Controller

Much as I like the Front Controller pattern, it is not always the right approach to take. The investment in up-front design tends to reward the larger system and penalize simple need-results-now projects. Page Controller probably does not need too much attention here, as I guess that it is the default approach for most PHP developers. It is worth rehearsing some of the issues, though.

The Problem

Once again, the problem is your need to manage the relationship between request, domain logic, and presentation. This is pretty much a constant for Enterprise projects. What differs, though, are the constraints placed upon you.

If you have a relatively simple project, and one where the time spent on infrastructure design will impinge upon schedule, Page Controller can be a good option for managing requests and views.

Let's say that you want to present a page that displays a list of all venues in the WOO system. Even with the database retrieval code finished, without a Front Controller already in place, we have a daunting task to get just this simple result.

The view is a list of venues, the request is for a list of venues. Errors permitting, the request does not lead to a new view, as you might expect in a complex task. The simplest thing that works here is to associate the view and the controller—often in the same page.

Implementation

Although the practical reality of Page Controller projects can become fiendish, the pattern is simple. Control is related to a view, or to a set of views. In the simplest case, this means that the control sits in the view itself, although it can be abstracted, especially when a view is closely linked with others (that is when you might need to forward to different pages in different circumstances).

Here is the simplest flavor of Page Controller:

```php
try {
    $venues = woo_domain_Venue::findAll();
} catch ( Exception $e ) {
    include( 'error.php' );
    exit(0);
}

// default page follows
?>
<html>
<head>
<title>Venues</title>
</head>
<body>
<h1>Venues</h1>

<?php foreach( $venues as $venue ) { ?>
    <?php print $venue->getName(); ?><br />
<?php } ?>

</body>
</html>
```

This document has two elements to it. The view element handles display, whilst the controller element manages the request, and invokes application logic. Even though view and controller inhabit the same page, they are rigidly separated.

There is very little to this example (aside from the database work going on behind the scenes, of which more in the section "The Data Layer"). The PHP block at the top of the page attempts to get a list of Venue objects, which it stores in the $venues global variable.

If an error occurs, then the page delegates to a page called "error.php" by using include(), followed by exit() to kill any further processing on the current page. I prefer this mechanism to an HTTP forward, which is much more expensive, and loses you any environment you may have set up in memory. If no include takes place, then the HTML at the bottom of the page (the view) is shown.

Figure 12-7 shows this crude model.

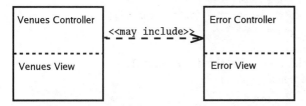

Figure 12-7. *Page Controllers embedded in views*

This will do as a quick test, but a system of any size or complexity will probably need more support than that.

The Page Controller code was previously implicitly separated from the view. Here I make the break starting with a rudimentary Page Controller base class:

```
abstract class woo_controller_PageController {
    private $request;
    function __construct() {
        $request = woo_base_RequestRegistry::getRequest();
        if ( ! $request ) { $request = new woo_controller_Request(); }
        $this->request = $request;
    }

    abstract function process();

    function forward( $resource ) {
        include( $resource );
        exit( 0 );
    }

    function getRequest() {
        return $this->request;
    }
}
```

This class uses some of the tools that we have already looked at, in particular the Request and RequestRegistry classes. The PageController class's main roles are to provide access to a Request object, and to manage the including of views. This list of purposes would quickly grow in a real project as more child classes discover a need for common functionality.

A child class could live inside the view, and thereby display it by default as before, or it could stand separate from the view. The latter approach is cleaner, I think, so that's the path I take. Here is a PageController that attempts to add a new venue to the system:

```
class woo_controller_AddVenueController extends woo_controller_PageController {
    function process() {
        try {
            $request = $this->getRequest();
            $name = $request->getProperty( 'venue_name' );
            if ( ! $request->getProperty('submitted') ) {
                $request->addFeedback("choose a name for the venue");
                $this->forward( 'add_venue.php' );
            } else if ( ! $name ) {
                $request->addFeedback("name is a required field");
                $this->forward( 'add_venue.php' );
            }
            // just creating the object is enough to add it
            // to the database
            $venue = new woo_domain_Venue( null, $name );
            $this->forward( "ListVenues.php" );
        } catch ( Exception $e ) {
            $this->forward( 'error.php' );
        }
    }
}
$controller = new woo_controller_AddVenueController();
$controller->process();
```

The AddVenueController class only implements the process() method. process() is responsible for checking the user's submission. If the user has not submitted a form, or has completed the form incorrectly, the default view (add_venue.php) is included, providing feedback and presenting the form. If we successfully add a new user, then the method invokes forward() to send the user to the ListVenues Page Controller.

Note the format I used for the view. I tend to differentiate view files from class files by using all lowercase file names in the former and camel case in the latter.

Here is the view associated with the AddVenueController class:

```
<?php
require_once( "woo/base/Registry.php" );
$request = woo_base_RequestRegistry::getRequest();
?>
<html>
<head>
<title>Add Venue</title>
</head>
```

```
<body>
<h1>Add Venue</h1>

<table>
<tr>
<td>
<?php
print $request->getFeedbackString("</td></tr><tr><td>");
?>
</td>
</tr>
</table>

<form action="AddVenue.php" method="get">
    <input type="hidden" name="submitted" value="yes"/>
    <input type="text" name="venue_name" />
</form>

</body>
</html>
```

As you can see, the view does nothing but display data and provide the mechanism for generating a new request. The request is made to the PageController, not back to the view. Remember, it is the PageController class that is responsible for processing requests.

You can see an overview of this more complicated version of the Page Controller pattern in Figure 12-8.

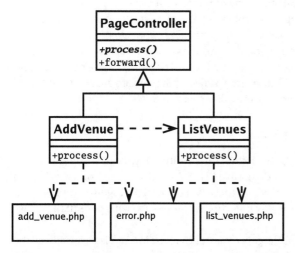

Figure 12-8. *A Page Controller class hierarchy and its include relationships*

Consequences

This approach has the great benefit that it makes sense to anyone with any Web experience straightaway. We make a request for venues.php, and that is precisely what we get. Even an error is within the bounds of everyday expectation, with "server error" and "page not found" pages an everyday reality.

Things get a little more complicated if you separate the view from the Page Controller, but the near one-to-one relationship between the participants is clear enough.

One potential area of confusion lies with the inclusion of views. A Page Controller includes its view once it has completed processing. In some circumstances, though, it might use the same inclusion code to include another Page Controller. So, for example, when AddVenue successfully adds a venue, it no longer needs to display the addition form. Instead it delegates to another Page Controller called ListVenues. You need to be clear about when you are delegating to a view, and when you are delegating to another Page Controller. It is the responsibility of the Page Controller to ensure that its views have the data they need to do their job.

Although a Page Controller class might delegate to Command objects, the benefit of doing so is not so marked as it is with Front Controller. Front Controller classes need to work out what the purpose of a request is; Page Controller classes already know this. The light request checking and logic layer calls that you would put in a Command sit just as easily in a Page Controller class, and you benefit from the fact that you do not need a mechanism to select your Command objects.

Duplication can be a problem, but the use of a common super class can factor away a lot of that. You can also save on setup time, because you can avoid loading data you won't be needing in the current context. Of course, you could do that with Front Controller too, but the process of discovering what is and is not needed would be much more complicated.

The real drawback to the pattern lies in situations where the paths through your views are complex—especially when the same view is used in different ways at different times (add and edit screens are a good example of this). You can find that you get tangled up in conditionals and state checking, and it becomes hard to get an overview of your system.

It is not impossible to start with a Page Controller and move toward a Front Controller, however. This is especially true if you are using a PageController super class.

As a rule of thumb, if I estimate a system should take me less than a week or so to complete, and that it isn't going to need more phases in the future, I would choose a Page Controller, and benefit from fast turnaround. If I were building a large project that needs to grow over time and has complex view logic, I would go for a Front Controller every time.

Template View and View Helper

Template View is pretty much what you get by default in PHP, in that we can commingle presentation markup (HTML) and system code (native PHP). As I have said before, this is both a blessing and a curse, because the ease with which these can be brought together represents a temptation to combine application and display logic in the same place with potentially disastrous consequences.

In PHP then, programming the view is largely a matter of restraint. If it isn't strictly a matter of display, then treat any code with the greatest suspicion.

To this end, the View Helper pattern (Alur et al.) provides for a helper class that may be specific to a view or shared between multiple views to help with any tasks that require more than the smallest amount of code.

The Problem

These days it is becoming rarer to find SQL queries and other business logic embedded directly in display pages, but it still happens. I have covered this particular evil in great detail in previous chapters, so let's keep this brief.

Web pages that contain too much code can be hard for Web producers to work with, as presentation components become tangled up in loops and conditionals.

Business logic in the presentation forces you to stick with that interface. You can't switch in a new view easily without porting across a lot of application code too.

With many operations recurring from view to view, systems that embed application code in their templates tend to fall prey to duplication as the same code structures are pasted from page to page. Where this happens, bugs and maintenance nightmares surely follow.

To prevent this happening, you should handle application processing elsewhere, and allow views to manage presentation only. This is often achieved by making views the passive recipients of data. Where a view does need to interrogate the system, it is a good idea to provide a View Helper object to do any involved work on the view's behalf.

Implementation

Once you have created a wider framework, the View layer is not a massive programming challenge. Of course, it remains a huge design and information architecture issue, but that's another book!

Template View was so named by Martin Fowler. It is a staple pattern used by most Enterprise programmers. In some languages an implementation might involve cooking up a templating system that translates tags to values set by the system. We have that option in PHP too. We could use a templating engine like the excellent Smarty. My preferred option, though, is to use PHP's existing functionality, but to use it with care.

In order for a view to have something to work with, it must be able to acquire data. I like to define a View Helper that views can use. From this, they can get access to the Request object and through it to any other objects that they need to do their job.

Here is a simple View Helper class:

```
class VH {
    static function getRequest() {
        return woo_base_RequestRegistry::getRequest();
    }
}
```

All this class does at present is to provide access to a Request object. You can extend it to provide additional functionality as your application evolves. If you find yourself doing something in a view that takes up more than a couple of lines, chances are it belongs in the View Helper. In a larger application, you may provide multiple View Helper objects in an inheritance hierarchy in order to provide different tools for different parts of your system.

Here is a simple view that uses both the View Helper and the Request object:

```php
<?php
require_once( "woo/view/ViewHelper.php" );
$request = VH::getRequest();
$venue = $request->getObject('venue');
?>

<html>
<head>
<title>Add a Space for venue <?php echo $venue->getName() ?></title>
</head>
<body>
<h1>Add a Space for Venue '<?php print $venue->getName() ?>'</h1>

<table>
<tr>
<td>
<?php print $request->getFeedbackString("</td></tr><tr><td>"); ?>
</td>
</tr>
</table>

<form method="post">
    <input type="text"
     value="<?php echo $request->getProperty( 'space_name' ) ?>" name="space_name"/>
    <input type="hidden" name="venue_id" value="<?php echo $venue->getId() ?>" />
    <input type="submit" value="submit" />
</form>

</body>
</html>
```

The view (add_space.php) gets a Request object from the View Helper (VH) and uses its methods to supply the dynamic data for the page. In particular, the getFeedback() method returns any messages set by commands, and getObject() acquires any objects cached for the View layer. getProperty() is used to access any parameters set in the HTTP request.

You could simplify things still further here by making the View Helper a proxy that delegates for the Request object's most useful methods, saving the View layer the bother of even acquiring a reference to Request.

Clearly this example doesn't banish code from the view, but it does severely limit the amount and kind of coding that needs to be done. The page contains simple print statements and a few method calls. A designer should be able to work around code of this kind with little or no effort.

Slightly more problematic are if statements and loops. These are difficult to delegate to a View Helper because they are usually bound up with formatted output. I tend to keep both simple conditionals and loops (which are very common in building tables that display rows of data) inside the Template View, but to keep them as simple as possible, delegating things like test clauses where possible.

Consequences

There is something slightly disturbing about the way that data is passed to the view layer, in that a view doesn't really have a fixed interface that guarantees its environment. I tend to think of every view as entering into a contract with the system at large. The view effectively says to the application, "If I am invoked, then I have a right to access object `This`, object `That`, and object `TheOther`." It is up to the application to ensure that this is the case.

Surprisingly, I have always found that this works perfectly well for me, though you could make views stricter by adding assertions to view-specific helper classes. If you go as far as this, you could go for complete safety and provide accessor methods in the helper classes that do away with the need for the evil `Request::getObject()` method, which is clearly just a wrapper around an associative array.

While I like type safety where I can get it, I find the thought of building a parallel system of views and View Helper classes exhausting in the extreme. I tend to register objects dynamically for the view layer, whether through a `Request` object, a `SessionRegistry`, or a `RequestRegistry`.

While templates are often essentially passive, populated with data resulting from the last request, there may be times when the view may need to make an ancillary request. The View Helper is a good place to provide this functionality, keeping any knowledge of the mechanism by which data is required hidden from the view itself. Even the View Helper should do as little work as possible, delegating to a command or contacting the domain layer via a Facade.

▓**Note** We saw the Facade pattern in Chapter 10. Alur et al. look at one use of Facades in Enterprise programming in the Session Facade pattern (which is designed to limit fine-grained network transactions). Martin Fowler also describes a pattern called Service Layer which provides a simple point of access to the complexities within a layer.

The Business Logic Layer

If the control layer orchestrates communication with the outside world and marshals a system's response to it, the logic layer gets on with the *business* of an application. This layer should be as free as possible of the noise and trauma generated as query strings are analyzed, HTML tables are constructed, and feedback messages composed. Business logic is about doing the "stuff" that needs doing—the true purpose of the application. Everything else exists just to support these tasks.

In a classic object-oriented application, the Business Logic layer is often composed of classes that model the problems that the system aims to address. As we shall see, this is a flexible design decision. It also requires significant up-front planning.

Let's begin, then, with the quickest way of getting a system up and running.

Transaction Script

The Transaction Script pattern (*Patterns of Enterprise Application Architecture*) describes the way that many systems evolve of their own accord. It is simple, intuitive, and effective, although it becomes less effective as systems grow. It is also a hard pattern to categorize, because it combines elements from other layers in this chapter. I have chosen to present it as part of the Business Logic layer because the pattern's motivation is to achieve the business aims of the system.

The Problem

Every request must be handled in some way. As we have seen, many systems provide a layer that assesses and filters incoming data. Ideally, though, this layer should then call on classes that are designed to fulfill the request. Each of these classes will provide a set of methods, and each method will be crafted to handle a particular request.

The problem then is the need to provide a fast and effective mechanism for fulfilling a system's objectives.

The great benefit of this pattern is the speed with which you can get results. Each script takes input, and manipulates the database to ensure an outcome. Beyond organizing related methods within the same class, and keeping the Transaction Script classes in their own tier (that is, as naive as possible of the Command and Controller and View layers), there is little up-front design required.

While Business Logic layer classes tend to be clearly separated from the Presentation layer, they are often more embedded in the Data layer. This is because retrieving and storing data is key to the tasks that such classes often perform. We will see mechanisms for decoupling logic objects from the database later in the chapter. Transaction Script classes, though, usually know all about the database (though they can use gateway classes to handle the details of their actual queries).

Implementation

Let's return to our events listing example. In this case, the system supports three relational database tables: venue, space, and event. A venue may have a number of spaces (a theater can have more than one stage, for example, a dance club may have different rooms, and so on). Each space plays host to many events. Here is the schema:

```
CREATE TABLE venue
( id INT PRIMARY KEY, name TEXT );
CREATE TABLE space
( id INT PRIMARY KEY, venue INT, name TEXT );
CREATE TABLE event
( id INT PRIMARY KEY, space INT, start long, duration int, name text );
```

Clearly our system will need mechanisms for adding both venues and events. Each of these represents a single transaction. We could give each method its own class (and organize our classes according to the Command pattern that we encountered in the last chapter). In this case, though, we are going to place the methods in a single class, albeit as part of an inheritance hierarchy. You can see the structure in Figure 12-9.

So why does this example include an abstract super class? In a script of any size, we would be likely to add more concrete classes to this hierarchy. Since most of these will work with the database, a common super class is an excellent place to put core functionality for making database requests.

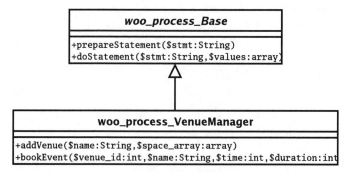

Figure 12-9. *A Transaction Script class with its super class*

In fact, this is a pattern in its own right (Martin Fowler has named it Layer Supertype), albeit one that most programmers use without thinking. Where classes in a layer share characteristics, it makes sense to group them into a single type, locating utility operations in the base class. We will see this a lot in this chapter.

In this case, the base class acquires a DB object, which it stores in a static property. It also provides methods for caching database statements and making queries.

```
abstract class woo_process_Base {
    static $DB;
    static $stmts = array();

    function __construct() {
        self::$DD - woo_base_RequestRegistry::getDB( "DB" );
        if ( ! self::$DB ) {
            throw new woo_base_AppException( "No DB object" );
        }
        if ( DB::isError( self::$DB ) ) {
            throw new woo_base_DBException( self::$DB );
        }
    }


    protected function prepareStatement( $stmt_s ) {
        if ( self::$stmts[$stmt_s] ) {
            return self::$stmts[$stmt_s];
        }
        $stmt_handle = self::$DB->prepare($stmt_s);
        if ( DB::isError( $stmt_handle ) ) {
            throw new woo_base_DBException( $stmt_handle );
        }
        self::$stmts[$stmt_s] = $stmt_handle;
        return $stmt_handle;
    }
```

```
    protected function doStatement( $stmt_s, $values_a ) {
        $st_handle = $this->prepareStatement( $stmt_s );
        $db_result = self::$DB->execute( $st_handle, $values_a );
        if ( DB::isError( $db_result ) ) {
            throw new woo_base_DBException( $db_result );
        }
        return $db_result;
    }
}
```

There's less to this class than meets the eye. Most of the bulk you can see is code for throwing exceptions when things go wrong.

We use the RequestRegistry class to acquire a DB_common object, which we store in the static $DB property. If we fail to acquire a DB_common object, we throw an exception, ensuring that the type can only be used with a valid database connection.

The prepareStatement() method simply calls DB_Common class's prepare() method, which returns a statement handle. This is eventually passed to the execute() method. To run a query though in this method, we simply cache the resource in a static array called $stmts. We use the SQL statement itself as the array element's index.

prepareStatement() can be called directly by child classes, but it is more likely to be invoked via doStatement(). This accepts an SQL statement, and a mixed array of values (strings and integers). This array should contain the values that are to be passed to the database in executing the statement. The method then uses the SQL statement in a call to prepareStatement(), acquiring a statement resource that it uses with the DB_common::execute() method. If an error occurs, we throw an exception. As we will see, all this work is hidden from our transaction scripts. All they need to do is formulate the SQL and get on with business logic.

Here is the start of the VenueManager class, which sets up our SQL statements:

```
class woo_process_VenueManager extends woo_process_Base {
    static $add_venue =  "INSERT INTO venue
                          ( id, name )
                          values( ?, ? )";
    static $add_space  = "INSERT INTO space
                          ( id, name, venue )
                          values( ?, ?, ? )";
    static $check_slot = "SELECT id, name
                          FROM event
                          WHERE space=?
                          AND (start+duration) > ?
                          AND start < ?";
    static $add_event =  "INSERT INTO event
                          ( id, name, space, start, duration )
                          values( ?, ?, ?, ?, ? )";
    //...
```

Not much new here. These are the SQL statements that the transaction scripts will use. They are constructed in a format accepted by the DB package's prepareStatement() method. The question marks are placeholders for the values that will be passed to doStatement().

Let's look at the first method designed to fulfill a specific business need:

```
function addVenue( $name, $space_array ) {
    // check input here
    $ret = array();
    $v_id = self::$DB->nextId('venue');
    $ret['venue'] = array( $v_id, $name );
    $this->doStatement( self::$add_venue, $ret['venue']);
    $ret['spaces'] = array();
    foreach ( $space_array as $space_name ) {
        $s_id = self::$DB->nextId('space');
        $values = array($s_id, $space_name, $v_id );
        $this->doStatement( self::$add_space, $values);
        $ret['spaces'][] = $values;
    }
    return $ret;
}
```

As you can see, addVenue() requires a venue name, and an array of space names. It uses these to populate the venue and space tables. It also creates a data structure that contains this information, along with the newly generated ID values for each row.

This method is spared lots of tedious database work by the super class. We acquire a table-unique ID value from the database and pass that, along with the venue name provided by the caller, to doStatement(). If there's an error with this, remember, an exception is thrown. We don't catch any exceptions here, so anything thrown by doStatement() or (by extension) prepareStatement() will also be thrown by this method. This is the result we want, although we should be careful to make it clear that this method throws exceptions in our documentation.

Having created the venue row, we loop through $space_array, adding a row in the space table for each element. Notice that we include the venue ID as a foreign key in each of the space rows we create, associating the row with the venue.

The second Transaction Script is similarly straightforward:

```
function bookEvent( $space_id, $name, $unixtime, $duration ) {
    $result =
        $this->doStatement( self::$check_slot,
            array( $space_id, $unixtime, ($unixtime+$duration) ) );
    if ( $result->numRows() > 0 ) {
        throw new woo_base_AppException( "double booked!
            try again" );
    }
    $e_id = self::$DB->nextId('event');
    $this->doStatement( self::$add_event,
        array( $e_id, $name, $space_id, $unixtime, $duration ) );
}
```

The purpose of this script is to add an event to the events table, associated with a space. Notice that we use the SQL statement contained in $check_slot to make sure that the proposed event does not clash with another in the same space.

Consequences

The Transaction Script pattern is an effective way of getting good results fast. It is also one of those patterns many programmers have used for years without imagining it might need a name. With a few good helper methods like those we added to the base class, you can concentrate on application logic without getting too bogged down in database fiddle-faddling.

I have seen Transaction Script appear in a less welcome context. I thought I was writing a much more complex and object-heavy application than would usually suit this pattern. As the pressure of deadlines began to tell, I found that I was placing more and more logic in what was intended to be a thin facade onto a Domain Model (see the next section). Although the result was less elegant than I had wanted, I have to admit that the application did not appear to suffer for its implicit redesign.

In most cases, you would choose a Transaction Script approach with a small project when you are certain it isn't going to grow into a large one. The approach does not scale well, because duplication often begins to creep in as the scripts inevitably cross one another. You can go some way to factoring this out, of course, but you probably will not be able to excise it completely.

In our example, we decide to embed database code in the Transaction Script classes themselves. As you saw, though, the code wants to separate the database work from the application logic. We can make that break absolute by pulling it out of the class altogether and creating a gateway class whose role it is to handle database interactions on the system's behalf.

Domain Model

The Domain Model is the pristine logical engine that many of the other patterns in this chapter strive to create, nurture, and protect. It is an abstracted representation of the forces at work in your project. A kind of plane of forms, where your business problems play out their nature unencumbered by nasty material issues like databases and Web pages.

If that seems a little flowery, let's bring it down to reality. A Domain Model is a representation of the real-world participants of your system. It is in the Domain Model that the object-as-thing rule of thumb is truer than elsewhere. Everywhere else, objects tend to embody responsibilities. In the Domain Model, they often describe a set of attributes, with added agency. They are *things* that do *stuff*.

The Problem

If you have been using Transaction Scripts, you may find that duplication becomes a problem as different scripts need to perform the same tasks. That can be factored out to a certain extent, but over time it's easy to fall into cut-and-paste coding.

You can use a Domain Model to extract and embody the participants and process of your system. Rather than using a script to add space data to the database, and then associate event data with it, you can create Space and Event classes. Booking an event in a space can then become as simple as a call to Space::bookEvent(). A task like checking for a time clash becomes Event::intersects(), and so on.

Clearly, with an example as simple as Woo, a Transaction Script is more than adequate, but as domain logic becomes more complex, it becomes much easier to handle, and less riddled with conditional code if the problems are rendered as a model.

Implementation

Domain Models can be relatively simple to design. Most of the complexity around the subject lies with the patterns that are designed to keep the model pure—that is, to separate it from the other tiers in the application.

Separating the participants of a Domain Model from the presentation layer is largely a matter of ensuring that they keep to themselves. Separating the participants from the Data layer is much more problematic. Although the ideal is to consider a Domain Model only in terms of the problems it represents and resolves, the reality of the database is hard to escape.

It is common for Domain Model classes to map fairly directly to tables in a relational database, and this certainly makes life easier. Figure 12-10, for example, shows a class diagram that sketches some of the participants of the Woo system.

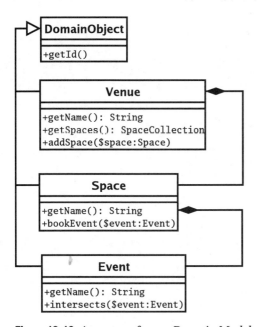

Figure 12-10. *An extract from a Domain Model*

The objects in Figure 12-10 mirror the tables that were set up for the Transaction Script example. This direct association makes a system easier to manage, but it is not always possible, especially if you are working with a database schema that precedes your application.

Just because a Domain Model often mirrors the structure of a database does not mean that its classes should have any knowledge of it. By separating the model from the database, you make the entire tier easier to test, and less likely to be affected by changes of schema, or even changes of storage mechanism. It also focuses the responsibility of each class upon its core tasks.

Here is a simplified Venue object:

```
class woo_domain_Venue extends woo_domain_DomainObject {
    private $name;
    private $spaces;

    function __construct( $id=null, $name=null ) {
        $this->name = $name;
        $this->spaces = self::getCollection("woo_domain_Space");
        parent::__construct( $id );
    }

    function setSpaces( woo_domain_SpaceCollection $spaces ) {
        $this->spaces = $spaces;
    }

    function getSpaces() {
        return $this->spaces;
    }

    function addSpace( woo_domain_Space $space ) {
        $this->spaces->add( $space );
        $space->setVenue( $this );
    }

    function setName( $name_s ) {
        $this->name = $name_s;

        $this->markDirty();
    }

    function getName( ) {
        return $this->name;
    }
}
```

There a few points that distinguish this class from one intended to run without persistence. Instead of an array, we are using an object of type SpaceCollection to store any Space objects the Venue might contain. (Though we could argue that a type-safe array is a bonus whether you are working with a database or not!) Because this class works with a special collection object rather than an array of Space objects, the constructor needs to instantiate an empty collection on startup. It does this by calling a static method on the Layer Supertype.

```
$this->spaces = self::getCollection("woo_domain_Space");
```

I will return to this system's collection objects shortly.

We expect an $id parameter in the constructor that we pass to the super class for storage. It should come as no surprise to learn that the $id parameter represents the unique ID of a row in the database. Notice also that we call a method on the super class called markDirty() (this will covered when we encounter the Unit of Work pattern).

Consequences

The design of a Domain Model needs to be as simple or complicated as the business processes you need to emulate. The beauty of this is that you can focus on the forces in your problem as you design the model, and handle issues like persistence and presentation in other layers. In theory, that is.

In practice I think that most developers design their domain models with at least one eye on the database. No one wants to design structures that will force you (or, worse, your colleagues) into somersaults of convoluted code when it comes to getting your objects in and out of the database.

This separation between Domain Model and the Data layer comes at a considerable cost in terms of design and planning. It is possible to place database code directly in the model (although you would probably want to design a gateway to handle the actual SQL). For relatively simple models, and especially if each class broadly maps to a table, this approach can be a real win, saving you the considerable design overhead of devising an external system for reconciling your objects with the database.

The Data Layer

In discussions with clients, it's usually the Presentation layer that dominates. Fonts, colors, and ease of use are the primary topics of conversation. Amongst developers it is often the database that looms large. It's not the database itself that concerns us; we can trust that to do its job unless we're very unlucky. No, it's the mechanism we use to translate the rows and columns of a database table into data structures that cause the problems. In this section, we look at code that can help with this process.

Not everything presented here sits in the Data layer itself. Rather I have grouped here some of the patterns that help to solve persistence problems.

Data Mapper

If you thought I glossed over the issue of saving and retrieving Venue objects from the database in the "Domain Model" section, here is where you might find at least some answers. The Data Mapper pattern is described by both Alur et al. (as Data Access Object) and Martin Fowler. (In fact, Data Access Object is not an exact match as it generates data transfer objects, but since such objects are designed to become the real thing if you add water, the patterns are close enough.)

As you might imagine, a Data Mapper is a class that is responsible for handling the transition from database to object.

The Problem

Objects are not organized like tables in a relational database. As you know, database tables are grids made up of rows and columns. One row may relate to another in a different (or even the same) table by means of a foreign key. Objects, on the other hand, tend to relate to one another more organically. One object may "contain" another, and different data structures will organize the same objects in different ways, combining and recombining objects in new relationships at runtime.

So how do we make that transition? One answer is to give a class (or a set of classes) responsibility for just that problem, effectively hiding the database from the Domain Model, and managing the inevitable rough edges of the translation.

Implementation

Although with careful programming it may be possible to create a single Mapper class to service multiple objects, it is common to see an individual Mapper for a major class in the Domain Model.

Figure 12-11 shows three concrete Mapper classes and an abstract super class.

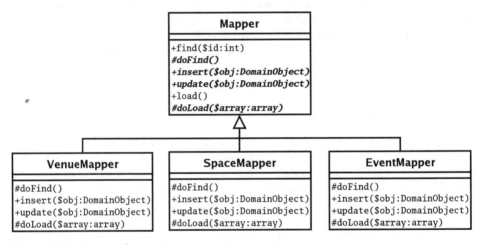

Figure 12-11. *Mapper classes*

In fact, since the Space objects are effectively subordinate to Venue objects, it may be possible to factor the SpaceMapper class into VenueMapper. For the sake of these exercises, I'm going to keep them separate.

As you can see, the classes present common operations for saving and loading data. The base class stores common functionality, delegating to its children to handle object-specific operations. Typically these operations include actual object generation and constructing queries for database operations.

The base class often performs housekeeping before or after an operation, which is why Template Method is used for explicit delegation (calls from concrete methods like load() to abstract ones like doLoad(), etc.). Implementation determines which of the base class methods are made concrete in this way, as you will see later in the chapter.

Here is a simplified version of a Mapper base class:

```
abstract class woo_mapper_Mapper {
    protected static $DB;
    function __construct() {
        if ( ! self::$DB ) {
            self::$DB = woo_controller_ApplicationHelper::
                           instance()->DB( );
        }
    }


    function load( DB_Result $result ) {
        $array = $result->fetchRow( DB_FETCHMODE_ASSOC );
        if ( ! is_array( $array ) ) { return null; }
        if ( ! $array['id'] ) { return null; }
        $object = $this->loadArray( $array );
        return $object;
    }

    function loadArray( $array ) {
        $obj = $this->doLoad( $array );
        return $obj;
    }

    function find( $id ) {
        return $this->doFind( $id );
    }

    protected function doStatement( $sth, $values ) {
        $db_result = self::$DB->execute( $sth, $values );
        if ( DB::isError( $db_result ) ) {
            throw new woo_base_DBException( $db_result );
        }
        return $db_result;
    }
    abstract function insert( woo_domain_DomainObject $obj );
    abstract function update( woo_domain_DomainObject $object );
    protected abstract function doLoad( $array );
    protected abstract function doFind( $id );
}
```

The constructor method uses an ApplicationHelper to get a DB_common object. A stand-alone Singleton or a request-scoped Registry really come into their own for classes like this. There isn't always a sensible path from the presentation layer to a Mapper along which data can be passed. I have omitted code to test the DB_common object for validity, although in fact the ApplicationHelper object does this and throws an exception if it has problems, so we are safe enough.

The find() method does nothing but delegate to doFind(). This would be something that I would factor out in favor of an abstract find() method were it not for the fact that I know that the implementation will be useful here in due course.

doFind() is responsible for constructing and running any queries that are needed. Individual child classes take responsibility for that, finishing up by calling load(). load() is responsible for extracting an associative array from the DB_result object. Having acquired the array, it calls a method named loadArray(), which is responsible for transforming an associative array into a DomainObject instance. loadArray() does this by delegating to the child class's implementation of doLoad().

Child classes will also implement custom methods for finding data according to specific criteria (we will want to locate Space objects that belong to Venue objects, for example).

The doStatement() method is a utility method. It accepts a statement handle and an array of values, and invokes the DB_common::execute() method, returning a DB_result handle, all being well. This method is called by all mapper code that needs to make a database query.

You can take a look at the process from the child's perspective here:

```
class woo_mapper_VenueMapper extends woo_mapper_Mapper {
    private $selectStmt;
    private $updateStmt;
    private $insertStmt;

    function __construct() {
        parent::__construct();
        $this->selectStmt = self::$DB->prepare(
                            "SELECT * FROM venue WHERE id=?");
        $this->updateStmt = self::$DB->prepare(
                            "UPDATE venue SET name=?, id=? WHERE id=?");
        $this->insertStmt = self::$DB->prepare(
                            "INSERT into venue (name, id)
                             values( ?, ?)");
    }

    function doFind( $id ) {
        $result = $this->doStatement( $this->selectStmt, array( $id ) );
        return $this->load( $result );
    }

    protected function doLoad( $array ) {
        $obj = new woo_domain_Venue( $array['id'] );
        $obj->setName( $array['name'] );
        return $obj;
    }
```

```
function insert( woo_domain_DomainObject $object ) {
    $id = $this->newId();
    $object->setId( $id );
    $values = array( $object->getname(), $object->getid() );
    $this->doStatement( $this->insertStmt, $values );
}

public function newId() {
    return self::$DB->nextId('venue');
}

function update( woo_domain_DomainObject $object ) {
    $values = array( $object->getname(),
                     $object->getid(), $object->getId() );
    $this->doStatement( $this->updateStmt, $values );
}
}
```

Once again, this class is stripped of some of the goodies that are still to come. Nonetheless, it does its job. The constructor prepares some SQL statements for use later on. These could be made static and shared across VenueMapper instances, or a single Mapper object could be stored in a Registry, thereby saving the cost of repeated instantiation. These are refactorings I will leave to you!

The doFind() method uses the $selectStmt property and the user-supplied $id to invoke doStatement() on the super class. This should result in a result handle that is passed on to load(). As you have seen, load() delegates to doLoad() where a Venue object is created.

From the point of view of the client, this process is simplicity itself:

```
$mapper = new woo_mapper_VenueMapper();
$venue = $mapper->find( 39 );
print_r( $venue );
```

The print_r() method is a quick way of confirming that find() was successful. In my system (where there is a row in the venue table with ID 39), the output from this fragment is

```
woo_domain_Venue Object
(
    [name:private] => The Hairy Arms
    [spaces:private] =>
    [id:private] => 39
)
```

The insert() and update() methods reverse the process established by find(). Each accepts a DomainObject, extracts row data from it, and calls doStatement() with the resulting information. Notice that the insert() method sets an ID on the provided object. Remember that objects are passed by reference in PHP 5, so the client code will see this change via its own reference.

Another thing to note is that insert() and update() are not really type safe. They will accept any DomainObject subclass without complaint. You should probably perform an instanceof test, and throw an Exception if the wrong object is passed. This will guard against unfortunate but inevitable bugs.

Once again, here is a client perspective on inserting and updating:

```
$venue = new woo_domain_Venue();
$venue->setName( "The Likey Lounge" );
// add the object to the database
$mapper->insert( $venue );
// find the object again - just prove it works!
$venue = $mapper->find( $venue->getId() );
print_r( $venue );
// alter our object
$venue->setName( "The Bibble Beer Likey Lounge" );
// call update to enter the amended data
$mapper->update( $venue );
// once again, go back to the database to prove it worked
$venue = $mapper->find( $venue->getId() );
print_r( $venue );
```

Handling Multiple Rows

The find() method is pretty straightforward because it only needs to return a single object. What do you do though if you need to pull lots of data from the database? Your first thought may be to return an array of objects. This will work, but there is a major problem with the approach.

If you return an array, each object in the collection will need to be instantiated first, which, if you have a result set of 1,000 objects, may be needlessly expensive. An alternative would be to simply return an array and let the calling code sort out object instantiation. This is possible, but it violates the very purpose of our Mapper classes.

There is one way we can have our cake and eat it. It is a feature new to PHP 5 called the Iterator interface.

The Iterator interface requires implementing classes to define methods for querying a list. If you do this, then your class can be used in foreach loops just like an array. There are some people who say that iterator implementations are unnecessary in a language like PHP with such good support for arrays. Tish and piffle! I will show you at least three good reasons for using PHP's built-in Iterator interface in this chapter.

Table 12-1 shows the methods that the Iterator interface requires.

Table 12-1. *Methods Defined by the Iterator Interface*

Name	Description
rewind()	Send pointer to start of list.
current()	Return element at current pointer position.
key()	Return current key (i.e., pointer value).
next()	Return element at current pointer and advance pointer.
valid()	Confirm that there is an element at the current pointer position.

So in order to implement an Iterator, you need to implement its methods, and keep track of a pointer with relation to some kind of set of data. How you acquire that data, or order it, or otherwise filter it is hidden from the client.

Here is an Iterator implementation that works like an array, but also accepts DB_Result and Mapper objects in its constructor for reasons that will become apparent:

```php
abstract class woo_mapper_Collection implements Iterator {
    private $mapper;
    private $result;
    private $total = 0;
    private $pointer = 0;
    private $objects = array();
    private $raw = array();

    function __construct( $result=null, $mapper=null ) {
        if ( $result && $mapper ) {
            $this->init_db( $result, $mapper );
        }
    }

    protected function init_db( DB_Result $result,
                    woo_mapper_Mapper $mapper ) {
        $this->result = $result;
        $this->mapper = $mapper;
        $this->total  += $result->numrows();
        while ( $row = $this->result->fetchRow( DB_FETCHMODE_ASSOC ) ) {
            $this->raw[] = $row;
        }
    }

    protected function doAdd( woo_domain_DomainObject $object ) {
        $this->notifyAccess();
        $this->objects[$this->total] = $object;
        $this->total++;

    }

    protected function notifyAccess() {
        // deliberately left blank!
    }

    private function getObjectAt( $num ) {
        $this->notifyAccess();
        if ( $num >= $this->total || $num < 0 ) {
            return null;
        }
```

```
        if ( $this->objects[$num] ) {
            return $this->objects[$num];
        }

        if ( $this->raw[$num] ) {
            $this->objects[$num]=$this->mapper->loadArray( $this->raw[$num] );
            return $this->objects[$num];
        }
    }

    public function rewind() {
        $this->pointer = 0;
    }

    public function current() {
        return $this->getObjectAt( $this->pointer );
    }

    public function key() {
        return $this->pointer;
    }

    public function next() {
        $row = $this->getObjectAt( $this->pointer );
        if ( $row ) { $this->pointer++; }
        return $row;
    }

    public function valid() {
        return ( ! is_null( $this->current() ) );
    }
}
```

The constructor expects to be called with no arguments or with two. Because the constructor accepts null values, it defers type checking to the init_db() method (if you use a type hint, then your method will not accept a null value for that argument).

Assuming that the client has set the $result and $mapper arguments (it will be a Mapper object that does this), then init_db() is invoked. init_db() acquires all rows from the result set and stores them in an array property called $raw. In fact, there is no really compelling reason why this operation needs to take place inside the Iterator. It could be done inside the Mapper and the resulting multidimensional array passed to the Iterator. Feel free to refactor!

If no arguments were passed to the constructor, the class starts out empty, though note that there is the doAdd() method for adding to the collection.

The class maintains two arrays, $objects and $raw. If a client requests a particular element, then the getObjectAt() method looks first in $objects to see if it has one already instantiated.

If so, that gets returned. Otherwise, the method looks in $raw for the row data. $raw data is only present if a Mapper object is also present, so the raw data can be passed to a new Mapper method, loadArray(), which is simply the array loading stage of the find process pulled out into a separate operation. This returns a DomainObject object, which is cached in the $objects array with the relevant index. The object is returned to the user.

The rest of the class is simple manipulation of the $pointer property, and calls to getObjectAt(). Apart, that is, from the notifyAccess() method, which will become important when we encounter the Lazy Load pattern.

You may have noticed that the Collection class is abstract. You need to provide specific implementations for each domain class:

```
class woo_mapper_VenueCollection
        extends woo_mapper_Collection
 {

    function add( woo_domain_Venue $venue ) {
        $this->doAdd( $venue );
    }
}
```

The VenueCollection class simply extends Collection, and implements an add() method that ensures that only Venue objects can be added to the collection. You could provide additional checking in the constructor as well if you wanted to be even safer. Clearly this class should only work with a VenueMapper. In practical terms, though, this is a reasonably type-safe collection, especially as far as the Domain Model is concerned.

Because the Domain Model needs to instantiate Collection objects, and because we may need to switch the implementation at some point (especially for testing purposes), we provide a factory class in the Domain layer for generating Collection objects on a type-by-type basis. Here's how we get an empty VenueCollection object:

```
$collection = woo_domain_HelperFactory::getCollection("woo_domain_Venue");
```

You can then add values to it and loop through it as if it were an array:

```
$collection->add( new woo_domain_Venue( null, "Loud and Thumping" ) );
$collection->add( new woo_domain_Venue( null, "Eeezy" ) );
$collection->add( new woo_domain_Venue( null, "Duck and Badger" ) );

foreach( $collection as $venue ) {
    print $venue->getName()."\n";
}
```

With the implementation we have built here, there isn't much else you can do with this collection, but adding elementAt(), deleteAt(), count(), etc. methods is a trivial exercise. (And fun, too! Enjoy!)

The DomainObject super class is a good place for convenience methods that acquire collections.

```
// DomainObject

    static function getCollection( $type ) {
        return woo_domain_HelperFactory::getCollection( $type );
    }

    function collection() {
        return self::getCollection( get_class( $this ) );
    }
```

The class supports two mechanisms for acquiring a Collection object: static and instance. In both cases, the methods simply call HelperFactory::getCollection() with a class name. We saw the static getCollection() method used in the Domain Model example earlier in the chapter.

In light of all this, the Venue class can be extended to manage the persistence of Space objects. The class initializes itself with an empty SpaceCollection object like this:

```
    function __construct( $id=null, $name=null ) {
        $this->name = $name;
        $this->spaces = self::getCollection("woo_domain_Space");
        parent::__construct( $id );
    }
```

Venue provides methods for adding individual Space objects to its SpaceCollection, or for switching in an entirely new SpaceCollection.

```
    function setSpaces( woo_domain_SpaceCollection $spaces ) {
        $this->spaces = $spaces;
    }

    function getSpaces() {
        return $this->spaces;
    }

    function addSpace( woo_domain_Space $space ) {
        $this->spaces->add( $space );
        $space->setVenue( $this );
    }
```

The setSpaces() operation is really designed to be used by the VenueMapper class in constructing the Venue. It takes it on trust that all Space objects in the collection refer back to the current Venue. It would be easy enough to add checking to the method. This version keeps things simple though.

The VenueMapper needs to set up a SpaceCollection for each Venue object it creates.

```
// VenueMapper
    protected function doLoad( $array ) {
        $obj = new woo_domain_Venue( $array['id'] );
        $obj->setname( $array['name'] );
        $space_mapper = new woo_mapper_SpaceMapper();
        $space_collection = $space_mapper->findByVenue( $array['id'] );
        $obj->setSpaces( $space_collection );
        $obj->markClean();
        return $obj;
    }
```

The VenueMapper::doLoad() method gets a SpaceMapper, and acquires a SpaceCollection from it. As you can see, the SpaceMapper class implements a findByVenue() method. This is identical to findAll() except for the SQL statement used. The resulting collection is set on the Venue object via Venue::setSpaces().

So Venue objects now arrive fresh from the database, complete with all their Space objects in a neat type-safe list. None of the objects in that list are instantiated before requested.

Figure 12-12 shows the process by which a client class might acquire a SpaceCollection, and how the SpaceCollection class interacts with SpaceMapper::loadArray() to convert its raw data into an object for returning to the client.

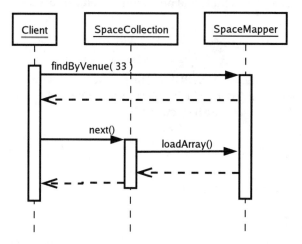

Figure 12-12. *Acquiring a SpaceCollection, and using it to get a Space object*

Consequences

The drawback with the approach we took to adding Space objects to Venue ones is that we had to take two trips to the database. In most instances, I think that is a price worth paying. If efficiency becomes an issue, however, it should be easy enough to factor out SpaceMapper altogether and retrieve all the data you need in one go using an SQL join.

Of course, your code may become less portable as a result of that, but efficiency optimization always comes at a price!

Ultimately, the granularity of your Mapper classes will vary. If an object type is stored solely by another, then you may consider only having a Mapper for the container.

The great strength of this pattern is the strong decoupling it effects between Domain layer and database. The Mapper objects take the strain behind the scenes and can adapt to all sorts of relational twistedness.

Perhaps the biggest drawback with the pattern is the sheer amount of slog involved in creating the implementing Mapper classes. However, there is a large amount of boilerplate code that can be automatically generated. A neat way of generating the common methods for Mapper classes is through reflection. You can query a domain object, discover its setter and getter methods (perhaps in tandem with an argument naming convention), and generate basic Mapper classes ready for amendment. This is how all the Mapper classes featured in this chapter were initially produced.

One issue to be aware of with mappers is the danger of loading too many objects at one time. The Iterator implementation helps us here, though. Because a Collection object only holds row data at first, the secondary request (for a Space object) is only made when a particular Venue is accessed and converted from array to object. This form of lazy loading can be enhanced even further, as we shall see.

You should be careful of ripple loading. Be aware as you create your mapper that the use of another one to acquire a property for your object may be the tip of a very large iceberg. This secondary mapper may itself use yet more in constructing its own object. If you are not careful, you could find that what looks on the surface like a simple find operation sets off tens of other similar operations.

Identity Map

Do you remember the nightmare of pass-by-value errors in PHP 4? The sheer confusion that ensued when two variables that you thought pointed to a single object turned out to refer to different but cunningly similar ones? Well, the nightmare has returned.

The Problem

Let's look back to some test code created to try out the Data Mapper example.

```
$venue = new woo_domain_Venue();
$venue->setName( "The Likey Lounge" );
$mapper->insert( $venue );
$venue = $mapper->find( $venue->getId() );
print_r( $venue );
$venue->setName( "The Bibble Beer Likey Lounge" );
$mapper->update( $venue );
$venue = $mapper->find( $venue->getId() );
print_r( $venue );
```

The purpose of this code was to demonstrate that an object that we add to the database could also be extracted via a Mapper, and would be identical. Identical, that is, in every way except for being the *same* object. I cheated this problem by assigning the new Venue object over the old. Unfortunately, you won't always have that kind of control over the situation. The same object may be referenced at several different times within a single request. If you alter one version of it, and save that to the database, can you be sure that another version of the object (perhaps stored already in a Collection object) won't be written over your changes?

Not only are duplicate objects risky in a system, they also represent a considerable overhead. Some popular objects could be loaded three or four times in a process, with all but one of these trips to the database entirely redundant.

Fortunately, fixing this problem is relatively straightforward.

Implementation

An Identity Map is simply an object whose task it is to keep track of all the objects in a system, and thereby help to ensure that nothing that should be one object becomes two.

In fact, the Identity Map itself does not prevent this from happening in any active way. Its role is to manage information about objects. Here is a simple Identity Map:

```
class woo_domain_ObjectWatcher {
    private $all = array();
    private static $instance;

    private function __construct() { }

    static function instance() {
        if ( ! self::$instance ) {
            self::$instance = new woo_domain_ObjectWatcher();
        }
        return self::$instance;
    }

    function globalKey( woo_domain_DomainObject $obj ) {
        $key = get_class( $obj ).".".$obj->getId();
        return $key;
    }

    static function add( woo_domain_DomainObject $obj ) {
        $inst = self::instance();
        $inst->all[$inst->globalKey( $obj )] = $obj;
    }

    static function exists( $classname, $id ) {
        $inst = self::instance();
        $key = "$classname.$id";
        return $inst->all[$key];
    }
}
```

The main trick with an Identity Map is, pretty obviously, identifying objects. This means that you need to tag each object in some way. There are a number of different strategies you can take here. The database table key that all objects in the system already use is no good because the ID is not guaranteed to be unique across all tables.

The DB package supports unique database-wide keys as standard (by means of managing a key table), so this is one candidate solution. You would need to add a field to the database for each object, and generate a key whenever an object is inserted. The overheads of this are relatively slight, and it would be easy to do.

As you can see, I have gone for an altogether simpler approach. I concatenate the name of the object's class with its table ID. There can be no two objects of type woo_domain_Event with an ID of 4, so my key of "woo_domain_Event.4" is safe enough for my purposes.

The globalKey() method handles the details of this. The class provides an add() method for adding new objects. Each object is labeled with its unique key in an array property: $all.

The exists() method accepts a class name and an $id rather than an object. We don't want to have to instantiate an object to see whether or not it already exists! The method builds a key from this data and checks to see if it indexes an element in the $all property. If an object is found, a reference is duly returned.

There is only one class where I work with the ObjectWatcher class in its role as an Identity Map. The Mapper class provides functionality for generating objects, so it makes sense to add the checking there.

```
// Mapper
    function getFromMap( $id ) {
        return woo_domain_ObjectWatcher::exists
                ( $this->targetClass(), $id );
    }

    function addToMap( woo_domain_DomainObject $obj ) {
        return woo_domain_ObjectWatcher::add( $obj );
    }

    function find( $id ) {
        $old = $this->getFromMap( $id );
        if ( $old ) { return $old; }

        return $this->doFind( $id );
    }

    function loadArray( $array ) {
        $old = $this->getFromMap( $array['id']);
        if ( $old ) { return $old; }
        $obj = $this->doLoad( $array );
        $this->addToMap( $obj );
        return $obj;
    }
    protected abstract function targetClass();
```

The class provides two convenience methods: addToMap() and getFromMap(). These save the bother of remembering the full syntax of the static call to ObjectWatcher. More importantly, they call down to the child implementation (VenueMapper, etc.) to get the name of the class currently awaiting instantiation.

This is achieved by calling targetClass(), an abstract method that is implemented by all concrete Mapper classes. It should return the name of the class that the Mapper is designed to generate. Here is the SpaceMapper class's implementation of targetClass():

```
protected function targetClass() {
    return "woo_domain_Space";
}
```

Both find() and loadArray() first check for an existing object by passing the table ID to getFromMap(). If an object is found, it is returned to the client and method execution ends. If, however, there is no version of this object in existence yet, object instantiation goes ahead. In loadArray() the new object is passed to addToMap() to prevent any clashes in future.

So why are we going through part of this process twice, with calls to getFromMap() in both find() and loadArray()? The answer lies with Collections. When these generate objects, they do so by calling loadArray(). We need to make sure that the row encapsulated by a Collection object is not stale, and ensure that the latest version of the object is returned to the user.

Consequences

As long as you use the Identity Map in all contexts in which objects are generated from the database, the possibility of duplicate objects in your process is practically zero.

Of course, this only works *within* your process. Different processes will inevitably access versions of the same object at the same time. It is important to think through the possibilities for data corruption engendered by concurrent access. If there is a serious issue, you may need to consider a locking strategy.

Unit of Work

When do you save your objects? Until I discovered the Unit of Work pattern (written up by David Rice in Martin Fowler's *Patterns of Enterprise Application Architecture*), I sent out save orders from the Presentation layer upon completion of a command. This turned out to be an expensive design decision.

The Unit of Work pattern helps you to save only those objects that need saving.

The Problem

One day I echoed my SQL statements to the browser window to track down a problem and had a shock. I found that I was saving the same data over and over again in the same request. I had a neat system of composite commands, which meant that one command might trigger several others, and each one was cleaning up after itself.

Not only was I saving the same object twice, I was saving objects that didn't need saving.

This problem then is similar in some ways to that addressed by Identity Map. That problem involved unnecessary object loading, this problem lies at the other end of the process. Just as these issues are complementary, so are the solutions.

Implementation

To determine what database operations are required, you need to keep track of various events that befall your objects. Probably the best place to do that is in the objects themselves.

You also need to maintain a list of objects scheduled for each database operation (insert, update, delete). I am only going to cover insert and update operations here. Where might be a good place to store a list of objects? It just so happens that we already have a ObjectWatcher object, so we can develop that further:

```
// ObjectWatcher
// ...
    private $all = array();
    private $dirty = array();
    private $new = array();
    private $delete = array(); // unused in this example
    private static $instance;
// ...

    static function addDirty( woo_domain_DomainObject $obj ) {
        $inst = self::instance();
        if ( ! $inst->new[$inst->globalKey( $obj )] ) {
            $inst->dirty[$inst->globalKey( $obj )] = $obj;
        }
    }

    static function addNew( woo_domain_DomainObject $obj ) {
        $inst = self::instance();

        $inst->new[$inst->globalKey( $obj )] = $obj;
    }

    static function addClean(woo_domain_DomainObject $obj ) {
        $self = self::instance();
        // unset( $self->delete[$self->globalKey( $obj )] );
        // not implementing deletes in this example!
        unset( $self->dirty[$self->globalKey( $obj )] );
    }

    function performOperations() {
        foreach ( $this->dirty as $key=>$obj ) {
            $obj->finder()->update( $obj );
        }
        foreach ( $this->new as $key=>$obj ) {
            $obj->finder()->insert( $obj );
        }
        $this->dirty = array();
        $this->new = array();
    }

    function __destruct() {
        $this->performOperations();
    }
```

The `ObjectWatcher` class remains an Identity Map, and continues to serve its function of tracking all objects in a system via the `$all` property. This example simply adds more functionality to the class.

Objects are described as "dirty" when they have been changed since extraction from the database. A dirty object is stored in the `$dirty` array property (via the `addDirty()` method) until the time comes to update the database. Client code may decide that a dirty object should not undergo update for its own reasons. It can ensure this by marking the dirty object clean (via the `addClean()` method). As you might expect, a newly created object should be added to the `$new` array (via the `addNew()` method). Objects in this array are scheduled for insertion into the database. We are not implementing delete functionality in these examples, but the principle should be clear enough.

The `addDirty()` and `addNew()` methods each add an object to their respective associative array properties, using the `globalKey()` method covered in the last pattern. `addClean()`, on the other hand *removes* the given object from the `$dirty` array, marking it as no longer pending update.

When the time finally comes to process all objects stored in these arrays, the `performOperations()` method is invoked. This loops through the `$dirty` and `$new` arrays either updating or adding the objects. We can call the `performOperations()` method from client code at any time, but we have also added an invocation to the magic `__destruct()` method. As you know, `__destruct()` is called automatically whenever an object is deleted. This means that object update and insertion is entirely automated by this class!

The `ObjectWatcher` class now provides a mechanism for updating and inserting objects. The code is still missing a means of adding objects to the `ObjectWatcher` object.

Since it is these objects that are operated upon, they are probably best placed to perform this notification. Here are some utility methods we can add to the `DomainObject` class. Notice also the constructor method.

```
// DomainObject
    function __construct( $id=null ) {
        $this->id = $id;
        if ( ! $this->id ) {
            $this->id = $this->finder()->newId();
            $this->markNew();
        }
    }

    function finder() {
        return self::getFinder( get_class( $this ) );
    }

    static function getFinder( $type ) {
        return woo_domain_HelperFactory::getFinder( $type );
    }

    function markNew() {
        woo_domain_ObjectWatcher::addNew( $this );
    }
```

```
function markDirty() {
    woo_domain_ObjectWatcher::addDirty( $this );
}

function markClean() {
    woo_domain_ObjectWatcher::addClean( $this );
}
```

Before looking at the Unit of Work code, it is worth noting that Domain object here has finder() and getFinder() methods. These work in exactly the same way as collection() and getCollection(), querying a simple factory class, HelperFactory, in order to acquire Mapper objects when needed.

As you can see, the constructor method marks the current object as new (by calling markNew()) if no $id property has been passed to it. First, though, it acquires a new $id from its Mapper. This is where the DB object's ID generation mechanism works in our favor; we can generate a new ID *before* entering the related row into the database. Here is the implementation of newID() in VenueMapper:

```
public function newId() {
    return self::$DB->nextId('venue');
}
```

We also need to add some code to the Mapper class:

```
// Mapper
    function loadArray( $array ) {
        $old = $this->getFromMap( $array['id']);
        if ( $old ) { return $old; }
        $obj = $this->doLoad( $array );
        $this->addToMap( $obj );
        $obj->markClean();
        return $obj;
    }
```

Because setting up an object involves marking it new via the constructor's call to ObjectWatcher::addNew(), we must call markClean(), or every single object extracted from the database will be saved at the end of the request, which is not what we want.

The only thing remaining to do is to add markDirty() invocations to methods in the Domain Model classes. Remember, a "dirty" object is one that has been changed since it was retrieved from the database. This is the one aspect of this pattern that has a slightly fishy odor. Clearly it's important to ensure that all methods that mess up the state of an object are marked dirty, but the manual nature of this task means that the possibility of human error is all too real.

Here are some methods in the Space object that call markDirty():

```
function setName( $name_s ) {
    $this->name = $name_s;
    $this->markDirty();
}
```

```
function setVenue( woo_domain_Venue $venue ) {
    $this->venue = $venue;
    $this->markDirty();
}
```

The results of this pattern, combined with some of the others in this chapter, are truly marvelous. This at least looks like the Shangri-la of the persistent model with a magically invisible persistence layer.

Here is some code for adding a new Venue and Space to the database, taken from a Command class:

```
$venue = new woo_domain_Venue( null, "The Green Trees" );
$venue->addSpace(
    new woo_domain_Space( null, 'The Space Upstairs' ) );
$venue->addSpace(
    new woo_domain_Space( null, 'The Bar Stage' ) );
```

I have added some debug code to the ObjectWatcher so you can see what happens at the end of the request:

```
inserting The Green Trees
inserting The Space Upstairs
inserting The Bar Stage
```

Because the ObjectWatcher object calls the performOperations() method from its __destruct() method, all you need to do is create or modify an object, and the Unit of Work class (ObjectWatcher) will do its job behind the scenes.

Consequences

This pattern is very useful, but there are a few issues to be aware of. You need to be sure that all modify operations actually do mark the object in question dirty. Failing to do this can result in hard-to-spot bugs.

You may like to look at other options for testing for modified objects. Reflection sounds like a good option there, but you should look into the performance implications of such testing—the pattern is meant to improve efficiency, not undermine it.

You need to watch out for temporary objects as well. You may wish to create an Event object in order to test it against an existing object (using a method such as intersects()), for example. You don't want this added to the database in error. In this situation, you could explicitly mark your temporary objects for deletion, or perhaps have a setTemporary() method on the DomainObject class.

Lazy Load

Lazy Load is one of those core patterns most Web programmers learn for themselves very quickly, simply because it's such an essential mechanism for avoiding massive database hits, which is something we all want to do.

The Problem

In the example that has dominated this chapter, we have set up a relationship between Venue, Space, and Event objects. When a Venue object is created, it is automatically given a SpaceCollection object. If we were to list every Space object in a Venue, this automatically kicks off a database request to acquire all the Events associated with each Space. These are stored in an EventCollection object. If we don't wish to view any events, we have nonetheless made several journeys to the database for no reason. With many venues, each with a two or three spaces, and with each space managing tens, perhaps hundreds, of events, this is a costly process.

Clearly we need to throttle back on this automatic inclusion of collections in some instances.

Here is the code in SpaceMapper that acquires Event data:

```
protected function doLoad( $array ) {
    $obj = new woo_domain_Space( $array['id'] );
    $obj->setname( $array['name'] );
    $ven_mapper = new woo_mapper_VenueMapper();
    $venue = $ven_mapper->find( $array['venue'] );
    $obj->setVenue( $venue );

    $event_mapper = new woo_mapper_EventMapper();
    $event_collection = $event_mapper->findBySpaceId( $array['id'] );

    $obj->setEvents( $event_collection );
    $obj->markClean();
    return $obj;
}
```

The doLoad() method first acquires the Venue object with which the space is associated. This is not costly, because it is almost certainly already stored in the ObjectWatcher object. Then the method calls the EventMapper::findBySpaceId() method. This is where the system could run into problems.

Implementation

As you may know, a Lazy Load means to defer acquisition of a property until it is actually requested by a client.

The easiest way of doing this is to make the deferral explicit in the containing object. Here's how we might do this in the Space object:

```
// Space
function getEvents() {
    if ( is_null($this->events) ) {
        $this->events = self::getFinder('woo_domain_Event')
            ->findBySpaceId( $this->getId() );
    }
    return $this->events;
}
```

This method checks to see whether or not the $events property is set. If it isn't set, then the method acquires a Finder (that is, a Mapper) and uses its own $id property to get the EventCollection with which it is associated. Clearly, for this method to save us a potentially unnecessary database query, we would also need to amend the SpaceMapper code so that it does not automatically preload an EventCollection object as it does in the preceding example!

This approach will work just fine, although it is a little messy. Wouldn't it be nice to tidy the mess away?

This brings us back to the Iterator implementation that goes to make the Collection object. We are already hiding one secret behind that interface (the fact that raw data may not yet have been used to instantiate a domain object at the time a client accesses it), perhaps we can hide still more.

The idea here is to create an EventCollection object that defers its database access until a request is made of it. This means that a client object (such as Space, for example) need never know that it is holding an empty Collection in the first instance. As far as a client is concerned, it is holding a perfectly normal EventCollection.

Here is the DeferredEventCollection object:

```
class woo_mapper_DeferredEventCollection
        extends woo_mapper_EventCollection {
    private $stmt;
    private $valueArray;
    private $mapper;
    private $run=false;

    function __construct( woo_mapper_EventMapper $mapper,
                          $stmt_handle, $valueArray ) {
        parent::__construct( );
        $this->stmt = $stmt_handle;
        $this->valueArray = $valueArray;
        $this->mapper = $mapper;
    }

    function notifyAccess() {
        if ( ! $this->run ) {
            $result =
                $this->mapper->doStatement( $this->stmt,
                            $this->valueArray );
            $this->init_db( $result, $this->mapper );
        }
        $this->run=true;
    }
}
```

As you can see, this class extends a standard EventMapper. Its constructor requires an EventMapper object and a primed DB statement handle. In the first instance, the class does nothing but store its properties, and wait. No query has been made of the database.

You may remember that the Collection base class defines the empty method called notifyAccess() that I mentioned in the "Data Mapper" section. This is called from any method whose invocation is the result of a call from the outside world.

DeferredEventCollection overrides this method. Now if someone attempts to access the Collection, the class knows it is time to end the pretense and acquire some real data. It does this by passing the statement handle to the VenueMapper's doStatement() method. This yields a DB_result object that can then be passed to the init_db() method. Remember that init_db() simply decants a database result set into an array, and does some other housekeeping.

Here is the method in EventMapper that instantiates a DeferredEventCollection:

```
function findBySpaceId( $s_id ) {
    return new woo_mapper_DeferredEventCollection(
            $this,
            $this->selectBySpaceStmt, array( $s_id ) );
}
```

Consequences

Lazy loading is a good habit to get into, whether or not you explicitly add deferred loading logic to your domain classes.

Over and above type safety, the particular benefit of using a collection rather than an array for your properties is the opportunity this gives you to retrofit lazy loading should you need it.

Summary

This is the longest chapter in this book, and for good reason. PHP is a Web-oriented language before it is an object-oriented language. You are probably reading this now because you are involved in coding for the Web at some level.

I have covered an enormous amount of ground here (although I have also left a lot out). You should not feel daunted by the sheer volume of code in this chapter. Patterns are meant to be used in the right circumstances and combined when useful. Here is a list of the patterns I covered. Raid from them when you feel that the needs of your project are matched by a summary, and do not feel that you must build an entire framework before embarking upon a project.

We examined the following patterns:

- *Registry*: This pattern is useful for making data available to all classes in a process. Through careful use of serialization, it can also be used to store information across a session, or even across instances of an application.

- *Front Controller*: Use this for larger systems in which you know that you will need as much flexibility as possible in managing many different views and commands.

- *Application Controller*: Create a class to manage view logic and command selection.

- *Template View*: Create pages that manage display and user interface only, incorporating dynamic information into display markup with as little raw code as possible.

- *Page Controller*: Lighter-weight but less flexible than Front Controller, Page Controller addresses the same need. Use this pattern to manage requests and handle view logic if you want fast results and your system is unlikely to grow substantially in complexity.

- *Transaction Script*: When you want to get things done fast, with minimal up-front planning, fall back on procedural library code for your application logic. This pattern does not scale well.

- *Domain Model*: On the opposite pole from Transaction Script, use this pattern to build object-based models of your business participants and processes. This pattern requires a relatively complex framework to decouple it from quotidian concerns of presentation and persistence.

- *Data Mapper*: Create specialist classes for mapping Domain Model objects to and from relational databases.

- *Identity Map*: Keep track of all the objects in your system to prevent duplicate instantiations and unnecessary trips to the database.

- *Unit of Work*: Automate the process by which objects are saved to the database, ensuring that only objects that have been changed are updated and only those that have been newly created are inserted.

In the next chapter, we take a welcome break from code and introduce some of the wider practices that can contribute to a successful project.

PART FOUR

Practice

CHAPTER 13

■ ■ ■

Good (and Bad) Practice

So far this in this book, we have focused on coding, concentrating particularly on the role of design in building flexible and reusable tools and applications. Development doesn't end with code, however. It is possible to come away from books and courses with a solid understanding of a language, and yet still run into trouble when it comes to running and deploying a project.

In this chapter, we will move beyond code to introduce some of the tools and techniques that form the underpinnings of a successful development process. This chapter will cover

- *Third-party packages*: Where to get them, when to use them

- *Version control*: Bringing harmony to the development process

- *Documentation*: Writing code that is easy to understand, use, and extend

- *Unit testing*: A tool for automated bug prevention

Beyond Code

When I first graduated from working on my own and took a place in a development team, I was astonished at how much *stuff* other developers seemed to have to know. Good-natured arguments simmered endlessly over issues of vital-seeming importance: Which is the best text editor? Should the team standardize on an integrated development environment? Should we impose a coding standard? How should we test our code? Should we document as we develop? Sometimes these issues seemed more important than the code itself, and my colleagues seemed to have acquired their encyclopedic knowledge of the domain through some strange process of osmosis.

The books I had read on PHP, Perl, and Java certainly didn't stray from the code itself to any great extent. As I have already discussed, most books on programming platforms rarely divert from their tight focus on functions and syntax to take in code design. If design is off topic, you can be sure that version control and code documentation are rarely discussed. This is not a criticism—if a book professes to cover the main features of a language, it should be no surprise that this is what it does.

In learning about code, however, I found that I had neglected many of the mechanics of a project's day-to-day life. I discovered that some of these details were critical to the success or failure of projects I helped develop. In this chapter, and in more detail in coming chapters, we will look beyond code to explore some of the tools and techniques upon which the success of your projects may depend.

Borrowing a Wheel

When faced with a challenging but discrete aspect to a project, there is a lot to be said for building a component that addresses the need. It can be one of the best ways to learn your craft. In creating a package, you gain insight into a problem, and file away new techniques that might have wider application. You invest at once in your project and in your own skills. By keeping your functionality internal to your system, you can avoid the need for your users to download third-party packages, and occasionally sidestep thorny licensing issues. There's nothing like the sense of satisfaction you can get when you test a component you designed yourself and find that, wonder of wonders, it works—it does exactly what *you* wrote on the tin.

There is a dark side to all this, of course. Many packages represent an investment of thousands of man-hours: a resource that you may not have on hand. You may be able to address this by developing only the functionality needed specifically by your project, while a third-party tool might fulfill a myriad of other needs as well. The question remains though, If a freely available tool exists, why are you squandering your talents in reproducing it? Do you have the time and resources to develop, test, and debug your package? Might not this time be better deployed elsewhere?

I am one of the worst offenders when it comes to wheel reinvention. Picking apart problems and inventing solutions to them is a fundamental part of what we do as coders. Getting down to some serious architecture is a more rewarding prospect than writing some glue to stitch together three or four existing components. When this temptation comes over me, I remind myself of projects past. Although the choice to build from scratch has never killed a project in my experience, I have seen it devour schedules and murder profit margins. There I sit with a manic gleam in my eye, hatching plots and spinning class diagrams, failing to notice as I obsess over the details of my component that the big picture is now a distant memory.

Now when I map out a project, I try to develop a feel for what belongs inside the codebase, and what should be treated as a third-party requirement. For example, your application may generate (or read) an RSS feed, you may need to validate e-mail addresses and automate mail-outs, authenticate users, or read from a standard format configuration file. All of these needs can be fulfilled by external packages.

Once you have defined your needs, your first stop should be the PEAR Web site at `http://pear.php.net`. PEAR stands for the PHP Extension and Application Repository, and is an officially maintained and quality-controlled repository of packages. It is also a mechanism for installing packages seamlessly, and managing package interdependencies. I will cover PEAR in more detail in the next chapter, in which I look at the way that you can use PEAR functionality to prepare your own packages. To give you some idea of what's available in the PEAR repository, here are just a very few of the things you can do with PEAR packages:

- Cache output with Cache_Lite.

- Test the efficiency of your code with Benchmark.

- Abstract the details of database access with DB.

- Manipulate Apache `.htaccess` files with File_HtAccess.

- Extract or encode news feeds with XML_RSS.

- Send mail with attachments with Mail_Mime.

- Parse configuration file formats with Config.

- Password protected environments with Auth.

The PEAR Web site provides a list of packages categorized by topic. You may find packages that broadly address your needs here, or you may need to cast your net wider (using the major search engines). Either way, you should always take time to assess existing packages before setting out to potentially reinvent that wheel.

The fact that you have a need, and that a package exists to address it, should not be the start and end of your deliberations. Although it is preferable to use a package where it will save you otherwise unnecessary development, in some cases it can add an overhead without real gain. Your client's need for your application to send mail, for example, does not mean that you should automatically use PEAR's Mail package. PHP provides a perfectly good mail() function, so to start with all the benefit lies with a simple internal implementation. As soon as you realize that you have to validate all e-mail addresses according to the RFC822 standard, and that the design team wants to send image attachments with the mails, you may begin to weigh the options differently. As it happens there are PEAR packages for both these features.

Many programmers, myself included, often place too much emphasis upon the creation of original code, sometimes to the detriment of their projects. This emphasis upon authorship may be one reason that there often seems to be more creation than actual use of reusable code.

Effective programmers see original code as just one of the tools available to aid them in engineering a project's successful outcome. Such programmers look at the resources they have at hand and deploy them effectively. If a package exists to take some strain, then that is a win. To steal and paraphrase an aphorism from the Perl world: good coders are lazy.

Playing Nice

The truth of Sartre's famous dictum that "Hell is other people" is proved on a daily basis in some software projects. This might describe the relationship between clients and developers, symptomized by the many ways that lack of communication leads to creeping features and skewed priorities. But the cap fits too for happily communicative and cooperative team members when it comes to sharing code.

As soon as a project has more than one developer, version control becomes an issue. A single coder may work on code in place, saving a copy of her working directory at key points in development. Introduce another programmer to this mix, and this strategy breaks down in minutes. If the new developer works in the same development directory, then there is a real chance that one programmer will overwrite the work of his colleague when saving, unless both are very careful to always work on different files.

Alternatively, our two developers can each take a version of the codebase to work on separately. That works fine until the moment comes to reconcile the two versions. Unless the developers have worked on entirely different sets of files, the task of merging two or more development strands rapidly becomes an enormous headache.

This is where Concurrent Versions System (CVS) and similar tools come in. Using CVS you can check out your own version of a codebase and work on it until you are happy with the result. You can then update your version with any changes that your colleagues have been making. CVS will automatically merge these changes into your files, notifying you of any conflicts it cannot handle. Once you have tested this new hybrid, you can save it to the central CVS repository, making it available to other developers.

CVS provides you with other benefits. It keeps a complete record of all stages of a project, so you can roll back to, or grab a snapshot of, any point in the project's lifetime. You can also create branches, so that you can maintain a public release at the same time as a bleeding-edge development version.

Once you have used version control on a project, you will not want to attempt another without it. Despite the mind-numbing tangle of revisions and branches you will occasionally have to conceptualize, version control is just too useful to live without. I cover CVS in Chapter 16.

■**Note** CVS isn't the only game in town when it comes to version control. A newer package called Subversion has made a relatively recent debut. It is free of some of the eccentricities of the more venerable CVS. Subversion is covered in detail by Garrett Rooney in *Practical Subversion* (Apress, 2004).

Giving Your Code Wings

Have you ever seen your code grounded because it is just too hard to install? This is especially true for projects that are developed in place. Such projects settle into their context, with passwords and directories, databases and helper application invocations programmed right into the code. Deploying a project of this kind can be a major undertaking, with teams of programmers picking through source code to amend settings so that they fit the new environment.

This problem can be eased to some degree by providing a centralized configuration file or class so that settings can be changed in one place, but even then installation can be a chore. The difficulty or ease of installation will have a major impact upon the popularity of any application you distribute. It will also impede or encourage multiple and frequent deployment during development.

As with any repetitive and time-consuming task, installation should be automated. An installer can determine default values for install locations, check and change permissions, create databases, and initialize variables, among other tasks. In fact, an installer can do just about anything you need to get an application from a source directory in a distribution to full deployment.

This doesn't absolve the user from the responsibility for adding information about his environment to the code, of course, but it can make the process as easy as answering a few questions or providing a few command line switches.

For developers, installers have the further virtue of memory. Once an installer has been run from a distribution directory, it can cache many of its settings, making subsequent installations even easier. So the second time you install from a distribution directory, you may not need to provide configuration information like database names and install directories. These are remembered from the first installation. This is important for developers who frequently update their local development space using version control. Version control makes it easy to acquire the latest version of a project. There is little point, however, to removing impedence from the acquisition of code if you have a bottleneck restricting its deployment.

There are various build tools available to the developer. PEAR, for example, is, in part, an installation solution. Most of the time, you will use the PEAR installer to deploy code from the official PEAR repository. It is possible, however, to create your own PEAR packages that can be downloaded and installed by users with ease. The PEAR installer is best suited to self-enclosed, functionally focused packages. It is relatively rigid about the role and install locations of the files a package should contain, and it tends to concentrate upon the process of placing file A in location B. I cover this aspect of PEAR in detail in Chapter 14.

If you need greater flexibility than this, as you might for application installation, you may need an installer that is more scriptable. In Chapter 17 we will look at an application called Phing. This open source project is a port of the popular Ant build tool that is written in and for Java. Phing is written in and for PHP, though in either case you can easily perform any task that you could on the command line or programmatically. Where PEAR does a few things very well, and offers the simplest possible configuration, Phing is more daunting at first, but with the tradeoff of immense flexibility. Not only can you use Phing to automate anything from file copying to XSLT transformation, you can easily write and incorporate your own tasks should you need to extend the tool. Phing is written using PHP 5's object-oriented features, and its design emphasizes modularity and ease of extension.

Documentation

My code is so sparse and elegant that it doesn't need documenting. Its purpose is luminously clear at the slightest of glances. I know your code is the same. The others, though, have a problem.

All irony aside, it is true that good code documents itself to some extent. By defining a clear interface and well-defined responsibility for each class and method, and naming each descriptively, you communicate your code's intent. However, you can improve the transparency of your work still further by avoiding unnecessary obfuscation: clarity beats cleverness unless cleverness brings with it immense, and required, gains in efficiency.

The naming of properties, variables, and arguments, too, can play a tremendous role in making your code easy for others to read. Choose descriptive names, where possible. I often add information about the type of a variable to the name—especially for argument variables.

```
public function setName( $name_str, $age_int ) {
    //...
}
```

No matter how clear your code is, though, it can never be quite clear enough on its own. We have seen that object-oriented design often involves combining many classes together in relationships of inheritance, aggregation, or both. When you look at a single class in such a structure, it is often very hard to extrapolate the bigger picture without some kind of explicit pointer.

At the same time, every programmer knows what a pain it is to write documentation. You tend to neglect it during development because the code is in flux, and really your project is about getting the code right. Then when you have reached a point of stability, you suddenly see the enormity of the task of documenting your work. Who would have thought that you would create so many classes and methods? Now your deadline is looming, so it's time to cut your losses and concentrate on quality assurance.

This is an understandable but shortsighted attitude, as you will discover when you return to your code for a second phase in a year's time. Here's a programmer quoted on the popular repository for Internet Relay Chat (IRC) witticism http://www.bash.org:

<@Logan> *I spent a minute looking at my own code by accident.*
<@Logan> *I was thinking "What the hell is this guy doing?"*
                                                    —http://www.bash.org/?6824

Without documentation, you are destined to play out that story: wasting your time second-guessing decisions you probably made for very good reasons (if you only knew what they were). This is bad enough, but the situation becomes worse, and more expensive, when you hand off your work to a colleague. Undocumented code will cost you expensive work days, as your new hire is forced to pepper your code with debug messages, and work her way through fat printouts of promiscuously interrelated classes.

Clearly the answer is to document, and to do it as you code, but can the process be streamlined? As you might imagine, the answer is "yes" and once again the solution is borrowed from a Java tool. phpDocumentor (http://www.phpdoc.org/) is a reimplementation of JavaDoc, the documentation application that ships with the Java SDK. From a coder's perspective, the principle is simple. Add specially formatted comments above all classes, most methods, and some properties, and phpDocumentor will incorporate them into a hyperlinked web of documents. Even if you omit these comments, the application will read the code, summarizing and linking up the classes it finds. This is a benefit in itself, allowing you to click from class to class, and to observe inheritance relationships at a glance.

We examine phpDocumentor in Chapter 15.

Testing

Every component in a system depends for its continued smooth running upon the consistency of operation and interface of its peers. By definition, then, development breaks systems. As you improve your classes and packages, you must remember to amend any code that works with them. For some changes, this can create a ripple effect, affecting components far away from the code we originally changed. Eagle-eyed vigilance and an encyclopedic knowledge of a system's dependencies can help to address this problem. Of course, while these are excellent virtues, systems soon grow too complex for every unwanted effect to be easily predicted, not least because systems often combine the work of many developers. To address this problem, it is a good idea to test every component regularly. This, of course, is a repetitive and complex task and as such it lends itself well to automation.

Testing is essential in any project. Even if you don't formalize the process, you must have found yourself developing informal lists of actions that put your system through its paces. This process soon becomes wearisome, and that can lead to a fingers-crossed attitude to programming.

One approach to testing starts at the interface of a project, modeling the various ways in which a user might negotiate the system. This is probably the way you would go when testing by hand, although there are various frameworks for automating the process. These functional tests are sometimes called acceptance tests because a list of actions performed successfully can be used as criteria for signing off a project phase.

While functional tests work from the top down, unit tests, the subject of this section, work from the bottom up. Unit testing tends to focus on classes, with test methods grouped together in test cases that put a class through a rigorous workout, checking that each method performs as advertised, and that it fails as it should. These test cases are then grouped together into test suites. Tests can be run as part of the build process, directly from the command line, or even via a Web page.

Unit testing is a good way of ensuring the quality of design in a system. Tests reveal the responsibilities of classes and functions. Some programmers even advocate a test-first approach. You should, they say, write the tests before you even begin work on a class. This lays down a class's purpose, ensuring a clean interface and short, focused methods. Personally, I have never attained this level of purity, but I do attempt to write tests as I go.

So, let's create some classes to test. Here is a class that places user information in persistent storage. For the sake of demonstration, it saves the information in an array:

```php
class UserStore {
    private $users = array();
    function addUser( $name=null, $mail=null, $pass=null ) {
        if ( is_null( $name ) || is_null( $mail ) || is_null( $pass ) ) {
            return false;
        }

        if ( strlen( $pass ) < 5 ) {
            throw new Exception(
                "Password must have 5 or more letters");
        }

        $this->users[$mail] = array( 'pass' => $pass,
                                     'mail' => $mail,
                                     'name' => $name );
        return true;
    }

    function getUser( $mail ) {
        return ( $this->users[$mail] );
    }
}
```

This class accepts user data with the addUser() method, and retrieves it via getUser(). The user's e-mail address is used as the key for retrieval.

Here is a client class. It uses UserStore to confirm that a user has provided the correct authentication information.

```php
class Validator {
    private $store;
    public function __construct( UserStore $store ) {
        $this->store = $store;
    }

    public function validateUser( $mail, $pass ) {
        if ( ! is_array($user = $this->store->getUser( $mail )) ) {
            return false;
        }
        if ( $user['pass'] == $pass ) {
            return true;
        }
        return false;
    }
}
```

The class requires a UserStore object, which it saves in the $store property. This property is used by the validateUser() method first of all to ensure that the user referenced by the given e-mail address exists in the store, and secondly that the user's password matches the provided argument. If both these conditions are fulfilled, the method returns true.

In order to test these classes, we need a PEAR package called PHPUnit2. The original PHPUnit package is no longer maintained, and does not use PHP 5. We will deal with PEAR installation in the next chapter, but in most cases you need only type the following at the command line in order to acquire a package:

```
$ pear install PHPUnit2
```

Note I show commands that are input at the command line in bold to help distinguish them from any output they may produce.

Armed with PHPUnit2, we can write tests for the UserStore class. Tests should be collected in a single class that extends PHPUnit2_Framework_TestCase, one of the classes made available by the PHPUnit2 package. Here's how to create a minimal test case class:

```
require_once('PHPUnit2/Framework/TestCase.php');

class UserStoreTest extends PHPUnit2_Framework_TestCase {
    public function setUp() {
    }

    public function tearDown() {
    }
    //...
}
```

I named the test case class UserStoreTest. You are not obliged to use the name of the class you are testing in the test's name, though that is what most developers do. Each test in a test case class is run in isolation of its siblings. The setUp() method is automatically invoked for each test, allowing us to set up a sane environment for the test. tearDown() is invoked after each test method is run. If your tests change the wider environment of your system, you can use this method to reset state.

In order to test the UserStore class, we need an instance of it. We can instantiate this in setUp() and assign it to a property. Let's create a test method as well:

```php
require_once('UserStore.php');
require_once('PHPUnit2/Framework/TestCase.php');


class UserStoreTest extends PHPUnit2_Framework_TestCase {
    private $store;

    public function setUp() {
        $this->store = new UserStore();
    }

    public function tearDown() {
    }
     public function  testGetUser() {
        $this->store->addUser(  "bob williams",
                                "bob@example.com",
                                "12345" );
        $user = $this->store->getUser(  "bob@example.com" );
        $this->assertEquals( $user['name'], "bob williams" );
        $this->assertEquals( $user['mail'], "bob@example.com" );
        $this->assertEquals( $user['pass'], "12345" );
    }
}
```

Test methods should be named to begin with the word "test" and should require no arguments. This is because the test case class is manipulated using reflection.

Note Reflection is covered in detail in Chapter 5.

The object that runs the tests looks at all the methods in the class and only invokes those that match this pattern. In the example, we test the retrieval of user information. First we invoke UserStore::addUser() with dummy data, then we retrieve that data and test each of its elements. For each individual test, we use an inherited method: assertEquals(). This compares the two provided arguments and checks them for equivalence. If they do not match, then the test method will be deemed a failure. Having subclassed PHPUnit2_Framework_TestCase, we have access to a set of assert methods. These methods are listed in Table 13-1.

Table 13-1. *The PHPUnit2_Framework_TestCase Assert Methods*

Method	Description
assertEquals($val1, $val2, $delta, $message)	Fail if $val1 is not equivalent to $val2. ($delta represents an allowable margin of error.)
assertFalse($expression, $message)	Evaluate $expression. Fail if it does *not* resolve to false.
assertTrue($expression, $message)	Evaluate $expression. Fail if it does *not* resolve to true.
assertNotNull($val, $message)	Fail if $val is null.
assertNull($val, $message)	Fail if $val is anything other than null.
assertSame($obj1, $obj2, $message)	Fail if $obj1 and $obj2 are *not* references to the same object.
assertNotSame($obj1, $obj2, $message)	Fail if $obj1 and $obj2 are references to the same object.
assertRegExp($regexp, $val, $message)	Fail if $val is not matched by regular expression $regexp.
assertType($typestring, $val, $message)	Fail if $val is not the type described in $type.
fail()	Fail.

Here is a test that checks the behavior of the UserStore class when an operation fails:

```
//...
public function  testAddUser_ShortPass() {
    try {
        $this->store->addUser(  "bob williams", "bob@example.com", "ff" );
    } catch ( Exception $e ) { return; }
    $this->fail("Short password exception expected");
}
//...
```

If you look back at the UserStore::addUser() method, you will see that we throw an exception if the user's password is less than 5 characters long. Our test attempts to confirm this. We add a user with an illegal password in a try clause. If the expected exception is thrown, then all is well and we return silently. The final line of the method should never be reached, and we therefore invoke the fail() method there. If the addUser() method does not throw an exception as expected, the catch clause is not invoked, and the fail() method is called.

If we are testing the UserStore class, we should also test Validator. Here is a cut-down version of a class called ValidateTest that tests the Validator::validateUser() method:

```
require_once('UserStore.php');
require_once('Validator.php');
require_once('PHPUnit2/Framework/TestCase.php');
```

```
class ValidatorTest extends PHPUnit2_Framework_TestCase {
    private $validator;

    public function setUp() {
        $store = new UserStore();
        $store->addUser( "bob williams", "bob@example.com", "12345" );
        $this->validator = new Validator( $store );
    }
    public function tearDown() {
    }
    public function testValidate_CorrectPass() {
        $this->assertTrue(
            $this->validator->validateUser( "bob@example.com", "12345" ),
            "Expecting successful validation"
            );
    }
}
```

So now that we have written some tests, how do we go about running them? We must first give the names of our TestCase classes to a PHPUnit2_Framework_TestSuite object. This class has an addTestSuite() method for this purpose. Here is some code that runs our UserStoreTest and ValidatorTest classes:

```
define('PHPUnit2_MAIN_METHOD', 'AppTests::main');

require_once( "PHPUnit2/Framework/TestSuite.php" );
require_once( "PHPUnit2/TextUI/TestRunner.php" );

require_once( "tests/UserStoreTest.php" );
require_once( "tests/ValidatorTest.php" );


class AppTests {
    public static function main() {
        $ts = new PHPUnit2_Framework_TestSuite( 'User Classes');
        $ts->addTestSuite('UserStoreTest');
        $ts->addTestSuite('ValidatorTest');
        PHPUnit2_TextUI_TestRunner::run( $ts );
    }
}

AppTests::main();
```

We begin by defining a constant: PHPUnit2_MAIN_METHOD. We set this to refer to our static AppTests::main() method. This tells the PHPUnit2_TextUI_TestRunner class that we have defined our own main() method in place of its default, which gathers information about the test it wants to run from the command line. If we did not reset PHPUnit2_MAIN_METHOD, the static method PHPUnit2_TextUI_TestRunner::main() would be run as soon as the TestRunner class was included.

In the main() method we instantiate a PHPUnit2_Framework_TestSuite object and call its addTestSuite() method for each of the test case classes we wish to run. Once we have set up our TestSuite object, we pass it to the static run() method of the PHPUnit2_TextUI_TestRunner class. This runs all tests and writes the results to standard output. Finally we invoke our main() method. If we run this code from the command line, this is the output:

```
$ php tests/AllTests.php
PHPUnit 2.0.1 by Sebastian Bergmann.

...

Time: 0.0572509765625

OK (3 tests)
```

Tests Succeed When They Fail

While everyone agrees that testing is a fine thing, it is generally only after it has saved your bacon a few times that you grow to really love it. Let's simulate a situation where a change in one part of a system has an unexpected effect elsewhere.

Our UserStore class has been running for a while, when during a code review it is agreed that it would be neater for the class to generate User objects rather than associative arrays. Here is the new version:

```php
class UserStore {
    private $users = array();
    function addUser( $name=null, $mail=null, $pass=null ) {
        if ( is_null( $name ) || is_null( $mail ) || is_null( $pass ) ) {
            return false;
        }

        $this->users[$mail] = new User( $name, $mail, $pass );

        if ( strlen( $pass ) < 5 ) {
            throw new Exception("Password must have 5 or more letters");
        }
        return true;
    }

    function getUser( $mail ) {
        return ( $this->users[$mail] );
    }
}
```

Here is the simple User class:

```
class User {
    private $name;
    private $mail;
    private $pass;

    function __construct( $name, $mail, $pass ) {
        $this->name     = $name;
        $this->mail     = $mail;
        $this->pass     = $pass;
    }

    function getMail() {
        return $this->mail;
    }
}
```

Of course, we amend the UserStoreTest class to account for these changes. So code designed to work with an array like this:

```
public function testGetUser() {
    $this->store->addUser( "bob williams", "bob@example.com", "12345" );
    $user = $this->store->getUser( "bob@example.com" );
    $this->assertEquals( $user['mail'], "bob@example.com" );
```

is converted into code designed to work with an object like this:

```
public function testGetUser() {
    $this->store->addUser( "bob williams", "bob@example.com", "12345" );
    $user = $this->store->getUser( "bob@example.com" );
    $this->assertEquals( $user->getMail(), "bob@example.com" );
```

When we come to run our test suite however, we are rewarded with a warning that our work is not yet done:

```
$ php5 tests/AllTests.php
PHPUnit 2.0.1 by Sebastian Bergmann.

.......F

Time: 0.061473846435547
There was 1 failure:
1) testvalidate_correctpass
Expecting successful validation
/home/projects/556/tests/ValidatorTest.php:25
/home/projects/556/tests/AllTests.php:17
/home/projects/556/tests/AllTests.php:21
```

```
FAILURES!!!
Tests run: 7, Failures: 1, Errors: 0, Incomplete Tests: 0.
```

There is a problem with TestValidate. Let's take another look at the Validator::validateUser() method:

```php
public function validateUser( $mail, $pass ) {
    if ( ! is_array($user = $this->store->getUser( $mail )) ) {
        return false;
    }
    if ( $user['pass'] == $pass ) {
        return true;
    }
    return false;
}
```

We invoke getUser(). Although getUser() now returns an object and not an array, our method does not generate a warning. getUser() originally returned the requested user array on success or null on failure, so we validated users by checking for an array using the is_array() function. Now of course, getUser() returns an object, and our validateUser() method will always return false. Without the test framework, the Validator would have simply rejected all users as invalid without fuss or warning.

Now imagine making this neat little change on a Friday night without a test framework in place. Think about the frantic pager messages that would drag you out of your pub, armchair or restaurant—"*What have you done? All our customers are locked out!*"

The worst bugs don't cause the interpreter to report that something is wrong. They take the form of perfectly legal code and they silently break the logic of your system. The worst bugs don't manifest where you are working, they are caused there, but the effects pop up elsewhere, days or even weeks later. A test framework can help you catch at least some of these insidious bugs.

Write tests as you code, and run them often. If someone reports a bug, first add a test to your framework to confirm it, then fix the bug so that the test is passed—bugs have a funny habit of recurring.

Summary

A coder's aim is always to deliver a working system. Writing good code is an essential part of this aim's fulfillment, but it is not the whole story.

In this chapter, I introduced PEAR (which is also the subject of the next chapter). We discussed two great aids to collaboration: documentation and version control. We saw that version control requires automated build, and I introduced Phing, a PHP implementation of Ant, a Java build tool. Finally, we discussed unit testing, and since this is the only topic to which we will not return, I offered an example demonstrating its power to catch and prevent bugs.

CHAPTER 14

■ ■ ■

An Introduction to PEAR

Programmers aspire to produce reusable code. This is one of the great goals of object orientation. We like to abstract useful functionality from the messiness of specific context, turning it into a tool that can be used again and again. To come at this from another angle, if programmers love the reusable, they hate duplication. By creating libraries that can be reapplied, programmers avoid the need to implement similar solutions across multiple projects. Even if we avoid duplication in our own code, though, there is a wider issue. For every tool you create, how many other programmers have implemented the same solution? This is wasted effort on an epic scale: wouldn't it be much more sensible for programmers to collaborate, and to focus their energies on making a single tool better, rather than producing hundreds of variations on a theme? This is where PEAR (PHP Extension and Application Repository) comes in.

PEAR is a repository of quality-controlled PHP packages that extend the functionality of PHP. It is also a client-server mechanism for distributing and installing packages, and for managing interpackage dependencies.

This chapter will cover

- *PEAR basics*: What is this strange fruit?

- *Installing PEAR packages*: All it takes is one command.

- *Adding PEAR packages to your projects*: An example, some notes on error handling.

- *package.xml*: The anatomy of a build file.

- *Automation*: Programmatic generation of the `package.xml` file.

What Is PEAR?

At its core PEAR is a collection of packages, organized into broad categories, such as networking, mail, and XML. The PEAR repository is managed centrally, so that when you use an official PEAR package, you can be sure of its quality.

You can browse the available packages at `http://pear.php.net`. Before you create a tool for a project, you should get into the habit of checking the PEAR site to see if someone has got there first.

Support for PEAR comes bundled with PHP, which means that some of the core packages are available on your system straightaway (unless PHP was compiled to exclude it using the `–without-pear` configure flag). Packages are installed in a configurable location (on Unix systems this will often be /usr/local/lib/php). You can check this using the pear command line application:

```
$ pear config-get php_dir
/usr/local/lib/php
```

The core packages (known as the PHP Foundation Classes) provide a backbone for the wider repository—including core functions such as error handling and the processing of command line arguments.

We have already seen the pear application in action. This is a tool for interacting with all aspects of PEAR, and as such it is an important part of PEAR in itself. The pear application supports a number of subcommands. We used config-get, which shows the value of a particular configuration setting. You can see all settings and their values with the config-show subcommand:

```
$ pear config-show
Configuration:
==============
PEAR executables directory    bin_dir  /usr/local/bin
PEAR documentation directory  doc_dir  /usr/local/lib/php/doc
...
```

Although pear supports many subcommands, you will probably get the most use out of one in particular. pear install is used for installing PEAR packages.

Installing a Package with PEAR

Once you have selected your package, you can download and install it with a single command. Here is the process for installing Log, a package that provides enhanced support for error logging:

```
pear install log
```

It really is as simple as that. The PEAR installer is bundled with PHP and locates, downloads, and installs the Log package on your behalf. If the package you wish to install depends upon others, the installation will fail with a warning message by default:

```
requires package 'Fandango' >= 10.5
dialekt: Dependencies failed
```

You can either install the required package before trying again, or you could run pear install with the -o flag.

```
pear install -o log
```

The -o flag ensures that the PEAR installer will automatically install any required dependencies for you. Some PEAR packages specify optional dependencies, and these are ignored if -o is specified. To have all dependencies installed automatically, use the -a flag instead.

Although the PEAR repository exists in a particular location online, you will find that many developers produce PEAR-compatible packages for ease of installation. You may be given the location of a tarball (a tarred and gzipped package). Installing this using PEAR is almost as easy as installing an official package:

```
$ pear install -o http://www.example.com/MegaQuiz-1.2.tgz
downloading MegaQuiz-1.2.tgz ...
Starting to download MegaQuiz-1.2.tgz (592 bytes)
....done: 592 bytes
install ok: MegaQuiz 1.2
```

You can also download a package and install it from the command line. Here we use a Unix command called wget to fetch the MegaQuiz package before installing it from the command line:

```
$ wget -nv http://127.0.1.2/MegaQuiz-1.2.tgz
09:40:36 URL:http://127.0.1.2/MegaQuiz-1.2.tgz [592/592]
    -> "MegaQuiz-1.2.tgz" [1]
$ pear install MegaQuiz-1.2.tgz
install ok: MegaQuiz 1.2
```

You can also install a PEAR package by referencing an XML file (usually named package.xml), which provides information about what files are to be installed where.

```
$ pear install package.xml
install ok: MegaQuiz 1.2
```

Using a PEAR Package

Once you have installed a PEAR package, you should be able to use it in your projects immediately. Your PEAR directory should already be in your include path—there should be no problem including the package. Here's how you might work with the bundled DB package, for example:

```
require_once("DB.php");
$dsn = "mysql://bob:pib44@localhost/test";
$db = DB::connect($dsn);

//drop and re-create table 'scores'
$db->query( "DROP TABLE scores" );
$db->query( "CREATE TABLE scores (  id INT PRIMARY KEY,
                                    name VARCHAR
                                    score INT )");

//add some rows
foreach ( array(
            array( 'harry', 44),
            array( 'mary', 66 ) ) as $row ) {
    $id = $db->nextId('score_sequence');
    $ret = $db->query( "insert into scores values( $id, '$row[0]', $row[1])" );
}
```

```
// output the rows
$query_result = $db->query( "SELECT * FROM scores");
while ( $row = $query_result->fetchRow( DB_FETCHMODE_ASSOC ) ) {
    print "row: {$row['id']} {$row['name']} {$row['score']}\n";
}

$query_result->free();
$db->disconnect();
```

Although the details of individual PEAR packages are beyond the scope of this chapter, it would be perverse not to explain this example.

We begin by including DB.php. Most PEAR packages work in this way, providing a single top-level point of access. All further require statements are then made by the package itself.

We construct a DSN (which stands for Data Source Name). A DSN is a URL-like string that includes the database type, the user name, the password, the host, and the database name. This string is passed to DB::connect(). DB::connect() uses it to determine the correct subclass of DB_Common to return.

We then use the query() method to pass various SQL statements to the database platform: we drop the scores table, and re-create it. We add some rows using INSERT statements. Rather than using MySQL's auto-increment feature to generate row IDs, we implement a sequence table. The DB package automatically creates this for us, and generates a unique ID when we call nextID(). This mechanism ensures that our SQL will be portable across platforms, because SQLite, in particular, does not support AUTOINCREMENT fields.

The argument to our final query() invocation is an SQL SELECT statement. query() returns a DB_Result object, which provides methods for working with our database result set. We call the fetchRow() method, passing it a constant that specifies the format we would like. Finally, we print each row.

The DB package is worth mastering. It provides a platform-agnostic interface to multiple databases. The idea is that you write code to work with the DB API, and it handles the database-specific syntax. The package will be used again in later examples, so you might want to take a look at the documentation at http://pear.php.net/DB.

This is an excellent example of good object-oriented design—an abstract class called DB_common defines an interface that supports the operations we have illustrated (in particular query() and nextIndex()), and a set of concrete children provide the implementation. In this way your application is ready to work with MySQL, SQLite, MSSQL, or Oracle with no change in your code (as long as you use standard SQL syntax). Our preceding example is designed to work with MySQL, but we can change it to work with SQLite simply by changing the DSN:

```
$dsn = "sqlite://./test.db";
$db = DB::connect($dsn);
```

Every PEAR package is different, of course, and each one should be associated with complete usage instructions. In the case of official PEAR packages, you will find API instructions on the Web site at http://pear.php.net/. In all cases you should expect to be able to add the functionality of PEAR package to your script with minimal effort. The package should provide you with a clear, well-documented API.

Handling PEAR Errors

Many, if not most, PEAR packages use the standard PEAR error class PEAR_Error. This is often returned in place of the expected return value if something goes wrong in an operation. If this is the case, it will be documented, and you should test return values using the static PEAR::isError() method.

```
$dsn = "qlite://./test.db";
$db = DB::connect($dsn);

if ( PEAR::isError( $db ) ) {
    print "message:    ". $db->getMessage()    ."\n";
    print "code:       ". $db->getCode()       ."\n\n";
    print "Backtrace:\n";

    foreach ( $db->getBacktrace() as $caller ) {
        print $caller['class'].$caller['type'];
        print $caller['function']."() ";
        print "line ".$caller['line']."\n";
    }
    die;
}
```

Here we test the return value from DB::connect() after making a deliberate mistake with the DSN.

```
PEAR::isError( $db )
```

is the functional equivalent of

```
$db instanceof PEAR_Error
```

So within our conditional block we know that $db is a PEAR_Error rather than a DB_Common object. This pollution of a method's return value was an unfortunate necessity before the advent of PHP 5. More packages are likely to use Exceptions as well as or instead of return values in the future.

Once we are sure we have a PEAR_Error object, we can interrogate it for more information about the error. In our example, we have three of the most useful methods: getMessage() returns a message that describes the error, getCode() returns an integer corresponding to the error type (this is an arbitrary number that the package author will have declared as a constant and, we hope, documented), and finally, getBacktrace() returns an array of the methods and classes that lead to the error. This enables us to work our way back through our script's operation and locate the root cause of the error. As you can see, getBacktrace() is itself an array, which describes each method or function that led to the error. The elements are described in Table 14-1.

Table 14-1. *Fields Provided by PEAR_Error::getBacktrace()*

Field	Description
file	Full path to PHP file
args	The arguments passed to the method or function
class	The name of the class (if in class context)
function	The name of the function or method
type	If in class context, the nature of the method call (:: or ->)
line	The line number

Working with the PEAR Installer

Packages from the PEAR repository are well documented and designed to be easy to use. How easy are they to create, though, and how do you go about creating your own? In this section, we will look at the anatomy of a PEAR package.

package.xml

The package.xml file is the heart of any PEAR package. It provides information about a package, determines where and how its participants should be installed, and defines its dependencies. Whether it operates upon a URL, the local file system, or a tarred and gzipped archive, the PEAR installer needs the package.xml file to acquire its instructions.

No matter how well designed and structured your package is, if you omit the build file, the install will fail. Here's what happens if you attempt to install an archive that does not contain package.xml:

```
$ pear install megafail.tgz
Unable to open /tmp/pearzd890n/package.xml

User Warning: Could not open dir /tmp/pearzd890n in System.php on line 87
```

The PEAR installer first unpacks our archive to the temporary directory, and then looks for package.xml. Here it falls at the first hurdle. So if package.xml is so important, what does it consist of?

Package Elements

The package file must begin with an XML declaration. All elements are then enclosed by the root package element:

```
<?xml version="1.0" encoding="ISO-8859-1" ?>
<!DOCTYPE package SYSTEM "http://pear.php.net/dtd/package-1.0">
<package version="1.0">

<!-- additional elements here -->

</package>
```

This example would fail with an error. The PEAR installer requires a number of elements to work with. To start with, we must provide overview information.

```
<?xml version="1.0" encoding="ISO-8859-1" ?>
<!DOCTYPE package SYSTEM "http://pear.php.net/dtd/package-1.0">
<package version="1.0">
  <name>Dialekt</name>
  <summary>
              A package for translating text and web pages
              into silly tones of voice
  </summary>
  <description>
              Be the envy of your friends with this
              hilarious dialect translator. Easy to extend
              and altogether delightful.
  </description>

<!-- additional elements here -->

</package>
```

These new elements should be pretty self-explanatory. The name element defines the handle by which the user will refer to the package. The summary element contains a one-line overview of the package, and description provides a little more detail. All these elements should be regarded as compulsory (although you can force the PEAR installer to attempt to install without them).

Next, you should provide information about the team behind your package. The maintainers element is used for this purpose. It should contain at least one maintainer element:

```
<maintainers>
  <maintainer>
    <user>mattz</user>
    <name>Matt Zandstra</name>
    <email>matt@example.com</email>
    <role>developer</role>
  </maintainer>
</maintainers>
```

Once again the elements used here should be fairly clear. The value you choose for the role element should be one of lead, developer, contributor, or helper. These are designations recognized by the PEAR community, but they should adequately cover most non-PEAR projects too. The user element refers to the contributor's user name with PEAR. Most teams use similar handles to allow users to log in to CVS, a development server, or both.

The release Element

The real heart of a package document is to be found in its release element. This provides information about the current version of your package, as well as instructions for installing its components. Let's look at the information side of release first of all:

```
<release>
  <version>0.2</version>
  <date>2004-01-01</date>
  <license>PHP License</license>
  <state>beta</state>
  <notes>initial work</notes>

  <!-- additional elements here -->

</release>
```

The version element is used by PEAR in dependency calculations. If another system claims to require Dialekt 1.0, and the installing user only has version 0.2 on her system, PEAR will halt its installation, or attempt to fetch a later version, depending upon the mode in which it was run. If you are releasing your package according to specific license terms (such as GNU's GPL license, for example) you should add this information to the license element. The state element can be one of dev, devel, alpha, beta, snapshot, or stable; you should choose the one that best describes your project.

Working with Files and Directories

Now that we've described the package, its contributors, and the current release, we are finally ready to talk about the files and directories in the package. Every file in a PEAR package has a role. Every role is associated with a default (configurable) location. Table 14-2 describes the common roles.

Table 14-2. *Some Common PEAR File Roles*

Role	Description	PEAR Config Name	Example Location
php	PHP file	php_dir	/usr/local/lib/php
test	Unit test file	test_dir	/usr/local/lib/php/test/<package>
script	Command line script	bin_dir	/usr/local/bin
data	Resource file	data_dir	/usr/local/lib/php/data/<package>
doc	Documentation file	doc_dir	/usr/local/lib/php/doc/<package>

When installation takes place, files of role, doc, data, and test, are not dropped directly into their respective directories. Instead a subdirectory named after the package is created in the test_dir and data_dir directories, and files are installed into this.

In a PEAR project, everything must have a role, and every role has its place. If you do not have the correct privileges to work with the default role locations, you can set your own locations using the pear command line tool:

```
$ pear config-set php_dir ~/php/lib/
$ pear config-set data_dir ~/php/lib/data/
$ pear config-set bin_dir ~/php/bin/
$ pear config-set doc_dir ~/php/lib/doc/
$ pear config-set test_dir ~/php/lib/test/
```

Now PEAR will use your directories rather than those described in Table 14-2. Remember that if you do this, you should add the lib directory to your include path: either in the php.ini file, an .htaccess file, or using the ini_set() function in your scripts. You should also ensure that the bin directory is in your shell's path so that command line commands can be found.

Our example revolves around a fictitious package called Dialekt. Here is the package's directory and file structure:

```
./package.xml
./data
    ./data/dalek.txt
    ./data/alig.txt
./script
    ./script/dialekt.sh
    ./script/dialekt.bat
./cli-dialekt.php
./Dialekt.php
./Dialekt
    ./Dialekt/AliG.php
    ./Dialekt/Dalek.php
```

As you can see, we have mirrored some of the standard PEAR roles in our data structure. So we include data and script directories. The top-level directory contains two PHP files. These should be installed in the PEAR directory (/usr/local/php/lib by default). Dialekt.php is designed to be the first port of call for client code. The user should be able to include Dialekt with

```
require_once("Dialekt.php");
```

Additional PHP files (Dalek.php and AliG.php) are stored in a Dialekt directory that will be added to the PEAR directory (these are responsible for the detailed process of translating Web pages and text files into oh-so-funny versions of themselves). Dialekt.php will include these on behalf of client code. In order that the Dialekt package can be used from the command line, we have included a shell script that will be moved to PEAR's script directory. Dialekt uses configuration information stored in text files. These will be installed in PEAR's data directory.

When we last looked at our package.xml file, we had reached the release element. In addition to general information, the release element must contain a filelist element, which in turn must contain file elements that describe the files in the release.

```
<filelist>
    <file role="php" name="cli-dialekt.php" />
</filelist>
```

Now, for the first time in this chapter, package.xml is legal! We can run it from the command line, and a single file will be installed. As you can see, we have defined a file with the role php. The file is named cli-dialekt.php and can be found on the same level as package.xml. Let's run the package.xml file:

```
$ pear install package.xml
```

cli-dialekt.php should now appear in the PEAR directory (whether that's ~/php/lib or /usr/local/php/lib). If you change your mind about the package, you can uninstall it from the command line like this:

```
$ pear uninstall dialekt
```

You do not need to specify a package.xml file in order to uninstall—PEAR maintains a registry of installed packages.

Now let's include Dialekt.php in the package:

```
<file role="php" name="Dialekt.php">
    <replace type="pear-config"
             from="@bin_dir@" to="bin_dir"/>
</file>
```

We have included a new element in this fragment. The replace element causes the PEAR installer to search the file for the trigger string given in the from attribute, replacing it with the PEAR config setting in the to attribute. So our Dialekt.php file might start out looking like this:

```
<?php
/*
 * Use this from PHP scripts, for a CLI implementation use
 * @bin_dir@/dialekt
 */
class Dialekt {
    const DIALEKT_ALIG=1;
    const DIALEKT_DALEK=2;
//...
}
```

After installation, the same class comment should look something like this:

```
/*
 * Use this from PHP scripts, for a CLI implementation use
 * /home/mattz/php/bin/dialekt
 */
```

In order to install our command line tool, we need to set the role attribute for the file to script. This ensures that the file is copied to the directory specified in the bin_dir setting.

```
<file role="script"
    platform="(.*nix|.*nux)"
    install-as="dialekt"
    name="script/dialekt.sh">
    <replace type="pear-config"
            from="@php_dir@" to="php_dir"/>
    <replace type="pear-config"
            from="@bin_dir@" to="bin_dir"/>
    <replace type="pear-config"
            from="@php_bin@" to="php_bin"/>
</file>
```

The install-as attribute specifies that the file dialekt.sh should be renamed dialekt on installation. We also introduce the platform attribute in which you can define a regular expression test. If the current platform matches this test, then the file is installed; otherwise the entire element is ignored.

Although you must specify every individual file in a package, you can apply some attributes to multiple files. For this you must use the dir element. Here we use dir to group php and data files:

```
<dir name="Dialekt" role="php">
    <file name="Dalek.php" />
    <file name="AliG.php" />
</dir>

<dir name="data" role="data">
    <file install-as="dalek" name="dalek.txt" />
    <file install-as="alig" name="alig.txt" />
</dir>
```

In each instance, we specify a role in the dir element rather than in the file elements it contains. This saves us from specifying the role for every file element. We also define the common part of the name attribute for each file. The dir element saves typing and makes file elements clearer, both by shortening and grouping them. Here is an equivalent to the preceding fragment that does not use the dir element:

```
<file role="php" name="Dialekt/Dalek.php" />
<file role="php" name="Dialekt/AliG.php" />
<file role="data"
        install-as="dalek" name="data/dalek.txt" />
<file role="data"
        install-as="alig" name="data/alig.txt" />
```

We specify that our data files should be installed without the .txt suffix. This means that they will be installed as <data_dir>/dialekt/dalek and <data_dir>/dialekt/alig. We do not need to specify the dialekt subdirectory—this is automatically included for files with a data role.

In the case of the data files, however, the situation is more involved. They are stored locally in ./data/dalek.txt and ./data/alig.txt. We want them to end up in a directory called Dialekt in PEAR's data directory. We can't use their local path to determine their output directory, so we set baseinstalldir to "Dialekt". If we simply left it at that, though, PEAR would still use the local path: the files would be saved to <data_dir>/Dialect/data/. To prevent this we set the install-as attribute. This transforms the data files' names (stripping the .txt extension), but it also removes the directory path. If we want to keep the full path, we would have to specify it in install-as.

Dependencies

Although packages are generally stand-alone entities, they often make use of one another. Any use of another package introduces a dependency. If the used package is not present on the user's system, then the package that uses it will not run as expected.

You can specify dependencies in package.xml. If these are not satisfied, PEAR will refuse to install the package by default. A package can depend upon another package, a PHP extension (such as zlib or gd) or a particular version of PHP. Here we insist that Dialekt has access to PHP 5 or greater and the DB package:

```
<deps>
<dep type="php" rel="ge" version="5.0.0"/>
<dep type="pkg" rel="ge" version="1.5"
 optional="yes">DB</dep>
</deps>
```

As you can see, dependencies are defined by the dep element. dep elements are organized by the deps element. Each dep element must define a type attribute. Table 14-3 lists dependency types.

Table 14-3. *package.xml Dependency Types*

Type	Description
php	The PHP application
pkg	A PEAR package
sapi	A server API ("apache", for example)
ext	A PHP extension (a capability compiled into PHP such as zlib or GD)
prog	A third-party program (such as cp or cvs)
os	An operating system
zend	A version of the Zend Engine (either 1 or 2 at time of writing)
doc	Documentation file

In addition to a type of dependency, you can define the dependency relationship. This defaults to has. By setting the rel attribute of the dep element to "has", you are requiring that the user has a particular package, extension, or program, regardless of version number. All other values to rel require that a version attribute is also set. You can insist that a particular version of a package is installed by setting rel to "eq". If you need the version to be less than a particular value, you would specify a rel of "lt". For a version less than or equal to a particular value, you would use "le". To require a version greater than, or greater than or equal to, a particular value, you would use "gt" or "ge" respectively.

We also used the optional attribute in our example. When PEAR encounters an unfilled optional dependency, it will raise a warning, but will continue to install nonetheless. You should set optional to "yes", where your package can limp along adequately without the preferred package or extension.

If the user runs the pear install command with the -o flag:

```
pear install -o package.xml
```

then PEAR will attempt to download and install all unmet *required* dependencies. Running the command with the -a flag also automates the download of dependencies, but will take in optional as well as required packages.

Automating package.xml Generation with PEAR_PackageFileManager

PEAR provides a package for generating the package.xml file. This might seem needlessly convoluted at first glance, but if you are managing a package that is set to evolve and grow over time, it could save you maintenance headaches. As we have seen, in order to install a package you must use the package.xml file to describe every individual file that belongs to it. This process is clearly ripe for automation.

The PEAR_PackageFileManager package provides a mechanism for describing every aspect of a package.xml file, and for adding every file in a directory structure to it. The package is not bundled with PHP by default, so you may need to install it:

```
$ pear install PEAR_PackageFileManager
```

You can then include and instantiate the PEAR_PackageFileManager class:

```
require_once('PEAR/PackageFileManager.php');
$pkg_man = new PEAR_PackageFileManager();
```

PEAR_PackageFileManager accepts a large number of options that equate to package.xml elements. Here we use some of these to describe the dialekt package:

```
$pkg_man->setOptions(
    array(
    'baseinstalldir'     => '/',
    'version'            => '0.1',
    'packagedirectory'   => '.',
    'simpleoutput'       =>  true,
    'state'              => 'beta',
    'package'            => 'dialekt',
    'summary'            => 'A package for translating text '.
                            'and web pages into silly tones '.
                            'of voice',
```

```
    'description'        => 'Be the envy of your friends with '.
                            'this hilarious dialect translator. '.
                            'Easy to extend and altogether'.
                            'delightful.',
    'notes'              => 'autogenerated build',
    'dir_roles'          => array(       'script' => 'script',
                                          'data' => 'data'),
    'installas'          => array( 'data/alig.txt' => 'alig',
                                  'data/dalek.txt' => 'dalek',
                               'script/dialekt.bat' => 'dialekt',
                                'script/dialekt.sh' => 'dialekt',
                            )

    )
);
```

Options are passed to the PEAR_PackageFileManager object via the setOptions() method, which accepts an associative array. Like most methods in this package, setOptions() returns a PEAR_Error object if it encounters any problems, so it is safest to test the return value with PEAR::isError(). We will omit this for the sake of brevity.

Many of the options accepted by setOptions() such as package, summary, and description, refer directly to package.xml elements that we have already encountered. The packagedirectory element includes a path to the package's development folder. PEAR_PackageFileManager needs this path in order to construct the release element with its file and dir elements. We have used a single dot for the path, because we intend to run this code from within the package directory.

The dir_roles element allows you to associate the contents of a directory with a particular role. We ensure that the contents of the script and data directories take on the right roles.

The installas option is like a centralized version of the install-as attribute we encountered previously. It consists of an array whose keys are the paths to the files affected, with the values the new file names. We reproduce the transformations we set up manually.

Some features of PEAR_PackageFileManager can be set through their own methods. Here we add our sole maintainer:

```
$pkg_man ->addMaintainer (
    'mattz    'Matt Zandstra', 'matt@example.com');
```

The addMaintainer() method accepts a user name, a maintainer role, a full name, and an e-mail address.

In our package.xml file, we used the platform attribute to make the installation of certain files dependent upon operating system. We achieve the same effect in PEAR_PackageFileManager with the addPlatformException() method.

```
$pkg_man->addPlatformException('script/dialekt.bat', 'windows');
$pkg_man->addPlatformException('script/dialekt.sh', 'linux');
```

addPlatformException() requires a file path and a platform. The file will only be installed if the platform matches the current operating system.

The other operation we describe in package.xml is keyword replacement. PEAR_PackageFileManager provides the addReplacement() method.

```
$pkg_man->addReplacement(
    'script/dialekt.sh', 'pear-config',
    '@php_dir@', 'php_dir');
```

This method requires a file path, a type, the string to replace, and the name of the replacement. In this case, we have chosen the pear-config type, and elect to replace the target string with the php_dir pear-config variable. Other types include php-const, where the replacement value should be a PHP constant, and package-info, where the value is a package value such as summary.

Having configured our PEAR_PackageFileManager object, we need to provide a mechanism for generating the package.xml file. There are two methods of note here. The first writes the contents of package.xml to standard output:

```
$pkg_man->debugPackageFile();
```

This is very useful for checking your configuration before writing your file. Once you have checked your output, it is time to write the file:

```
 $pkg_man->writePackageFile();
```

Preparing a Package for Shipment

Now that we have created our package and generated a package.xml file, whether manually or automatically, it is time to generate an archived and compressed product.

There is a single PEAR command to achieve this. We ensure we are in the root directory of our project and run this subcommand:

```
$ pear package
```

This will generate a tarred and gzipped archive suitable for distribution.

Summary

PEAR is extensive almost by definition, and I have only had space to provide an introduction here. Nevertheless, you should leave this chapter with a sense of how easy it is to leverage PEAR packages to add power to your projects. Through the package.xml file and the PEAR installer, you can also make your code accessible to other users.

PEAR is best suited for relatively self-enclosed packages with well-defined functionality. For larger applications, other build solutions come into their own. We will be looking at Phing, a powerful tool for building applications, later in the book.

■ ■ ■

CHAPTER 15

Generating Documentation with phpDocumentor

Remember that tricky bit of code? The one in which you treated that method argument as a string, unless it was an integer? Or was it a Boolean? Would you recognize it if you saw it? Maybe you tidied it up already? Coding is a messy and complex business, and it's hard to keep track of the way your systems work and what needs doing. The problem becomes worse when you add more programmers to the project. Whether you need to signpost potential danger areas or fantastic features, documentation can help you. For a large codebase, documentation or its absence can make or break a project.

This chapter will cover

- *The phpDocumentor application*: Installing phpDocumentor, running it from the command line

- *Documentation syntax*: The DocBlock comment, documentation tags

- *Documenting your code*: Using DocBlock comments to provide information about classes, properties, and methods

- *Creating links in documentation*: Linking to Web sites and to other documentation elements

Why Document?

Programmers love and loathe documentation in equal measure. When you are under pressure from deadlines, with managers or customers peering over your shoulders, documentation is often the first thing to be jettisoned. The overwhelming drive is to get results. Write elegant code, certainly (though that can be another sacrifice), but with a codebase undergoing rapid evolution, documentation can feel like a real waste of time. After all, you'll probably have to change your classes several times in as many days. Of course, everyone agrees that it's desirable to have good documentation. It's just that no one wants to undermine productivity in order to make it happen.

Imagine a very large project. The codebase is enormous, consisting of very clever code written by very clever people. The team members have been working on this single project (or set of related subprojects) for over five years. They know each other well, and they understand the code absolutely. Documentation is sparse, of course. Everyone has a map of the project in their heads, and a set of unofficial coding conventions that provide clues as to what is going on in any particular area. Then the team is extended. The two new coders are given a good basic introduction to the complex architecture and thrown in. This is the point at which the true cost of undocumented code begins to tell. What would otherwise have been a few weeks of acclimatization soon becomes months. Confronted with an undocumented class, the new programmers are forced to trace the arguments to every method, track down every referenced global, check all the methods in the inheritance hierarchy. And with each trail followed, the process begins again. If, like me, you have been one of those new team members, you soon learn to love documentation.

Lack of documentation costs. It costs in time, as new team members join a project, or existing colleagues shift beyond their area of specialization. It costs in errors as coders fall into the traps that all projects set. Code that should be marked private is called, argument variables are populated with the wrong types, functionality that already exists is needlessly re-created.

Documentation is a hard habit to get into because you don't feel the pain of neglecting it straightaway. Documentation needn't be difficult, though, if you work at it as you code. This process can be significantly eased if you add your documentation in the source itself as you code. You can then run a tool to extract the comments into neatly formatted Web pages. This chapter is about just such a tool.

phpDocumentor is based on a Java tool called JavaDoc. Both systems extract special comments from source code, building sophisticated application programming interface (API) documentation from both the coder's comments and the code constructs they find in the source.

Installation

The easiest way to install phpDocumentor is by using the PEAR command line interface. First, though, you need to get your hands on the package. You can find the phpDocumentor Web site at http://www.phpdoc.org. Once you have the package on your file system, you should decompress it. Assuming that you have downloaded the tarred and gzipped version, and that you are on a Unix-like command line, you might use the following command:

```
tar -xvzf phpdocumentor-1.3.0rc3.tar.gz
```

Note There is also a distribution of phpDocumentor archived in Zip format available for Windows users.

Of course, by the time you read this, the version number of phpDocumentor may have changed. Substitute the current name of the package for the one just quoted. Once you have unpacked the package, change your current working directory to the package root:

```
cd phpdocumentor-1.3.0rc3
```

At this level you should see a file named `package.xml`. This is used by PEAR to install phpDocumentor.

```
pear install package.xml
```

That should be that! PEAR prints a confirmation message, and we are ready to get started. If you have any problems with installation, the phpDocumentor package includes a file named `INSTALL`, which contains extensive instructions and troubleshooting hints.

Generating Documentation

It might seem odd to generate documentation before we have even written any, but phpDocumentor parses the code structures in our source code, so it can gather information about our project before we even start.

We are going to document aspects of an imaginary project called "megaquiz." It consists of two directories, `command` and `quiztools`, which contain class files. These are also the names of packages in the project. phpDocumentor can be run as a command line tool, or through a slick Web GUI. We will concentrate on the command line, because it's easy then to embed documentation updates into build tools or shell scripts. The command to invoke phpDocumentor is `phpdoc`. You will need to run the command with a number of arguments in order to generate documentation. Here's an example:

```
phpdoc -d /home/projects/megaquiz/ \
       -t /home/projects/docs/megaquiz/ \
       -ti 'Mega Quiz' \
       -dn 'megaquiz'
```

The `-d` flag denotes the directory whose contents you intend to document. `-t` denotes your target directory (the directory to which you wish to write the documentation files). Use `-ti` to set a project title, and `-dn` to define the default package name.

If we run this command on our undocumented project, we get a surprising amount of detail. You can see the menu page of our output in Figure 15-1.

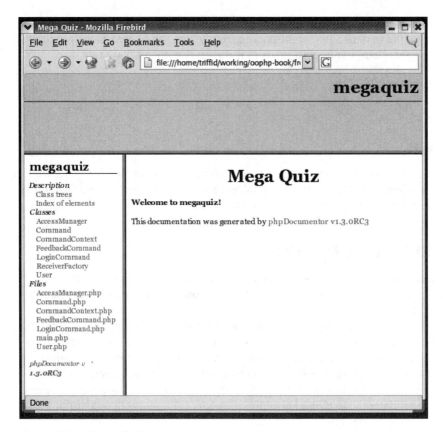

Figure 15-1. *A basic phpDocumentor output menu*

As you can see, all the classes and files in the project are listed in the left-hand frame. Both the project name and the package name are incorporated into the documentation. The class names are all hyperlinks. In Figure 15-2, you can see some of the documentation for the Command class that we created in Chapter 11.

phpDocumentor is smart enough to recognize that Command is an abstract class, and that it is extended by FeedbackCommand and LoginCommand. Notice also that it has reported both the name and the type of the argument required by the execute() method.

Because this level of detail alone is enough to provide an easily navigable overview of a large project, it is a huge improvement upon no documentation at all. However, we can improve it significantly by adding comments to our source code.

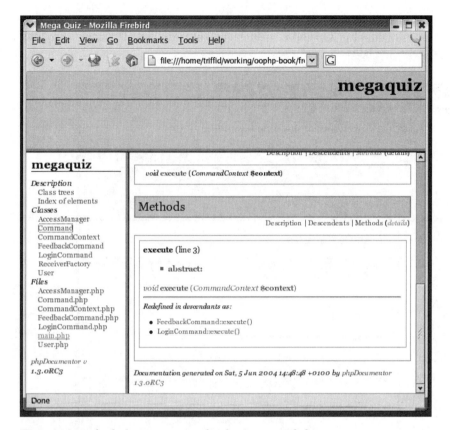

Figure 15-2. *Default documentation for the Command class*

DocBlock Comments

DocBlock comments are specially formatted to be recognized by a documentation application. They take the form of standard multiline comments. Standard, that is, with the single addition of an asterisk to each line within the comment:

```
/**
 * My DocBlock comment
 */
```

phpDocumentor is designed to expect special content within DocBlocks. This content includes normal text descriptive of the element to be documented (for our purposes, a file, class, method, or property). It also includes special keywords called tags. Tags are defined using the at sign (@), and may be associated with arguments. So the following DocBlock placed at the top of a class tells phpDocumentor the package to which it belongs:

```
/**
 * @package command
 */
```

If we add this comment to every class in our project (with the appropriate package name, of course), phpDocumentor will organize our classes for us. You can see phpDocumentor output that includes packages in Figure 15-3.

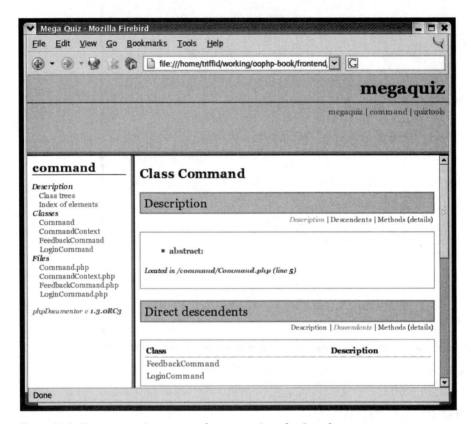

Figure 15-3. *Documentation output that recognizes the @package tag*

In Figure 15-3, notice that packages have been added to the navigation (top-right corner). In addition to the default megaquiz package we defined as a command line switch, we can now click command or quiztools. Because we are currently examining classes in the command package, the links that form the left-hand navigation list only those classes.

Generally, packages in documentation will mirror your directory structure. So the command package maps to a command directory. That isn't necessary, however. A third-party developer may wish to create a Command class that is part of the command package but lives in her own directory, for example. So the @package tag makes you take responsibility for associating classes with packages, but it also affords you flexibility that would not be available by using the file system to guess at package names.

Documenting Classes

Let's add some more tags and text that are useful in class- or file-level DocBlocks. We should identify the class, explain its uses, and add authorship and copyright information.

Here is the Command class in its entirety:

```
/**
 * Defines core functionality for commands.
 * Command classes perform specific tasks in a system via
 * the execute() method
 *
 * @package command
 * @author  Clarrie Grundie
 * @copyright 2004 Ambridge Technologies Ltd
 */
abstract class Command {
    abstract function execute( CommandContext $context );
}
```

The DocBlock comment has grown significantly. The first sentence is a one-line summary. This is emphasized in the output, and also extracted for use in overview listings. The subsequent lines of text contained more detailed description. It is here that you can provide detailed usage information for the programmers who come after you. As we will see, this section can contain links to other elements in the project, fragments of code in addition to descriptive text. We also include @author and @copyright tags, which should be self-explanatory. You can see the effect of our extended class comment in Figure 15-4.

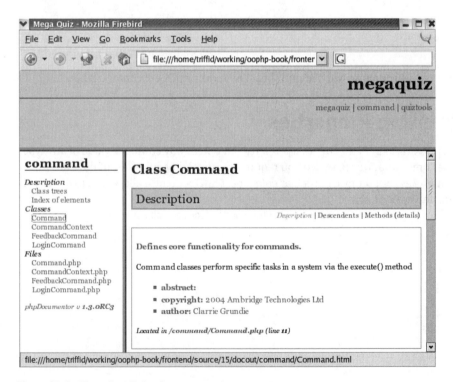

Figure 15-4. *Class details in documentation output*

Notice that we didn't need to tell phpDocumentor that the `Command` class is abstract. This confirms something that we already know, that phpDocmentor interrogates the classes it works with even without our help. But it is also important to see that DocBlocks are contextual. phpDocumentor understands that we are documenting a class in the previous listing, because the DocBlock it encounters immediately precedes a class declaration.

File-Level Documentation

Although I tend to think in terms of classes rather than of the files that contain them, there are good reasons in some projects for providing a layer of documentation at the file level.

First of all, phpDocumentor likes file comments. If you fail to include a DocBlock for a file in your project, a warning is raised that can clutter up the application's reporting, especially in large projects. A file comment should be the first DocBlock in a document. It should contain a `@package` tag, and it should not directly precede a coding construct. In other words, if you add a file-level DocBlock, you should ensure that you also add a class-level comment before the first class declaration.

Many open source projects require that every file includes a license notice, or a link to one. Page-level DocBlock comments can be used, therefore, for including license information that you do not want to repeat on a class-by-class basis. You can use the `@license` tag for this. `@license` should be followed by a URL, pointing to a license document, and a description:

```
/**
 * @license http://www.example.com/lic.html Borsetshire Open License
 * @package command
 */
```

The URL in the license tag will become clickable in the phpDocumentor output.

Documenting Properties

All properties are mixed in PHP. That is, a property can potentially contain a value of any type. There may be some situations in which you require this flexibility, but most of the time you think of a property as containing a particular data type. phpDocmentor allows you to document this fact using the `@var` tag.

Here are some properties documented in the `CommandContext` class:

```
class CommandContext {
/**
 * The application name.
 * Used by various clients for error messages, etc.
 * @var string
 */
    public $applicationName;

/**
 * Encapsulated Keys/values.
 * This class is essentially a wrapper for this array
 * @var array
 */
    private $params = array();

/**
 * An error message.
 * @var string
 */
    private $error = "";
// ...
```

As you can see, we provide a summary sentence for each property, and fuller information for the first two. We use the @var tag to define each property's type. If we were to use the same phpdoc command line arguments as usual to generate output at this point, we would only see documentation for the public $applicationName property. This is because private methods and properties do not appear in documentation by default.

Whether or not you choose to document private elements depends in large part upon your intended audience. If you are writing for client coders, then you should probably hide your classes' internals. If, on the other hand, your project is under development, your team members may need more detailed documentation. You can make phpDocumentor include private elements by using the -pp (--parseprivate) command line argument when you invoke the script:

```
phpdoc -d /home/projects/megaquiz/ \
       -t /home/projects/docs/megaquiz/ \
       -ti 'Mega Quiz' \
       -dn 'megaquiz' \
       -pp on
```

Notice that you must explicitly set the -pp flag to on; it is not enough to include the flag on its own. You can see our documented properties in Figure 15-5.

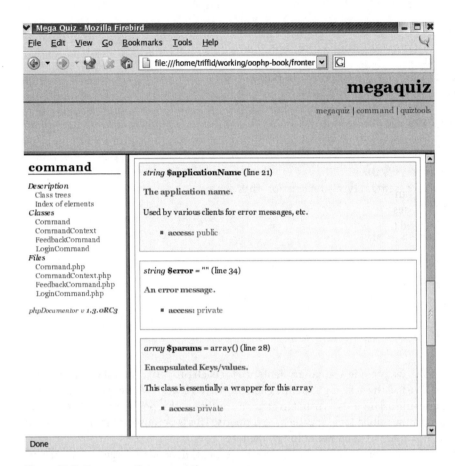

Figure 15-5. *Documenting properties*

Documenting Methods

Together with classes, methods lie at the heart of a documentation project. At the very least, readers need to understand the arguments to a method, the operation performed, and its return value.

As with class-level DocBlock comments, method documentation should consist of two blocks of text: a one-line summary and an optional description. You can provide information about each argument to the method with the @param tag. Each @param tag should begin a new line, and should be followed by the argument name, its type, and a short description.

Because PHP 5 does not constrain return types, it is particularly important to document the value a method returns. You can do this with the @return tag. @return should begin a new line, and should be followed by the return value's type and a short description. We put these elements together here:

```
/**
 * Perform the key operation encapsulated by the class.
 * Command classes encapsulate a single operation. They
 * are easy to add to and remove from a project, can be
 * stored after instantiation and execute() invoked at
 * leisure.
 * @param  $context CommandContext Shared contextual data
 * @return bool     false on failure, true on success
 */
    abstract function execute( CommandContext $context );
```

It may seem strange to add more documentation than code to a document. Documentation in abstract classes is particularly important, though, because it provides directions for developers who need to understand how to extend the class. If you are worried about the amount of dead space the PHP engine must parse and discard for a well-documented project, it is a relatively trivial matter to add code to your build tools to strip out comments on installation. You can see our documentation's output in Figure 15-6.

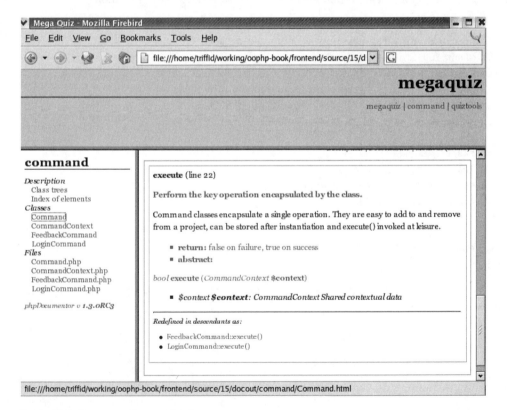

Figure 15-6. *Documenting methods*

Creating Links in Documentation

phpDocumentor generates a hyperlinked documentation environment for you. Sometimes, though, you will want to generate your own hyperlinks, either to other elements within documentation or to external sites. In this section we will look at the tags for both of these and encounter a new syntax: the inline tag.

As you construct a DocBlock comment, you may want to talk about a related class, property, or method. To make it easy for the user to navigate to this feature, you can use the @see tag. @see requires a reference to an element in the format

```
class
class::method()
```

or

```
class::$property
```

So in the following DocBlock comment, we document the CommandContext object, and emphasize the fact that it is commonly used in the Command::execute() method:

```
/**
 * Encapsulates data for passing to, from and between Commands.
 * Commands require disparate data according to context. The
 * CommandContext object is passed to the Command::execute()
 * method, and contains data in key/value format. The class
 * automatically extracts the contents of the $_REQUEST
 * superglobal.
 *
 * @package command
 * @author  Clarrie Grundie
 * @copyright 2004 Ambridge Technologies Ltd
 * @see Command::execute()
 */

class CommandContext {
// ...
```

As you can see in Figure 15-7, the @see tag resolves to a link. Clicking this will lead you to the execute() method.

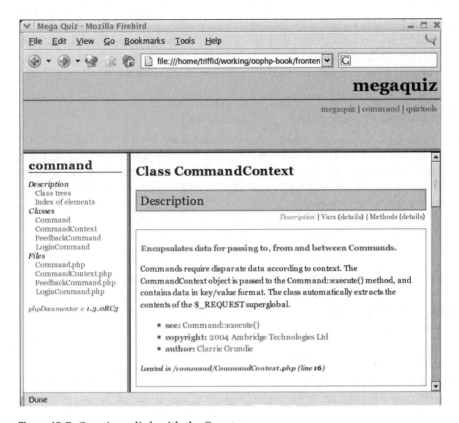

Figure 15-7. *Creating a link with the @see tag*

Notice, though, that we also embedded a reference to Command::execute() in the DocBlock description text. We can transform this into a live link by using the @link tag. @link can be added at the beginning of a line, as @see is, but it can also be used inline. In order to differentiate inline tags from their surroundings, you must surround them with curly brackets. So, to make our embedded reference to Command::execute() clickable, we would use the following syntax:

```
// ...
 * Commands require disparate data according to context. The
 * CommandContext object is passed to the {@link Command::execute()}
 * method, and contains data in key/value format. The class
//...
```

Because the @link tag in the previous fragment includes only the element reference (Command::execute()), it is this string that becomes clickable. If we were to add some description here, it would become clickable instead.

@link can be used to refer to URLs as well. Simply replace the element reference with a URL:

```
@link http://www.example.com More info
```

Once again, the URL is the target, and the description that follows it is the clickable text.

You may want to make a reciprocal link. Command uses CommandContext objects so we might decide to create a link from Command::execute() to the CommandContext class, and a reciprocal link in the opposite direction. We could, of course, do this with two @link or @see tags. @uses handles it all with a single tag, however:

```
/**
 * Perform the key operation encapsulated by the class.
 *
 * ...
 * @param  $context {@link CommandContext} Shared contextual data
 * @return bool     false on failure, true on success
 * @link http://www.example.com More info
 * @uses CommandContext
 */
    abstract function execute( CommandContext $context );
```

In adding the @uses tag, we create a link in the Command::execute() documentation: "Uses: CommandContext". In the CommandContext class documentation, a new link will appear: "Used by: Command::execute()".

You can see the latest output in Figure 15-8. Note that we have not used @link inline, so it is output in list format.

Summary

In this chapter, I covered the core features of phpDocumentor. We encountered the DocBlock comment syntax and the tags that can be used with it. We looked at approaches to documenting classes, properties, and methods, providing you with enough material to transform your documentation, and so to improve collaborative working immeasurably (especially when used in conjunction with build tools and version control). There is a lot more to this fantastic application than I have space to cover, though, so be sure to check the phpDocumentor homepage at http://www.phpdoc.org.

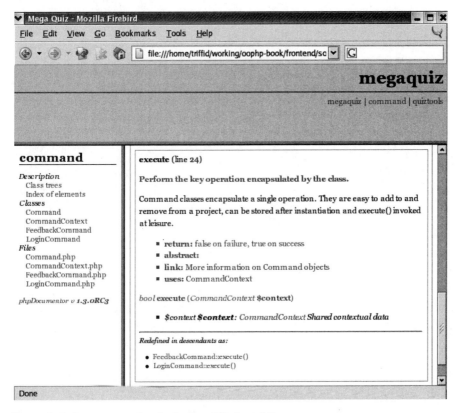

Figure 15-8. *Documentation including @link and @uses tags*

CHAPTER 16

Version Control with CVS

Have you ever noticed a particular moment at which a project seems to run out of control? Perhaps it's when you make "just a couple of changes" and find that you have brought everything crashing down around you (and even worse, you're not quite sure how to get back to the point of stability you have just destroyed). It could be when you realize that three members of your team have been working on the same set of classes and merrily saving over each other's work. Or perhaps it's when you discover that a bug fix you have implemented twice has somehow disappeared from the codebase yet again. Wouldn't it be nice if there was a tool to help you manage collaborative working, allowing you to take snapshots of your projects and roll them back if necessary, and to merge multiple strands of development? In this chapter, we look at CVS, a tool that does all that and more.

This chapter will cover

- *Basic configuration*: Some tips for setting up CVS

- *Importing*: Starting a new project

- *Committing changes*: Saving your work to the repository

- *Updating*: Merging other people's work with your own

- *Branching*: Maintaining parallel strands of development

Why Use Version Control?

If it hasn't already, version control will change your life (if only your life as a developer). How many times have you reached a stable moment in a project, drawn a breath, and plunged onward into development chaos once again? How easy was it to revert to the stable version when it came time to demonstrate your work in progress? Of course, you may have saved a snapshot of your project when it reached a stable moment, probably by duplicating your development directory. Now, imagine that your colleague is working on the same codebase. Perhaps she has saved a stable copy of the code as you have. The difference is that her copy is a snapshot of her work, not yours. Of course, she has a messy development directory too. So you have four versions of your project to coordinate. Now imagine a project with four programmers and a Web developer. You're looking pale. Perhaps you would like to lie down?

CVS stands for Concurrent Versions System, and it exists exclusively to address this problem. Using CVS, all your developers check out their own copies of the codebase from a central repository. Whenever they reach a stable point in their code, they update their copy. This merges any changes in the shared code with their own recent work. After they fix any conflicts, they can check their new stable version back into the shared repository. There is now only one authoritative source of code in your project. The fact that each developer merges his work into the central repository means that you no longer have to worry about reconciling multiple strands of development by hand. Even better, you can check out versions of your codebase based upon a date or a label. So when your code reaches a stable point, suitable for showing to a client as work in progress, for example, you can tag that with an arbitrary label. You can then use that tag to check out the correct codebase when your client swoops into your office looking to impress an investor.

Wait! There's more! You can also manage multiple strands of development at the same time. If this sounds needlessly complicated, imagine a mature project. You have already shipped the first version, and you're well into development of version 2. Does version 1.n go away in the meantime? Of course not. Your users are spotting bugs and requesting enhancements all the time. You may be months away from shipping version 2, so where do you make and test the changes? CVS will let you maintain distinct branches of the codebase. So you might create a bug-fix branch of your version 1.n for development on the current production code. At key points this branch can be merged back into the version 2 code (the "trunk"), so that your new release can benefit from improvements to version 1.n.

Let's get on and look at some of these features in practice.

Getting CVS

If you are working on a Unix machine, you will almost certainly already have a CVS client installed and ready to use.

Try typing

```
$ cvs
```

from the command line. You should see some usage information that will confirm that you are ready to get started.

■Note Throughout this chapter, I denote command line input by displaying it in bold text. A dollar sign ($) represents the command prompt.

If you get an error message, you may need to download and install CVS yourself. You can acquire both source and binaries from `https://www.cvshome.org/`.

CVS graphical user interface clients for Windows and MacOS can be downloaded from `http://www.wincvs.org/`. These will need to be used in conjunction with a CVS server installed on a Unix or Linux machine.

Note If you have no access to Unix, there are server solutions you can deploy on Windows that are compatible with CVS clients. You may like to take a look at CVSNT (`http://www.cvsnt.org/wiki`).

CVS is by its nature a network application. Although this chapter is written from the perspective of the Linux command line, you will find menu items that match the commands we examine.

Configuring a CVS Repository

Whether you are running CVS locally or across multiple clients, you must have a repository in place before you can start work. What's more, every user's CVS process must know where that repository is. In this section, we look at the steps necessary to get CVS up and running, either on a single machine or over the Internet. We assume root access to a Linux machine.

Creating a Repository

You can create a CVS repository with a simple CVS subcommand: `init`. This will create a properly configured CVS repository directory.

Here we create a repository in the directory /usr/local/cvs. We must use the flag -d to tell CVS which directory we wish to work with. Generally speaking, only the root user can create and modify directories in /usr/local, so we run the following command as root:

```
$ cvs -d /usr/local/cvs init
```

This command will execute silently, but you should find that it has created a directory called cvs in the /usr/local directory. The cvs directory should contain a directory called CVSROOT that contains configuration information.

Let's assume that you have multiple users on this Linux machine, all of whom will need to commit to and update from this repository. We need to ensure that they can all write to the /usr/local/cvs directory. We can do this by adding these users to a common group and making the directory writable by this group.

You can create a new group (called "cvsusers") on the command line like this:

```
$ groupadd cvsusers
```

You must run the groupadd command as root. You should now have this group on your system.

First let's add a user on the current host, "bob," to the cvsusers group. We do this by editing a special file called /etc/group. In /etc/group you should find a line that looks like this:

```
cvsusers:x:504:
```

We can add "bob" to the group:

```
cvsusers:x:504:bob,
```

Now we need to ensure that /etc/local/cvs is writable by anyone in the cvsusers group. We can do this by changing the group of /usr/local/cvs to cvsusers.

```
$ cd /usr/local/cvs
$ chgrp -R cvsusers .
$ chmod g+s .
```

The final line in the previous fragment causes all directories created here to take on the wheel group. We should also ensure that the cvs directory is group writable.

```
$ chmod 775 .
```

Configuring the Client

So how does a CVS process know where to find the repository we have just created? You could tell it on the command line as part of every CVS command you invoke, but it is easier to set an environment variable called CVSROOT and forget about it until you need to make a change.

If you are using the Bash shell, you can set CVSROOT in a file called .bash_profile, which should be found in (or can be added to) your home directory and is executed automatically on login (other shells have equivalent files). Simply add this line:

```
export CVSROOT=/usr/local/cvs
```

That should be all you need to start working with CVS. Remember that any users who want to use the repository must have write access to the repository directory. You achieve this by adding them to the wheel group.

Running CVS Across Multiple Machines

CVS works fine locally, of course, but for any serious work, you are likely to have a central CVS server managing code for developers on any number of client machines. We need a strategy to enable remote users to connect to the CVS repository and to work with it. The approach we take here is by no means the only one, so if you are taking on ownership of a CVS repository, you would be well advised to spend some time reading up on the subject. https://www.cvshome.org/ is a good starting point.

CVS includes a password server, called "pserver," that can be configured to allow remote access. However, I prefer the security of SSH, which encrypts all data it transfers. Setting up CVS for working with SSH is relatively trivial, although there are a couple of annoyances. It is hard, for example, to allow users full access to your repository without first giving them a shell account on the CVS machine. (If you are allowing nontrusted users, you could look into setting up a "chroot jail," which supports an extremely restricted environment for user accounts.

This strays too far into the realms of system administration for this chapter!) Also annoying for users is the requirement to continually type in their password or pass phrase for every CVS command. We will summarize a solution to the latter problem at least later in the section.

We have already set user "bob" up on our CVS machine. Now he tells us he wants to access the repository and install a working directory on another machine. In fact, all he needs to do is to set up the .bash_profile file on his remote machine:

```
export CVS_RSH=ssh
export CVSROOT=:ext:bob@the-cvs-server.com:/usr/local/cvs
```

This is enough to get him up and running. The finer details of SSH configuration are beyond the scope of this book. In brief, though, Bob should generate a public key with a program called ssh-keygen on his client machine. He will be prompted to create a pass phrase. He should copy the generated public key, which he will find in .ssh/id_rsa.pub (where .ssh is in his client home directory), and append it to a file called .ssh/authorized_keys (where .ssh is in his home directory) on the CVS server. He can now use a program called ssh-agent to handle the details of authentication for him.

Beginning a Project

In order to work with a project using CVS, you must add it to the repository. You can do this by importing a project directory and any contents you might already have.

Before you start, take a good look at your files and directories, removing any temporary items you might find. Failure to do this is a common and annoying mistake. Temporary items to watch for include automatically generated files such as phpDocumentor output, build directories, installer logs, and so on.

Once your project is clean, ensure that your current working directory is the project directory, and not its parent. This is another gotcha: importing from the directory that holds your project will add *everything at that level* to the repository. Let's say that we want to import a directory: /home/harry/projects/megaquiz.

```
$ cd /home/harry/projects/megaquiz
$ cvs import megaquiz harry release0
```

Let's break down this use of the cvs command. CVS is a very big package consisting of many subcommands and switches. The purpose of the import subcommand should be clear enough. import requires three arguments: the name of the project, a vendor name, and a release tag. For your own projects, the vendor and release tag arguments are immaterial; the project name is, of course, vitally important—it is the name that everyone on your team will use to acquire their copies of the codebase (their "sandboxes").

When you run the import subcommand, you will be presented with an editor window and instructed to provide an import message. In Figure 16-1, you can see vi, my default editor, demanding just such input.

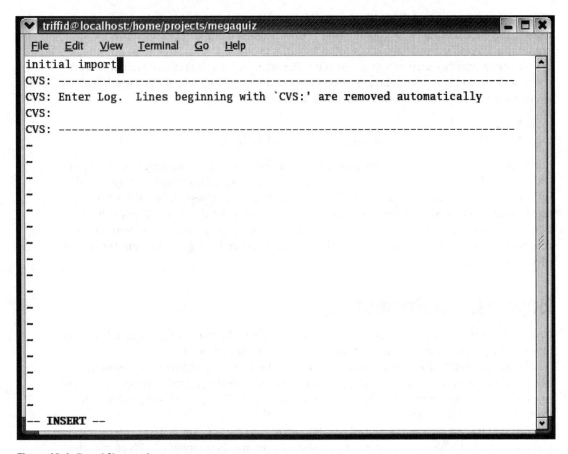

Figure 16-1. *Providing an import message*

The import subcommand should generate output that looks something like this:

```
N megaquiz/main.php
cvs import: Importing /usr/local/cvs/megaquiz/command
N megaquiz/command/Command.php
N megaquiz/command/FeedbackCommand.php
N megaquiz/command/LoginCommand.php
N megaquiz/command/CommandContext.php
cvs import: Importing /usr/local/cvs/megaquiz/quiztools
N megaquiz/quiztools/AccessManager.php
cvs import: Importing /usr/local/cvs/megaquiz/quizobjects
N megaquiz/quizobjects/User.php

No conflicts created by this import
```

As you can see, CVS generates a report for every directory and file it encounters in your project directory.

Now that you have imported your project, you should move your source directory out of the way. If you're feeling bold, you could delete it; otherwise rename it. I generally add the extension .orig to the directory name:

```
$ cd ..
$ mv megaquiz megaquiz.orig
```

The point to remember here is that importing a project does not in any way transform the source directory. If you want to use version control, you must check your project out from the repository after you have imported it. We can check out a project with the checkout subcommand.

```
$ cvs checkout megaquiz
```

Remember, the dollar sign at the beginning of the line represents the shell prompt. The rest of the line is what a user might type. CVS will re-create the megaquiz directory, reporting as it does so:

```
cvs checkout: Updating megaquiz
U megaquiz/main.php
cvs checkout: Updating megaquiz/command
U megaquiz/command/Command.php
U megaquiz/command/CommandContext.php
U megaquiz/command/FeedbackCommand.php
U megaquiz/command/LoginCommand.php
cvs checkout: Updating megaquiz/quizobjects
U megaquiz/quizobjects/User.php
cvs checkout: Updating megaquiz/quiztools
U megaquiz/quiztools/AccessManager.php
```

If you look into the newly created megaquiz directory, you will see that it, and all of its subdirectories, contain a folder called CVS. This contains metadata about your project and its repository. You can pretty much ignore the CVS directories, but you should not delete any of them.

Now that you have a sandbox set up, it is time to start work. You can edit and save your files as normal, but remember, you are no longer alone! You need to keep your work synchronized with the central repository, or you will lose the benefits afforded by CVS.

Updating and Committing

For the purposes of this chapter, we have invented a team member named Bob. Bob is working with us on the MegaQuiz project. Bob is, of course, a fine and talented fellow. Except, that is, for one common and highly annoying trait: he cannot leave other people's code alone.

Bob is smart and inquisitive, easily excited by shiny new avenues of development, and keen to help optimize new code. As a result, everywhere we turn, we seem to see the hand of Bob. Bob has added to our documentation, Bob has implemented an idea we mentioned over coffee. We may have to kill Bob. In the meantime, though, we must handle the fact that the code we are working on needs to be merged with Bob's input.

Here's a file called `quizobjects/User.php`. At the moment, it contains nothing but the barest of bones:

```php
<?php
class User {}
?>
```

We have decided to add some documentation. As you know from the last chapter, we should add file and class comments. We begin by adding the file comment:

```php
<?php
/**
 * @license   http://www.example.com Borsetshire Open License
 * @package   quizobjects
 */

class User {}
?>
```

Meanwhile, Bob is keen as ever, and he has created the class comment:

```php
<?php

/**
 * @package   quizobjects
 */
class User {}
?>
```

So we now have two distinct versions of `User.php`. At this time, the CVS repository contains only the recently imported version of MegaQuiz. We decide to add our changes to the CVS repository. This requires only one command, but two are advisable:

```
$ cvs update User.php
M User.php
```

The update subcommand instructs CVS to merge any changes stored in the repository into your local document or documents. Before we commit our own work, it is good practice to first see if anyone else's changes conflict with our own, resolving any such conflicts in our own space. The "M" character at the start of the command's output means that we have modified `User.php`, but no third-party changes need be applied. We can now go ahead and commit our changes:

```
$ cvs commit -m'added doc level comment' User.php
Checking in User.php;
/usr/local/cvs/megaquiz/quizobjects/User.php,v  <--  User.php
new revision: 1.2; previous revision: 1.1
done
```

As you can see, we use the commit subcommand to check new data into the CVS repository. CVS tells us where the version information for User.php is stored, and the new revision number for the document. Notice that we have used a new command line switch with commit. -m allows us to add a message on the command line, rather than via an editor.

Now it's Bob's turn to update and commit:

$ cvs update User.php
```
RCS file: /usr/local/cvs/megaquiz/quizobjects/User.php,v
retrieving revision 1.1
retrieving revision 1.2
Merging differences between 1.1 and 1.2 into User.php
rcsmerge: warning: conflicts during merge
cvs update: conflicts found in User.php
C User.php
```

Take a close look at the output generated by the update subcommand. It helpfully tells us exactly what it is doing. First it identifies the data from the repository it needs to merge with Bob's additions. This data is the difference between revision 1.1 (the initial import, and the version that Bob checked out) and 1.2 (the document-level comment we added previously). It then takes this information and attempts to merge it into Bob's amended version of User.php. But then disaster strikes! CVS has no means of handling changes that affect the same lines. How can it decide what is to have priority? Should the repository overwrite Bob's changes, or the other way around? Should both changes coexist? Which should go first? CVS has no choice but to report a conflict and let Bob sort out the problem. Here's what CVS has done to Bob's document:

```
<?php
<<<<<<< User.php

/**
 * @package   quizobjects
 */
=======
/**
 * @license    http://www.example.com Borsetshire Open License
 * @package   quizobjects
 */

>>>>>>> 1.2
class User {}
?>
```

As you can see, CVS includes both Bob's comment and our own, together with metadata that tells us which part originates where. The conflicting information is separated by a line of equals signs. Bob's input is signaled by a line of lesser-than signs followed by the name of the document. Data pulled from the repository is delineated by a line of greater-than signs and the version number. It is up to Bob to resolve the conflict, which he does by deleting the metadata and arranging the content in the right order:

```
<?php
/**
 * @license   http://www.example.com Borsetshire Open License
 * @package   quizobjects
 */

/**
 * @package   quizobjects
 */
class User {}
?>
```

Bob can now commit as normal:

```
$ cvs commit -m'added class comment' User.php
Checking in User.php;
/usr/local/cvs/megaquiz/quizobjects/User.php,v  <--  User.php
new revision: 1.3; previous revision: 1.2
done
```

So far we have updated and committed a single file only. By omitting the file argument altogether, we can apply these commands to every file and directory in the project. Here we run update from the root directory of the project:

```
$ cvs update
cvs update: Updating .
cvs update: Updating command
cvs update: Updating quizobjects
U quizobjects/User.php
cvs update: Updating quiztools
```

CVS visits every directory in our project, finding nothing to update until it encounters the document User.php. Bob's changes are then incorporated into our version of the document.

We can commit globally in the same way. In this example, we have made minor changes to two documents, command/Command.php and quiztools/AccessManager.php:

```
$ cvs commit -m'documentation amendments'
cvs commit: Examining .
cvs commit: Examining command
cvs commit: Examining quizobjects
cvs commit: Examining quiztools
Checking in command/Command.php;
/usr/local/cvs/megaquiz/command/Command.php,v  <--  Command.php
new revision: 1.2; previous revision: 1.1
done
Checking in quiztools/AccessManager.php;
/usr/local/cvs/megaquiz/quiztools/AccessManager.php,v  <--  AccessManager.php
new revision: 1.2; previous revision: 1.1
done
```

Once again, CVS works through every directory below our current working directory. It takes no action until it encounters a changed file. At this point it checks the changes in to the repository.

Adding and Removing Files and Directories

Projects change shape as they develop. Version control software must take account of this, allowing users to add new files and remove deadwood that would otherwise get in the way.

Adding a File

You can add a new document to CVS with the add subcommand. Here we add a document called Question.php to the project:

```
$ touch Question.php
$ cvs add Question.php
cvs add: scheduling file 'Question.php' for addition
cvs add: use 'cvs commit' to add this file permanently
```

In a real-world situation, we would probably start out by adding some content to Question.php. Here we confine ourselves to creating an empty file using the standard touch command. As the output from add tells us, once we have added a document, we must still invoke the commit subcommand to complete the addition.

```
$ cvs commit -m'initial check in' Question.php
RCS file: /usr/local/cvs/megaquiz/quizobjects/Question.php,v
done
Checking in Question.php;
/usr/local/cvs/megaquiz/quizobjects/Question.php,v  <--  Question.php
initial revision: 1.1
done
```

Question.php is now in the repository.

Removing a File

Should we discover that we have been too hasty and need to remove the document, it should come as no surprise to learn that we can use a subcommand called remove.

```
$ cvs remove Question.php
cvs remove: file 'Question.php' still in working directory
cvs remove: 1 file exists; remove it first
```

CVS is cautious by nature, and requires that you remove the file from your sandbox before it will go ahead and mark it as removed from the repository. Alternatively, you can force CVS to remove the document from your sandbox as well as the repository by passing it the -f flag.

```
$ cvs remove -f Question.php
cvs remove: scheduling 'Question.php' for removal
cvs remove: use 'cvs commit' to remove this file permanently
```

Once again a `commit` is required to finish the job.

Adding a Directory

We can also add and remove directories with `add` and `remove`.

```
$ mkdir resources
$ cvs add resources/
Directory /usr/local/cvs/megaquiz/resources added to the repository
```

When you add a directory, CVS makes the change straightaway with no `commit` required. If you take a look inside the `resources` directory, you will see that CVS has created a utility folder inside it.

Now when Bob updates, he should get a `resources` directory of his own. Shouldn't he?

```
$ cvs update
cvs update: Updating .
U README
cvs update: Updating command
U command/Command.php
cvs update: Updating quizobjects
U quizobjects/Question.php
cvs update: Updating quiztools
U quiztools/AccessManager.php
$ ls
command  CVS  main.php  quizobjects  quiztools  README
```

If you look carefully at the output in the preceding example, you will see that the `resources` directory has not appeared. The `update` command does not add directories to a sandbox by default. To ensure that new directories are added, Bob should use the `-d` flag with the `update` command.

```
$ cvs update -d
cvs update: Updating .
cvs update: Updating command
cvs update: Updating quizobjects
cvs update: Updating quiztools
cvs update: Updating resources
$ ls
command  CVS  main.php  quizobjects  quiztools  README  resources
```

Adding Binary Files

CVS evolved to work with text files. As we will see, in addition to its key tasks of finding and merging textual information, CVS looks for special flags in documents and substitutes timely information such as dates and revision numbers. Clearly this behavior could be positively harmful in a GIF file. It is lucky then that CVS allows us to flag files as binary when we add them.

We can ensure that a file is treated as binary by using the -kb flag. Here we add a GIF to the resources directory:

```
$ cvs add -kb resources/logo.gif
cvs add: scheduling file 'resources/logo.gif' for addition
cvs add: use 'cvs commit' to add this file permanently

$ cvs commit -m'import of logo' resources/logo.gif
RCS file: /usr/local/cvs/megaquiz/resources/logo.gif,v
done
Checking in resources/logo.gif;
/usr/local/cvs/megaquiz/resources/logo.gif,v  <--  logo.gif
initial revision: 1.1
done
```

Notice that CVS is pretty silent about our use of the -kb flag. It has nonetheless flagged the file as binary, and won't attempt to merge differences or perform substitutions.

It is easy to forget to import binary files correctly, especially when you are adding entire directories or importing a project. Luckily, you can set the -kb flag after the event with the admin subcommand. Let's say we have already added a binary file, resources/correct.gif, as text. Here we correct our mistake with admin:

```
$ cvs admin -kb resources/correct.gif
RCS file: /usr/local/cvs/megaquiz/resources/correct.gif,v
done
```

Removing Directories

As you might expect, you can remove directories with the remove subcommand. There are a couple of issues to watch out for, though.

Let's try to remove the resources directory:

```
$ cvs remove resources
cvs remove: Removing resources
cvs remove: file 'resources/correct.gif' still in working directory
cvs remove: file 'resources/logo.gif' still in working directory
cvs remove: 2 files exist; remove them first
```

As you can see, we cannot remove a directory that has contents (other than the CVS directory). We should remove the contents first:

```
$ cvs remove -f resources/*.*
cvs remove: scheduling 'resources/correct.gif' for removal
cvs remove: scheduling 'resources/logo.gif' for removal
cvs remove: use 'cvs commit' to remove these files permanently
$ cvs commit -m'removing res files' resources
cvs commit: Examining resources
Removing resources/correct.gif;
/usr/local/cvs/megaquiz/resources/correct.gif,v  <--  correct.gif
new revision: delete; previous revision: 1.1
done
Removing resources/logo.gif;
/usr/local/cvs/megaquiz/resources/logo.gif,v  <--  logo.gif
new revision: delete; previous revision: 1.1
done
```

Once we have emptied the resources directory, we can tell CVS that we want to remove the directory itself.

```
$ cvs remove resources
cvs remove: Removing resources
```

Finally, we must delete it from our sandbox.

```
$ rm -rf resources
```

Now that we have removed the resources directory, our changes should be reflected in Bob's sandbox when he next updates. Or should they?

```
$ cvs update -d
cvs update: Updating .
cvs update: Updating command
cvs update: Updating quizobjects
cvs update: Updating quiztools
cvs update: Updating resources
cvs update: resources/correct.gif is no longer in the repository
cvs update: resources/logo.gif is no longer in the repository
$ ls resources/
CVS
```

CVS removes the files in resources, but leaves the directory in place. So that deleted directories are removed from his sandbox, Bob should use the -P flag ("P" stands for "prune") with the update subcommand.

```
$ cvs update -Pd
cvs update: Updating .
cvs update: Updating command
cvs update: Updating quizobjects
cvs update: Updating quiztools
cvs update: Updating resources
$ ls resources
ls: resources: No such file or directory
```

It is a good idea to foster the habit of including -d and -P whenever you use update.

Tagging and Exporting a Release

All being well, a project will eventually reach a state of readiness, and you will want to ship it or deploy it. CVS can help you here in two ways. Firstly, you can generate a version of the project that does not contain CVS metadata. Secondly, you can freeze this moment in your project's development so that you can always return to it later on.

Tagging a Project

A tag is simply a handle that is attached to a moment in your project's development. Once you have applied a tag, you can use it to acquire a copy of your project as it existed at that time.

You can apply a tag with the tag subcommand, passing it a label:

```
$ cvs tag MegaQuiz_1_0_0
cvs tag: Tagging .
T README
T main.php
cvs tag: Tagging command
T command/Command.php
T command/CommandContext.php
T command/FeedbackCommand.php
T command/LoginCommand.php
cvs tag: Tagging quizobjects
T quizobjects/User.php
cvs tag: Tagging quiztools
T quiztools/AccessManager.php
```

As you can see from the output in the previous example, CVS responds to the tag subcommand by applying the tag individually to every file below the current working directory.

Retrieving a Project by Tag

Releasing a project does not generally end its development. Your current project directory will likely evolve as you fix bugs, add new features, and so on. If you need to access your first release, however, you can do so easily by using the checkout subcommand with the -r flag.

Here, Bob retrieves MegaQuiz release 1:

```
$ cvs checkout -r MegaQuiz_1_0_0 megaquiz
cvs checkout: Updating megaquiz
U megaquiz/README
U megaquiz/main.php
cvs checkout: Updating megaquiz/command
U megaquiz/command/Command.php
U megaquiz/command/CommandContext.php
U megaquiz/command/FeedbackCommand.php
U megaquiz/command/LoginCommand.php
cvs checkout: Updating megaquiz/quizobjects
U megaquiz/quizobjects/User.php
cvs checkout: Updating megaquiz/quiztools
U megaquiz/quiztools/AccessManager.php
cvs checkout: Updating megaquiz/resources
```

As you can see, Bob uses checkout in the usual way, except for the addition of the -r flag, which is used here in conjunction with the tag label. By now, of course, Bob may be suffering from a confusing multiplicity of directories called megaquiz. He can require that checkout generates a differently named directory by specifying a new flag: -d.

```
$ cvs checkout -r MegaQuiz_1_0_0 -d megaquiz_release_1 megaquiz
```

When used with the checkout subcommand, the -d flag causes a project to be output to a specified directory rather than the default.

Exporting a Project

As we have seen, a checked-out project includes administrative directories (named CVS, appropriately enough). These will clutter up an official release of your project. CVS provides the export subcommand to generate clean release versions of your codebase.

export requires an -r flag with revision information (a tag label in our example). The -d flag works as it does with checkout. Finally, the command requires the name of the project. Here we generate a distribution directory ready for tarballing:

```
$ cvs export -r MegaQuiz_1_0_0 -d megaquiz-release-1_0_0 megaquiz
```

The output from this command looks similar to that generated by checkout, but when we peek into the new directory, we see no CVS directories.

```
$ ls megaquiz-release-1_0_0/
command  main.php  quizobjects  quiztools  README
```

Because this output now bears no relation at all to our CVS repository, it is important to remember not to make any changes here.

Branching a Project

Now that our project has been released, we can pack it away, and wander off to do something new, right? After all, it was so elegantly written that bugs are an impossibility, and so thoroughly specified that no user could possibly require any new features!

Meanwhile, back in the real world, we must continue to work with the codebase on at least two levels. Bug reports should be trickling in right about now, and the wish list for version 1.2.0 swelling with demands for fantastic new features. How do we reconcile these forces? We need to fix the bugs as they are reported, and we need to push on with primary development. We could fix the bugs as part of development, and release in one go when the next version is stable. But then users may have a long wait before they see any fixes. This is plainly unacceptable. On the other hand, we could release as we go. Here we risk shipping broken code. Clearly, we need two strands to our development.

CVS allows us to maintain parallel strands of development in a project. We continue working on as before in our main strand (known as the trunk). It is here that we will add new and experimental code. Let's use a particular file, command/FeedbackCommand.php, as an example.

```php
class FeedbackCommand extends Command {

    function execute( CommandContext $context ) {
        // new and risky development
        // goes here
        $msgSystem = ReceiverFactory::getMessageSystem();
        $email = $context->get( 'email' );
        $msg = $context->get( 'pass' );
        $topic = $context->get( 'topic' );
        $result = $msgSystem->despatch( $email, $msg, $topic );
        if ( ! $user ) {
            $this->context->setError( $msgSystem->getError() );
            return false;
        }
        $context->addParam( "user", $user );
        return true;
    }
}
```

All we have done here is to add a comment to simulate an addition to the code. Meanwhile, users begin to report that they are unable to use the feedback mechanism in our system. We locate the bug in this very file:

```php
//...
$result = $msgSystem->despatch( $email, $msg, $topic );
if ( ! $user ) {
    $this->context->setError( $msgSystem->getError() );
//...
```

We should, in fact, be testing $result, and not $user. We could fix this here, of course, but the users would not see the fix until our experimental code is stable. Instead, let's create a branch of our project.

We need to fix the code as it stood at the point of last release. We move out of the development project directory (so that our current working directory does not contain a CVS administration directory), and then check out the project.

```
$ cvs checkout -d megaquiz-bugfix -r MegaQuiz_1_0_0 megaquiz
cvs checkout: Updating megaquiz-bugfix
U megaquiz-bugfix/README
U megaquiz-bugfix/main.php
cvs checkout: Updating megaquiz-bugfix/command
U megaquiz-bugfix/command/Command.php
U megaquiz-bugfix/command/CommandContext.php
U megaquiz-bugfix/command/FeedbackCommand.php
U megaquiz-bugfix/command/LoginCommand.php
cvs checkout: Updating megaquiz-bugfix/quizobjects
U megaquiz-bugfix/quizobjects/User.php
cvs checkout: Updating megaquiz-bugfix/quiztools
U megaquiz-bugfix/quiztools/AccessManager.php
cvs checkout: Updating megaquiz-bugfix/resources
```

We modify checkout with two flags. -d allows us to define a directory name for the checked-out project, and -r determines the revision we are checking out. We use the release tag we set up in the previous section. Before we can go ahead and work in this directory, we need to create a branch to work with.

```
$ cd megaquiz-bugfix
$ cvs tag -b MegaQuiz_bugbranch
```

We move into our bug-fix directory. Notice that we use a new flag with the tag subcommand. The -b flag that ensures that changes made to a project checked out under this tag will not affect the trunk. Creating the branch only affects the repository, and not our current working directory. To begin working with the branch, we need either to check out a new working directory (using the -r flag) or to update the megaquiz-bugfix directory to shift it over to the branch. Just as we can check out a tagged project with the -r flag, we can use it with update to convert a project:

```
$ cvs update -r MegaQuiz_bugbranch
cvs update: Updating .
cvs update: Updating command
cvs update: Updating quizobjects
cvs update: Updating quiztools
```

Now we are ready to fix our bug:

```
class FeedbackCommand extends Command {

    function execute( CommandContext $context ) {
        $msgSystem = ReceiverFactory::getMessageSystem();
        $email = $context->get( 'email' );
        $msg = $context->get( 'pass' );
        $topic = $context->get( 'topic' );
        $result = $msgSystem->despatch( $email, $msg, $topic );
        if ( ! $result ) {
            $this->context->setError( $msgSystem->getError() );
            return false;
        }
        $context->addParam( "user", $user );
        return true;
    }
}
```

We have changed

```
if ( ! $user ) {
```

to

```
if ( ! $result ) {
```

Notice, though, that there is no sign of our "experimental" comments—these were committed to the trunk, and bear no relation to this document. Let's commit the code, and create a new distribution (this example omits the output):

```
$ cvs commit -m'fixed result test'
$ cvs tag MegaQuiz_1_0_2
$ cd ..
$ cvs export -r  MegaQuiz_1_0_2 -d megaquiz-release-1_0_2 MegaQuiz
```

It doesn't end there, though. Now that we have fixed our bug, we need to apply the change to our main development strand (the trunk).

The update subcommand supports the -j flag, which stands for "join." Using this, we can join our bug branch back into the trunk:

```
$ cd megaquiz
$ cvs update -j MegaQuiz_bugbranch
cvs update: Updating .
cvs update: Updating command
RCS file: /usr/local/cvs/megaquiz/command/FeedbackCommand.php,v
retrieving revision 1.1
retrieving revision 1.1.1.1.4.1
Merging differences between 1.1 and 1.1.1.1 into FeedbackCommand.php
cvs update: Updating quizobjects
cvs update: Updating quiztools
cvs update: Updating resources
```

Now, when we look at the version of FeedbackCommand in the trunk, we see that all changes have been merged.

```
function execute( CommandContext $context ) {
    // new and risky development
    // goes here
    $msgSystem = ReceiverFactory::getMessageSystem();
    $email = $context->get( 'email' );
    $msg = $context->get( 'pass' );
    $topic = $context->get( 'topic' );
    $result = $msgSystem->despatch( $email, $msg, $topic );
    if ( ! $result ) {
        $this->context->setError( $msgSystem->getError() );
        return false;
    }
    $context->addParam( "user", $user );
    return true;
}
```

The execute() method includes both our simulated trunk development:

```
// new and risky development
// goes here
```

and our bug fix:

```
if ( ! $result ) {
```

Branches are often seen as an advanced CVS topic, largely because of the difficulty of some of the concepts involved. For large or long-lived projects, though, branching soon becomes an essential technique.

Summary

CVS comprises an enormous number of tools, each with a daunting range of options and capabilities. I can only hope to provide a brief introduction in the space available. Nonetheless, if you only use the features I have covered in this chapter, you should see the benefit in your own work, whether through protection against data loss or improvements in collaborative working.

In this chapter, we took a tour through the basics of CVS. We looked briefly at configuration, before importing a project. We checked out, committed, and updated code, finally tagging and exporting a release. We ended the chapter with a brief look at branches, demonstrating their usefulness in maintaining concurrent development and bug-fix strands in a project.

There is one issue that we have glossed over here to some extent. We established the principle that developers should check out their own versions of a project. On the whole, though, projects will not run in place. In order to test their changes, developers need to deploy code locally. Sometimes this is as simple as copying over a few directories. More often, though, deployment must address a whole range of configuration issues. In the next chapter, we will look at some techniques for automating this process.

CHAPTER 17

■ ■ ■

Automated Build with Phing

If version control is one side of the coin, then automated build is the other. Version control allows multiple developers to work collaboratively on a single project. With many coders each deploying a project in her own space, automated build soon becomes essential. One developer may have her Web-facing directory in /usr/local/apache/htdocs, another might use /home/bibble/public_html. Developers may use different database passwords, library directories, or mail mechanisms. A flexible codebase might easily accommodate all of these differences, but the effort of changing settings and manually copying directories around your file system to get things working would soon become tiresome—especially if you need to install code in progress several times a day (or several times an hour).

And then there are your users. The elegance of your code is irrelevant if it takes a degree in computer science to install it. Your customers may be willing to type a command or two on the command line in order to get your system running, but that is about as far as it goes.

Wouldn't it be nice if you could automate installation, and do it in such a way that it can be customized for your own particular project, for the needs of your developers, and for the ease of your customers? In this chapter, I introduce you to Phing, which is just such a tool. This chapter will cover

- *Getting and installing Phing*: Who builds the builder?

- *Properties*: Setting and getting data.

- *Types*: Describing complex parts of a project.

- *Targets*: Breaking a build into callable, interdependent sets of functionality.

- *Tasks*: The things that get stuff done.

What Is Phing?

Phing is a PHP tool for building projects. It is very closely modeled on a hugely popular (and very powerful) Java tool called Ant. Ant was so named because, like an ant, the application is relatively small but capable of constructing things that are very large indeed. Both Phing and Ant use an XML file (usually named build.xml) to determine what to do in order to install or otherwise work with a project.

The PHP world *really* needs a good install solution. Serious developers have had a number of options in the past. Firstly, it is possible to use make, the ubiquitous Unix build tool that is still used for most C and Perl projects. make is extremely picky about syntax, however, and requires quite a lot of shell knowledge, up to and including scripting—this can be a steep learning curve for many PHP programmers. What's more, make provides very few built-in tools for common build operations such as transforming file names and contents. It is really a glue for shell commands. This makes it hard to write programs that will install across platforms. Not all environments will have the same version of make, or even have it at all. Even if you have make, you may not have all the commands the makefile (the configuration file that drives make) requires.

Phing's relationship with make is illustrated in its name: Phing stands for PHing Is Not Gnu make. This playful recursion is a common coder's joke (for example, GNU itself stands for Gnu is Not Unix).

Phing is a native PHP application that interprets a user-created XML file in order to perform operations upon a project. Such operations would typically involve the copying of files from a distribution to various destination directories, but there is much more to Phing. Phing can be used to generate documentation, run tests, invoke commands, run arbitrary PHP code, create PEAR packages, replace keywords in files, strip comments, and generate tar-gzipped package releases. If Phing does not yet do what you need, it is easy to extend by design.

Because Phing is itself a PHP application, all you need to run it is a recent PHP engine. Since Phing is an application for installing PHP applications, the presence of a PHP executable is a pretty safe bet.

We have seen that PEAR packages are breathtakingly easy to install. PEAR supports its own automated build mechanism. Since PEAR is bundled with PHP, should we not use the PEAR mechanism to install our own projects? At the time of writing, PEAR is primarily (and rightly) designed for the installation of PEAR packages. It has, in other words, a very specific purpose. It assumes a particular set of destination directories, and provides a limited feature set. It does not handle applications well. Applications tend to be messy, requiring that files are installed in nonstandard places, needing support from databases and other third-party tools. The PEAR installer is not designed to be easy to extend. Phing begins and ends with flexibility and extensibility. Because PEAR installation is so easy and increasingly familiar for the end user, one useful technique is to use Phing for project development, but to have it generate a PEAR package upon release. This approach is used in building the Phing application itself.

Getting and Installing Phing

If it is difficult to install an install tool, then something is surely wrong! However, assuming that you have PHP 5 on your system (and if you haven't, this isn't the book for you!), installation of Phing could not be easier.

You can acquire and install Phing with a single command.

```
$ pear install http://phing.info/pear/phing-current.tgz
```

This will install Phing as a PEAR package. You should have write permission for your PEAR directories, which, on most Unix systems, will mean running the command as the root user.

If you run into any installation problems, you should download and unpack the release at http://phing.info/pear/phing-current.tgz. You will find plenty of installation instructions there.

build.xml: The Build Document

You should now be ready to get cracking with Phing! Let's test things out:

```
$ phing -v
Phing version 2.0.0b3
```

The -v flag to the phing command causes the script to return version information. By the time you read this, the version number may have changed, but you should see a similar message when you run the command on your system.

Now let's run the phing command without arguments:

```
$ phing
Buildfile: build.xml does not exist!
```

As you can see, Phing is lost without instructions. By default it will look for a file called build.xml. Let's build a minimal document so that we can at least make that error message go away:

```
<?xml version="1.0"?>
<!-- build xml -->

<project name="megaquiz" default="main">
    <target name="main"/>
</project>
```

This is the bare minimum you can get away with in a build file. If we save the previous example as build.xml, and run phing again, we should get some more interesting output.

```
$ phing
Buildfile: /home/bob/working/megaquiz/build.xml

megaquiz > main:

BUILD FINISHED

Total time: 0.2557 seconds
```

A lot of effort to achieve precisely nothing, you may think, but we have to start somewhere! Let's look again at that build file. Because we are dealing with XML, we include an XML declaration. As you probably know, XML comments look like this:

```
<!-- Anything here is ignored. Because it's a comment. OK? -->
```

The second line in our build file is ignored. You can put as many comments as you like in your build files, and as they grow, you should make full use of this fact. Large build files can be hard to read.

The real start of any build file is the `project` element. The `project` element can include up to three attributes. Of these, name and `default` are compulsory. The name attribute establishes the project's name. `default` defines a target to run if none are specified on the command line. You can specify the context directory for the build using a `basedir` attribute. If this is omitted, the current working directory will be assumed. You can see these attributes summarized in Table 17-1.

Table 17-1. *The Attributes to the* project *Element*

Attribute	Required	Description	Default Value
name	Yes	The name of the project	
default	Yes	The default target to run	
basedir	No	The file system context in which build will run	Current directory (.)

Once we have defined our `project` element, we must create at least one target—the one we reference in the `default` attribute.

Targets

Targets are similar in some senses to functions. A target is a set of actions grouped together to achieve an objective: to copy a directory from one place another, for example, or to generate documentation.

In our previous example, we included a bare-minimum implementation for a target:

```
<target name="main"/>
```

As you can see, a target must define at least a name attribute. We have made use of this in the `project` element. Because the default element points to the main target, this target will be invoked whenever Phing is run without command-line arguments. This was confirmed by our output:

```
megaquiz > main:
```

Targets can be organized to depend upon one another. By setting up a dependency between targets, you tell Phing that one target should not run before the target it depends upon has been run. Let's add a dependency to our build file:

```
<?xml version="1.0"?>
<!-- build xml -->

<project name="megaquiz"
        default="main"
>
    <target name="runfirst" />
    <target name="runsecond" depends="runfirst"/>
    <target name="main" depends="runsecond"/>
</project>
```

As you can see, we have introduced a new attribute for the target element. depends tells Phing that the referenced target should be executed before the current one. So we might want a target that copies certain files to a directory to be invoked before one that runs a transformation on all files in that directory. We added two new targets in the example: runsecond, upon which main depends, and runfirst, upon which runsecond depends. Let's see what happens when we run Phing with this build file:

```
$ phing
Buildfile: /home/bob/working/megaquiz/build.xml

megaquiz > runfirst:

megaquiz > runsecond:

megaquiz > main:

BUILD FINISHED

Total time: 0.3029 seconds
```

As you can see, the dependencies are honored. Phing encounters the main target, sees its dependency, and moves back to runsecond. runsecond has its own dependency and Phing invokes runfirst. Having satisfied its dependency, Phing can invoke runsecond. Finally, main is invoked. The depends attribute can reference more than one target at a time. A comma-separated list of dependencies can be provided, and each will be honored in turn.

Now that we have more than one target to play with, let's override the project element's default attribute from the command line:

```
$ phing runsecond
Buildfile: /home/bob/working/megaquiz/build.xml

megaquiz > runfirst:

megaquiz > runsecond:

BUILD FINISHED

Total time: 0.2671 seconds
```

By passing in a target name, we cause the default attribute to be ignored. The target matching our argument is invoked instead (as well as the target upon which it depends).

The target element also supports an optional description attribute, to which you can assign a brief description of the target's purpose:

```
<?xml version="1.0"?>
<!-- build xml -->

<project name="megaquiz"
        default="main"
        basedir=".">
    <target name="runfirst"
            description="The first target" />
    <target name="runsecond"
            depends="runfirst"
            description="The second target" />
    <target name="main"
            depends="runsecond"
            description="The main target" />
</project>
```

Adding a description to your targets makes no difference to the normal build process. If the user runs Phing with a -projecthelp flag, however, the descriptions will be used to summarize the project.

```
$ phing -projecthelp
Buildfile: /home/bob/working/megaquiz/build.xml
Default target:
------------------------------------------------------------
 main      The main target

Main targets:
------------------------------------------------------------
 main      The main target
 runfirst  The first target
 runsecond The second target
```

Properties

Most projects of any complexity will require local configuration values: a database name, and its host and password, for example, or a nonstandard public HTML directory. Phing allows you to set such values using the property element.

Properties are similar to global variables in a script. As such, they are often declared toward the top of a project to make it easy for developers to work out what's what in the build file. Here we create a build file that works with database information:

```xml
<?xml version="1.0"?>
<!-- build xml -->

<project name="megaquiz"
        default="main"
        basedir=".">

    <property name="dbname"  value="megaquiz" />
    <property name="dbpass"  value="default" />
    <property name="dbhost" value="localhost" />

    <target name="main">
        <echo>database: ${dbname}</echo>
        <echo>pass:     ${dbpass}</echo>
        <echo>host:     ${dbhost}</echo>
    </target>
</project>
```

We introduced a new element: property. property requires name and value attributes. Notice also that we have added to the main target. echo is an example of a task. We will explore tasks more fully in the next section. For now, though, it's enough to know that echo does exactly what you would expect—it causes its contents to be output. Notice the syntax we use to reference the value of a property here: by using a dollar sign, and wrapping the property name in curly brackets, you tell Phing to replace the string with the property value.

${propertyname}

All this build file achieves is to declare three properties, and to print them to standard output. Let's see this in action:

$ phing
```
Buildfile: /home/bob/working/megaquiz/build.xml

megaquiz > main:
    [echo] database: megaquiz
    [echo] pass:     default
    [echo] host:     localhost

BUILD FINISHED

Total time: 0.4402 seconds
```

Now that I have introduced properties, we can wrap up our exploration of targets. The target element accepts two additional attributes: if and unless. Each of these should be set with the name of a property. When you use if with a property name, the target will only be executed if the given property is set. If the property is not set, the target will exit silently. Here we comment out the dbpass property and make the main task require it using the if attribute:

```
<property name="dbname"  value="megaquiz" />
<!--<property name="dbpass"  value="default" />-->
<property name="dbhost" value="localhost" />

<target name="main" if="dbpass">
    <echo>database: ${dbname}</echo>
    <echo>pass:     ${dbpass}</echo>
    <echo>host:     ${dbhost}</echo>
</target>
```

Let's run phing again:

```
$ phing
Buildfile: /home/bob/working/megaquiz/build.xml

megaquiz > main:

BUILD FINISHED

Total time: 0.2628 seconds
```

As you can see, we have raised no error, but the main task did not run. Why might we want to do this? There is another way of setting properties in a project. They can be specified on the command line. You tell Phing that you are passing it a property with the -D flag followed by a property assignment. So the argument should look like this:

```
-Dname=value
```

In our example, we want the dbname property to be made available via the command line. Let's try it:

```
$ phing -Ddbpass=userset
Buildfile: /home/bob/working/megaquiz/build.xml

megaquiz > main:
    [echo] database: megaquiz
    [echo] pass:     userset
    [echo] host:     localhost

BUILD FINISHED

Total time: 0.4611 seconds
```

The if attribute of the main target is satisfied that the dbpass property is present, and the target is allowed to execute.

As you might expect, the unless attribute is the opposite of if. If a property is set and it is referenced in a target's unless attribute, then the target will not run. This is useful if you want to make it possible to suppress a particular target from the command line. So we might add something like this to the main target:

```
<target name="main" unless="suppressmain">
```

main will be executed unless a suppressmain property is present:

```
$ phing -Dsuppressmain=yes
```

Now that we have wrapped up the target element, let's take a look at a summary of its attributes as presented in Table 17-2.

Table 17-2. *The Attributes to the target Element*

Attribute	Required	Description
name	Yes	The name of the target.
depends	No	Targets upon which the current depends.
if	No	Execute target only if given property is present.
unless	No	Execute target only if given property is not present.
description	No	A short summary of the target's purpose.

When a property is set on the command line, it overrides any and all property declarations within the build file. There is another condition in which a property value can be overwritten. By default, if a property is declared twice, the original value will have primacy. You can alter this behavior by setting an attribute called override in the second property element. Here's an example:

```
<?xml version="1.0"?>
<!-- build xml -->

<project name="megaquiz"
        default="main"
        basedir=".">

    <property name="dbpass"  value="default" />

    <target name="main">
        <property name="dbpass" override="yes" value="specific" />
        <echo>pass:      ${dbpass}</echo>
    </target>

</project>
```

We set a property called dbpass, giving it the initial value "default". In the main target we set the property once again, adding an override attribute set to "yes" and providing a new value. The new value is reflected in the output:

```
$ phing
Buildfile: /home/bob/working/megaquiz/build.xml

megaquiz > main:
    [echo] pass:     specific

BUILD FINISHED

Total time: 0.3802 seconds
```

If we had not set the override element in the second property element, the original value of "default" would have stayed in place. It is important to note that targets are not functions: there is no concept of local scope. If you override a property within a task, it remains overridden for all other tasks throughout the build file. You could get around this, of course, by storing a property value in a temporary property before overriding, and then resetting it when you have finished working locally.

So far we have dealt with properties that you define yourself. Phing also provides built-in properties. You reference these in exactly the same way that you would reference properties you have declared yourself. Here's an example:

```
<?xml version="1.0"?>
<!-- build xml -->

<project name="megaquiz"
        default="main"
        basedir=".">

    <target name="main">
        <echo>name:     ${phing.project.name}</echo>
        <echo>base:     ${project.basedir}</echo>
        <echo>home:     ${user.home}</echo>
        <echo>pass:     ${env.DBPASS}</echo>
    </target>

</project>
```

We reference just a few of the built-in Phing properties. phing.project.name resolves to the name of the project as defined in the name attribute of the project element; project.basedir gives the starting directory; user.home provides the executing user's home directory (this is useful for providing default install locations). Finally, the env prefix in a property reference indicates an operating system environment variable. So by specifying ${env.DBPASS}, we are looking for an environment variable called DBPASS. Let's run Phing on this file:

```
$ phing
Buildfile: /home/bob/working/megaquiz/build.xml

megaquiz > main:
     [echo] name:     megaquiz
     [echo] base:     /home/bob/working/oophp-book-phing
     [echo] home:     /home/bob
     [echo] pass:     ${env.DBPASS}

BUILD FINISHED

Total time: 0.5190 seconds
```

Notice that the final property has not been translated. This is the default behavior when a property is not found—the string referencing the property is left untransformed. If we set the DBPASS environment variable and run again, we should see the variable reflected in the output:

```
$ export DBPASS=wooshpoppow
$ phing
Buildfile: /home/bob/working/megaquiz/build.xml

megaquiz > main:
     ...
     [echo] pass:     whooshpoppow

BUILD FINISHED

Total time: 0.2852 seconds
```

So now we have seen three ways of setting a property: the property element, a command line argument, and an environment variable.

You can use targets to ensure that properties are populated. Let's say, for example, that our project requires a dbpass property. We would like the user to set dbpass on the command line (this always has priority over other property assignment methods). Failing that, we should look for an environment variable. Finally, we should give up and go for a default value:

```
<?xml version="1.0"?>
<!-- build xml -->

<project name="megaquiz"
         default="main"
         basedir=".">

    <target name="setenvpass" if="env.DBPASS" unless="dbpass">
        <property name="dbpass" override="yes" value="${env.DBPASS}" />
    </target>
```

```
<target name="setpass" unless="dbpass" depends="setenvpass">
    <property name="dbpass" override="yes" value="default" />
</target>

<target name="main" depends="setpass">
    <echo>pass:      ${dbpass}</echo>
</target>
```

```
</project>
```

So, as usual the default target, main is invoked first. This has a dependency set, so Phing goes back to the setpass target. setpass, though, depends on setenvpass, so we start there. setenvpass is configured to run only if dbpass has not been set, and if env.DBPASS is present. If these conditions are met, then we set the dbpass property using the property element. At this stage then, dbpass is populated either by a command line argument or by an environment variable. If neither of these were present, then the property remains unset at this stage. The setpass target is now executed, but only if dbpass is not yet present. In this case, it sets the property to the default string: "default".

Types

You may think that by looking at properties, we are through with data. In fact, Phing supports a set of special elements called types that encapsulate different kinds of information useful to the build process.

FileSet

Let's say that you need to represent a directory in your build file, a common situation as you might imagine. You could use a property to represent this directory, certainly, but you'd run into problems straightaway if your developers use different platforms that support distinct directory separators. The answer is the FileSet data type. FileSet is platform independent, so if you represent a directory with forward slashes in the path, they will be automatically translated behind the scenes into backslashes when the build is run on a Windows machine. You can define a minimal FileSet element like this:

```
<fileset dir="src/lib" />
```

As you can see, we use the dir attribute to set the directory we wish to represent. You can optionally add an id attribute, so that you can refer to the FileSet later on.

```
<fileset dir="src/lib" id="srclib">
```

The FileSet data type is particularly useful in specifying types of documents to include or exclude. When installing a set of files, you may not wish those that match a certain pattern to be included. You can handle conditions like this in an excludes attribute:

```
<fileset dir="src/lib" id="srclib"
        excludes="**/*_test.php **/*Test.php" />
```

Notice the syntax we have used in the excludes attribute. Double asterisks represent zero or more directories. A single asterisk represents zero or more characters. So we are specifying that we would like to exclude files that end in "_test.php" or "Test.php" in all directories below the starting point defined in the dir attribute. The excludes attribute accepts multiple patterns separated by white space.

We can apply the same syntax to an includes attribute. Perhaps our src/lib directories contain many non-PHP files that are useful to developers but should not find their way into an installation. We could exclude those files, of course, but it might be simpler just to define the kinds of files we *can* include. In this case, if a file doesn't end in ".php", it isn't going to be installed:

```
<fileset dir="src/lib" id="srclib"
        excludes="**/*_test.php **/*Test.php"
        includes="**/*.php" />
```

As you build up include and exclude rules, your fileset element is likely to become overly long. Luckily, you can pull out individual exclude rules and place each one in its own exclude subelement. You can do the same for include rules. We can now rewrite our FileSet like this:

```
<fileset dir="src/lib" id="srclib">
    <exclude name="**/*_test.php" />
    <exclude name="**/*Test.php" />
    <include name="**/*.php" />
</fileset>
```

You can see some of the attributes of the fileset element in Table 17-3.

Table 17-3. *Some Attributes of the fileset Element*

Attribute	Required	Description
id	No	A unique handle for referring to the element.
dir	No	The fileset directory.
excludes	No	A list of patterns for exclusion.
includes	No	A list of patterns for inclusion.
refid	No	Current fileset is a reference to fileset of given ID.

PatternSet

As we build up patterns in our fileset elements (and in others), there is a danger that we will begin to repeat groups of exclude and include elements. In our previous example, we defined patterns for test files and regular code files. We may add to these over time (perhaps we wish to include .conf and .inc extensions to our definition of code files). If we define other fileset elements that also use these patterns, we will be forced to make any adjustments across all relevant fileset elements.

We can overcome this problem by grouping patterns into patternset elements. The patternset element groups include and exclude elements so that they can be referenced later from within other types. Let's extract the include and exclude elements from our fileset example and add them to patternset elements.

```
<patternset id="inc_code">
    <include name="**/*.php" />
    <include name="**/*.inc" />
    <include name="**/*.conf" />
</patternset>

<patternset id="exc_test">
    <exclude name="**/*_test.php" />
    <exclude name="**/*Test.php" />
</patternset>
```

We create two patternset elements, setting their id attributes to inc_code and exc_test respectively. inc_code contains the include elements for including code files, and exc_test contains the exclude files for excluding test files. We can now reference these patternset elements within a fileset:

```
<fileset dir="src/lib" id="srclib">
    <patternset refid="inc_code" />
    <patternset refid="exc_test" />
</fileset>
```

To reference an existing patternset, you must use another patternset element. The second element must set a single attribute: refid. The refid attribute should refer to the id of the patternset element you wish to use in the current context. In this way, we can reuse patternset elements:

```
<fileset dir="src/views" id="srcviews">
    <patternset refid="inc_code" />
</fileset>
```

Any changes we make to the inc_code patternset will automatically update any types that use it. As with FileSet, you can place exclude rules either in an excludes attribute or a set of exclude subelements. The same is true of include rules.

The patternset element's attributes are summarized in Table 17-4.

Table 17-4. *Some Attributes of the patternset Element*

Attribute	Required	Description
id	No	A unique handle for referring to the element.
excludes	No	A list of patterns for exclusion.
includes	No	A list of patterns for inclusion.
refid	No	Current patternset is a reference to patternset of given ID.

FilterChain

The types that we have encountered so far have provided mechanisms for selecting sets of files. FilterChain, by contrast, provides a flexible mechanism for transforming the contents of text files.

In common with all types, defining a filterchain element does not in itself cause any changes to take place. The element and its children must first be associated with a task—that is, an element that tells Phing to take a course of action. We will return to tasks a little later.

A filterchain element groups any number of filters together. Filters operate on files like a pipeline—the first alters its file, and passes its results on to the second, which makes its own alterations, and so on. By combining multiple filters in a filterchain element, you can effect flexible transformations.

Let's dive straight in and create a filterchain that removes PHP comments from any text passed to it:

```
<filterchain>
    <stripphpcomments />
</filterchain>
```

The StripPhpComments task does just what the name suggests. If you have provided detailed API documentation in your source code, you may have made life easy for developers, but you have also added a lot of dead weight to your project. Since all the work that matters takes place within your source directories, there is no reason why you should not strip out comments upon installation.

■**Note** If you use a build tool for your projects, ensure that no one makes changes in the installed code. The installer will copy over any altered files, and the changes will be lost. I have seen it happen.

Let's sneak a preview of the next section and place the filterchain element in a task:

```
<target name="main">
    <copy todir="build/lib">
        <fileset refid="srclib"/>
        <filterchain>
            <stripphpcomments />
        </filterchain>
    </copy>
</target>
```

The Copy task is probably the one you get most use out of. It copies files from place to place. As you can see, we define the destination directory in the todir attribute. The source of the files is defined by the fileset element we created in the previous section. Then comes the filterchain element. Any file copied by the Copy task will have this transformation applied to it.

Phing supports filters for many operations including stripping new lines (StripLineBreaks), replacing tabs with spaces (TabToSpaces). There is even an XsltFilter! Perhaps the most commonly used filter, though, is ReplaceTokens. This allows you to swap tokens in your source code for properties defined in your build file, pulled from environment variables, or passed in on the command line. This is very useful for customizing an installation.

ReplaceTokens optionally accepts two attributes, begintoken and endtoken. You can use these to define the characters that delineate token boundaries. If you omit these, Phing will assume the default character of "@". In order to recognize and replace tokens, you must add token elements to the replacetokens element. Let's add a replacetokens element to our example:

```
<copy todir="build/lib">
        <fileset refid="srclib"/>
        <filterchain>
            <stripphpcomments />
            <replacetokens>
                <token key="dbname" value="${dbname}" />
                <token key="dbhost" value="${dbhost}" />
                <token key="dbpass" value="${dbpass}" />
            </replacetokens>
        </filterchain>
    </copy>
```

As you can see, token elements require key and value attributes. Let's see the effect of running this task with its transformations upon a file in our project. The original file lives in a source directory: src/lib/Config.php:

```
/*
 * Quick and dirty Conf class
 */
class Config {
    public $dbname ="@dbname@";
    public $dbpass ="@dbpass@";
    public $dbhost ="@dbhost@";
}
```

Running our main target containing the Copy task defined previously gives the following output:

```
$ phing
Buildfile: /home/bob/working/megaquiz/build.xml

megaquiz > main:
   [delete] Deleting directory /home/bob/working/megaquiz/build
     [copy] Copying 8 files to /home/bob/working/megaquiz/build/lib
[filter:ReplaceTokens] Replaced "@dbname@" with "megaquiz"
[filter:ReplaceTokens] Replaced "@dbpass@" with "pass"
[filter:ReplaceTokens] Replaced "@dbhost@" with "localhost"

BUILD FINISHED

Total time: 1.1186 second
```

The original file is untouched, of course, but thanks to the Copy task it has been reproduced at build/lib/Config.php:

```
class Config {
    public $dbname ="megaquiz";
    public $dbpass ="pass";
    public $dbhost ="localhost";
}
```

Not only has the comment been removed, but the tokens have been replaced with their property equivalents.

Tasks

Tasks are the elements in a build file that get things done. You won't achieve much without using a task, which is why we have cheated and used a couple already. Let's reintroduce these.

Echo

The Echo task is perfect for the obligatory "Hello World" example. In the real world you can use it to tell the user what you are about to do or what you have done. You can also sanity-check your build process by displaying the values of properties. As we have seen, any text placed within the opening and closing tags of an echo element will be printed to the browser:

```
<echo>The pass is '${dbpass}', shhh!</echo>
```

Alternatively, you can add the output message to a msg attribute.

```
<echo msg="The pass is '${dbpass}', shhh!" />
```

This will have the identical effect of printing the following to standard output:

```
[echo] The pass is 'pass', shhh!
```

Copy

Copying is really what installation is all about. Typically, you will create one target that copies files from your source directories and assembles them in a temporary build directory. You will then have another target that copies the assembled (and transformed) files to their output locations. Breaking the installation into separate build and install phases is not absolutely necessary, but it does mean that you can check the results of the initial build before committing to overwriting production code. You can also change a property and install again to a different location without the need to run a potentially expensive copy/replace phase again.

At its simplest, the Copy task allows you to specify a source file and a destination directory or file:

```
<copy file="src/lib/Config.php" todir="build/conf" />
```

As you can see, we specify the source file using the file attribute. You may be familiar already with the todir attribute, which is used to specify the target directory. If the target directory does not exist, Phing will create it for you.

If you need to specify a target file, rather than a containing directory, you can use the tofile attribute instead of todir.

```
<copy file="src/lib/Config.php" tofile="build/conf/myConfig.php" />
```

Once again the build/conf directory is created if necessary, but this time Config.php is renamed to myConfig.php.

As we have seen, to copy more than one file at a time, you need to add a fileset element to copy:

```
<copy todir="build/lib">
    <fileset refid="srclib"/>
</copy>
```

The source files are defined by the srclib fileset element, so all we have to set in copy is the todir attribute.

Phing is smart enough to test whether or not your source file has been changed since the target file was created. If no change has been made, then Phing will not copy. This means that you can build many times and only the files that have changed in the meantime will be installed. This is fine, as long as other things are not likely to change. If a file is transformed according to the configuration of a replacetokens element, for example, you may want to ensure that the file is transformed every time that the Copy task is invoked. You can do this by setting an overwrite attribute:

```
<copy todir="build/lib" overwrite="yes">
    <fileset refid="srclib"/>
    <filterchain>
        <stripphpcomments />
        <replacetokens>
            <token key="dbpass" value="${dbpass}" />
        </replacetokens>
    </filterchain>
</copy>
```

Now whenever copy is run, the files matched by the fileset element are replaced whether or not the source has been recently updated.

You can see the copy element summarized in Table 17-5.

Table 17-5. *The Attributes to the copy Element*

Attribute	Required	Description	Default Value
todir	Yes (if tofile not present)	Directory to copy into.	
tofile	Yes (if todir not present)	The file to copy to.	
file	No	Source file.	
overwrite	No	Overwrite target if it already exists.	no

Input

We have seen that the echo element is used to send output to the user. To gather input *from* the user, we have used separate methods involving the command line, and an environment variable. These mechanisms are neither very structured nor interactive, however.

■**Note** One reason for allowing users to set values at build time is to allow for flexibility from build environment to build environment. In the case of database passwords, another benefit is that this sensitive data is not enshrined in the build file itself. Of course, once the build has been run, the password will be saved into a source file, so it is up to the developer to ensure the security of his system!

The input element allows you to output a prompt message. Phing then awaits user input, and assigns it to a property. Let's see it in action:

```
<target name="setpass" unless="dbpass">
    <input message="You don't seem to have set a db password"
           propertyName="dbpass"
           defaultValue="default"
           promptChar=" >" />
</target>

<target name="main" depends="setpass">
    <echo>pass:      ${dbpass}</echo>
</target>
```

Once again, we have a default target: main. This depends upon another target, setpass, which is responsible for ensuring that the dbpass property is populated. To this end, we use the target element's unless attribute, which ensures that it will not run if dbpass is already set.

The setpass target consists of a single input task element. An input element can have a message attribute, which should contain a prompt for the user. The propertyName attribute is required, and defines the property to be populated by user input. If the user hits Enter at the prompt without setting a value, the property is given a fallback value if the defaultValue attribute is set. Finally, you can customize the prompt character using the promptChar attribute—this provides a visual cue for the user to input data. Let's run Phing using the previous targets:

```
$ phing
Buildfile: /home/bob/working/megaquiz/build.xml

megaquiz > setpass:
You don't seem to have set a db password [default] > mypass

megaquiz > main:
    [echo] pass:      mypass

BUILD FINISHED

Total time: 6.0322 seconds
```

We summarize the `input` element in Table 17-6.

Table 17-6. *The Attributes to the input Element*

Attribute	Required	Description
propertyName	Yes	The property to populate with user input
message	No	The prompt message
defaultValue	No	A value to assign to the property if the user does not provide input
promptChar	No	A visual cue that the user should provide input

Delete

Installation is generally about creating, copying, and transforming files. Deletion has its place as well, though. This is particularly the case when you wish to perform a clean install. As we have already discussed, files are generally only copied from source to destination for source files that have changed since the last build. By deleting a build directory, you ensure that the full compilation process will take place.

Let's delete a directory:

```
<target name="clean">
    <delete dir="build" />
</target>
```

When we run `phing` with the argument `clean` (the name of the target), our `delete` task element is invoked. Here's Phing's output:

```
$ phing clean
Buildfile: /home/bob/working/megaquiz/build.xml

megaquiz > clean:
    [delete] Deleting directory /home/bob/working/megaquiz/build

BUILD FINISHED
```

The `delete` element accepts an attribute, `file`, which can be used to point to a particular file. Alternatively, you can fine-tune your deletions by adding a `fileset` subelement to `delete`.

Summary

Serious development rarely happens in one place. A codebase needs to be separated from its installation, so that work in progress does not pollute production code that needs to remain functional at all times. Version control allows developers to check out a project and work on it in their own space. This requires that they should be able to configure the project easily for their environment. Finally, and perhaps most importantly, the customer (even if the "customer" is you in a year's time when you've forgotten the ins and outs of your code) should be able to install your project after a glance at a README file.

In this chapter, I have covered some of the basics of Phing, a fantastic tool, which brings much of the functionality of Jakarta Ant to the PHP world. With this chapter, we have really only seen a few of Phing's capabilities. Nevertheless, once you are up and running with the targets, tasks, types, and properties discussed here, you'll find it easy to bolt on new elements for advanced features, like creating tar/gzipped distributions, automatically generating PEAR package installations, and running PHP code directly from the build file. If you find that Phing does not satisfy all your build needs, you will discover that, like Ant, it is designed to be extensible—get out there and build your own tasks! Even if you don't add to Phing, you should take some time out to examine the source code. Phing is written entirely in object-oriented PHP 5, and the code is chock full of design examples.

PART FIVE

■■■

Conclusion

CHAPTER 18

■ ■ ■

Objects, Patterns, Practice

From object basics through design pattern principles, and on to tools like phpDocumentor, CVS, and Phing, this book has concentrated on two aspects of the journey to meet a single objective: the successful PHP project.

In this chapter, I recap some of the topics I have covered and points made throughout the book:

- *PHP 5 and objects*: How the Zend Engine 2 ushers in an object-oriented future for PHP

- *Objects and design*: Summarizing some OO design principles

- *Patterns*: What makes them cool

- *Pattern principles*: A recap of the guiding object-oriented principles that underlie many patterns

- *The tools for the job*: Revisiting the tools I have described, and checking out a few I haven't

Objects

As we saw in Chapter 2, for a long time objects were something of an afterthought in the PHP world. Support was rudimentary to say the least in PHP 3, with objects barely more than associative arrays in fancy dress. Although things improved radically for the object enthusiast with PHP 4, there were still significant problems, the default behavior that objects were assigned and passed by reference not the least of them.

The introduction of PHP 5 (powered by the Zend Engine 2) has finally dragged objects center stage. You can still program in PHP without ever declaring a class, of course, but there can be no doubt that the language is optimized for object-oriented design.

In Chapters 3, 4, and 5, we looked at PHP 5's improved object-oriented support in detail. Objects are now passed by reference, and the complexity of object copying is acknowledged with the introduction of the __clone() method. Here are some of the new features PHP 5 has brought us: reflection, exceptions, private and protected methods and properties, the __toString() method, the `static` modifier, abstract classes and methods, final methods and properties, interfaces, iterators, type hinting, the `const` modifier, and the __construct() method. The extensive nature of this list reveals the degree to which object-oriented programming is now bound up with the future of PHP.

I would have liked to have seen a few features included that did not make it to the final list, such as hinting for primitive types as well as object types. I would also like to be able to hint return values as well as method arguments, and I would have loved to see package namespaces supported.

These are quibbles, though. The Zend Engine 2 and PHP 5 have made object-oriented design central to the PHP project, opening up the language to a new set of developers and opening up new possibilities for existing devotees.

In Chapter 6, we looked at the benefits that objects can bring to the design of your projects. Since objects and design are one of the central themes of this book, it is worth recapping some conclusions in detail.

Choice

There is no law that says you have to develop with classes and objects only. Well-designed object-oriented code provides a clean interface that can be accessed from any client code, whether procedural or object oriented. Even if you have no interest in writing objects (unlikely if you are still reading this book), you will probably find yourself using them, if only as a client of PEAR packages.

Encapsulation and Delegation

Objects mind their own business and get on with their allotted tasks behind closed doors. They provide an interface through which requests and results can be passed. Any data that need not be exposed, and the dirty details of implementation, are hidden behind this facade.

This gives object-oriented and procedural projects different shapes. The controller in an object-oriented project is often surprisingly sparse, consisting of a handful of instantiations that acquire objects, and invocations that call up data from one set and pass it on to another.

A procedural project, on the other hand, tends to be much more interventionist. The controlling logic descends into implementation to a greater extent, referring to variables, measuring return values, taking turns along different pathways of operation according to circumstance.

Decoupling

To decouple is to remove interdependence between components, so that making a change to one component does not necessitate changes to others. Well-designed objects are self-enclosed. That is, they do not need to refer outside of themselves to recall a detail they learned in a previous invocation.

By maintaining an internal representation of state, objects reduce the need for global variables—a notorious cause of tight coupling. In using a global variable, you bind one part of a system to another. If a component (whether a function, a class, or a block of code) refers to a global variable, there is a risk that another component will accidentally use the same variable name and pollute its value for the first. There is a chance that a third component will come to rely on the value in the variable as set by the first. Change the way that the first component works, and you may cause the third to stop working. The aim of object-oriented design is to reduce such interdependence, making each component as self-sufficient as possible.

Another cause of tight coupling is code duplication. Where you must repeat an algorithm in different parts of your project, you will find tight coupling. What happens when you come to change the algorithm? Clearly you must remember to change it everywhere it occurs. Forget to do this, and your system is in trouble.

A common cause of code duplication is the parallel conditional. If your project needs to do things in one way according to a particular circumstance (running on Linux, for example), and another according to an alternative circumstance (running on Windows), you will often find the same if/else clauses popping up in different parts of your system. If we add a new circumstance together with strategies for handling it (MacOS), then we must ensure that all conditionals are updated.

Object-oriented programming provides a technique for handling this problem. You can replace conditionals with polymorphism. Polymorphism, otherwise known as class switching, is the transparent use of different subclasses according to circumstance. Because each subclass supports the same interface as the common super class, the client code neither knows nor cares which particular implementation it is using.

Conditional code is not banished from object-oriented systems, it is merely minimized and centralized. Conditional code of some kind must be used to determine which particular subtypes are to be served up to clients. This test, though, generally takes place once, and in one place, thus reducing coupling.

Reusability

Encapsulation promotes decoupling, which promotes reuse. Components that are self-sufficient and communicate with wider systems only through their public interface can often be moved from one system and used in another without change.

In fact, this is rarer than you might think. Even nicely orthogonal code can be project specific. When creating a set of classes for managing the content of a particular Web site, for example, it is worth taking some time in the planning stage to look at those features that are specific to your client, and those that might form the foundation for future projects with content management at their heart.

Another tip for reuse: centralize those classes that might be used in multiple projects. Do not, in other words, copy a nicely reusable class into a new project. This will cause tight coupling on a macro level as you will inevitably end up changing the class in one project, and forgetting to do so in another. You would do better to manage common classes in a central repository that can be shared by your projects.

Aesthetics

This is not going to convince anyone who is not already convinced, but to me object-oriented code is aesthetically pleasing. The messiness of implementation is hidden away behind clean interfaces, making an object a thing of apparent simplicity to its client.

I love the neatness and elegance of polymorphism, so that an API allows you to manipulate vastly different objects that nonetheless perform interchangeably, and transparently—the way that objects can be stacked up neatly or slotted into one another like children's blocks.

Of course, there are those who argue that the converse is true. Object-oriented code can lead to torturous class names that must be combined with method names to form even more labored invocations. This is especially true of PEAR where class names include their package names to make up for PHP's lack of support for namespaces.

Another fair criticism is that object-oriented code can dissolve into a babel of classes and objects that can be very hard to read. There is no denying that this can be the case, although matters can be eased considerably through careful documentation containing usage examples.

Patterns

Recently a Java programmer applied for a job in a company with which I have some involvement. In his cover letter, he apologized for only having used patterns for a couple of years. This assumption that design patterns are a recent discovery—a transformative advance—is testament to the excitement they have generated. In fact, it is likely that this experienced coder has been using patterns for a lot longer than he thinks.

Patterns describe common problems and tested solutions. Patterns name, codify, and organize real-world best practice. They are not components of an invention, or clauses in a doctrine. A pattern would not be valid if it did not inscribe practices that are already common at the time of hatching.

Remember that the concept of a pattern language originated in the field of architecture. People were building courtyards and arches for many thousands of years before patterns were proposed as a means of describing solutions to problems of space and function.

Having said that, it is true that design patterns often provoke the kind of emotions associated with religious or political disputes. Devotees roam the corridors with an evangelistic gleam in their eye and a copy of the Gang of Four book under their arm. They accost the uninitiated and reel off pattern names like articles of faith. It is little wonder that some critics see design patterns as hype.

In languages such as Perl and PHP, patterns are also controversial because of their firm association with object-oriented programming. In a context in which objects are a design decision and not a given, associating oneself with design patterns amounts to a declaration of preference, not least because patterns beget more patterns, and objects beget more objects.

What Patterns Buy Us

I introduced patterns in Chapter 7. Let's reiterate some of the benefits that patterns can buy us.

Tried and Tested

First of all, as I've noted, patterns are proven solutions to particular problems. Drawing an analogy between patterns and recipes is dangerous: recipes can be followed blindly, whereas patterns are "half-baked" (Martin Fowler) by nature and need more thoughtful handling. Nevertheless, both recipes and patterns share one important characteristic: they have been tried out, and tested thoroughly before inscription.

Patterns Suggest Other Patterns

Patterns have grooves and curves that fit one another. Certain patterns slot together with a satisfying click. Solving a problem using a pattern will inevitably have ramifications. These consequences can become the conditions that suggest complementary patterns. It is important, of course, to be careful that you are addressing real needs and problems when you choose related patterns, and not just building elegant but useless towers of interlocking code. It is tempting to build the programming equivalent of the architectural folly.

A Common Vocabulary

Patterns are a means of developing a common vocabulary for describing problems and solutions. Naming is important—it stands in for describing, and therefore lets us cover lots of ground very quickly. Naming, of course, also obscures meaning for those who do not yet share the vocabulary, which is one reason why patterns can be so infuriating at times.

Patterns Promote Design

As discussed in the next section, patterns can encourage good design when used properly. It is, of course, important to hedge statements like that with plenty of caveats. Patterns are not fairy dust.

Patterns and Principles of Design

Design patterns are, by their nature, concerned with good design. Used well, they can help you build loosely coupled and flexible code. Pattern critics have a point, though, when they say that patterns can be overused by the newly infected. Because pattern implementations form pretty and elegant structures, it can be tempting to forget that good design always lies in fitness for purpose. Remember that patterns exist to address problems.

When I first started working with patterns, I found myself creating Abstract Factories all over my code. I needed to generate objects, and Abstract Factory certainly helped me to do that.

In fact, though, I was thinking lazily and making unnecessary work for myself. The sets of objects I needed to produce were indeed related, but they did not yet have alternative implementations. The classic Abstract Factory pattern is ideal for situations in which you have alternative sets of objects to generate according to circumstance. To make Abstract Factory work, you need to create factory classes for each type of object and a class to serve up the factory class. It's exhausting just describing the process.

My code would have been much cleaner had I created a basic factory class, only refactoring to implement Abstract Factory if I found myself needing to generate a parallel set of objects.

The fact that you are using patterns does not guarantee good design. When developing, it is a good idea to bear in mind two expressions of the same principle: KISS ("Keep it simple, stupid") and "Do the simplest thing that works." eXtreme programmers also give us another, related, acronym: YAGNI: "You aren't going to need it," meaning that you should not implement a feature unless it is truly required.

With the warnings out of the way, we can resume the tone of breathless enthusiasm. As I laid out in Chapter 9, patterns tend to embody a set of principles that can be generalized and applied to all code.

Favor Composition over Inheritance

Inheritance relationships are powerful but inflexible. By relying on inheritance in design, we produce either limited structures or torturous inheritance hierarchies infested with duplication.

Avoid Tight Coupling

I have already talked about this issue in this chapter, but it is worth mentioning here for the sake of completeness. You can never escape the fact that change in one component may require changes in other parts of your project. You can, however, minimize this by avoiding duplication (typified in our examples by parallel conditionals), overuse of global variables (or Singletons), and use of concrete subclasses when abstract types can be used to promote polymorphism. This last point leads us to another principle:

Code to an Interface, Not an Implementation

Design your software components with clearly defined public interfaces that make the responsibility of each transparent. If you define your interface in an abstract super class and have client classes demand and work with this abstract type, you then decouple clients from specific implementations.

Having said that, remember the YAGNI principle. If you start out with the need for only one implementation for a type, there is no immediate need to create an abstract super class. You can just as well define a clear interface in a single concrete class. As soon as you find that your single implementation is trying to do more than one thing at the same time, you can redesignate your concrete class as the abstract parent of two subclasses. Client code need be none the wiser, since it continues to work with a single type.

A classic sign that you may need to split an implementation and hide the resultant classes behind an abstract parent is the emergence of conditional statements in the implementation.

Encapsulate the Concept That Varies

If you find that you are drowning in subclasses, it may be that you should be extracting the reason for all this subclassing into its own type. This is particularly the case if the reason is a means to achieving an end that is incidental to your type's main purpose.

Given a type `UpdatableThing`, for example, you may find yourself creating `FtpUpdatableThing`, `HttpUpdatableThing`, and `FileSystemUpdatableThing` subtypes. The responsibility of your type, though, is to be a *thing* that is *updatable*—the mechanism for storage and retrieval are incidental to this purpose. `Ftp`, `Http`, and `FileSystem` are the things that vary here, and they belong in their own type—let's call it `UpdateMechanism`. `UpdateMechanism` will have subclasses for the different implementations. You can then add as many update mechanisms as you want without disturbing the `UpdatableThing` type, which remains focused on its core responsibility.

Notice also that we have replaced a static compile-time structure with a dynamic runtime arrangement here, bringing us (as if by accident) back to our first principle: "Favor composition over inheritance."

Practice

The issues that I covered in this section of the book (and introduced in Chapter 13) are often ignored by texts and coders alike. In my own life as a programmer, I discovered that these tools and techniques were at least as relevant to the success of a project as design. There is little doubt that issues like documentation and automated build are less revelatory in nature than wonders such as the Composite pattern.

■**Note** Let's just remind ourselves of the beauty of Composite: a simple inheritance tree whose objects can be joined at runtime to form structures that are also trees, but are orders of magnitude more flexible and complex. Multiple objects that share a single interface by which they are presented to the outside world. The interplay between simple and complex, multiple and singular, has got to get your pulse racing—that's not just software design, it's poetry.

Even if issues like documentation and build, testing, and version control are more prosaic than patterns, they are no less important. In the real world, a fantastic design will not survive if multiple developers cannot easily contribute to it or understand the source. Systems become hard to maintain and extend without automated testing. Without build tools, no one is going to bother to deploy your work. As PHP's user base widens, so does our responsibility as developers to ensure quality and ease of deployment.

A project exists in two modes. It is its structures of code and functionality, and it is a set of files and directories, a ground for cooperation, a set of sources and targets, a subject for transformation. In this sense, a project is a system from the outside as much as it is within its code. Mechanisms for build, testing, documentation, and version control require equal attention to detail as the code such mechanisms support. Focus on the meta-system with as much fervor as you do the system itself.

Testing

Although testing is part of the framework that one applies to a project from the outside, it is intimately integrated into the code itself. Because total decoupling is not possible, or even desirable, test frameworks are a powerful way of monitoring the ramifications of change. Altering the return type of a method could influence client code elsewhere, causing bugs to emerge weeks or months after the change is made. A test framework gives you half a chance of catching errors of this kind.

Testing is also credited as a tool for improving object-oriented design. Testing first (or at least concurrently) helps to focus the coder on a class's interface, and to think carefully about the responsibility and behavior of every method. I introduced the PHPUnit2 package in Chapter 13.

Documentation

Your code is not as clear as you think it is. A stranger visiting a codebase for the first time can be faced with a daunting task. Even you, as author of the code, will eventually forget how it all hangs together. In Chapter 15, I covered phpDocumentor, which allows you to document as you go, and automatically generates hyperlinked output.

The output from phpDocumentor is particularly useful in an object-oriented context, as it allows the user to click around from class to class. As classes are often contained in their own files, reading the source directly can involve complex trails from source file to source file.

Version Control

Collaboration is hard. Let's face it, people are awkward. Programmers are even worse than people. Once you've sorted out the roles and tasks on your team, the last thing you want to deal with is clashes in the source code itself. As we saw in Chapter 16, CVS (and similar tools such as Subversion) enable you to merge the work of multiple programmers into a single repository. Where clashes are unavoidable, CVS flags the fact and points you to the source to fix the problem.

Even if you are a solo programmer, version control is a necessity. It supports branching, so that you can maintain a software release and develop the next version at the same time, merging bug fixes from the stable release to the development branch.

CVS also provides a record of every commit ever made on your project. This means that you can roll back by date or tag to any moment. This will save your project one day—believe me.

Automated Build

Version control without automated build is of limited use. A project of any complexity takes work to deploy. Various files need to be moved to different places on a system, configuration files need to be transformed to have the right values for the current platform and database, database tables need to be set up or transformed. I covered two tools designed for installation. The first, PEAR (Chapter 14), is ideal for standalone packages and small applications. The second build tool I covered was Phing (Chapter 17), which is a tool with enough power and flexibility to automate the installation of the largest and most labyrinthine project.

Automated build transforms deployment from a chore to a matter of a line or two at the command line. With little effort, you can invoke your test framework and your documentation output from your build tool. If the needs of your developers do not sway you, bear in mind the pathetically grateful cries of your users as they discover that they need no longer spend an entire afternoon copying files and changing configuration fields every time you release a new version of your project.

What We Missed

A few tools I have had to omit from this book due to time and space constraints are, nonetheless, supremely useful in any project.

Perhaps foremost amongst these is Bugzilla. Its name should suggest two things to you. Firstly, it is a tool concerned with bug tracking. Secondly, it is part of the Mozilla project.

Like CVS, Bugzilla is one of those productivity tools that, once you have tried it on a project, you cannot imagine not using. Bugzilla is available for download from `http://www.bugzilla.org`.

It is designed to allow users to report problems with a project, but in my experience it is just as often used as a means of describing required features, and allocating their implementation to team members.

You can get a snapshot of open bugs at any time, narrowing the search according to product, bug owner, version number, and priority. Each bug has its own page, in which you can discuss any ongoing issues. Discussion entries and changes in bug status can be copied by mail to team members, so it's easy to keep an eye on things without going to the Bugzilla URL all the time.

Trust me. You want Bugzilla in your life.

Every serious project needs at least one mailing list so that users can be kept informed of changes and usage issues, and developers can discuss architecture and allocation of resources. My favorite mailing list software is Mailman (`http://www.gnu.org/software/mailman/`), which is free, relatively easy to install, and highly configurable. If you don't want to install your own mailing list software, however, there are plenty of sites that allow you to run mailing lists or newsgroups for free.

Although inline documentation is important, projects also generate a broiling heap of written material. This includes usage instructions, consultation on future directions, client assets, meeting minutes, and party announcements. During the lifetime of a project such materials are very fluid, and a mechanism is often needed to allow people to collaborate in their evolution.

Wiki (which is apparently Hawaiian for "very fast") is the perfect tool for creating collaborative webs of hyperlinked documents. Pages can be created or edited at the click of a button, and hyperlinks are automatically generated for words that match page names. Wiki is another one of those tools that seems so simple, essential, and obvious that you are sure you probably had the idea first but just didn't get around to doing anything about it. There are a number of Wikis to choose from. I have had good experience with one called TWiki, which is available for download from `http://www.twiki.org`. TWiki is written in Perl. Naturally, there is a Wiki written in PHP. It is called PhpWiki and can be downloaded from `http://phpwiki.sourceforge.net`.

Summary

In this chapter, we wrapped things up, revisiting the core topics that make up the book. Although we haven't tackled any concrete issues such as individual patterns or object functions here, this chapter should serve as a reasonable summary of this book's concerns.

There is never enough room or time to cover all the material that one would like. Nevertheless, I hope that this book has served to make one argument. PHP is growing up. It is now one of the most popular programming languages in the world, and with the advent of PHP 5 it is fully object oriented. I hope that PHP remains the hobbyist's favorite language, and that many new PHP programmers are delighted to discover how far they can get with just a little code. At the same time, though, more and more professional teams are building large commercial and open source systems with PHP. Such projects deserve more than a just-do-it approach. PHP has given us the power to develop at the highest level; it is our responsibility to meet that challenge with careful design and good practice.

PART SIX

Appendixes

APPENDIX A

■ ■ ■

Bibliography

Books

Applied Java Patterns:

Stelting, Stephen and Olav Maasen, *Applied Java Patterns*. Sun Microsystems Press, 2002.

Building Parsers with Java:

Metsker, Steven John, *Building Parsers with Java*. Addison-Wesley, 2001.

Core J2EE Patterns:

Alur, Deepak, John Crupi, and Dan Malks, *Core J2EE Patterns: Best Practices and Design Strategies*. Prentice Hall PTR, 2001.

Design Patterns:

Gamma, Erich, Richard Helm, Ralph Johnson, and John Vlissides, *Design Patterns: Elements of Reusable Object-Oriented Software*. Addison-Wesley, 1995.

Design Patterns Explained:

Shalloway, Alan and James R. Trott, *Design Patterns Explained: A New Perspective on Object-Oriented Design*. Addison-Wesley, 2002.

Data Access Patterns:

Nock, Clifton, *Data Access Patterns: Database Interactions in Object-Oriented Applications*. Addison-Wesley, 2004.

Extreme Programming Explained:

Beck, Kent, *Extreme Programming Explained: Embrace Change*. Addison-Wesley, 1999.

Open Source Development with CVS:

Fogel, Karl and Moshel Bar, *Open Source Development with CVS*, 2nd Edition. Coriolis Group, 2001.

A Pattern Language:

Alexander, Christopher, Sara Ishikawa, Murray Silverstein, Max Jacobson, Ingrid Fiksdahl-King and Shlomo Angel, *A Pattern Language: Towns, Buildings, Construction*. Oxford University Press, 1977.

Patterns of Enterprise Application Architecture:

Fowler, Martin, *Patterns of Enterprise Application Architecture*. Addison-Wesley, 2003.

The Pragmatic Programmer:

Hunt, Andrew and David Thomas, *The Pragmatic Programmer: From Journeyman to Master*. Addison-Wesley, 2000.

Refactoring:

Fowler, Martin, Kent Beck, John Brant, William Opdyke, and Don Roberts, *Refactoring: Improving the Design of Existing Code*. Addison-Wesley, 1999.

UML Distilled:

Fowler, Martin and Kendall Scott, *UML Distilled: A Brief Guide to the Standard Object Modeling Language*, Second Edition. Addison-Wesley, 1999.

Articles

"Applying patterns to PHP":

Atkinson, Leon, `http://www.zend.com/zend/trick/tricks-app-patt-php.php`

"The Object-Oriented Evolution of PHP":

Zeev Suraski, Zeev, `http://www.devx.com/webdev/Article/10007/0/page/1`

"PHP/FI Brief History":

Lerdorf, Rasmus, `http://www.php.net//manual/phpfi2.php#history`

"Test Infected: Programmers Love Writing Tests":

Beck, Kent and Erich Gamma, `http://junit.sourceforge.net/doc/testinfected/testing.htm`

Sites

BinaryCloud:

`http://www.binarycloud.com/`

CVS:

`https://www.cvshome.org/`

Phing:

`http://phing.info/wiki/index.php`

::PHPPatterns():

Harry Fuecks, `http://www.phppatterns.com`

PEAR:

`http://pear.php.net`

PHP:

http://www.php.net

PHPDocumentor:

http://www.phpdoc.org/

Portland Pattern Repository's Wiki:

Ward Cunningham, http://www.c2.com/cgi/wiki

Zend:

http://www.zend.com

■■■

A Simple Parser

The Interpreter pattern discussed in Chapter 11 does not cover parsing. An interpreter without a parser is pretty incomplete, unless you persuade your users to write PHP code to invoke the interpreter! Third-party parsers are available that could be deployed to work with the Interpreter pattern, and that would probably be the best choice in a real-world project. This appendix, however, presents a very simple object-oriented parser designed to work with the MarkLogic interpreter built in Chapter 11. Be aware that these examples are no more than a proof of concept. They are not designed for use in real-world situations.

> ■**Note** The interface and broad structure of this parser code are based on Steven John Metsker's *Building Parsers with Java* (Addison-Wesley, 2001). The brutally simplified implementation is my fault, however, and any mistakes should be laid at my door. John has given kind permission for the use of his original concept.

The Scanner

In order to parse a statement, we must first break it down into a set of words and characters (known as tokens). The following class uses a number of regular expressions to define tokens. It also provides a convenient result stack that we will be using later in this section. Here is the Scanner class:

```
class Scanner {
    const WORD        = 1;
    const QUOTE       = 2;
    const APOS        = 3;
    const WHITESPACE  = 6;
    const EOL         = 8;
    const CHAR        = 99;
    const EOF         = 0;
```

```php
        protected $in;
        protected $line_no = 1;
        protected $char_no = 0;
        protected $token;
        protected $token_type;
        protected $regexps;
        public $resultstack = array();

        function __construct( $in_str ) {
            $this->in = $in_str;
            $this->setRegexps();
            $this->nextToken();
            $this->eatWhiteSpace();
        }

        // push a result on to the result stack
        function pushResult( $mixed ) {
            array_push( $this->resultstack, $mixed );
        }

        // remove and return result from result stack
        function popResult( ) {
            return array_pop( $this->resultstack );
        }

        // number of items on the result stack
        function resultCount() {
            return count( $this->resultstack );
        }

        // return the last item on the result stack but
        // don't remove
        function peekResult( ) {
            if ( empty( $this->resultstack ) ) {
                throw new Exception( "empty resultstack" );
            }
            return $this->resultstack[count( $this->resultstack ) -1 ];
        }

        // set up regular expressions for tokens
        private function setRegexps() {
            $this->regexps = array(
                        self::WHITESPACE => '[ \t]',
                        self::EOL => '\n',
                        self::WORD => '[a-zA-Z0-9_-]+\b',
                        self::QUOTE => '"',
                        self::APOS => "'",
            );
```

```php
        $this->typestrings = array(
                    self::WHITESPACE => 'WHITESPACE',
                    self::EOL => 'EOL',
                    self::WORD => 'WORD',
                    self::QUOTE => 'QUOTE',
                    self::APOS => "APOS",
                    self::CHAR  => 'CHAR',
                    self::EOF => 'EOF'
        );
}

// skip through any whitespace
function eatWhiteSpace( ) {
    $ret = 0;
    if ( $this->token_type != self::WHITESPACE &&
         $this->token_type != self::EOL ) {
        return $ret;
    }
    // by calling nextToken() we gobble up any
    // whitespace
    while ( $this->nextToken() == self::WHITESPACE ||
            $this->token_type == self::EOL ) {
        $ret++;
    }
    return $ret;
}

// given a constant number, return a
// string version
// eg 1 => 'WORD',
function getTypeString( $int=-1 ) {
    if ( $int<0 ) {
        $int=$this->token_type();
    }
    return $this->typestrings[$int];
}

// the type of the current token
function token_type() {
    return $this->token_type;
}
```

```php
// the text being scanned
// gets shorter as the tokens are
// pulled from it
function input() {
    return $this->in;
}

// the current token
function token() {
    return $this->token;
}

// the current line number (great for error messages)
function line_no() {
    return $this->line_no;
}

// current char_no
function char_no() {
    return $this->char_no;
}

// attempt to pull another token from
// the input. If no token match is found then
// it's a character token
function nextToken() {
    if ( ! strlen( $this->in ) ) {
        return ( $this->token_type = self::EOF );
    }

    $ret = 0;
    foreach ( $this->regexps as $type=>$regex ) {
        if ( $ret = $this->testToken( $regex, $type ) ) {
            if ( $ret == self::EOL ) {
                $this->line_no++;
                $this->char_no = 0;
            } else {
                $this->char_no += strlen( $this->token() );
            }
            return $ret;
        }
    }
    $this->token = substr( $this->in, 0, 1 );
    $this->in    = substr( $this->in, 1 );
    $this->char_no += 1;
    return ( $this->token_type = self::CHAR );
}
```

```
    // given a regular expression check for a match
    private function testToken( $regex, $type ) {
        $matches = array();
        if ( preg_match( "/^($regex)(.*)/s", $this->in, $matches ) ) {
            $this->token = $matches[1];
            $this->in    = $matches[2];
            return ( $this->token_type  = $type );
        }
        return 0;
    }


    // given another scanner, make this one a clone
    function updateToMatch( Scanner $other ) {
        $this->in = $other->in;
        $this->token = $other->token;
        $this->token_type = $other->token_type;
        $this->char_no = $other->char_no;
        $this->line_no = $other->line_no;
        $this->resultstack = $other->resultstack;
    }
}
```

First off we set up constants for the tokens we care about. We are going to match characters, words, whitespace, and quote characters. We define regular expressions for these in the setRegexps() method. The heart of the class is the getToken() method. This attempts to match the next token in a given string. Perhaps the best way to see how this class might be used is to use it. Here is some code to break up our example statement into tokens:

```
$user_in = "\$input equals '4' or \$input equals 'four'";
$scanner = new Scanner( $user_in );
do {
    print $scanner->token();
    print "\t{$scanner->char_no()}";
    print "\t{$scanner->getTypeString()}\n";
} while ( $scanner->nextToken() != Scanner::EOF );
```

When we initialize the Scanner object, it automatically moves to the first token in the given string. So we use a do...while statement to eat up all the tokens. The token() method returns the current portion of the input matched. char_no() tells us where we are in the string, and getTypeString() returns a string version of the constant flag representing the current token. This is what the output should look like:

$	1	CHAR
input	6	WORD
	7	WHITESPACE
equals	13	WORD
	14	WHITESPACE
'	15	APOS
4	16	WORD
'	17	APOS
	18	WHITESPACE
or	20	WORD
	21	WHITESPACE
$	22	CHAR
input	27	WORD
	28	WHITESPACE
equals	34	WORD
	35	WHITESPACE
'	36	APOS
four	40	WORD
'	41	APOS

We could, of course, match finer-grained tokens than this, but this is good enough for our purposes. Breaking up the string is the easy part. How do we build up a grammar in code?

The Parser

One approach is to build a tree of Parser objects. Here is the abstract Parser class that we will be using:

```
abstract class Parser {
    protected $debug = false;
    private   $discard = false;
    protected $name;

    function __construct( $name=null ) {
        if ( is_null( $name ) ) {
            $this->name = (string)$this;
        } else {
            $this->name = $name;
        }
    }

    function setHandler( Handler $handler ) {
        $this->handler = $handler;
    }
```

```
function invokeHandler( Scanner $scanner ) {
    if ( ! empty( $this->handler ) ) {
        if ( $this->debug ) {
            $this->report( "calling handler: ".get_class( $this->handler ) );
        }
        // delegate to a handler on successful match
        $this->handler->handleMatch( $this, $scanner );
    }
}

function report( $msg ) {
    print "<{$this->name}> ".get_class( $this )."  : $msg\n";
}

function push( Scanner $scanner ) {
    if ( $this->debug ) {
        $this->report("pushing {$scanner->token()}");
    }
    // push the current from Scanner to the
    // scanner's result stack
    $scanner->pushResult( $scanner->token() );
}

function scan( Scanner $scanner ) {
    // delegate to child class for real scan
    $ret = $this->doScan( $scanner );
    // on a match push the current token to the scanner's
    // result stack (if we are a terminal and we haven't
    // been told to discard the result)
    if ( $ret &&  ! $this->discard && $this->term() ) {
        $this->push( $scanner );
    }
    // on a match call the handler if assigned
    if ( $ret ) {
        $this->invokeHandler( $scanner );
    }
    if ( $this->debug ) {
        $this->report("::scan returning $ret");
    }
    // move on to the next token
    if ( $this->term() && $ret ) {
        $scanner->nextToken();
        // gobble up any unused space
        $scanner->eatWhiteSpace();
    }
```

```
            return $ret;
    }

    function discard() {
        // if this is set, the matching token won't be
        // pushed onto the scanner's result stack
        $this->discard = true;
    }

    // are the conditions right to attempt match?
    abstract function trigger( Scanner $scanner );

    abstract protected function doScan( Scanner $scan );

    function term() {
        // distinguish between collections and terminals.
        // if this method returns true, then the
        // implementation is a leaf.
        return true;
    }
}
```

The place to start with this class is the scan() method. It is here that most logic resides. scan() is given a Scanner object to work with. The first thing that the Scanner does is to defer to a concrete child class, calling the abstract doScan() method. doScan() returns true or false, and we will see a concrete example later in the section.

If doScan() reports success, and a couple of other conditions are fulfilled, then the results of the parse are pushed to the Scanner object's result stack. The scanner object maintains a stack that is used by Parser objects to communicate results. The actual pushing of the successful parse takes place in the Parser::push() method.

```
    function push( Scanner $scanner ) {
        $this->report("pushing {$scanner->token()}");
        $scanner->pushResult( $scanner->token() );
    }
```

In addition to a parse failure, there are two conditions that might prevent the result being pushed to the scanner's stack. Firstly, client code can ask a parser to discard a successful match by calling the discard() method. This toggles a property called $discard to true. Secondly, only terminal parsers (that is, parsers that are not composed of other parsers) should push their result to the stack. Composite parsers (instances of CollectionParser and often referred to in the following text as collection parsers) will instead let their successful children push their results. We test whether or not a parser is terminal using the isTerm() method, which is over-ridden to return false by collection parsers.

If the concrete parser has been successful in its matching, then we call another method: invokeHandler(). This is passed the Scanner object. If a Handler (that is an object that implements the Handler interface) has been attached to Parser (using the setHandler() method), then its handleMatch() method is invoked here. We use handlers to make a successful grammar actually do something, as we shall see shortly.

Back in the scan() method, we call on the Scanner object to advance its position by calling its nextToken() and eatWhiteSpace() methods before returning the value it was given by doScan().

In addition to doScan(), notice the abstract trigger() method. This is used to determine whether a parser should bother to attempt a match. If trigger() returns false, then the condition is not right for parsing. Let's take a look at a concrete terminal Parser. CharacterParse is designed to match a particular character:

```
class CharacterParse extends Parser {
    private $char;

    function __construct( $char, $name=null ) {
        parent::__construct( $name );
        $this->char = $char;
    }

    function trigger( Scanner $scanner ) {
        return ( $scanner->token() == $this->char );
    }

    protected function doScan( Scanner $scanner ) {
        return ( $this->trigger( $scanner ) );
    }
}
```

The constructor accepts a character to match, and an optional parser name for debugging purposes. The trigger() method simply checks whether the scanner is pointing to a character token that matches the sought character. Because no further scanning than this is required, the doScan() method simply invokes trigger().

Terminal matching is a reasonably simple affair, as you can see. Let's look now at a collection parser. Firstly we'll define a common super class, and then go on to create a concrete example.

```
// This abstract class holds subparsers
abstract class CollectionParse extends Parser {

    protected $parsers = array();

    function add( Parser $p ) {
        if ( is_null( $p ) ) {
            throw new Exception( "argument is null" );
        }
        $this->parsers[]= $p;
        return $p;
    }
```

```
    function term() {
        return false;
    }
}

class SequenceParse extends CollectionParse {

    function trigger( Scanner $scanner ) {
        if ( empty( $this->parsers ) ) {
            return false;
        }
        return $this->parsers[0]->trigger( $scanner );
    }

    protected function doScan( Scanner $scanner ) {
        foreach( $this->parsers as $parser ) {
            if ( ! ( $parser->trigger( $scanner ) &&
                    $scan=$parser->scan( $scanner )) ) {
                return false;
            }
        }
        return true;
    }
}
```

The abstract CollectionParse class simply implements an add() method that aggregates Parsers and overrides isTerm() to return false.

The SequenceParse::trigger() method tests only the first child Parser it contains, invoking its trigger() method. The calling Parser will first call CollectionParse::trigger() to see if it is worth calling CollectionParse::scan(). If CollectionParse::scan() is called, then doScan() is invoked, and the trigger() and scan() methods of all Parser children are called in turn. A single failure results in CollectionParse::doScan() reporting failure.

For the sake of completeness, here are all the remaining Parser classes:

```
// This matches if one or more subparsers match
class RepetitionParse extends CollectionParse {
    function trigger( Scanner $scanner ) {
        return true;
    }

    protected function doScan( Scanner $scanner ) {
        if ( empty( $this->parsers ) ) {
            return true;
        }
        $parser = $this->parsers[0];
```

```php
        if ( ! $parser->trigger( $scanner ) ) {
            // no initial match is fine
            return true;
        }
        if ( $parser->scan( $scanner ) ) {
            // all is well. go again
            $this->scan( $scanner );
        } else {
            // we got a partial match but failed
            return false;
        }
        return true;
    }
}


// This matches if one or other of two subparsers match
class AlternationParse extends CollectionParse {
    function trigger( Scanner $scanner ) {
        foreach ( $this->parsers as $parser ) {
            if ( $parser->trigger( $scanner ) ) {
                return true;
            }
        }
        return false;
    }

    protected function doScan( Scanner $scanner ) {
        $type = $scanner->token_type();
        foreach ( $this->parsers as $parser ) {
            $s_copy = clone $scanner;
            if ( $type == $parser->trigger( $s_copy ) &&
                $parser->scan( $s_copy ) ) {
                $scanner->updateToMatch($s_copy);
                return true;
            }
        }
        return false;
    }
}


// this terminal parser matches a string literal
class StringLiteralParse extends Parser {
    function trigger( Scanner $scanner ) {
        return ( $scanner->token_type() == Scanner::APOS ||
                $scanner->token_type() == Scanner::QUOTE );
    }
```

```
        function push( Scanner $scanner ) {
            if ( $this->debug ) {
                $this->report("pushing {$this->string}");
            }
            $scanner->pushResult( $this->string );
        }

        protected function doScan( Scanner $scanner ) {
            $quotechar = $scanner->token_type();
            $this->string = "";
            while ( $token = $scanner->nextToken() ) {
                if ( $token == $quotechar ) {
                    return true;
                }
                $this->string .= $scanner->token();
            }
            return false;
        }
    }

// this terminal parser matches a word token
class WordParse extends Parser {
    function WordParse( $word=null, $name=null ) {
        parent::__construct( $name );
        $this->word = $word;
    }

    function trigger( Scanner $scanner ) {
        if ( $scanner->token_type() != Scanner::WORD ) {
            return false;
        }
        if ( is_null( $this->word ) ) {
            return true;
        }
        return ( $this->word == $scanner->token() );
    }

    protected function doScan( Scanner $scanner ) {
        $ret = ( $this->trigger( $scanner ) );
        return $ret;
    }
}
```

By combining terminal and nonterminal Parser objects, we can build a reasonably sophisticated parser. You can see all the Parser classes we use for our example in Figure B-1.

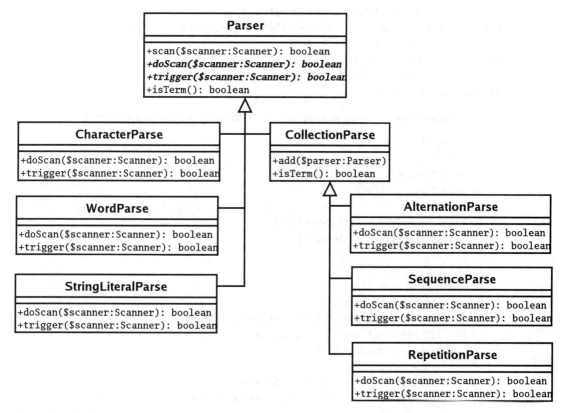

Figure B-1. *The Parser classes*

The idea behind this use of the Composite pattern is that a client can build up a grammar in code that closely matches EBNF notation. Table B-1 shows the parallels between these classes and EBNF fragments.

Table B-1. *Composite Parsers and EBNF*

Class	EBNF Example	Description
AlternationParse	orExpr | andExpr	Either one or another
SequenceParse	'and' operand	A list (all required in order)
RepetitionParse	(eqExpr)*	Zero or more required

So let's build some client code to implement our mini-language. As a reminder, here is the EBNF fragment I presented in Chapter 11:

```
expr      ::= operand (orExpr | andExpr )*
operand   ::= ( '(' expr ')' | <stringLiteral> | variable ) ( eqExpr )*
orExpr    ::= 'or' operand
andExpr   ::= 'and' operand
eqExpr    ::= 'equals' operand
variable ::= '$' <word>
```

This simple class builds up a grammar based upon this fragment and runs it:

```php
class MarkParse {
    private $expression;
    private $operand;
    private $interpreter;

    function __construct( $statement ) {
        $this->compile( $statement );
    }

    function evaluate( $input ) {
        $context = new Context();
        $prefab = new VariableExpression('input', $input );
        // add the input variable to Context
        $prefab->interpret( $context );

        $this->interpreter->interpret( $context );
        $result = $context->lookup( $this->interpreter );
        return $result;
    }

    function compile( $statement ) {
        // build parse tree
        $scanner = new Scanner( $statement );
        $statement = $this->expression();
        $scanresult = $statement->scan( $scanner );

        if ( ! $scanresult || $scanner->token_type() != Scanner::EOF ) {
            $msg  = "";
            $msg .= " line: {$scanner->line_no()} ";
            $msg .= " char: {$scanner->char_no()}";
            $msg .= " token: {$scanner->token()}\n";
            throw new Exception( $msg );
        }

        $this->interpreter = $scanner->popResult();
    }
```

```php
function expression() {
    if ( ! isset( $this->expression ) ) {
        $this->expression = new SequenceParse();
        $this->expression->add( $this->operand() );
        $bools = new RepetitionParse();
        $whichbool = new AlternationParse();
        $whichbool->add( $this->orExpr() );
        $whichbool->add( $this->andExpr() );
        $bools->add( $whichbool );
        $this->expression->add( $bools );
    }
    return $this->expression;
}

function orExpr() {
    $or = new SequenceParse( );
    $or->add( new WordParse('or') )->discard();
    $or->add( $this->operand() );
    $or->setHandler( new BooleanOrHandler() );
    return $or;
}

function andExpr() {
    $and = new SequenceParse();
    $and->add( new WordParse('and') )->discard();
    $and->add( $this->operand() );
    $and->setHandler( new BooleanAndHandler() );
    return $and;
}

function operand() {
    if ( ! isset( $this->operand ) ) {
        $this->operand = new SequenceParse( );
        $comp = new AlternationParse( );
        $exp = new SequenceParse( );
        $exp->add( new CharacterParse( '(' ))->discard();
        $exp->add( $this->expression() );
        $exp->add( new CharacterParse( ')' ))->discard();
        $comp->add( $exp );
        $comp->add( new StringLiteralParse() )
            ->setHandler( new StringLiteralHandler() );
        $comp->add( $this->variable() );
        $this->operand->add( $comp );
        $this->operand->add( new RepetitionParse() )->add($this->eqExpr());
    }
    return $this->operand;
}
```

```
    function eqExpr() {
        $equals = new SequenceParse();
        $equals->add( new WordParse('equals') )->discard();
        $equals->add( $this->operand() );
        $equals->setHandler( new EqualsHandler() );
        return $equals;
    }

    function variable() {
        $variable = new SequenceParse();
        $variable->add( new CharacterParse( '$' ))->discard();
        $variable->add( new WordParse());
        $variable->setHandler( new VariableHandler() );
        return $variable;
    }
}
```

This may seem like a complicated class, but all it is doing is building up the grammar we have already defined. Most of the methods are analogous to production names (that is, the names that begin each production line in EBNF, such as eqExpr and andExpr). If you look at the expression() method, you should see that we are building up the same rule as we defined in EBNF earlier:

```
// expr    ::= operand (orExpr | andExpr )*
    function expression() {
        if ( ! isset( $this->expression ) ) {
            $this->expression = new SequenceParse();
            $this->expression->add( $this->operand() );
            $bools = new RepetitionParse();
            $whichbool = new AlternationParse();
            $whichbool->add( $this->orExpr() );
            $whichbool->add( $this->andExpr() );
            $bools->add( $whichbool );
            $this->expression->add( $bools );
        }
        return $this->expression;
    }
```

In both the code and the EBNF notation, we define a sequence that is formed of a reference to an operand, followed by zero or more instances of an alternation between orExpr and andExpr. Notice that we are storing the Parser returned by this method in a property variable. This is to prevent infinite loops as methods invoked from expression() themselves reference expression().

The only methods that are doing more than just building the grammar are compile() and evaluate(). compile() can be called directly or automatically via the constructor, which accepts a statement string and uses it to create a Scanner object. It calls the expression() method, which returns a tree of Parser objects that make up the grammar. It then calls Parser::scan(), passing it the Scanner object. If the raw code does not parse, the compile() method throws an exception. Otherwise it retrieves the result of compilation as left on the

Scanner object's result stack. As we will see shortly, this should be an Expression object. This result is stored in a property called $interpreter.

The evaluate() method makes a value available to the Expression tree. It does this by predefining a VariableExpression object named "input" and registering it with the Context object that is then passed to the main Expression object. As with variables like $_REQUEST in PHP, this $input variable is always available to MarkLogic coders. evaluate() calls the Expression::interpret() method to generate a final result. Remember, we need to retrieve interpreter results from the Context object.

So far we have seen how we parse text and how we build a grammar. We have also seen how we combine Expression objects to process a query. We have not yet seen, though, how we relate the two processes. How do we get from a parse tree to our interpreter? The answer lies in the Handler objects that can be associated with Parser objects using Parser::setHandler(). Let's take a look at the way we manage variables. We associate a VariableHandler with the Parser in the variable() method:

```
$variable->setHandler( new VariableHandler() );
```

Here is the VariableHandler (and the interface it implements):

```
interface Handler {
    abstract function handleMatch( Parser $parser, Scanner $scanner );
}
class VariableHandler implements Handler {
    function handleMatch( Parser $parser, Scanner $scanner ) {
        $varname = $scanner->popResult();
        $scanner->pushResult( new VariableExpression( $varname ) );
    }
}
```

If the Parser with which VariableHandler is associated matches on a scan operation, then handleMatch() is called. By definition the last item on the stack will be the name of the variable. We remove this, and replace it with a new VariableExpression object with the correct name. Similar principles are used to create EqualsExpression, LiteralExpression objects, and so on.

Here are the remaining handlers:

```
class StringLiteralHandler implements Handler {
    function handleMatch( Parser $parser, Scanner $scanner ) {
        $value = $scanner->popResult();
        $scanner->pushResult( new LiteralExpression( $value ) );
    }
}

class EqualsHandler implements Handler {
    function handleMatch( Parser $parser, Scanner $scanner ) {
        $comp1 = $scanner->popResult();
        $comp2 = $scanner->popResult();
        $scanner->pushResult( new EqualsExpression( $comp1, $comp2 ) );
    }
}
```

```
class VariableHandler implements Handler {
    function handleMatch( Parser $parser, Scanner $scanner ) {
        $varname = $scanner->popResult();
        $scanner->pushResult( new VariableExpression( $varname ) );
    }
}

class BooleanOrHandler implements Handler {
    function handleMatch( Parser $parser, Scanner $scanner ) {
        $comp1 = $scanner->popResult();
        $comp2 = $scanner->popResult();
        $scanner->pushResult( new BooleanOrExpression( $comp1, $comp2 ) );
    }
}

class BooleanAndHandler implements Handler {
    function handleMatch( Parser $parser, Scanner $scanner ) {
        $comp1 = $scanner->popResult();
        $comp2 = $scanner->popResult();
        $scanner->pushResult( new BooleanAndExpression( $comp1, $comp2 ) );
    }
}
```

Bearing in mind that you also need the Interpreter example from Chapter 11 at hand, we can work with the MarkParse class like this:

```
$input     = '4';
$statement = "( \$input equals '4' or  \$input equals 'four' )";

$engine = new MarkParse( $statement );
$result = $engine->evaluate( $input );
print "input: $input evaluating: $statement\n";
if ( $result ) {
    print "true!\n";
} else {
    print "false!\n";
}
// output: input: 4 evaluating: ( $input equals '4' or  $input equals 'four' )
// output: true!
```

INDEX

forums.apress.com

FOR PROFESSIONALS BY PROFESSIONALS™

JOIN THE APRESS FORUMS AND BE PART OF OUR COMMUNITY. You'll find discussions that cover topics of interest to IT professionals, programmers, and enthusiasts just like you. If you post a query to one of our forums, you can expect that some of the best minds in the business—especially Apress authors, who all write with *The Expert's Voice*™—will chime in to help you. Why not aim to become one of our most valuable participants (MVPs) and win cool stuff? Here's a sampling of what you'll find:

DATABASES
Data drives everything.

Share information, exchange ideas, and discuss any database programming or administration issues.

INTERNET TECHNOLOGIES AND NETWORKING
Try living without plumbing (and eventually IPv6).

Talk about networking topics including protocols, design, administration, wireless, wired, storage, backup, certifications, trends, and new technologies.

JAVA
We've come a long way from the old Oak tree.

Hang out and discuss Java in whatever flavor you choose: J2SE, J2EE, J2ME, Jakarta, and so on.

MAC OS X
All about the Zen of OS X.

OS X is both the present and the future for Mac apps. Make suggestions, offer up ideas, or boast about your new hardware.

OPEN SOURCE
Source code is good; understanding (open) source is better.

Discuss open source technologies and related topics such as PHP, MySQL, Linux, Perl, Apache, Python, and more.

PROGRAMMING/BUSINESS
Unfortunately, it is.

Talk about the Apress line of books that cover software methodology, best practices, and how programmers interact with the "suits."

WEB DEVELOPMENT/DESIGN
Ugly doesn't cut it anymore, and CGI is absurd.

Help is in sight for your site. Find design solutions for your projects and get ideas for building an interactive Web site.

SECURITY
Lots of bad guys out there—the good guys need help.

Discuss computer and network security issues here. Just don't let anyone else know the answers!

TECHNOLOGY IN ACTION
Cool things. Fun things.

It's after hours. It's time to play. Whether you're into LEGO® MINDSTORMS™ or turning an old PC into a DVR, this is where technology turns into fun.

WINDOWS
No defenestration here.

Ask questions about all aspects of Windows programming, get help on Microsoft technologies covered in Apress books, or provide feedback on any Apress Windows book.

HOW TO PARTICIPATE:
Go to the Apress Forums site at **http://forums.apress.com/**.
Click the New User link.